Edmund Charles Cox

A Short History of the Bombay Presidency

Edmund Charles Cox

A Short History of the Bombay Presidency

ISBN/EAN: 9783743325685

Manufactured in Europe, USA, Canada, Australia, Japa

Cover: Foto ©ninafisch / pixelio.de

Manufactured and distributed by brebook publishing software (www.brebook.com)

Edmund Charles Cox

A Short History of the Bombay Presidency

A SHORT HISTORY

OF THE

BOMBAY PRESIDENCY.

BY

EDMUND C. COX

(TRIN. COLL., CAMB.),
BOMBAY DISTRICT POLICE.

Bombay:
THACKER & Co., Ld.
Calcutta :—THACKER, SPINK & Co.
London :—W. THACKER & Co., 87, Newgate Street.

1887.

BOMBAY:
PRINTED AT THE EDUCATION SOCIETY'S PRESS, BYCULLA.

TO MY FATHER,

The Rev. Sir GEORGE W. COX, Bart., M.A.,

RECTOR OF SCRAYINGHAM, YORK,

WHOSE EARLIEST WORKS WERE WRITTEN FOR HIS CHILDREN,

I DEDICATE THIS HISTORY

OF THE PRESIDENCY

IN WHICH I HAVE THE HONOUR TO SERVE.

A brief introductory sketch has been given of the time before the roll of European conquest to the East, and a more detailed description of the course of events between the coming of the Portuguese and ourselves. I have written a tolerably full account of the process by which the West of India came under the British flag, bringing in what happened in other parts of the Peninsula so far only as to elucidate the events that took place in Bombay. With this object, and to give a greater degree of continuity to the narrative, there runs through the book a short account of the supreme power whether at Delhi or Calcutta.

E. C. COX.

ALIBÁG, KOLÁBA, *August* 29*th*, 1886.

Postscript.—My best thanks are due to K. M. Chatfield, Esq., M.A., Director of Public Instruction, for his kind aid in the publication of this book.

E. C. C.

NOTE ON THE SPELLING OF INDIAN NAMES.

As a general rule, the authorised Government spelling has been followed, and the subjoined table explains the system:—

A unaccented	as	u	in	fun.
A accented	as	a	in	father.
Ai, Ay, Y	as	ai	in	aisle.
E	as	ê	in	fête.
I	as	i	in	fill.
or	as	ee	in	feel.
U	as	u	in	full.
or	as	oo	in	stool.
G	as	g	in	get.
J	as	j	in	jail.

An exception has been made in the following names, which are spelt in the older English way:—

Jumna.
Indus.
Delhi.
Comorin.
Deccan.
Oudh.
Ganges.
Bengal.
Calcutta.
Madras.
Bombay.
Salsette.
Colaba (Bombay).

Mazagon.
Sindia.
Indore.
Carnatic.
Arcot.
Plassey.
Cambay.
Travancore.
Assaye.
Vellore.
Cawnpore.
Lucknow.

CONTENTS.

CHAPTER I.—PAGE 1.

Description of the Bombay Presidency.

India a continent rather than a country.—The term "Indian People" a misleading one.—India as a whole.—Component parts of the Bombay Presidency.—The climates.—The food of the people.—The scenery and appearance of the country.—The vernacular languages.

CHAPTER II.—PAGE 9.

Description of the People.

Details of the population.—The majority descended from the Aryan tribes who dwelt in Central Asia.—The aboriginal tribes.—The early Aryans.—The Weds (Vedas).—The four original castes.—The Institutes of Manu.—Castes in their later form.—Their religious nature.—Superstition.—Buddha and his creed.—Predominance of Buddhism as a state religion.—Its downfall.—Food, dress, and marriage customs of Hindus and Muhammadans.

CHAPTER III.—PAGE 26.

Early Hindu Civilisation.

Invasions of Darius and Alexander.—State of the country during the latter.—Megasthenes at Patna.—Village communities—Tenure of the land.—The village officers.

Chapter V.—Page 35.

Establishment of Muhammadan Rule.

Mission of Muhammad.—Muhammadan expedition into Sind in 700.—Its failure.—Invasions from the Áfghán mountains.—Mahmoud of Ghazni.—Muhammad Ghori.—Conquest of Northern India by the Muhammadans.—The Slave and Khiljy dynasties.—Extension of Muhammadan conquest to the Deccan by Alla-ud-din in 1295.—The Toghlak dynasty.—Rebellion of Záffar Khán in the Deccan and foundation of the Bahmani Muhammadan dynasty of the Deccan.—Muhammadan kingdoms of Gujárát, Khándesh and Sind.—Invasion of Taimur the Tártár.—End of the Toghlak dynasty.—Bábar the descendant of Taimur invades India and founds the Moghal Empire in 1526.—Character of Muhammadan rule prior to the establishment of the Moghal empire.

Chapter V.—Page 51.

Conquests of the Portuguese.

Vasco da Gama reaches Kálikat in 1498.—The state of Western India at the time.—The Bahmani dynasty of the Deccan breaking up into five independent kingdoms, chief of which are Áhmadnagar, Bijápur and Golkonda.—Destruction of the Hindu kingdom of Bijanagar.—The Maráthas employed largely in the armies of the Muhammadan states of the Deccan, and the Brahmans as men of business.—Relations of Da Gama and his successors with the Zámorin of Kálikat and the rulers of Káchin and Kánnanur.—Factories founded and a large trade created.—Albuquerque makes Goa the capital of Portuguese India.—Character of the Portuguese rule.—Vicissitudes in their fortunes.—Their wars with Gujárát and Bijápur.—Acquisitions of Bombay, Salsette and Diu.

Chapter VI.—Page 67.
Foundation of the Moghal Empire.

Búbar invades India.—His success at Pánipat in 1526.—His son Humáyun succeeds him in 1530.—Humáyun driven into exile for fifteen years by the Sur dynasty.—His return in triumph.—Succeeded by Akbar in 1556.—Continued success of the Portuguese at the time of his accession.—Increase of Akbar's power.—His policy of conciliation.—He calls upon the Muhammadan kingdoms of the Deccan to acknowledge his supremacy.—Their refusal.—Akbar's forces invade the Deccan.—Chánd Bibi repels the invaders.—Akbar himself takes the field.—His death in 1605.—His policy and character.

Chapter VII.—Page 83.
Coming of the English.

The Emperor Jahángir.—The East India Company.—Captain Hawkins at Ágra.—Sir Henry Middleton and the "Trades' Increase."—Defeat of the Portuguese fleet by the English at Surat in 1612.—Jahángir invades the Deccan accompanied by Sir Thomas Roe the English ambassador.—Málik Ambar and Sháhji Bhonsli.

Chapter VIII.—Page 91.
Rise of the Maráthas.

Sháh Jahán suppresses the rebellion of Khán Jahán Lodi in the Deccan—End of the kingdom of Áhmadnagar in 1633.—State of Muhammadan power in the Deccan at the time.—Progress of the English.—The rival Company.—Shiwáji son of Sháhji Bhonsle.—His plan to drive the Muhammadans from the country.—Encouragement of his mother.—Shiwáji seizes the fort of Torna.—He builds a fort at Rájgahr.—He obtains a series of forts on the Western Ghâts.—He seizes treasure of the Bijápur Government.—Aurangzib viceroy of the Deccan.—He goes to Delhi on the illness of his father Sháh Jahán and usurps the throne.—Shiwáji defies the Moghal Government, but Aurangzib grants him forgiveness.—Aurangzib encourages him as the means of putting pressure on his Muhammadan vassals.

Chapter IX.—Page 104.

Expansion of Marátha Power.

Aurangzíb Emperor.—His great object.—His character and policy.—Afzul Khán sent against Shiwáji from Bijápur.—His death and the destruction of his army at Pratápgahr.—Failure of the Bijápur avenging army.—Shiwáji makes his head-quarters at Raygahr.—Strength of his army.—The English obtain Bombay.—Their liberal policy.—Shiwáji attacks Surat, but is firmly resisted by the English under Oxenden.—He seizes the Moghal pilgrim vessels.—Extraordinary successes.—Rája Jay Singh sent against him by Aurangzíb.—His submission and journey to Delhi.—His disgust at his treatment there.—He is imprisonned but escapes.—He obtains tribute from Bijápur and Golkonda.—He works up his army and civil government.—He defeats an army sent against him by Aurangzíb.—The English strengthen Bombay.—Gerald Aungier.—An attack of the Dutch repulsed.—Officers of the Company formed into four grades.—Splendid coronation of Shiwáji.—Treaty between him and the English.—His death.

Chapter X.—Page 119.

Decline of the Moghal Empire.

Sambháji succeeds Shiwáji.—He attacks Goa.—Reprisals of the Portuguese.—Aurangzíb at the aged of 63 marches against Bijápur—Golkonda and the Maráthas.—Rebellion of Captain Keigwin in Bombay.—Spirited foreign policy of the Childs.—Its failure.—The English seize the Moghal pilgrim vessels.—They sue for peace.—The Scotch East Indian Company.—Its union with the English one.—Calcutta founded in 1670.—Aurangzíb destroys Bijápur and Golkonda.—He captures and kills Sambháji.—Rájárám, son of Shiwáji, rules on behalf of Sáhu (Shiwáji), son of Sambháji.—Rise of the Ángria family.—Death of Rájárám.—His wife Tárábai becomes regent on behalf of his son Shiwáji.—Struggle between the Emperor and the Maráthas.—Death of Aurangzíb.

CHAPTER XI.—PAGE 128.

Rise of the Peshwas and the great Marátha Houses.

Bahádur Sháh becomes Emperor.—He releases Sáhu, and then arise the two great Marátha factions of Sáhu of Sátára and Sambháji, son of Rájárám, at Kolhápur.—Ultimate success of Sáhu.—Comparative tranquillity in the Deccan.—Death of Bahádur Sháh.—The emperors Jahándár and Farokhsir.—Intrigues of the Syads.—Rise of Nizám-ul-Mulk founder of the Nizáms of Hydarúbád.—Báláji Wishwánáth founder of the Brahman dynasty of the Peshwas.—The Peshwa, in alliance with Hussein Ali, viceroy of the Deccan, leads an army against Delhi.—The emperor killed.—Succeeded by Muhammad Sháh.—Marátha revenue system.—Kanhoji Ángria's piracies on the English ships.—Nizám-ul-Mulk asserts his independence, so there is nothing left to the Delhi empire of its possessions in the Deccan.—Báji Rao, son of Báláji Wishwánáth, becomes Peshwa.—Origin of Sindia, Holkar, the Gaikwár of Barodá and the Rájas of Barár.—Marátha campaigns against Delhi.—The Maráthas capture Thána and Salsette from the Portuguese.—Decline of the Portuguese power.—English embassies to the Maráthas.—Nádir Sháh massacres 30,000 men at Delhi.—Steady increase of Marátha power.—Báláji Báji Rao succeeds as Peshwa.—His brother Raghonáth Rao or Raghoba.—Deaths of Nizám-ul-Mulk, Sáhu, and the emperor.—Sáhu's rendition of Marátha power to the Peshwa.

CHAPTER XII.—PAGE 145.

Struggle between the English and the French.

The idea of an European empire in India originated by Duploix and worked out by Clive.—Struggles for the thrones of the Deccan and Carnatic.—Increasing military reputation of the English.—The seat of the Marátha power transferred to Puna.—Marátha power at its zenith.—Struggle between the Maráthas and the Áfghán—

Áhmad Abdali in Hindustán.—Terrible defeat of the Maráthas at Pánipat.—The hope of Hindu supremacy over India at an end.—Commodore James sent against the Ángrias.—His success at Sawarndrug.—Clive and Watson take Gheria.—Affairs in Bengal.—The battle of Plassey.—English conquest of Bengal.—Death of Báláji Báji Rao.—Political condition of India.—Dislike of the Court of Directors to territorial acquisition.

Chapter XIII.—Page 162.
First Marátha War.

Máhdu Rao son of Báláji Rao becomes Peshwa, but Raghoba is regent.—Nána Farnáwis is made minister.—Raghoba's disputes with the Peshwa.—He seeks aid from the English and the Nizám.—The result.—Rise of Hydar Ali of Mysur.—The strange series of alliances between the English, the Maráthas, the Nizám, and Hydar Ali.—The English dragged into the first Mysur war.—Its disastrous result.—Embassies to Puna.—Death of Máhdu Rao Peshwa.—His brother Nárayan Rao succeeds, but is murdered.—Raghoba assumes the Peshwaship, but a posthumous son is born to Nárayan Rao and two great parties are formed, that of Raghoba, and the ministerialists on behalf of the infant Peshwa.—The English take Surat and Broach.—The Governor of Bengal made Governor-General of India with authority over Bombay.—The English conquer Thána, and join in a campaign with Raghoba.—Treaty of Surat made with Raghoba who makes important cessions of territory.—Battle of Aras.—Naval battle with the Maráthas.—The Calcutta Council order the Bombay authorities to stop the war, and send Colonel Upton to make terms with the Maráthas.—Unsatisfactory treaty of Purandhar, which annulled that of Surat and broke off the alliance with Raghoba.—Mr. Hornby's minute that the English must interfere in Marátha affairs.—St. Lubin, the French envoy, at Puna.—Nána Farnáwis' negociations with him.—Hastings resolves to strike the first blow and sends an army across India under Colonel Leslie.—Colonel Egerton advances towards Puna from Panwel.—Miserable failure of the expedition.—Disgraceful convention of Wargaum.—Gallantry of Captain Hartley—Hasting sends Colonel Goddard to relieve Leslie.—Exploits of this officer.—He takes Ahmadábád.—Confederacy against the English.—Captain Popham's brilliant campaign in Málwa.—Hydar Ali commences the second Mysur war.—Hastings therefore endeavours to make peace with the Maráthas as soon as it can be honourably secured.—Goddard takes Basseid.—His rash advance towards Puna and retreat to Panwel.—Peace concluded with the Maráthas at Sálbai.—Its favourable nature to the English.—Alliance of the Maráthas and the English against Mysur.—New phase of the Marátha power which now consists of a lax confederacy.

CHAPTER XIV.—PAGE 187.

Theory of the Balance of Power.

The second Mysur war.—Death of Hydar.—Succession of his son Tipu.—The French under Bussy aid Tipu, but are defeated.—When success is assured the Madras Council make a disgraceful surrender.—Gallant action between the "Ranger" and the Marátha fleet.—Sindia's schemes in Hindustán.—Warren Hastings returns to England.—Sindia demands chauth from his successor, Mr. Macpherson.—He is forced to withdraw his demands.—Mr. Malet sent as envoy to Puna.—Arrival of Lord Cornwallis.—State of India at the time.—The third Mysur War.—Its successful result.—Annexation of Kánara.—Theory of the balance of power by which the English should hold the scales between the various powers of India.—Retirement of Lord Cornwallis.—Sindia at Puna.—He becomes a rival to Nána Farnáwis.—His death.—His character and policy.—Daolat Rao Sindia.—The pirates on the Western Coast.—Janjira never conquered.—Sir John Shore, Governor-General.—His return to the non-intervention policy.—

The Nizám defeated by the Maráthas at Khardla.—The young Peshwa in disgust at Nána's severity kills himself—Intrigues for the Peshwaship, which is at last given to Báji Rao II., a son of Raghoba.—Sindia plunders Puna.—Anarchy and confusion in the Deccan.

Chapter XV.—Page 205.
Second Marátha War.

Lord Mornington, subsequently Marquis of Wellesley, Governor-General.—His favourable treaty with the Nizám.—Tipu still bent on driving the English out of India, but he is defeated and killed in the fourth Mysur War.—Lord Wellesley sees that the English must be supreme in India.—Death of Nána Farnáwis.—Increased disorder in the Deccan.—Dhondia Wág's disturbances.—General Arthur Wellesley puts them down.—War between Sindia and Yeshwant Rao Holkar.—Murder of Wituji Holkar.—Yeshwant Rao takes Puna and Báji Rao flies to Bombay.—Treaty of Bassein, by which the English protect the Peshwa and station troops at Puna, and the Peshwa acknowledges British supremacy over Gujúrát.—The Peshwa, Sindia and Barár conspire against the English.—General Wellesley's forced march upon Puna.—The Peshwa reseated on his throne by the English.—Fruitless negociations with Sindia and Barár.—Lord Wellesley compelled to assume the offensive.—His plans.—General Wellesley takes Áhmadnagar and wins the battle of Assaye.—Mountstuart Elphinstone.—Victories of Woodington in Gujúrát and Lake in Hindustán.—General Wellesley's victory at Argaum.—Submission of Sindia and Barár.—Elphinstone resident at Puna and Malcolm at the Court of India.—General Wellesley's triumphant entry into Bombay.—His opinions of the Peshwa's government.—Further treaty with the Gaikwár.—English possessions in the West of India after the war still very small.

CONTENTS.

CHAPTER XVI.—PAGE.—227.
British Supremacy.

War with Yeshwant Rao Holkar.—Colonel Monson's disaster.—Colonel Ochterlony's successful resistance to Yeshwant Rao at Delhi.—Defeat of Yeshwant Rao's army.—Lord Lake unsuccessfully besieges Bhartpur, but the Rája submits.—The East India Company send out Lord Cornwallis to undo all that Lord Wellesley had done.—Nature of Oriental monarchies.—Lord Wellesley sees that the English power must be paramount.—Ignorance of the Directors concerning India.—Lord Cornwallis soon dies, but not before he has time to shatter his reputation as a statesman.—Sir George Barlow succeeds him and carries on his miserable policy.—The joy of Yeshwant Rao, and plots of other chiefs.—Barlow becomes Governor of Madras.

CHAPTER XVII —PAGE 234.
Pindhári or Third Marátha War.

Lord Minto, Governor-General.—His firm dealing in Bandalkand.—The Pindháris and Amir Khán.—Amir Khán driven back to Holkar's territory.—Goa garrisoned by British troops.—The Pindháris again.—Plots of Báji Rao.—Treatment of the Bhils by the Maráthas.—Elphinstone becomes resident at Puna.—His dealing with the Peshwa's feudatory chiefs.—Piracy stamped out on the Western Coast.—The Indian Navy.—Báji Rao's schemes.—Rise of Trimbakji Dainglia.—His hatred of the English.—Báji Rao's plan to make himself paramount over all the Maráthas and to shake off the British Yoke.—Lord Moira, or the Marquis of Hastings, Governor-General.—His conquest of Nepál.—Báji Rao's schemes with regard to Guzárát.—The Gaikwár sends Gangadhar Shástri as his envoy to Puna.—Murder of the Shástri by the agents of Trimbakji.—Trimbakji is given up and imprisoned but escapes.—Expedition to Kachh.—Heavy punishment of the Peshwa for his hostile actions.—Large cessions of territory to the English.—Lord Hasting's preparations to subdue the Pindháris and their supporters.—His successful dealings with Sindia.—Báji Rao's plan to murder Elphinstone.—Crisis at Puna.—The battle of Khirki and end of the Marátha Empire.—Battle of Korygaum.—Abolition of the Peshwaship.—Annexation of the Peshwa's territories.—Partial restoration of the Rája of Sátára.—Mr. Elphinstone, Commissioner of the Deccan.—Conclusion of the Campaign.—Battle of Ashta —Defence of Sitabaldi.—Battle of Mehidpur and destruction of Holkar's army.—Suppression of the Pindháris.—The Peshwa surrenders to Sir John Malcolm and is sent to Cawnpore.—Civil administration of the new acquisitions.—Elphinstone becomes Governor of Bombay.—Retirement of Lord Hastings.

Chapter XVIII.—Page 269.
Mountstuart Elphinstone.

State of the country.—Elphinstone's wise and liberal views.—Marátha justice.—Elphinstone's tours.—The regeneration of Khándesh.—Formation of the Bhil Corps.—Lord Amherst, Governor-General.—Bad feeling in the Bombay Presidency owing to the Burmese War.—Rámoshi insurrection.—Dealings with Sind and Persia.—Elphinstone's policy and views.—His retirement.

Chapter XIX—Page 281.
Policy of Self-Effacement.

Sir John Malcolm, Governor of Bombay.—Lord William Bentinck, Governor-General.—His reputation over-estimated.—Financial retrenchment.—Abolition of Sati.—Suppression of Thaggi.—Steam navigation.—Lord William Bentinck's reforms.—The miserable deficiency of his policy towards Native States.—Disturbances at Hydarábád.—Gwálior and Jaypur unchecked.—Natives of India unfit for European methods.

CONTENTS.

CHAPTER XX.—PAGE 291.
The Amirs of Sind.

Meeting between Lord William Beutinck and Ranjit Sing.—Lord Auckland, Governor-General.—The Rája of Sátára exiled to Banáras.—Sháh Suja and Dost Muhammad.—A Russian Envoy at Kábul.—Eldred Pottinger at Herat.—Expedition to the Persian Gulf. —Lord Auckland determines to restore Sháh Suja and depose Dost Muhammad.—The army advances through Sind.—The history of the Amirs of Sind.—English attempts to get a footing in that province.—Tripartite treaty between the English, Ranjit Sing, and Sháh Suja.—Dishonourable treatment of the Amirs.—Sir James Outram, Political Agent in Sind.—Conqest of Aden.

CHAPTER XXI.—PAGE 304.
Conquest of Sind.

Destruction of the British Army in the Khyber Pass.—Lord Ellenborough, Governor-General.—The Amirs break through the treaty. —A new treaty consequently insisted upon.—Ali Murád of Kyrpur joins the English.—Sir Charles Napier supersedes Outram, but recalls the latter as Commissioner.—Napier's march against Imámgahr.—Battle of Miáni.—Outram's futile negociations.— Battle of Hydarábád.—Annexation of Sind.—War with Holkar's Forces and battle of Máhárájpur.—Annexation of Kolúba.—War with Kolhápur.

CHAPTER XXII.—PAGE 322.
The Law of Lapse.

Lord Harding as Governor-General. — Succeeded by Lord Dalhousie.— Annexation of Sátára.—Death of Bájí Rao.—His adopted son Dhondu Pant, Nána Sahib.—Lord Dalhousie's policy and the annexation of various states.

CHAPTER XXIII.—PAGE 328.

The Sowing of the Wind.

Lord Canning, Governor-General.—The sepoys and their relations with the Government.—Professor Seely's incorrect theory.—The Duke of Wellington's opinion of British soldiers.—Complex causes of the Mutiny.—The Mutiny at Vellore.—Various other mutinies.—Sir Charles Napier's views.—Character of Lord Canning.—Grievances of the sepoys.—The prophecy.—The Delhi Princes.—The Sháh of Persia.—Nána Sáhib.—The Chapátíes.

CHAPTER XXIV.—PAGE 349.

The Reaping of the Whirlwind.

Outbreak of the Mutiny.—Willoughby at Delhi.—Tragedy at Jhánsi.—Inconsistent aims of the mutineers.—Nána Sáhib proclaims himself Peshwa.—The well of Cawnpore.—The two reliefs of Lucknow and the reconquest of Oudh.—The siege of Delhi.—Exile of the last Moghal Emperor Bahádur Sháh.—Campaign of Tántia Topi.—His success over General Windham and capture of Cawnpore.—His defeat by Sir Colin Campbell.

CHAPTER XXV.—PAGE 359.

The Mutinies in Bombay.

Lord Elphinstone, Governor of Bombay.—His unselfish policy.—Plot at Sátára.—Disaffection in the Southern Marátha Country.—Outbreak at Kolhápur.—Colonel Jacob at Kolhápur.—Plot at Belgaum.—Conspiracies in Bombay.—Bombay saved by Forjett.—Plots at Áhmadábád, and in Sind.—Second outbreak at Kolhápur.—Brave defence of Talliwára by the Police.—Rebellion of the Chief of Nargund.—Murder of Manson.—Sir Frank Souter.

CHAPTER XXVI.—PAGE 376.

Exploits of the Bombay Army.

Sir Hugh Rose's triumphant Campaign in Central India.—Defeats of the Ráni of Jhánsi and Tántia Topi.—End of the Mutiny.—Peace Proclamation.—Abolition of the Company.—The Company's European Troops.—Discordant aims of the Mutineers.

CHAPTER XXVII.—PAGE 392.

Internal Administration.

Steamers and Railways.—City of Bombay.—The Parsis.—The Departments, and District Officers.—Land Tenure.—The Survey Settlement.—Forest Policy.—Local Funds.—European Officers.—Condition of the people.—Facts about British rule.

SHORT HISTORY

OF

THE BOMBAY PRESIDENCY.

I.—DESCRIPTION OF THE BOMBAY PRESIDENCY.

INDIA is a name that has been given by Europeans to the vast Peninsula which lies between the Himalayas and the ocean. Neither to their country nor to themselves have the inhabitants of India ever given any one comprehensive name. Hence, if we wish to speak of them collectively, we are forced to call them natives of India, or simply Natives. The term Indian cannot be applied to them, as its use is popularly restricted to denote the aboriginal tribes of America. Hindustán means only the Gangetic plain and Central India north of the Narbada, and is in no way synonymous with India. But there is in truth nothing to wonder at in the absence of a name for the land and the people that dwell in it. The only bond that forms India in any sense into a country or a nation is British rule. Apart from this it is a continent rather than a country. It comprises an area equal to all Europe without Russia and the Scandinavian Peninsula. It contains a population greater than that of all the countries of Europe except Russia put together, a population composed of peoples that differ one from the other in race and in language, in religion and in custom, no less than the Spaniard from the Russian, or the Greek from the Turk. Living as they do in countries separated from each other by broad rivers, lofty mountains and dense forests, there is indeed but little reason why the isolated units that form the population of India should have ever been welded into one symmetrical whole. So to speak of the inhabitants of India as the Indian People is no more accurate than it would be to speak of Englishmen, Germans, and Italians as the European people; and the term would be absolutely devoid of significance to the great majority of those whom it is intended to include.

From the Himalayas in the north to Cape Comorin in the south, the length of the Peninsula is nineteen hundred miles; while from the mouth of the Indus in the west to the mouth of the Irawadi in the east, its breadth is fifteen hundred. Hindustán proper may be said to consist of the huge river basin of the Ganges. Springing from the snow-clad Himalayas, two hundred miles north of Delhi, this mighty river receives into its yellow waters at Allahábád the dark stream of the Jumna, and flows through lands of wonderful richness to the Bay of Bengal. To the north-west of Hindustán is the Panjáb or land of the five rivers (pánch-áb), the Indus and its tributaries, the Jhelam, the Chenáb, the Rawi and the Satlej. This land, which tempted the Aryan invaders to leave their rugged homes in Central Asia and make their dwelling-place in India, forms with Sind the river-basin of the Indus, whose waters rise in the mountains that enclose the beautiful region of Káshmir. South of Hindustán India is termed by Hindu geographers the Deccan (Dakshin and Dakhin), which means south; but the name is more usually limited to that part of Western India which lies above the Gháts, and which forms the chief part of the Presidency of Bombay. That Presidency corresponds in area and population with the Peninsula of Spain and Portugal, and to a certain extent resembles it in position. Excluding the large native state of Baroda it contains an area of close on 192,000 square miles, nearly one-third of which consists of feudatory states, and a population of twenty-three millions and a quarter, of whom nearly seven millions are in those states.

The northernmost portion of the Presidency is composed of Sind, a hot and arid country, watered by the Indus as it flows from the Panjáb to the Arabian Sea. South of Sind is the state of Kachh (Cutch), and next in position the group of states in the peninsula of Káthiáwár. The remaining and most important portion of the Presidency is divided into two distinct natural divisions by the range of Western Gháts. Between these mountains and the sea there runs a strip of land twenty-five to fifty miles wide, which has various characteristics, and is known by several names. East of Káthiáwár and south as far as the Portuguese city of Damán it forms the rich undulating plain of Guzárát. From Damán southwards to Goa it is known as the Konkan or rugged country. South of Goa is the district of Kánara which was formerly included in the Madras Presidency. With its splendid harbour at Kárwár, its magnificent mountains and deadly jungles, Kánara possesses a marked individuality. Southward from Kánara the coast land belongs to Madras, and bears the name of Málabár. East of the Gháts is the table-land or plateau of the Deccan, a region of wild and varying scenery in some places fertile, in others barren, at a general elevation of two thousand feet above the sea. The most northern part of the Deccan is called Khándesh, the greater part of which consists of the low-lying valley of the Tápti; but Khándesh, though strictly speaking in the Deccan, is generally regarded as separate from it.

The Sáhyádris, or Western Gháts, may be described as buttresses, which, rising from the coast lands of Guzárát, the Konkan and Kánara, support the elevated table-land of the Deccan. Springing from the slopes of the Narbada and Tápti valleys they trend southwards almost without a break to the highlands of Mysur, at a height generally of some 4,000 feet above the sea. But they attain nearly 5,000 feet among the peaks of Máhábleshwár where, within sight of the Arabian Sea, rises the mighty Krishna which flows across the continent into the Bay of Bengal. The pleasant and healthy climate of Máhábleshwár could hardly be neglected by Europeans; and in the hot summer months it forms a delightful playground and health-resort for those who can get away from the scorching winds of the Deccan or the steamy atmosphere of the coast.

The great diversity in natural features brings with it a corresponding variety in the climates of Western India. In the open plains that form the valley of the Indus there are intense extremes of heat and cold, the winter being severe even for those who have come from a northern clime, while the heat in the hot season nearly approaches the limit at which life becomes intolerable to the European. Nor is there a rainy season, such as is vouchsafed to most of India, to cool the heated atmosphere. The rainfall is limited to a very few inches a year, and cultivation depends upon irrigation by canals fed from the great river, and tanks in which every drop of the scanty rainfall is carefully collected. Passing to the south, the land between the Ghâts and the sea has a climate of which winter forms no part. The air is moist and steamy; and though from December to February the nights are in places cold, the sun is always hot, while above the Ghâts at the same season the air is comparatively cold and bracing. As the spring months come on the heat rapidly increases; in the Deccan hot scorching winds blow all day and often all night, filling the air with a kind of mirage which makes every outline heavy and indistinct. In the coast districts the hot wind is modified by moisture from the ocean; but the enervating languor of the damp climate is a hardly preferable equivalent to the dry heat. By the end of May the heat reaches its intensity; vegetation is parched up and the country looks like a desert. But early in June there comes a welcome change; piles of clouds rise in the sky, and with little warning the phenomenon known as the bursting of the monsoon takes place, abundant rain from the south-west bringing fresh life to the thirsty soil. Vegetation springs up everywhere with wonderful rapidity; and pleasant showery weather with cheerful sunshine lasts on until the latter part of September. In the Deccan this is far the pleasantest time of the year, and is not unlike a fine English summer. On the coast, though the atmosphere is fairly cool, the rain is too heavy for enjoyment; but even there, as elsewhere, it is felt as a great relief after the heat. Throughout the seven dry months European civil officers are engaged in travelling all over their districts, pitching their tents close to the villages, living amongst the people, and meeting one another only from time to time. But in the rains they come into the head-quarter station of the district, and have comparative leisure for social enjoyment and relaxation. When the rains cease it is usually hot again for a month or six weeks before the cold weather can be said to commence. The climate of the Deccan is on the whole the healthiest in India.

In the Konkan and other coast districts rice is the principal food of the people, there being abundance of water for its cultivation. But above the Ghâts rice is rather looked upon as a luxury, many kinds of millet and pulse, with some barley and wheat, forming a more substantial food for the hardier population of the Deccan. Some of these cereals are grown in the monsoon and are known as the rabi or early crop, while wheat and barley, forming the kharif or late crop, are sown in the rich black soil after the rainy season is over. Cotton and oil seeds are sown at this later period, while rice ripens at the close of the monsoon. Exaggerated as the hardships of the Deccan peasantry have been, their land undoubtedly cannot compete in the richness of its soil and products with the more fertile parts of India.

On the whole, there is much beauty in the Bombay Presidency. Upper Sind affords magnificent views of the mountains of Beluchistán. Lying between the sea and the Sáhyádri mountains, from which innumerable spurs run down and cross it in all directions, the Konkan unites wonderful grandeur with beauty of a softer kind. Monotonous as much of the Deccan must be confessed to be, few portions of it can be called uninteresting. Sometimes the traveller may go for miles and miles through an undulating country with poor features and little vegetation; but elsewhere bold ranges of hills, steep ravines and rich forests form a beautiful and attractive landscape. But the scenery of the Ghâts themselves, with their rugged peaks of basalt often scarped down to make the well-nigh impregnable strongholds of Marátha free-booters, their rocks and forests, and after the rains their streams and waterfalls, leaves nothing to be desired by the lover of nature, except a climate that will allow him to enjoy the beauty that meets his eye.

Generally speaking, the rivers of the Deccan are raging torrents for a few months of the year, and not much more than dry beds for the rest. But near the coast the rivers are for the most part tidal streams, and are much used for navigation; while they afford fertility to the picturesque country through which they take their course. Next to the Indus, the most important rivers that fall into the Western Ocean are the Narbada and Tápti, that flow half across India from the Central Provinces and empty themselves into the sea at Broach and Surat in Guzárát. Of those that take the contrary course from the Gháts to the Bay of Bengal the chief are the Godáwari and the Krishna, with its tributary the Bhima. Towns and villages are met with every few miles, those in the Deccan having strong walls that were once needed for their protection. The people have ever sought the security that a community affords, and the traditional custom has survived after its necessity has disappeared. Farmhouses and cottages scattered about like those in England are never to be seen in India.

Four languages besides Hindustáni are spoken in the Presidency. In Sind the language is Sindi, in which the Persian and Hindustáni elements predominate; in Guzárát Guzaráti, the language spoken by the Pársis, in which a Persian colouring is laid upon a Sánskrit foundation; in the Konkan and the Deccan, except in the extreme south and east, Maráthi, which, of all Indian languages, bears the closest resemblance to the Sánskrit from which it has sprung, the characters in which it is written being almost unaltered. The country in which Maráthi is spoken is commonly known as Máháráshtra, a name which covers a large area in the Central Provinces, Central India, Barár and Hydarábád, besides the Maráthi-speaking districts of Bombay. All these tongues are Aryan and have a certain family likeness; but in the south and east of the Presidency is spoken Kánarese, a language which has nothing in common with any Aryan tongue. It belongs to the group, largely used in Southern India, which is known as Dravidian, and includes Támil and Telagu. Hindustáni is nowhere in Bombay the vernacular language of the people, but it is spoken generally by Muhammadans, and is a kind of lingua franca which the traveller may find understood to some extent wherever he goes. And by a kind of tradition (dating from the era of Mussalmán conquest) that it is necessarily the language of the ruling race, Maráthas constantly reply to a European in a patois which they believe to be Hindustáni to a question which may be asked in the purest Maráthi. Hindustáni is a language of comparatively modern growth that sprang up in the armies of the early Moghal invaders, and is properly known as Urdu, or the language of the camp. Sánskrit is spoken freely in the households of educated Brahmans, and Persian has a like use among Muhammadans; while now all natives with any pretence to education have a fair knowledge of English. In Bombay itself the languages spoken may be counted by the score.

II.—DESCRIPTION OF THE PEOPLE.

THE British Empire in India contains a population of more than 253 millions, exclusive of the new acquisition of Upper Burma (Burmah). Of the twenty-three millions and a quarter that inhabit the Bombay Presidency, 35,000 are in Perim and Aden, and nearly seven millions in the Native States of the Presidency. The population of the British districts includes 12,300,000 Hindus, 3,020,000 Muhammadans, 216,000 Jains, 138,000 Christians, 127,000 Sikhs, 72,000 Parsis, half a million forest or aboriginal tribes, and 8,400 of other religions, chiefly Jews. Four-fifths of the population of India are directly under British rule, and the remaining one-fifth is comprised in the protected Native States. The administration of these states is closely supervised by British political officers, and tends more and more nearly to resemble that of British India. Of this immense mass of people the great majority, including all the Hindus and most of the Muhammadans, are descended from those Aryan tribes who, before the dawn of history, dwelt in the highlands of Central Asia with the forefathers of Latins, Teutons, and Scandinavians. Schoolboys are now taught not that Latin words are derived from Greek or Greek from Sánskrit, but that all alike have sprung from that common parent language which was spoken by the ancestors both of Hindus and Englishmen in their original home, before successive waves broke off from the population to found colonies in India, Greece, and Italy. It has been shown by the science of philology how far the language had grown up before there was any separation of the family at all, and at what stage of their wanderings each different wave of colonists split up into groups which settled down and grew up into nations. Those who turned southwards to India had the least distance to go from their common home. Their language has undergone the least modification, and the speech of the Marátha peasant comes nearest to the original tongue of his and our Aryan forefathers.

Some twelve millions of the total population of India consist of people commonly known as aboriginal tribes. Their forefathers were already in India before the Aryan invasion, and of any earlier inhabitants of the country we have no knowledge at all. These are wild and savage tribes, barely reclaimed from barbarism. They are scattered widely over the country, but all have some resemblance to each other in physical features, language, and habits. Though all of them are of a very low type of humanity, some from contact with Hinduism have advanced to a small degree of civilisation, possess habitations, and cultivate land. Others, of whom in a long series of generations the Hindus could make absolutely nothing, the British Government has enrolled as soldiers and police; and with judicious gifts of seed and cattle has induced them to settle down on land that has also been a gift. Others again are still virtually in their original state of savagedom, and live in the depths of forests whose noxious vapours bring death to other races. They wander from place to place, supporting themselves as best they can by the chase, or by the wild roots and berries of the jungle.

Though some of these tribes worship Hindu gods they cannot be classed as Hindus. In the Deccan these races are represented by Mhárs and Mángs, Chámárs, Wadars, and Rámoshis, and the Kolis of the Gháts; and by a tribe of rude musicians named Garsi, whom popular legend names as the descendants of the earliest inhabitants of all. They have, for the most part, regular occupations, and are superior to the forest tribes of whom the most wild and warlike are the Bhils of Khándesh; while below the Gháts in the Kátkaris of the Konkan and the Taláwias of Guzárát are found strictly forest tribes, who can by no means whatever be brought within the pale of civilisation. Such were the people inhabiting the country before the Aryan invasion. From beginning to end they have excited from the Hindus no other feeling than loathing and contempt. Their touch is held to defile, and the Hindus have always insisted on those, such as Mhárs and Chámárs, who settle down in one place, occupying a separate quarter apart from the rest of the town or village, like the Jews in Europe in the Middle Ages.

The contrast between the early invaders and the aboriginal population was, indeed, no less marked than that which existed thousands of years later between the European conquerors of India and the population which they found in the country; while in their treatment of the conquered the comparison is altogether in favour of the later conquerors. There are, it is true, no records or traditions of the personal or individual history of the Aryan people before they found their way into India from the North-west; but of the Aryans collectively we have no inconsiderable knowledge. Insisting upon a strict observance of the marriage law, they lived in families which formed the unit of society, and in which the *patria potestas* of the Romans was a vigorous institution;

while, as with modern natives of India, the various degrees of relationship were marked out with wonderful elaboration. Far from leading a nomadic life they dwelt together in towns and villages; and with the increase of population the families grew into clans and tribes which formed at least the basis of the present system of caste. The whole were subjects to a king who had priests and soldiers as his councillors. But their kings were no absolute and irresponsible monarchs, for there were codes of laws carefully drawn up. The people were not dependent on the chase for food. They had reached that stage in civilisation in which men plough the fields and sow the seeds that they may reap the crop, and spin wool and flax to make themselves clothes. Deeply impressed with the mystery of creation they worshipped in many forms the Maker of the Universe, and reverenced the priests that directed the worship.

How many years have passed since these people left their old homes to sweep down through the narrow and dangerous mountain passes upon the land of the five rivers it is impossible to say. It is probable that the work of conquest took a long time and was advanced by many expeditions, while the first arrivals would come as settlers rather than as conquerors. At the time of the conquest it is uncertain how far the division into caste had been developed; but it is clear that from the earliest times the Aryans had in their deep veneration for the sanctity of the family a strong predisposition to a system of that nature. Their contact with the original tribes of India could not but have the effect of enormously strengthening and developing such a system, both for purposes of defence and offence; and more especially to prevent the contamination that would come to their race by union with those beyond their caste. Their close organisation may have enabled them to crush with comparative ease all resistance on the part of the inhabitants; and by a more or less gradual process, of which no details whatever have come down to us, they extended their conquest throughout the country, driving back the aboriginal people to the depths of the jungles and their fastnesses on hills and mountains.

For the first information that exists about the Hindus in India we must look to the religious poems of the Weds (Vedas) composed from time to time, and compiled into four books at perhaps 2000 B.C. These are not, and were probably never intended to be, historic records; but while all their descriptions of kings and queens and their magnificent palaces are purely imaginary and fanciful, the Weds yet give a general idea of the state to which the people had advanced. When the compilation was made, the Aryans had formed themselves into various kingdoms, and were divided into the two chief sections of the solar and lunar races, the great war between which forms the epic of the Máhábhárat. Of the various dynasties the more important were at Oudh and Megadha in Bengal. The union of castes, which had sufficed to crush the resistance of the aboriginal tribes, had with the necessity caused by that resistance ceased to hold together its component units. It is evident that one of the most marked features of the Hindu character was then, as it has ever been, the inability to form any political combination otherwise than for mere temporary purposes. From the hymns of the Rig-Wed it appears that the original four castes, which form the foundation of the present complicated structure, whenever they may have first begun, were then existing in a clearly defined form. All alike were born from Brahma the Creator, the highest caste or Brahmans springing from his mouth, the Kshatrya (here called Rájánya) from his arms, the Waishya from his thigh, the Sudra from his feet. But the Rig-Wed gives no hint of the immeasurable supremacy of the Brahman and the corresponding degradation of the Sudra, which sprang up later on, and in spite of a long period of organised resistance has continued until now. Notwithstanding the claims of Rájputs and some few others to belong to the Kshatrya caste, and of some merchants who represent themselves as Waishyas, both these castes have practically ceased to be. The stringent ordinances of the Brahmans have enabled them to preserve their lineage in its purity, while the Sudras have split up into a multitude of castes, some of which are practically guilds or crafts, all alike maintaining a strict religious exclusiveness. To Europeans the system may appear an intolerable oppression; but it does not seem to be felt so even by the lowest castes of real Hindus, who, while looking up to the Brahman as the representative of God on earth, feel elevated rather by the sanctity of their own caste, than humiliated by the existence of other castes higher in the religious scale. Natives of India, it has been stated, have no nationality and no name for themselves as a people: the fact is that the functions of nationality have been usurped by caste. A child is brought up with the idea strongly developed in every possible way that he is a member of his particular caste, the idea of any higher unit in the scale of humanity never entering his head. A parallel would exist if in England a boy were to grow up by caste a mason or a carpenter, feeling that all his world was limited to his fellow caste-people, and having no notion of his nationality as an Englishman. To the Hindu all beyond the limits of his caste are beyond the reach of his sympathy. He may, of course, have dealings with them in the way of buying and selling and the ordinary business of life; but to eat with an outsider involves defilement from which he can only be cleansed by heavy fines and harsh penance. Marriage with such an one, even if possible, involves expulsion from the caste, together with all that for the Hindu makes life worth living. Excommunication to the Roman Catholic is a bitter thing; bitterer far to the Hindu, for whom every incident of his daily life is a religious ordinance. Accustomed as he is from his youth up to these exaggerated notions of the paramount importance of caste, it is little wonder that in a land of such vast size caste has left no room for any developement of nationality. The bonds of caste, instead of binding together the Hindus into a nation, have made such a union impossible, and rendered them an easy prey to every invader.

At an interval which has been calculated at six hundred years after the compilation of the Weds, there was written a very curious book called the institutes of Manu. It contained an elaborate system of social and religious polity with laws for men of each profession or occupation, from the prince to the peasant. There had been a considerable advance in civilisation since the time of the Weds, and the picture of Hindu society, as it existed three thousand years ago, scarcely differs from that which Englishmen found in India when the house of Stuart reigned in England. It is hard to say whether it is a more wonderful thing that while Europe was steeped in barbarism the Hindu had already arrived at such an advanced stage of civilisation, or that men, who had already done so much, should seemingly have lost the power of doing more. The laws of Manu show that the Hindus had acquired a thorough knowledge of the science of trading. Banking in nearly all its modern branches, book-keeping by double and single entry, simple and compound interest, bills of exchange and insurances, were intimately known, though neither then nor now had they arrived at that immense convenience of modern banking, the use of a cheque-book. The bonds of caste had been drawn much closer by the time when Manu drew up his codes. The Brahmans formed the higher orders of hereditary priesthood, though then as now it was possible for men of other castes to give up the cares of this world and enter inferior orders, or become ascetics and devotees. The Brahmans expounded the sacred books and performed all the chief religious offices, naming the people, marrying them, and performing their funeral rites; and throughout their life they acted as their spiritual guides. Astrology was part of their functions, and no orthodox Hindu could set out on a journey, or undertake any inportant business without consulting a Brahman as to a favourable conjunction of the planets. Under the laws of Manu there were the most odious distinctions between Brahmans and Sudras. If a Sudra sat on the same seat as a Brahman he was exiled or was branded upon his body; if he insulted one of them his tongue was slit; if he molested one he was put to death; if he learnt the sacred books he suffered the same fate, but if he was murdered by a Brahman the penalty was the same as that for killing a dog, a cat, or a crow. A labourer was by law forbidden to accumulate wealth, nor could even his master give him freedom, "for of a state which is natural to him, by whom can he be divested?"

The Kshatryas were the soldiers; but their caste has ceased to exist, and soldiers are enlisted from any caste, including Brahmans, whether in the British service or in the armies of native princes. But the hereditary principle in military employment survived the extinction of the caste, and among the Marāthas and others the Commander-in-Chief of the army was succeeded by his son as much by a matter of course as the political privileges of an English peer descend to his heir. To the Waishya caste belonged the professional and higher degrees of trade, and lawyers, bankers, clerks, agents, and such like were members of the order. But while the humbler castes or guilds have remained intact, there has been much change in the higher ones; and as any one can become a soldier, so there is nothing to prevent his becoming a physician, lawyer, or scribe.

The fourth, or Sudra caste, embraced the lower classes of traders, farmers, cultivators, and artisans. But though the word Sudra is used now as a collective term for these classes, it can hardly be said to be a caste, and no native would reply when asked about his caste that he was a Sudra. Goldsmiths, blacksmiths, carpenters, weavers, and multitudes of others, who are undoubted Sudras, form absolutely independent and exclusive castes; as do others also, the Wánis, for instance, or Banyas (grain merchants and money-lenders) who like to represent themselves as members of the Waishya caste but are nothing more than Sudras. All these and many others are good Hindus. After them come outcastes, who however by no means consent to an equality between themselves, but strictly preserve their own individual distinctions. Chief among these are tanners, leather-dressers, and shoemakers, any persons working in leather being particularly repulsive to the Hindu. Englishmen commonly speak of outcastes as Pariahs, but the word is not used by natives in that sense. "Pahárias" are wild hill people, from "Pahár," a hill, and it is only by Europeans that the use of the word has been extended to others. The native word for caste is "Ját" which the Portuguese from its similarity to the Latin castus converted into caste.

The affairs of each caste are administered by its elders in

conjunction on solemn occasions with Brahmans, the special object being to prevent immorality and to resist any breach or neglect of caste rules. Punishments usually take the form of fine and penance. Any harshness or cruelty is of course punishable by British law; but appeals are seldom made against caste decisions, and on the whole the system works well. If a Hindu is outcasted no lower caste will receive him; thus the overwhelming importance of preserving intact the necessary conditions of his life can hardly be appreciated by those who have had no personal experience of what this tremendous system involves. This control by caste for the purposes of checking immorality and social offences has extended not only to Muhammadans, but also in the south of India to Native Christians.

Though caste and religion are not one and the same, yet the one more or less includes the other, and they are indissolubly bound up together. The Hindu's every act of daily life is a religious observance, depending upon what has been written in his sacred books. His ablutions and sanitary observances are made not so much with any idea of their intrinsic value as because they have been ordained in the ancient writings of his religion. Rich Hindus support family priests; but all, down to almost the poorest, possess family gods, by worshipping whom they constantly purify themselves for taking their meals or going forth to their labour. Ostensibly resting their faith on the trinity of Brahma, Wishnu, and Shiwa—the creating, preserving and destroying deities—the Hindus have set up a whole pantheon of subordinate or local gods, each man or family putting an unreserved and childlike trust in some particular tutelary deity. Faith so implicit and credulity so absolute could hardly fail to degenerate into superstition; and the Hindu, not excepting the educated Brahman, is not free from the terrors of evil demons and spirits, who bring sickness and misfortune, of magic and the evil eye. Nothing in the way of supernatural agency is too gross to be believed. These ideas are deeply seated in all natives of India, including the Muhammadans; and some of the Himalayan wild tribes offer their worship solely to the spirits of evil, in order to avert their wrath. If there be a good god, they say, he will do them no harm, and needs no propitiation.

The natural effect of this credulity has been to raise to an immense height the popular idea of the importance of the Brahmanical priesthood. India is above all things a priest-ridden country, and the "twice-born" Brahmans are looked up to with boundless veneration by the vast mass of Hindus, nay even by Muhammadans, as the means by which the divine wrath may be averted and salvation attained. Brahmans were not likely to discourage notions which exalted them to a pitch unattainable by any others; and by binding tighter and tighter the bonds of the caste system they effectually secured the acceptance of the most preposterous claims to sanctity. But even the population of India, after a time, found the weight of the priestly yoke intolerable. The original purity of the Hindu faith became sullied in the hands of a self-seeking and oppressive priesthood; the spirit of the religion was neglected, its letter rigidly enforced. The sanctity claimed by the Brahmans as inherent to themselves whatever they might do could hardly be maintained, even in such an atmosphere of credulity, in the face of their flagrant licentiousness and immorality. The reaction came. Born the heir to a magnificent kingdom, there grew up in the sixth century before the Christian era a man who was to introduce into the world a religion destined to number amongst its adherents more than any other faith before or since. Prince Gautama was brought up in the height of luxury; he received the best education that was then possible; and he excelled in every manly sport. But the mystery of life under which the few had lives of ease and pleasure, while the masses had no prospect but that of ceaseless toil throughout their days, deeply affected him. He loathed the frivolity and vice which he saw on all sides, and he became convinced that in the hollow precepts and vain ceremonies of the Brahmans there was no help for mankind. Overwhelmed with immeasurable pity and sorrow for the toiling millions, he determined to devote his life to the task of finding out some means by which he might heal their misery and disease. At the age of twenty-eight the prince left his father's palace and dwelt alone in the wilderness, attaining sanctity as Sakya Muni, or the monk, and pondering how he might alleviate the mass of human misery. Gradually he worked out his faith, and emerging from the desert as Buddha, or the wise, he preached the gospel of divine grace for all alike. The Brahmans themselves could not answer his arguments when he told them that no man, whether priest or layman, might come between his fellow-man and his Maker; he crushed their pretensions to infallibility and made war on their oppression and exclusiveness. His doctrine, he said, was like the sky, and had room for all alike, men and women, boys and girls, rich and poor. He told them that as the rivers that fall into the Ganges lose their own names and become one, so all that believed in him ceased to be Brahmans, Kshatryas, Waishyas, and Sudras. As he himself had renounced the riches and the pleasures of this world, so every one, he said, must subdue his passions and renounce everything, even his own self. Each man could make his own deliverance, and by subduing all evil desires, and practising charity, overcome earthly sin and sorrow, and at last after death obtain everlasting rest by Nirwána or absorption into the divine essence. As each drop in the ocean forms part of it, so each man at last would form part of the Creator himself. There was endless hope for all. No one could do more than defer Nirwána for himself, though it might be ages and ages before he eventually attained it. Full of love and sympathy for all, he called down no imprecations and threatened no future punishment for those who disbelieved in him; sin, he said, was its own punishment, virtue its own reward. He laid infinite stress on each man's capability for good or evil; prayer was of no more avail than priestly mediation, each man was to work out his own salvation by his life and deeds. The attractions of Nirwána might seem scanty as compared with the promises made to their disciples by founders of other religions. Nirwána was neither life nor death; it was to be one with life yet not to live, to be blest by ceasing to be. Buddhism was, in fact, a melancholy negative based upon an exaggerated view of the miseries of mankind, and an inability to look upon the brighter side of human affairs. It had no conception of the quiet happiness that may be attained in a Christian household; it saw nothing but gross pleasures on the one side and helpless misery on the other. It assumed that the world was wholly evil, and aimed at a total emancipation from its bondage. For three centuries this theory made its way with wonderful success; the ascendancy of the Brahman priesthood seemed overthrown for ever; and though it did not interfere with the restrictions of caste, so long as they were harmless and inoffensive, yet Buddhism undoubtedly made the people freer and less exclusive. For three centuries it grew in India and spread to China and Ceylon, and at length Asoka, the powerful king of Megadha, who had made enormous sacrifices to the Brahmanical gods, made it the state religion, and Brahmanism seemed at an end. But its union with the state was no source of strength to the Buddhist Church. Instead of resting upon an independent foundation, it allowed itself to be supported by the civil power; and when the kingdom of Megadha, under successive dynasties, crumbled away and could no longer maintain the state church, the end of Buddhism as a predominant religion was assured. In the fourth century of our era Brahmanism was again raising its head, and two centuries later it reattained its supremacy, which it has never again lost. The gentle and loving though sombre creed of Buddha passed away, and the grotesque pantheon—with gods, demi-gods, miracles, heavens and hells, splendid festivals, and liturgies—which the Brahmans had pinned on to the simple faith of the Weds became again the religion of the land. Some princes indeed were strong enough to preserve Buddhism for several centuries, and a sect called the Jains, who are numerous in Western India, are in some respects successors of the Buddhists to this day. Many of the Buddhist tenets are incorporated into the teachings of this sect, which denies the exclusive supremacy of the Brahmans, but which, though formed as a protest against exclusiveness, is itself as exclusive as any. Another offshoot from orthodox Hinduism are the Lingayats, who arose in the Deccan in the 11th century A.D. They also reject the ministration of the Brahmans and worship the phallic emblem (the linga) and the bull. In the case of these revolts against caste and exclusiveness, as in those made by the Sikhs of the Panjáb in the seventeenth century and similar religious movements in other parts of the world, the new sect has but imposed upon itself the very same fetters as those against which it rebelled.

DESCRIPTION OF THE PEOPLE.

It has been stated that with the Hindu everything that he does is connected with his religion. This, of course, includes what he eats and drinks, and the manner in which he takes his meals. Brahmans eat no meat, but live on grain, vegetables, milk, and sweetmeats, their food being always cooked and their water brought by some one of their own caste. While taking their food they may only wear a dhotar or piece of cloth folded round the loins, a rule which they find extremely inconvenient when business takes them to the hills in the cold weather. Maráthas and other classes of Hindus eat meat, but rather as a luxury than as an ordinary rule, never eating the cow because it is sacred, or the pig because it is unclean. At their meals the Hindus are unsociable in the highest degree. Women never eat with men, not even the wife with her husband. The well-to-do Hindu generally sits down to his meal in a small and dingy room, with his legs folded under him, on a square board raised three or four inches from the cow-dunged floor, while a tray on which are various brass or silver pots containing the several portions of his meal is placed before him on his seat. The use of a knife, fork and spoon is unknown, the hands only being employed.

The proper costume of the Hindu consists of two broad pieces of cotton cloth one of which, called the dhotar, is folded round the waist, reaching well below the knee, and the end of it passed between the legs and secured to the waist behind; the other is thrown over the soulders, a paggri or turban completing the costume. But Hindus now generally wear over the dhotar a tunic modelled on that which Muhammadans wear over their loose drawers or trowsers. Shoes or sandals are properly never worn in the house; but there is some latitude in the observance of this custom. Most natives shave parts of their heads in styles varying with the different castes. Brahmans shave all but a pig-tail which is allowed to grow to its natural length from the upper part of the back of the head. To uncover the head in the presence of a superior, whether in or out of the house, is a mark of disrespect, unless it is meant as a sign of the most intense humility, in order to obtain a request. The houses of ordinary Hindus or Muhammadans are furnished in the most simple style, if indeed they can be said to be furnished at all. There are no chairs or tables; a carpet with a mattress or some pillows covered with white cloth forms sufficient accommodation for the household to sit upon by day and sleep upon by night, a rough charpoy or bedstead being sometimes used. Even for writing chairs and tables are unknown, Hindus sitting down on the ground with their legs folded under them in a way that would be impossible for Europeans, their writing materials being placed on the ground in front of them. In most of these customs the Muhammadans resemble the Hindus, except that there is no limitation to the clothes that they may wear when taking their meals. In the times of the Weds the seclusion of women does not seem to have been known, but most of the upper classes of Hindus, influenced in great measure by Muhammadan fashions, generally follow this custom. But it is not universally or uniformly adhered to, and in the Deccan among the Brahmans and Maráthas, it is often only nominally observed. It has not prevented ladies of rank emerging from time to time from their seclusion, and taking prominent places in Indian history. But it must be confessed that on the whole the Hindu's notions on the subject of marriage are diametrically opposed to those of the Englishman. Marriages amongst Hindus, and Muhammadans also, are arranged by the parents of the bride and bridegroom while those chiefly concerned are mere children, without their inclinations being consulted in the least. If a Hindu woman loses her husband, which may happen before either he or she is grown up, she has to pass the rest of her life, at all events in the higher castes, in enforced widow-hood, and is obliged to do all the drudgery of the household and undergo every kind of degradation. Often a young girl of twelve becomes the bride of a widower four or five times her age with the certain prospect in the ordinary course of nature of occupying this despised position for the greater part of her life. In truth, the fate of a Hindu widow of the higher castes seems hardly happier now than in the old days when she was forced on the death of her husband to cast herself upon his burning pyre, before the British Government put an end to the infamous rite of sati. Polygamy is not in the west of India followed to any great extent, but there is nothing to hinder the taking of a second or even a third wife by a man who is able to support her.

III.—EARLY HINDU CIVILISATION.

FOR a series of generations the Hindus were suffered to spread themselves all over India and develope their civilisation pretty much into its present shape, without let or hindrance from any but the aboriginal dwellers of the land. The time however was to come when other nations should attempt, one after the other with varying success, to wrest from them the sovereignty over their rich and fertile lands. The first recorded invasion was that of the great Persian king Darius, about half a century after Buddha preached and taught his law. His army is said to have reached the Indus and sailed down to the sea, and thence made its way back to Persia. About two centuries later Alexander the Great led his soldiers across the rugged mountains of the Hindu Kush and through the gloomy passes of Áfghánistán into the Panjáb and crossed the Indus at Átak. After being hospitably entertained by the ruler of the country he advanced across the Jhelam, and defeated king Porus who was ruler of the land as far as Delhi. Going on as far as the Satlej the conquerer hoped within a few days to see the Ganges; but his army, which is said to have numbered more than a hundred thousand men, refused to march further on his errand of exploration and conquest.

So Alexander was forced to return home by the route chosen by the soldiers of Darius, though he left behind in the Panjáb the so-called Greek kingdom of Bactria, which lasted for a short time after his death. The chief value of the history of his wonderful expedition consists in the accounts of the state of the country, and its people, left by the writers who accompanied him to India. There was no one supreme ruler in the country; many independent kingdoms existed, whose common origin availed but little to prevent them from warring against each other. There were no great buildings; and the cities, which were wealthy and prosperous, were chiefly of wood and clay. The system of caste was in full force, the trades especially forming separate bodies, and the members of each could not eat or marry with those of any other. The country was thickly inhabited and carefully cultivated, while military science was developed to a high extent. The people were said to be well clothed, intelligent, and law abiding, the higher classes skilled in astrology and mathematics. They had elaborate rules for prosody and prose composition, and appear indeed to have reached a level not much below that of the Greeks themselves. Self-governing village communities existed then much as now; the gulf between Brahmans, who were the chief possessors of learning, and the other castes was immense, the reformation of Buddha not having then reached the Panjáb. In short, in all essential particulars the description of Alexander might have been equally well written by Clive. A different estimate of skill and intelligence would naturally be arrived at by different races. It is probable also that if the middle and upper classes appeared well to do, the victorious army of a slave-holding people like the Greeks would take their prosperity as a type of the general condition of the population, and pay little regard to the state of the toiling masses.

Alexander failed to effect a permanent conquest in India; but his invasion tended in some measure to break through the exclusiveness of the Hindus. Traffic grew up between his great city of Alexandria and Indian ports; Greek and Persian merchants visited and sojourned in various parts of India. An attempt was made by Seleukos, the general of Alexander, to complete his leader's scheme of conquest; but it was unsuccessful, and on the ensuance of peace he sent the philosopher Megasthenes to the city of Palibothra or Patna, the capital of the great Bengal kingdom of Megadha. The ruler of Megadha was then Chandra Gupta, who had been a soldier in the army of Porus. The Greek philosopher, in those of his memoirs which have survived, gives a most interesting account of the rule of this monarch of whom he speaks in terms of high praise. Under his sway Hindustán and other parts of India were consolidated into one kingdom, commerce was increased by land and sea, and Java and Siam were colonised by Hindus. Of the roads and rest-houses, and of the police Megasthenes could not speak too highly.

Buddhism was at this time gaining strength, and the great and wise Asoka, the grandson of Chandra Gupta, became for Buddhism what Constantine was afterwards for Christianity. This enlightened monarch, as is known from the Páli inscriptions on rocks and pillars from Orissa to Kábul, instituted popular courts of justice, extended roads and traffic, and, probably from Greek ideas, introduced architecture and sculpture for religious and public buildings. Before his time the most populous cities had nothing more permanent than clay or wooden dwellings, no traces of which survive.

At the death of Asoka the kingdom of Megadha fell to pieces, and from that period up to the commencement of the Muhammadan invasions of India the only event that can be said to be of interest to any but professed historical students is the gradual decline of Buddhism. Roughly speaking, it may be stated that throughout Northern India there existed a number of dynasties, the strongest of whom for the time being assumed the title of Máhárāj Adiraj, or Emperor of India; that some of these lasted for a longer, others for a shorter period; that they rested upon force or cunning, the success or failure of the rival claimants to power being achieved on the simple principle by which "the people that followed Omri prevailed against them that followed Tibni, so Tibni died and Omri reigned." What has been said of Northern India may be applied also to Southern India. Various states existed which possessed no confederation, no sympathy, and no common bond of union, but which, on the contrary, waged a perpetual war for supremacy. But the country was populous and well tilled, village communities flourished, and the sea was freely used for commerce. For the first six centuries of the Christian era the Jain faith was the predominant one, and its votaries built temples of much architectural skill and beauty. Schools were founded and education encouraged; and civilisation in general appears to have kept pace with that of the north. But the schools and education were for the Brahmans, and the Sudras merely existed for their benefit.

Throughout the long series of wars and conquests and the rise and fall of successive dynasties one remarkable institution continued to flourish, unaffected by any change of rulers. This was the system of self-governing village communities, which appears to have been a recognised feature in Aryan political existence from the earliest times. Each village may be regarded as a miniature state, the whole land of the country being attached to some one village or another. The boundaries of all the lands, except inaccessible tracts, were carefully marked out and the plots or fields into which the country was divided known each by its own name. The owner of each particular field was intensely jealous of encroachment on his land, and there were, of course, constant disputes as to right of possession. This division of the land has been carefully preserved by the British Government, the whole country having been elaborately surveyed, maps of each village prepared, and boundary marks erected for each field. But the ownership of land has never been regarded as absolute, in the same sense that it has been in England. It has always been conjointly held by the landlord and the tenant, the landlord in nearly the whole of the Bombay Presidency being the Government, and the tenure styled ryotwár, the tenant or cultivator being known as the ryot. The ryot is not a tenant at will, he is the hereditary occupant of the land ; and the Government cannot eject him as long as he pays the rent or tax for his field which is assessed for a period of thirty years. This was not invariably the case, there having been a class of tenants called Upris, who under native rule held their lands on such terms as Government might impose from year to year, as distinguished from the Mirásdárs or part proprietors above described. But throughout Mahárúshtra the part proprietors were always much more numerous than the tenants-at-will, and it seems probable that originally all the land was held by them, the inferior tenure only coming in as the old proprietors were disturbed by the Muhammadans. The matter is at present of no practical importance, for by the terms of the Survey Settlement the British Government has secured the higher right to all alike. Each ryot has a separate settlement with Government, terminable by the cultivator at the expiration of each year, but by Government only on his failure to pay the assessment which is fixed at a uniform amount for thirty years. The cultivator may sell, let, or mortgage his right of occupancy, and at the end of the thirty years he has an absolute right to the renewal of the lease at revised rates, fixed not with reference to any improvements that he has made, but by general considerations of the increased value of land in the district, owing to the rise of prices or facilities of communication. So the old distinction between Mirásdárs and Upris is a thing of the past, and the original system of the Hindu Government of giving the whole land in mirás is again in force. Under this system the obsolute ownership of the land can be said to rest neither with the Government nor with the ryot; it is shared between the two, an idea strange as it may appear to Europeans, familiar to all Hindus. An ignorance of this fact caused the fatal mistake of Lord Cornwallis in Bengal, who in his permanent settlement conferred the ownership of the land permanently and absolutely on the Zemindárs, in imitation of the landlord system of Great Britain; thus robbing the cultivators of their rights, and discounting the future claims of the state upon the revenues of the land. Such errors have fortunately been avoided in Bombay, where the principle at the root of the matter has been thoroughly grasped and its working systematised. A certain amount of land, especially in the Deccan, has been what is called alienated, that is for services done to the state the Mussalmán or Marátha rulers gave up the whole or a portion of their claims to a village or villages as a reward in perpetuity to a successful soldier or statesman. But in this case no change takes place in the position of the ryot, and under the Survey Settlement, the whole of the assessment is collected by Government and handed over in whole or part as the case may be to the Inámdár, or descendant of the person to whom the land was originally granted.

Under this tenure of land, in conjunction with the system of caste, the independent and self-containing nature of the village community can well be imagined. The village was ruled by its headman or Pátil, an officer elected by the landholders of the village for a term of years or for life, and who had a subordinate establishment to aid him in managing the village affairs. The Pátil is a man of action rather than learning; and in order to keep the village accounts and carry on such correspondence as may be necessary, the village possesses an hereditary accountant called the Kulkarni, who is generally a Brahman. The Pátil had an immediate assistant called a Chawgla, but this officer is no longer so generally found. Besides these the complete establishment for a village originally consisted of twenty-four persons of whom twelve were of major and twelve of minor importance; but in very few villages was the establishment complete. All were hereditary as far as their family was concerned, but subject to election within its limits. The most important of these were the carpenter, the blacksmith, the shoemaker, and the Mhár, the latter, though an outcast, holding a responsible position in the village. It was his duty to watch over the boundaries of the village lands and individual fields and the growing crops, to look after travellers' horses and baggage, and be the public messenger and guide. When the ryot has paid his rent to the Pátil, and the Kulkarni has registered it in his account books, it is the Mhár who has to carry it to the nearest Government treasury. Next to the Mhár was the Máng, one of the lowest outcast races, who eat carcases of cattle that have died of disease. In old days he was the public executioner, and he made the leather whips and thongs used by the cultivators. Next came the potter and barber, the washerman and the trumpeter, the astrologer and the bard. Evidently by a late addition the superior establishment was completed by a Muhammadan priest, a very strange excrescence on the ancient Hindu village. Among the twelve who were considered of less importance were the butcher, the water carrier, and the oil-seller.

The Pátil was assisted by the rest of the establishment in discharging the duties attached to his office, and payment was made to each by the community for his services to it in land, money, or more commonly grain, each individual's share being fixed by the rules and regulations of the village. The twelve men of major importance were known as balutidárs from balut, a handful of grain, in allusion to the remuneration due to them by the villagers. In cases of serious disputes the Pátil could summon a council of five or more, called a panchayat, who formed a kind of jury. In some villages the Pátil had by grant or by usage the power of fine or imprisonment in criminal cases, but as a general rule he had to report such matters to a superior officer of Government. As intermediate agents between the Pátil and the Rája there were hereditary district officers, each in charge of a large number of villages. They were generally known as Deshmukhs and Deshpands, latterly assuming the title of Zemindár; and they performed for their districts duties corresponding to those of Pátils and Kulkarnis for the villages. While under British rule the village system has been retained, the duties of hereditary district officers became more and more nominal; and they were finally relieved of all liability for future service on condition of paying a quit-rent on their holdings, the remainder being granted to them as private property. But the immense value of the village system with especial reference to the Pátil, Kulkarni and Mhár was so obvious, and the harm that would accrue if the influence of Government over the Pátils or theirs over the people were once lost would be so great, that the integrity of the system has been jealously guarded.

The status of the Pátil as revenue officer and the responsible head of what is now known as the village police is clearly defined, and everything is done to support his dignity. He is no less the agent of the Government than the representative of the ryot. The village system exists most vigorously in the Deccan, but in all parts of the Presidency there is for each village a Pátil, an accountant, and a menial servant

V.—ESTABLISHMENT OF MUHAMMADAN RULE.

THUS for many centuries the Hindus had been suffered to go their own way, with little if any interference from without. They had attained a degree of civilisation which in contemporary Europe must be sought in vain, but which had already ceased to show any promise of future expansion. Their highest unit was in one sense the family and caste, in another the village. Beyond that, although a successful soldier or wise statesman might for a time unite under one rule a large extent of country, yet such a government lacked every element of stability and cohesion, its subjects having no common interests and no spirit of patriotism.

It was now to be seen whether these centrifugal tendencies could not be eradicated, and a spirit of union forced into being by the persistent pressure of foreign invasion. Early in the seventh century of our era there had arisen in Arabia a new teacher who called himself the last of the prophets; and Muhammad told his countrymen that he had received a divine mission to force upon the whole world the choice between the Korán tribute or the sword. Thirty years after the Hijira or flight from Mecca to Medina in 622, from which date the Muhammadan era is reckoned, the warriors of Islam, urged on no less by their fanatical zeal than by lust for plunder and conquest, made themselves masters of Syria, Persia, and Egypt. In 664 they overcame the hardy Afgháns of Kábul; and in the same year the Caliph Omar founded

Bassora on the south-west of Persia, from which place in 700 was despatched into Sind the first Muhammadan expedition against India. Its success was only partial; but it was followed up a few years later by a larger expedition which, under Kásim, nephew of the governor of Bassora, conquered Sind, and advanced to Multán. Within fifty years of Kásim's death the Muhammadans were expelled by the Rájputs, and the fame of the Arab invasion soon dwindled into a mere tradition. This was not the only unsuccessful enterprise made by the Muhammadans before the tide turned which was to carry the supremacy of Islam over the length and breadth of India. The ascendancy was of a religion rather than that of a nationality; if, indeed, it may not be better described as that of a religious nationality which received into itself every one irrespective of race or birth, who would assent to the formula that there is but one God and Muhammad is his prophet. Nothing could be more radically opposed to Hindu notions of the necessary connection between religion and birth than a creed which placed the convert on terms of absolute religious and social equality with those born in the faith. Cut off irrevocably from his own caste, the enthusiasm for his new religion of the forcibly converted Hindu often exceeded that of its original propagators. Christianity has signally failed to have a like effect, for a Hindu, though he may become a Christian, can no more become an Englishman than an Englishman can become a Hindu; and the convert to Christianity finds himself but too often an object of contempt alike to his former caste-people, and to the cold unsympathising Englishman.

The next serious invasion of the Muhammadans was not from the sea, but from their kingdom of Ghazni in the Áfghán mountains, of which Sabuktagin succeeded to the sovereignty

ESTABLISHMENT OF MUHAMMADAN RULE. 37

in A.D. 976. This brave and skilful soldier conquered first Kandahár, and then Káshmir and the Panjáb, both of which were under the rule of the Hindu king Jaypál. Sabuktagin, however, withdrew to Ghazni, and Jaypál, aided by the kings of Delhi, Ájmir, and Kanauj, led against him a vast army to avenge the invasion of their territories. The Muhammadan chieftain advanced to meet them, and crushed their united forces. He took possession of Pesháwar, and levied heavy contributions on the country west of the Indus. His son and successor, the famous iconoclast, Mahmoud of Ghazni, incited by the story of his father's victories, moved upon India in 1001, and, with a force numerically far inferior to that opposed to him, inflicted another crushing defeat on King Jaypál; and the Hindu Rája sought death in the flames of the funeral pyre which he had caused to be prepared for himself. Mahmoud is said to have made no less than thirteen invasions of India from Ghazni, his zeal for the destruction of idols being at least equalled by his thirst for booty. His cruelty established in the hearts of the Hindu races a hatred of Muhammadans which has never been eradicated. Yet they failed to see that union was strength; and their mutual rivalries and jealousies effectually prevented a coalition which, with their vast numbers, might have made them absolutely invincible to any invaders, whosoever they might be. The Ghaznevide dynasty of Sabuktagin and Mahmoud lasted for a century and a half, during which time a more or less permanent garrison was left in the Panjáb; but the people were not yet conquered, and the Muhammadans looked upon India not as their home, but as an appanage of their Afghán kingdom. In 1186 the rival Muhammadan dynasty of Ghor, after a struggle that had lasted for years, swept away the Ghazni family, and Muhammad Ghori, the brother of the Sultán of Ghor, overran the Panjáb, and after finally defeating the last Sultán of Ghazni at Láhur, established his brother's government. In an age when each successive ruler thought himself compelled to put to death all his relations who might be possible pretenders to the throne, the fidelity shown by Muhammad to his brother, and his brother's unbroken and deserved confidence in him until Muhammad himself succeeded to the throne in 1195, are not unworthy of record. Muhammad Ghori laid the foundation of Muhammadan rule in India. Hitherto the Muhammadans merely formed an army of occupation in a hostile country, but now the whole of Hindustán was permanently subjugated and colonised. Before his work of conquest was completed Muhammad Ghori made no less than six campaigns from Ghazni; and in his third he was utterly defeated by a combination of Hindu Rájas, awake for a moment to their common danger. The danger passed the combination melted away; and two years later the same battle-field saw the reputation of Muhammad Ghori re-established, and the King of Delhi slain. The conqueror returned to Ghazni, leaving as Viceroy of Delhi, Kutab-ud-din, who had been a slave, and who afterwards became the first of the Slave kings of Delhi. During his viceroyalty Kutab advanced to Anhulwára in Gujarát and defeated its king Bhim-Dew; but before he could annex the kingdom he was recalled by orders from Ghazni. Muhammad Ghori occupied each district that he overran, and arranged for its administration; and his early death alone prevented him from seeing with his own eyes the firm establishment of the Muhammadan empire which he had had the greatest share in founding.

At the time of his death three viceroys ruled in various parts of his possessions. Kutab, the viceroy of Delhi, was invested as king by Mahmoud the nephew and successor of

Muhammad Ghori. By his ability and strength of will Kutab managed to retain his hold upon all the territories to which he succeeded. But in his son's reign the viceroys of Sind and Bengal assumed independence, and other chiefs followed their example. In this way during the Slave and succeeding dynasties India became parcelled out into a number of Muhammadan and Hindu States which enjoyed a less or greater degree of independence, according as the nominally supreme power was wielded by a strong or weak ruler. Some of these kingdoms were set up by rebellious viceroys, others were created by the gift from the sovereign of portions of the empire to favourite ministers. While some of these passed away at once and left nothing to mark their existence, others became strong and powerful, and even rivalled Delhi itself. The series of Slave kings ended in 1288, and under these rulers India escaped a great danger, which threatened it on more than one occasion, of being altogether swamped by savage hordes of merciless marauders, who poured down from the wastes of Central Asia. Commonly known as Mongols or Moghals, they were under the command of Jangiz Khán, a conqueror whose power was acknowledged from the city of Pekin to the banks of the Volga. These savage tribes were pagans who had not yet come under the civilising influence of Islam, and whose one object was to murder, destroy, and plunder. They wasted India as far as Láhur and then withdrew to Ghazni.

The next dynasty after the Slave, known as the Khiljy lasted only from 1288 to 1321, but it possesses special importance as under its rule Muhammadan conquest spread for the first time into the Deccan. In order to quell a rebellion in Málwa, a province of Central India, which had been already brought under Muhammadan sway, the king Jalál-ud-din made an expedition against it, and reduced it to obedience in 1293. For his exertions in this campaign Alla-ud-din, the nephew of the king, was rewarded by permission to march upon the Deccan. He conquered Ellichpur in Barár, and Dewgahr, now called Daolatábád, a place not far from Aurangábád in the Nizam's dominions. Subsequently by the murder of his uncle Alla-ud-din became king of Delhi. In 1297 he sent an expedition into Guzárát, which, after again taking Anhulwára, and plundering the rich city of Cambay, returned to Delhi. The beautiful wife of the Hindu Rája of Anhulwára became the bride of Alla-ud-din. In the course of his reign he had to send several expeditions to Dewgahr to suppress rebellions and enforce payment of tribute; and one of them passing over the Deccan and down into the Konkan, reached the sea-coast. Several Mongol invasions were repressed by Alla-ud-din. He developed into a monster of cruelty, and was at last murdered in 1321.

The next dynasty at Delhi was that of Toghlak. Its second king, Muhammad Toghlak, who united extraordinary learning with the disposition of the tiger, reigned from 1325 to 1351. He subjugated most of the Deccan, and brought Guzárát under his dominion. He preferred the Deccan to Northern India, and moved his capital from Delhi to Dewgahr. The latter part of his reign was taken up in crushing or attempting to crush a series of rebellions provoked by his atrocious cruelty. But under his rule the Muhammadan empire in India reached a limit which was not exceeded till the emperor Aurangzeb brought almost the whole of India beneath his iron rule. In Western India Islam was now supreme through Guzárát, and Dewgahr with its dependencies extended west to the sea-coast. Barár and most of the Eastern Deccan, that is now Hydarábád, with the cities of Raichur,

Mudgal, Kulbarga, and Bidar were conquered, as well as Bijápur, the frontier district of Bombay. But the Muhammadan possession of Puna, Sátára, and Kolhápur is doubtful, the sway of the Hindu Rájas probably continuing to exist. Lower Sind was still held by Rájput chiefs.

But though the area of Muhammadan conquests had attained such vast dimensions the conquerors had but little stronger bonds of union than the Hindu kings and chiefs whom they had supplanted. Even the enthusiasm for their militant religion could only bind them together for the purpose of aggression against a common foe. Ere their victorious career was completed their empire, as we have seen, began to split up. The provinces could not be governed except by deputies of the supreme ruler at Delhi, and each deputy or viceroy as soon as his master was at a safe distance set up an independent rule of his own. The twenty-seven years of Muhammad Toghlak's reign formed a succession of rebellions and bloody reprisals, executions, and massacres, to which the world has seldom seen a parallel. The criminal law was brutally harsh, the ordinary punishments being the cutting off of hands and feet, of noses and ears, the putting out of eyes, burning, crucifixion, ham-stringing, and cutting to pieces. There were vexatious imposts upon trade and cultivation; and the canals, reservoirs, bridges, public baths, and hospitals for which later Muhammadan rulers achieved fame had not been commenced. In fact, Muhammadan rule, so far at all events, was a curse, and not a blessing. It did nothing to alleviate the condition of the great mass of the people, and by its intolerance consolidated the bonds of Brahmanical sacerdotalism.

Muhammad Toghlak died in Sind in 1351. Four years before that event Zaffar Khán, one of the most remarkable men of his times, accomplished a rebellion, which brought into independent existence a wealthy and powerful Muhammadan State in the Deccan. Zaffar Khán was once a menial servant of a Brahman at Delhi named Gangu, and by his signal honesty gained his master's favour and received great kindness at his hands. The Brahman is said to have prophesied that his servant should attain royal honours. He was recommended to the service of the king of Delhi, and rose to a high military command in the Deccan. The exactions of Muhammad Toghlak had in 1341 caused a widespread revolt in that province. It was put down with merciless cruelty, and the Delhi officers plundered and wasted the land. Hassan Gangu, as Zaffar Khán was also called, availed himself of the discontent thus caused against the house of Delhi to gather together in his own interests, both many Mussalmán nobles and Hindu chiefs. Feeling secure of his strength he attacked and defeated the royal troops at Bidar, and made himself ruler of all the Deccan possessions of Delhi. He was crowned king, and out of gratitude to his former master took the strange title for one of his faith of Alla-ud-din Hassan 'Gangu Bahmani' (Brahmani). Not only did he thus adopt his master's name but he made him his treasurer, the earliest instance of high office being conferred by Muhammadans upon a Hindu. The two incidents are the more remarkable when it is remembered that at that time Moslem nobles vied with each other in the fiercest fanaticism and hatred of Hindu idolators.

The Bahmani Muhammadan dynasty of the Deccan lasted from 1347 to 1526, or 19 years, for the most part in great glory and power. Its kings showed terrible and relentless cruelty to those who opposed them, but to those who submitted to their rule they were on the whole considerate and moderate in their treatment. Cultivation and trade increased, ships

ESTABLISHMENT OF MUHAMMADAN RULE. 43

sailed to Egypt and Arabia from the royal ports of Goa and Chaul in the Konkan, to return laden with the choicest productions of Europe. In wars waged with Hindu Rájas this dynasty showed great military genius and detestable cruelty; one king, Áhmad Sháh, in his operations against Bijanagar, a Hindu kingdom of comparatively late growth, halting wherever the slain amounted to 20,000, and making a festival in celebration of the bloody event. The Bahmani kings introduced many foreign troops such as Persians, Tartars, Moghals, and Arabs from whose union with the women of the country have descended the mixed Deccani Mussalmán breeds. These have in great measure merged into the agricultural classes, and lost the warlike spirit of their ancestors. The finances of the state were brought into fair order, education was promoted and the army raised to a high state of efficiency. The Bahmani territories were gradually extended from sea to sea, and the Konkan was thoroughly subdued. Bijápur and Belgaum were included in its limits, but Dhárwár belonged to Bijanagar. Like other eastern despotisms the strength of the Bahmani kingdom was purely personal; and the increasing feebleness of its later kings brought about its dissolution into five independent kingdoms. The chief historical records of this period that have come down to us are occupied mostly with wars, massacres, and intrigues; but there are occasional references to transactions of quieter times which show a more tolerable state of things than existed under the contemporary rule of Delhi. Hindus were not indeed employed in public affairs, other than in most inferior offices, but the title of the dynasty brought a certain consideration for the Brahman caste. No interference was attempted with the system of corporate village Government, a system which gave the people justice when they could not obtain it elsewhere. The ground was well tilled and travelling fairly secure. Architecture, except in the construction of fortresses, did not attain any particular excellency, though there was some improvement when the capital moved from its original seat of Kulbarga to Bidar. But the Bahmani fortresses ranging from the mountain strongholds of feudal chieftains to imperial forts of enormous strength exceeded those that existed in Europe. Most of these were in what is now Hydarábád territory, but Bombay possesses a specimen of them in Sholápur. Under the Bahmani Mussalman rule there is said to have been a considerable amelioration of manners; and in spite of the loathsome and abominable cruelty of its rulers to all who dared to resist them, its existence may not have been devoid of some beneficial effects.

During the independent existence of the Muhammadan kingdom of the Deccan, Guzárát, which Alla-ud-din Khilji had added to his dominions in 1297, but in which the Hindus were by no means permanently subjugated, became a separate Muhammadan kingdom in 1391. It was severed from the Delhi empire by the rebellious viceroy Mozaffar Khán, whose grandson Áhmad, on his succession in 1411, commenced building a new capital at Áhmadábád whose remarkable ruins bespeak its original grandeur. The architectural style was a transitional one from the Hindu or Jain to the Indo-Sarasenic, and it follows that as yet the Muhammadans had no architecture of their own. Guzárát nominally included the Rájput country of Káthiáwár, and the founder of Áhmadábád carried his arms into the peninsula and reduced the Hindu fortress of Junagahr. Like his grandfather in an age of intolerance this king distinguished himself by outrageous fanaticism against Hindus and their temples and religion. His dominions were invaded by one of the Bahmani kings Áhmad Sháh as an ally of the king of Khándesh, and after a fiercely contested struggle in the island of Salsette adjoining Bombay, the Deccan troops were forced to retreat. The kingdom of Guzárát was consolidated by its king Mahmoud, who came to the throne in 1459. He led successful campaigns into Kachh (Cutch) and the borders of Sind; reducing the fort of Champaner ; and extended his dominions to the Indus and the desert. He was a powerful and efficient ruler. In 1509 he received an embassy from Delhi, acknowledging his independence, an official recognition from the emperor always highly valued by Muhammadan kings. For though ready to support their independence by the sword, these rulers generally acknowledged the theoretical supremacy of the emperor. Mahmoud subsequently distinguished himself as a soldier against the Portuguese. Guzárát was still in enjoyment of the high position to which he had raised it when the empire of the grand Moghal came into being in 1526.

Khándesh, it has been stated, is a district or province which though according to the strict geographical definition included in the Deccan, practically does not form part of it. It is a low-lying country between the elevated plateau of Central India on the north and that of the Deccan on the south. It is bounded on the north by the Sátpura mountains; it is watered by the river Tápti which flows through it from east to west and by numerous small tributaries that fall into it. Naturally fertile it was well cultivated under the Muhammadans, but in after years famine and the raids of the Maráthas reduced it to a state of desolation from which it has needed all the efforts of the British Government to reclaim it to a state of prosperity. Its original capital was at Tálner.

The first Mussalmán governor of Khándesh was appointed by the Toghlak rulers of Delhi in 1370. Like neighbouring viceroys he proclaimed his independence. In 1400 his successor, Málik Nasir, seized the powerful fortress of Asirgahr on the eastern borders of Khándesh, now included in the Central Provinces. He founded near it on the banks of the Tápti the city of Burhánpur, which for many years formed the capital of Khándesh. This city became one of the most splendid and luxurious in India, and grew famous for the manufacture of gold and silver cloths, silks, and muslins. Khándesh, like other parts of India had no immunity from wars, both within its borders and with external enemies; and on a disputed succession Mahmoud, the great king of Guzárát, marched into the country and placed upon the throne one of the claimants named Ádil Khán. His son, Miran Muhammad, who succeeded in 1520 was the reigning prince when in 1526 the Moghal empire commenced.

In Sind the Muhammadans formed the supreme power from the early part of the 13th century, when an invader from Ghazni subdued the Rájput tribe of Sumeras and called himself king of Sind. But the Hindu dynasty of the Sumána Rájputs, entitled Jáins, succeeded, and paid tribute to Belhi up to 1360. On their refusal to do so any longer the Toghlak emperor invaded Sind from Guzárát, and a few years later the Jáins embraced the faith of Islam. Wars and invasions and changes of dynasty make up the history of Sind until shortly before the foundation of the Moghal empire; and at the beginning of that epoch Sind was under the rule of Sháh Beg Árghun, who had sprung from Khorássán and had made himself ruler of Multán in the Panjáb.

While what is now Bombay was split up into the Bahmani kingdom of the Deccan and the kingdoms of Guzárát, Khándesh, and Sind, all of which were Muhammadan, and the kingdom of Bijanagar, that was Hindu, things had not been going well

ESTABLISHMENT OF MUHAMMADAN RULE. 47

with the nominally supreme Government at Delhi. Factions, civil wars, and rebellions pursued their course, broken only for a while by the benevolent reign of Feroz, a monarch who besides executing many useful public works mitigated for a time the intolerant cruelty of Muhammadan law. But the empire such as it was could barely maintain a nominal supremacy over its rebellious vassals, and it was altogether impotent to ward off invasion from without. Attracted by the rumours of its growing confusion Taimur the Tártár or Tamerlane, as he is also called, marched into India from his home at Samárkand with hordes no less terrible than those of his ancestor Jangiz Khán. He advanced to Delhi in 1398 and there proclaimed himself emperor of India; and after ruthlessly massacring the inhabitants right and left returned to the wilds of Central Asia leaving as his deputy in India Khizr Khán, viceroy of Láhur. For a few years the dynasty of Toghlak continued to rule in name; but there soon ceased to be a king or emperor of Delhi at all, and Khizr Khán and his successors held the land in the name of Tamerlane. One more attempt was made at independent rule, and the Áfghán Lodi administration developed into a dynasty which with more or less success over recalcitrant viceroys lasted from 1478 to 1526. But it collapsed amidst general rebellion, the deputies as usual declaring their independence. One of these however thought that he might more effectually gain his ends in another way; and Daulat Khán Lodi of the Panjáb journeyed to Kábul, and thence brought back its ruler Bábar, the descendant of Tamerlane, to claim the empire of Delhi in virtue of his ancestor's conquest. In no way loath to put forward his claim Bábar advanced on Delhi, and in 1526 on the field of Pánipat inflicted a crushing defeat upon Ibráhim the last of the Lodis. Bábar's main work was still before him, but his victory made him the first of the so-called Moghal emperors of Delhi. His line continued to hold the nominal suzerainty of India, until Bahádur Sháh was removed from his throne by the British Government after the great mutiny of 1857.

I have now given a rough outline of the events that occurred in India from the earliest times up to the foundation of the empire of the Grand Moghal in 1526. One event of supreme importance which took place a little more than quarter of a century before the invasion of Bábar has as yet been omitted, and the story of the coming of the Portuguese must be told later on. I have selected certain names or incidents rather as links in the chain of history, or as landmarks to accentuate various stages in the general condition of the people, and as illustrations of the various phases of growth and stagnation, than from any inherent importance rendering them worthy of a place in our memory. I have laid greater stress on all that more especially relates to what is now Bombay, and made room for more incident in its narrative; but it has not been possible to avoid some description of contemporary events in other parts of India.

When Bábar won his victory at Pánipat more than eight centuries had passed since the first Muhammadan inroads. For a long time their invasions had been mere raids for plunder, and for a longer time still the position of the conquerors was only that of a military garrison in a foreign country. Yet for three hundred years Muhammadan rulers had reigned continuously, and their people had made their homes in the land. There were from time to time bright intervals in these dark ages; and the nobility of character of more than one sovereign prompted him to take some measures for the alleviation of the condition of the toiling masses over whom he ruled. Some benevolent monarch might regard the conquered races as human beings, possessing no less right to the protection of the law, and to the air which they breathed, than the followers of the prophet themselves. But, on the whole, the general condition of the country changed for the worse. The brilliancy, refinement, and learning of the future Moghal empire had not yet sprung up to relieve the hideous blackness of an uncompromising and intolerant faith. The unity of God was preached at the point of the sword; but ruthless massacres and the enslaving of the unbelievers, the sacking of their temples, and the destruction of their shrines, could not force the Hindus to give up their ancient worship. The obstinacy of their resistance to concede a single point in their religion, emphasises the more intensely their singular inability to unite for the purposes of driving out of the country the enemies of their faith. There was indeed no lack of cause to incite them to a common resistance. Their dynasties swept away, they were excluded from public employment except in the lowest grades; they were debarred from all influence as statesmen, and might utter no opinion reflecting on the dominant government. The government was in fact one of brute force with no further aim than conquest, and it was absolutely incapable of any enlightened progress.

But what made the position of the conquered less intolerable was the system of village communities that existed in its greatest strength in the Deccan and West of India. As long as the inhabitants of each village were left to manage their own affairs, and the rulers contented themselves with exacting a not intolerable land revenue, they could maintain an attitude of stoical indifference to any change of dynasty. Their temples might be destroyed; but while the priesthood remained, and each household possessed its family gods, there was but little harm done to the solaces of their religion. Tyranny in the long run can have but little effect upon these self-containing communities, and the most barbarous and vindictive ruler must sooner or later realise the invaluable aid which they afford to his authority. But while the people of each village might thus retain some substantial freedom which was denied to their race as a whole, the very fact of such a possibility inevitably increased the strength of those centrifugal forces which effectually prevented a common union against a common foe.

Clearly then Muhammadan rule at this period is weighed in the balance and found wanting. It must, however, be credited with one good result. The inroads of savage hordes of pagans under Jangiz and his successors might have overcome the disunited armies of Hindu princes, and effectually swamped the civilisation of India without replacing it by another from without. The military genius of Muhammadanism could unite under one banner all the fierce warriors of Islam, and drive from the land the wild tribes of the desert. And, later on, when Bábar brought his armies to conquer the lands which his pagan ancestors had ravaged, he and his people had long since become members of the faith which taught that there is one God, and Muhammad is his prophet.

V.—CONQUESTS OF THE PORTUGUESE.

IN the month of May, 1498, the famous Portuguese Admiral, Vasco da Gama, sighted the beautiful peaks of the Nilgiri hills that form the continuation of the Western Ghats; and sailing up to the shores of India he weighed anchor in the harbour of Kálikat. The way was now opened to successive expeditions from different European countries; and a series of traders and explorers, who did not so much as dream of founding an empire, was destined to effect in India a more tremendous revolution than had taken place since the first invasion of the Aryans.

There was nothing new in the idea of trade between India and the West. From the days of Alexander the goods of Northern India found their way to Europe by way of Kábul, Astrakhan, and the shores of the Caspian Sea. Another route was by way of Persia and Egypt to the Mediterranean ports. The goods that arrived at the Great Sea by this overland route were forwarded in ships of Genoese and Venetian merchants who possessed a monopoly of the traffic. For the export of merchandize to Egypt the ports of Káchin, Kálikat, Goa, Dábul, and Chául on the Konkan and Malabár coasts formed, with the harbours of Guzárát, the chief emporiums of trade. But India was a distant and mysterious land. The reputation of its wealth and splendour formed an irresistible attraction to the brave explorers of an adventurous age. While Columbus sailed across the Atlantic, and discovered a new world which he took to be the India upon which he had longed to feast his eyes, Bartholomew Diaz in 1486 voyaged from Lisbon unto the Southern Cape of Africa. He went so far as to discover that beyond it the land trended away to the north-east; and it is even said that one of his men found his way to India itself.

Diaz found the Southern cape of Africa a cape of storms. Eleven years later the peaceful weather that he met with in those regions caused Vasco da Gama to name it the Cape of Good Hope. On Christmas Day, 1497, he sighted the country which, from this circumstance, he called Natal. Sailing on to Zanzibar he found a fleet of merchant vessels from India, and securing the services of a pilot from Guzárát he crossed the Indian Ocean to Kálikat.

Less at that time than ever was India prepared to make a formidable resistance to an invader. The empire of the Grand Moghal was not to be founded for more than a quarter of a century later. The sovereignty of Delhi was at its last gasp, distracted by an interminable series of wars, and it had for many years been governed as a province of Tamerlane's dominions. Rebellious viceroys reigned over as much country as they could hold by force. Everywhere Muhammadan States were struggling for supremacy. Here and there Hindu kingdoms joined in the contest, but Bijanagar was well-nigh the sole independent Hindu State remaining in India. The powerful Bahmani dynasty of the Deccan was in the throes of dissolution; and on its ruins were springing up and taking form five separate States. Of these two in what is now Bombay, the Nizám Sháhi dynasty at Áhmadnagar, and the Ádil Sháhi at Bijápur, lasted as independent and powerful kingdoms until they were brought under the sway of Aurangzíb; and so also the Kutab Sháli dynasty of Golkonda, in what is now Hydarábád. An attempt was made to maintain the Bahmani dynasty in the Barid Sháhi family at Bidar, and Imád Sháhi kings reigned for a time in Barár. The future greatness of the Maráthas, who were afterwards to rise up in their strength from their mountain-homes and form a confederacy of states that it took all the power of the English to conquer, was not even foreshadowed. They had for generations remained passive beneath the rule of Islam, nay, had even served loyally in its armies. While the kingdoms that rose from the ashes of the Bahmani dynasty were engaged in endless mutual rivalry, and later on in their contests against Akbar and Aurangzíb, they little thought which while exhausting their own strength they were exciting in the Maráthas that spirit of rapine, plunder, and dominion, which was all the while latent in the race. In fact, the real greatness of native India had not begun. The popular idea of eastern magnificence and luxury is based on a state of things that for the most part grew up later.

For the century that succeeded the arrival of Vasco da Gama the chief interest in the history of Western India centres in the rise of the Portuguese commercial supremacy along the coast, conjointly with the expansion of the new Moghal empire. By the end of that century these two powers shared the whole of what is now Bombay, with the moribund kingdoms of Áhmadnagar and Bijápur. And to elucidate the growth of the Portuguese and Moghal powers it will be useful to sketch in advance the condition during this century of the states that confronted them in Western India. In Sind the independent viceroy being harassed by invaders from Kándahár had called in to his aid Sháh Beg Árghun, (page 36), who was independent at Multán. The invaders were driven out, but Sháh Beg Árghun had no intention of doing his work for nothing, and he retained Sind for himself. The former ruler, hopeless of regaining his kingdom, entered the service of the king of Guzárát. The Árghun family was succeeded by a Persian one which preserved the independence of the province until 1592, when it was subdued by the forces of Akbar, and its ruler enrolled among the nobles of his empire.

Guzárát, including Káthiáwár, was at the height of its eminence, and possessed the coast as far as Chául, twenty-eight miles south of Bombay. Its king, Bahádur Sháh, who succeeded Mozáffar Sháh in 1526, annexed Málwa in Central India, and his authority was acknowledged as paramount in the Deccan as far south as Áhmadnagar. But in 1535, in spite of his fine park of artillery manned by Portuguese gunners, he was overthrown and driven to flight by Humáyan. But the Moghals could not hold the kingdom long at that time, and an era of confusion and anarchy followed that lasted until 1572. In that year Mozáffar Sháh, the last claimant to the throne, submitted to Akbar at Áhmadábád. He was enrolled amongst Akbar's nobility, but afterwards made an impotent attempt to rebel, and ended his days in exile at Káthiáwár.

Khándesh succeeded in maintaining its existence as a separate State, though not without considerable interference from Guzárát on the one side and Áhmadnagar on the other, until 1594. Its ruler then submitted to the Moghal general, who was on his way to besiege Áhmadnagar, and joined his army with 6,000 horse.

The kingdom of Áhmadnagar was founded, and its capital built in 1494 by Málik Áhmad, who, together with his father, Nizam-ul-Mulk had managed the districts which comprised it when they formed part of the Bahmani kingdom. Málik Áhmad had for some time aspired at carving out a separate state, and in disgust at the murder of his father by the Bahmani authorities boldly asserted his independence and sustained it against all efforts made to subdue him. He moved his seat of government from Junnar in Puna to Bingár, where he built the city called after his name.

The rival kingdom of Bijápur was founded five years earlier by Yusuf Ádil Sháh, Commander-in-Chief of the Bahmani army. It had been the site of an ancient Hindu city, of which a few traces still remain, and was the seat of a provincial government of the Deccan kingdom.

These two kingdoms were constantly at war with one another, though it occasionally suited them to combine against outsiders. Their united armies on several occasions fought against Golkonda, the third of the kingdoms which arose on the fall of the Bahmani government, and succeeded in maintaining a separate existence. Golkonda was, however, to the east of the Bombay Presidency, and concerns us in less degree than its rivals.

Áhmadnagar and Bijápur practically divided between them so much of the Deccan as belongs to Bombay, and all the Konkan. Áhmadnagar possessed the coast-line from Chául to Bánkot, and south of that Bijápur held the sea-coast towns. Khándesh, it has been shown, was not included in this disposition of territory, and though Áhmadnagar held the inland Konkan Guzárát held its coast-line. Two strong and turbulent States like Áhmadnagar and Bijápur could not look with content on the proximity of the rich Hindu kingdom of Dijanagar. Religious fanaticism and hunger for its broad acres alike stimulated them to form a joint confederacy with Golkonda, Bidar, and Barár against the only state that had not bowed its head to the followers of the Prophet of Mecca. In 1564 the government of Bijanagar was crushed, and its capital destroyed. The parcelling out of its conquered lands proved a less easy matter; and while some of them became a fruitful source of dispute between its conquerors many remained in the hands of local chieftains, who, for the most part, became, in course of time, vassals of Bijápur. Meanwhile Áhmadnagar enlarged its dominions by swallowing up in 1572 the territories of its late ally Barár. The comparatively unimportant State of Bidar, which considered itself the representative of the Bahmani power, had been invaded and conquered by Bijápur in 1529, and the king deposed and given a command in the Bijápur army. He served the state well, and was therefore allowed a sort of spurious independence at Bidar until he was conquered by Akbar.

The boundaries between Áhmadnagar and Bijápur were constantly changing, and depended upon the strength for the time being of their mutual forces. The possession of Sholápur was a constant matter of dispute; but roughly speaking, Áhmadnagar held the modern districts of Násik, part of which, however, belonged to Khándesh, Áhmadnagar, Sátára, Puna, part of Thána, including Kályán, Kolába, and the State of Janjira, which was claimed also by Guzárát; and besides these a considerable slice of Hydarábád, including Aurangábád and Galna. Sholápur oscillated between the two, but Bijápur held Dhárwár, Belgaum, Bijápur, Ratnágiri and Kánara. But on both of these as well as on Guzárát the Portuguese before long steadily encroached. The confederacy which succeeded in crushing Bijanagar was of no avail against the European merchants who were establishing their factories along the seashore. East of Áhmadnagar and Bijápur the dominions of Golkonda extended to the Bay of Bengal.

Such were the rival powers that had to be dealt with on the one side by the Portuguese, on the other by the new Moghal empire of Delhi. Guzárát, Áhmadnagar, and Bijápur, each possessed a certain magnificence, each earned some reputation as a civilised government, and each produced some distinguished men. But in all alike the whole system of government was ephemeral. It depended not upon any permanent system or love of order; it rested solely upon the personal caprice of irresponsible despots. While most of these delighted in plunder and persecution, and gave themselves up to the vilest pleasures, it is recorded on the other hand that many of them devoted themselves to good government, the well-being of their subjects, and the encouragement of learning. But all the good done by one benevolent monarch might be undone by his successor. The want of a permanent and consistent policy embodied in a system of nationality caused the labours of the most enlightened rulers to have purely evanescent results.

For the magnificence of its buildings and the strength of its defences, Bijápur was without a rival. The mighty dome that covers the mausoleum of Sultán Máhmud exceeds in dimensions any other in the world, and in no country can the mosque and tomb of Ibráhim be surpassed for gracefulness of outline. On all sides palaces, tombs, reservoirs, and fortresses, even now almost perfect, convey to the beholder a sense of the majesty of a state that has long since passed away. Nor did its governors scorn to avail themselves of the aid of Portuguese painters and artizans to beautify their city, and these together with Christian missionaries were not only tolerated but encouraged in the Ádil Sháhi capital.

The unceasing wars between these Deccan kingdoms compelled them to keep up enormous forces. They all preferred to enlist Turks, Arabs, Moghals, and Portuguese; but they were compelled to fill up, in most part, the rank and file of their armies with the Marátha and other Hindu natives of the country. This necessity stimulated a martial spirit in the vanquished races, which might have no little danger for Muhammadans. It foreshadowed the imprudence of that policy of placing an excessive amount of power in the hands of conquered mercenaries which was well-nigh to prove fatal to British rule itself. But when in.1529 Burhán Nizám Sháh of Áhmadnagar bestowed the office of Peshwa, or prime minister, on a Brahman, and Ibráhim Ádil Sháh on his accession to the throne of Bijápur in 1555 showed his preference for the natives of Máhárásthra as men of business no less than as soldiers, by letting Maráthi take the place of Persian as the court and official language, the power and influence of the Marátha Brahmans were necessarily increased. And so in addition to the men who possessed physical strength and warlike training a class came to the front which, gifted with keen intellect, intense ambition, and unrivalled powers of machination and scheming, formed the head which could direct the movement of the giant limbs as yet unconscious of their strength. The Maráthas were more numerous in the armies of Bijápur and Áhmadnagar, but they also served under Golkonda, neither community of language and religion nor national sentiment preventing them from fighting against each other. In fact fighting and plunder were to them food and drink; they little recked under whose banner they were ranged, and if their rulers lacked quarrels of their own the Maráthas had an interminable series of hereditary feuds between individuals and families, in which they were always ready to fight to the death. The Deccan kings had no desire to heal their disputes which they believed would keep the Maráthas poised against each other and so prevent any lasting union against the sway of Islam.

Vasco da Gama on landing at Kálikat was well received by its ruler, who bore the title of Zámorin, and the Portuguese were greatly impressed by the magnificence with which he was surrounded. Permission to trade was granted, but obstruction and intrigue soon appeared; and owing to the detention by the Zámorin of two of their officers the Portuguese were unable to effect their departure for several months. The officers were at last released and Da Gama sailed away, but he had no little difficulty in escaping the fleet of forty ships which had been collected to capture his vessels.

The success of this expedition encouraged the Portuguese to send another under Pedro Cabral, which reached Kálikat in September, 1500. Cabral was received with no less pomp and dignity than his predecessor, and he was allowed to establish the first European factory in India. But disagreement soon arose with the intriguing Muhammadan population; the factory was stormed, and the commandant killed. The retribution was prompt. Cabral seized ten ships of the Muhammadan merchants, transferred their cargo to his own, and after burning the vessels bombarded the city. He then sailed south to Káchin, where he was well received, and he left some of his men in charge of the factory which he was permitted to establish at that place. He afterwards sailed to Kánnanur, a port north of Kálikat, completed his cargoes, and sailed for Europe.

Before his arrival a third expedition had been despatched under Juan de Nueva. The new commander first touched at Anjidiwa, an island near Goa, and then proceeded to Káchin where the men left at the factory had been well treated. The Zámorin of Kálikat sent a fleet to attack him, and the Káchin ruler advised him to stand on his defence. But scorning their counsel he boldly sailed against the Zámorin's ships, and with his guns inflicted on them a crushing defeat. The Zámorin afterwards invited De Nueva to visit Kálikat, but treachery was not without reason suspected, and the overtures were declined. The Portuguese obtained rich cargoes and made their way to Europe.

The experience of these three voyages convinced the Portuguese that their commercial enterprises to India must be supported by force of arms. It was essential that they should be able to protect their expeditions from the cupidity of sovereigns like the Zámorin of Kálikat, and ensure more than a mere tolerance from states such as Káchin and Kánnanur. Of the real rulers of Western India Áhmadnagar and Bijápur, or of the Bahmani kingdom which they were then supplanting, the Portuguese had thus far learnt nothing. But what they did learn was that there was a large trade between India and Arabia and Southern Persia in the hands of Muhammadans. This they determined to divert into their own, not by any legitimate competition, but by the simple process of wholesale destruction and murder.

In 1502 Vasco da Gama was sent out to subvert at all hazards the Muhammadan commercial supremacy. He commanded twenty ships, with a full complement of sailors and soldiers. His plan was that while he himself drove the Muhammadan vessels from the coasts of India, his captains should cut them off at the mouth of the Red Sea. He soon showed the spirit in which he meant to carry on his operations; and a deed of infamous and wanton cruelty was done off Kánnanur where he met with an Egyptian ship carrying pilgrims from India to Mecca. The details of his action are narrated by the Portuguese historian, Faria Y. Souza. Reserving the children as slaves and converts the crew and passengers numbering about three hundred were battened down, and the ship set on fire. But the behaviour of the Zámorin of Kálikat to the previous expeditions still rankled in Da Gama's breast. He sailed to Kálikat, and capturing the crews of fishing craft and small trading vessels, informed the Zámorin that unless his demands were instantly complied with these men would be executed. His demands were met with refusal, or delay and evasion that implied refusal. The prisoners were therefore hanged at the yard-arm of Da Gama's ships, and their hands and feet sent to the Zamorin. Such was the guise under which Christianity was presented to Hindus and Muhammadans; and to the former the creed which taught that all men were alike children of a merciful Father may have seemed hardly more seductive than the faith of the prophet which bade men choose between the Korán tribute and the sword. After further contests with the ruler of Kálikat, and cementing his alliance with the Rájas of Káchin and Kánnanur, Vasco da Gama sailed for Europe in 1503, leaving a viceroy to protect Portuguese interests in India.

For the next twelve years events followed each other with startling rapidity, and a Portuguese empire grew up both on land and sea with a magical swiftness, compared with which the efforts of early English merchants appear indeed poor and insignificant. On Da Gama's departure the Zámorin took up arms against Káchin, and demanded the surrender of the Portuguese. His demands were refused, and his forces defeated by the Káchin troops, the Portuguese remaining aloof in their ships. Before long powerful reinforcements arrived from Portugal under Alfonzo Albuquerque, and the Zámorin was defeated and compelled to sue for peace. Formal permission for the establishment of the Portuguese factory at Káchin was received from the Rája. Albuquerque now sailed for Portugal, and obtaining valuable aid from the Rája of Bijanagar, the Zámorin advanced against Káchin with 50,000 men and a large fleet. But the small Portuguese force defeated the Zámorin in several sanguinary engagements, and a further fleet of thirteen men-of-war arriving from Portugal the joint forces bombarded and destroyed Kálikat, and then captured the Zámorin's fleet of seventeen ships. In 1506 the Portuguese Admiral Soarez sailed home with a vast booty.

The next year Dom Francis Almeida arrived from Portugal with the rank of Viceroy of India, in command of a large fleet and fifteen hundred trained soldiers. He built a fort on the island of Anjidiwa and sailed to Káchin with a crown of gold and jewels especially manufactured for the Rája. Here he learnt of a powerful combination against him, the Muhammadans being now thoroughly aroused by Portuguese interference with their commerce. The king of Bijápur had united with Muhammad Sháh, the mighty king of Guzárát, and to their combined strength was added a fleet of twelve ships built in the Red Sea, and furnished by the Mameluke Sultan of Egypt. The opposing fleets met at Chául, which then belonged to Áhmadnagar. The enemy fought with an ardour and skill not hitherto experienced by the Portuguese in the East. The Portuguese suffered a reverse. Their flag-ship was sunk, and a decided blow dealt to their supremacy. But for the arrival of two more fleets, one of which was under Alfonzo Albuquerque, it would have been difficult for them to maintain their footing. With the aid of the fresh arrivals the Portuguese attacked the Muhammadan positions in the Persian Gulf and Red Sea, taking Ormuz and Muscat. Albuquerque was appointed Viceroy of India, but before he received charge of the vice-regal appointment Almeida destroyed the Áhmadnagar port of Dábul on the Ratnágiri coast, and sailing northwards obtained a magnificent victory over the combined Muhammadan fleets off Diu in the peninsula of Káthiáwár. But the fame of the victory was sullied by the brutal cruelty of Almeida, who put all his prisoners to death. Almeida perished afterwards on the African coast, and the great and chivalrous Albuquerque succeeded him in 1510.

Albuquerque took possession of Goa, with the beauty of whose port and island he was greatly impressed, from Ibráhim Ádil Sháh of Bijápur. For a short time, in 1511, it was again held by Bijápur troops, but Albuquerque speedily attacked them, and in spite of a brave defence took the city with a loss of 6,000 men to the garrison. Goa was declared the capital of Portuguese India, a title which it still preserves. From this time till 1515 the great viceroy was actively employed against Malacca, Pegu, Aden, Ormuz, and Diu. A fort was built at Ormuz in 1514, and the Portuguese power recognised by the king of Persia. But the work which Albuquerque did for his country was ill-rewarded, and before his death in 1515 he was superseded by his avowed rival Soarez ; a treatment similar to that which the founders of the French empire in India commonly met with, while the services of English soldiers and statesmen in the East have almost always received a noble recognition from their country. But before he died he left affairs in India in so firm a condition that, as he said, they could speak on his behalf with more eloquence than any words of his. He had in a wonderfully brief time accomplished the object of his mission. He had swept the Muhammadan trade from the seas, and the European emporium for the riches of the East was no longer at Genoa or Venice, but at Lisbon. To found a territorial empire was altogether beyond his aims. He wanted factories, and when he took Goa, believing that his proceedings would only be hampered by any acquisition of territory, he gave up all except the city and the fort to a native ally, Timoja of Kánara. Thus the aim and object of the Portuguese was absolutely and entirely selfish. Any idea of responsibility or duty to the inhabitants of India was not so much as dreamt of. Nor did it even dawn upon them that the commercial interests of the country were not necessarily incompatible with their own. A successful trade meant to them the monopoly of trade, and so, with their ledger in one hand and their sword in the other, they set to work to burn, plunder, and destroy every vessel that ventured to compete with them in the Indian seas. Albuquerque himself was a chivalrous and honourable gentleman. He was guilty of neither cruelty nor deceit, and he was respected as well as feared by his enemies. But his successors, though they possessed his courage lacked his scruples, and their actions present a terrible picture of intolerance, cruelty, and vindictiveness.

With some vicissitudes of fortune the affairs of the Portuguese continued, on the whole, to prosper. Such seaport towns as refused to acknowledge their supremacy they bombarded and sacked; but they protected those that submitted. A rich and prosperous city sprang up at Chául, the king of Áhmadnagar paying them a yearly tribute for its protection by their armies. In 1516 they established a factory there of their own. In 1521 they made an attempt to build a fort at Diu, but the Guzárát admiral drove them back to Chául, and his sailors burnt their newly founded settlement. This reverse led to the erection of a powerful Portuguese fortress at Chául; but the success of the Guzárát expedition was noised abroad, and in the following year an army was sent from Bijápur against Goa. Goa could defend itself, but the dominions of Timoja, the ally of the Portuguese at Kánara, were annexed to the Ádil Sháhi kingdom. The ease with which his fleet had driven off the Portuguese from Diu, encouraged the king of Guzárát to attack their settlement at Chául in 1527. But the Portuguese destroyed his ships, and followed up their success by a march by land. With the aid of Áhmadnagar troops they made Thána and the whole island of Salsette tributary. However, the Guzárát troops obtained a temporary success, and Áhmadnagar had to acknowledge Guzárát supremacy, and break off its alliance with the Portuguese. Three years later Antonio di Silviera burnt Damaun, and sacked the rich city of Surat. But it was against Diu that the Portuguese efforts were chiefly directed, and in 1531 they assembled in the spacious harbour of Bombay 400 vessels and 22,000 men, of whom 3,600 were Europeans. The expedition failed to effect its object, and the Portuguese returned to Goa, sacking many seaports on their way. They, however, determined to persevere in their attempt to acquire Diu. They obtained the aid of Prince Chánd of Guzárát, who was in rebellion against his father Bahádur Sháh. In return for his help they annexed, nominally on his behalf, but really on their own, the Northern Konkan, including Mumbadewi or Mumbé, which from some similarity of sound they transformed into Bombahia, the good harbour, or Bombay. Prince Chánd's rebellion failed, and they then allied themselves to his father and aided him in his defence against the Emperor Humáyun, who had invaded Guzárát. In return for this assistance the Guzárát ruler ceded to them Bassein, and the long-coveted Diu But they were not suffered to hold Diu in peace, and in 1537 by order of the Sultan of Turkey, an Egyptian fleet was sent to drive them out. The garrison made a noble defence during the eight months that the siege lasted. They underwent the utmost miseries, and their condition was almost desperate. At last the siege was raised by the arrival of an enormous fleet under Juan de Castro, with 1,000 guns and 5,000 men. The relieving fleet on its way from Goa and Chául inflicted wanton cruelties on the inhabitants of the coast, massacring without distinction men, women, and children. Thousands were sold into slavery, and the towns were pillaged and burnt. On his return to Goa with his victorious legions the viceroy made a triumphal entry into his capital, and the account of its magnificence stirred with wonder the citizens of Lisbon.

But the danger to the kingdoms of Western India from Portuguese ascendancy, formidable as it was, was of only a partial nature. Their fleets and armies might be conquered, their foreign trade destroyed, their sea-coast towns pillaged and burnt. But their territories were in no danger of falling into the hands of the marauders, who were content with building factories and forts upon the coast. But a mighty power was now established in the north of India which would spare no effort to bring them one and all beneath its iron sway.

VI.—FOUNDATION OF THE MOGHAL EMPIRE.

FIFTH in descent from Taimur the Tartar, himself sprung from the race of Jangiz Khán, Bábar is generally spoken of as a Moghal. But of this race Bábar always professed a horror, and it was probably not unmixed Moghal blood that flowed in his veins. Practically he was a Turk; his memoirs were written in Turkish, and his army was Turkish. He was, at any rate, not an Aryan, yet both in himself and his descendants were exhibited some of the best qualities of the Aryans, and a power of growth and civilisation of which his ancestors showed not the slightest trace. Bábar did not hesitate to accept the invitation of the rebellious viceroy of the Panjáb (page 47). His way was made easy by the tyranny of Ibráhim Lodi at Delhi, which was not calculated to stimulate the resistance of his subjects to a foreign invader under whom their lot could hardly be worse than it already was. He advanced upon Delhi; and at the fateful field of Pánipat Ibráhim was slain and his army utterly defeated. Thus in 1526 Bábar became the first of the so-called Moghal emperors. But his work was not yet completed; and though his soldiers thought that they had done enough when Delhi was in their hands Bábar was not content to rest upon his laurels. He encouraged his weary troops to march over Bengal and Bahár; and at Sikri he crushed a formidable confederacy of Rájput chieftains, who imagined that they possessed an opportunity of overthrowing the

Muhammadan power, and of restoring to its original position their own national faith. On his death in 1530 he was succeeded by his son Humáyun, who lacked his father's genius but resembled him in the chequered fortunes of his early career. On the accession of Humáyun Guzárát was at the height of its prosperity, and its king, Bahádur Sháh, incurred the anger of the emperor by harbouring a political offender. Humáyun resolved to march against him, and in 1535 in spite of the aid of the Portuguese, he utterly defeated the Guzárát army at Mandesar. Leaving Guzárát in charge of his brother, Mirza Askári, he proceeded against Sher Khán, a powerful Áfghán feudatory in Bengal. But Sher Khán's military capacity greatly exceeded Humáyun's. After two miserably unsuccessful campaigns, in which his armies were destroyed, the emperor became a fugitive; while his brother Kámrán, who was viceroy of the Panjáb, ceded that province to Sher Khán, and retired to Kábul.

Humáyun fled to Sind and attempted to excite its ruler Hussein Árghun to action on his behalf. But his hopes of succour were disappointed, and he determined to cross the desert to Jodhpur. After extraordinary sufferings he arrived there with a scanty band of followers. He found the Rája hostile to him, and was compelled to resume his wanderings in the desert between Jodhpur and the Indus. The miseries and privations of the march exceeded anything that he had before experienced. His route lay through a tract of burning sand with hardly a tree to give shelter from the furious sun; and the few wells were in the hands of hereditary robbers and marauders. After many weary marches his small party found themselves pursued by the Jodhpur cavalry under the son of the Rája who cut off access to water or food. But when all hope was lost the prince relented, and after reproaching Humáyun with what he chose to call the wantonness of his invasion, gave him food and water and let him go. At length with his wife and only seven followers he reached Umarkot in Sind, where in 1542 was born his illustrious son Akbar. Humáyun attempted once more to make himself master of Sind, but in 1543 he was compelled to return to Kándahár and give up for a time all hopes of recovering his power in India.

Meanwhile, for five years his successful rival Sher Sháh Sur ruled India firmly and well. But in the short space of ten years after his death the Áfghán dynasty came to an end in scenes of wild confusion and anarchy. Welcoming the opportunity the emperor Humáyun advanced in triumph from Kábul, which he had already recovered from his brother Kámrán; and a decisive battle at Sirhind in which his son Akbar fought in the thickest of the fight, placed him in firm possession of Delhi and Ágra. Thus, after an exile of fifteen years and extraordinary vicissitudes of fortune, Humáyun firmly re-established the most glorious and enduring of all eastern empires in India. But he was not to live long in the enjoyment of his prosperity. In 1556 he perished by an accidental fall over the parapet of his library at Delhi; and Akbar became emperor of Hindustán. In memory of his father Akbar built at Delhi the stately marble tomb from which three hundred years later, during the great mutiny, the last of the house of Bábar was dragged out as a prisoner of the British Government, and in the precincts of which his two sons were shot.

Meanwhile, since the relief of the siege of Diu, the success of the Portuguese had steadily increased. Subsequent attacks upon Diu by Máhmud Sháh of Guzárát were repulsed with heavy loss to his armies. In 1553 the brother of Ibráhim

Ádil Sháh of Bijápur took refuge at Goa, and the king offered the Portuguese viceroy both territory and money if he would give him up. Far from acceding to this request the Portuguese gave the prince an army to fight against the king, and the force took possession of the Phunda Ghat, or pass, over the mountains, on the way from Goa to the Deccan. Here however the intervention ceased. The Portuguese seemed to have a political objection to interference in the continent of India; and afterwards, as before, they limited their operations to the coast. Along the sea they had now a series of factories and defences with here and there, as at Goa, Chául, and Bassein, splendid cities where the remains of stately fabrics still attest the grandeur that once existed. In revenge for the aid afforded to his brother, the king of Bijápur sent an army against Goa. It was unsuccessful, but in 1570 a powerful combination was formed against the Portuguese by Bijápur, Áhmadnagar and Kálikat, whose immense forces hurled themselves in vain upon Goa and Chául. The gallant defence of the Portuguese inspired the Deccan kings with respect, and peace was made on favourable terms. During the latter half of this century the Portuguese were at the height of their success. They steadily avoided the acquisition of territorial or political influence, although they had admirable opportunities of both, alike in Guzárát and in the Deccan. But as a maritime and trading power they attained a supremacy which beat all local rivalry out of the field, and was only to fall before stronger powers from Europe. They were detested by the native races for their vindictiveness and avarice; and the execrable cruelty of the inquisition established at Goa for the propagation of peace on earth and goodwill towards men heightens the dark colouring of the glowing picture. Conversions were made by force, and the great missionary Xavier baptised people by the thousand, just in the same way that the Muhammadans brought the erring Hindus into their fold, whether they would or not. The baptismal ceremony was all-sufficient to render the neophyte a member of the Church, and any mental change or process was regarded as superfluous. The gates of caste were of course closed on all who, however reluctantly, submitted to the ceremony; and on the Western Coast of India there are many descendants of the converts of Xavier who have Portuguese names and some vague and distorted notions of legendary Christianity, but to all intents and purposes are Hindus.

When Akbar came to the throne in 1556 he was only thirteen years old. At the battle of Sirhind he had displayed undaunted courage, but there was at that time little apparent likelihood that he would have the ability to win for himself a real control over his nominal empire. He had from the first to contend with armies which were altogether out of proportion to those which he could put into the field. The usurping Sur dynasty though fallen, had yet to be subdued; the Rájputs and Hindus in Central India had no inclination to submit; the Patháns in Kábul and Kandahár were restless and mutinous. Towards Bombay, Guzárát alone had ever been under the Moghal sway, and for more than two centuries the Muhammadan States of the Deccan had owned no allegiance to Delhi. Thus in the consolidation of the Muhammadan power in India, Akbar had a great task to accomplish, and many years passed by before he could give his attention to the kingdoms of Western India. It was not till 1571 that he was able to march upon Ahmadábád to bring Guzárát under his control.

At Sirhind Akbar had fought under the guidance of his guardian Bahrám Khán. Bahrám possessed remarkable talents as a military leader. On coming to the throne Akbar made him his chief minister, both for civil and military affairs. The troops of Muhammad Sur Adite, the last of the Sur dynasty, under Hemu, his active Hindu minister, marched upon Delhi and Ágra; and Akbar set out to meet them from Ambálla, a city in the northern part of the Panjáb. He had 20,000 men, with which to meet 100,000 Patháns under Hemu. Nearly all Akbar's officers counselled retreat. But at the advice of Bahrám Khán, Akbar determined to fight, and Pánipat, the scene of many battles before and since, saw another complete triumph of the Moghal arms. Hemu was brought as a captive into the presence of the emperor; and Bahrám Khán bade Akbar slay the infidel with his own hand and so attain the title of Ghází, or Defender of the Faith. The boy burst into tears and would do no more than lightly touch the head of the captive with his sword. But the minister had no wish to let Hemu escape to bring another army against his master, and himself smote off the prisoner's head. So perished the first Hindu who by clearness of judgment and devotion to his master's cause had risen to distinction amongst Muhammadans. Akbar entered Delhi in triumph and ascended his father's throne; and after crushing a rebellion in the Pánjáb found himself in 1557 undisputed possessor of the whole of North-Western India.

As the emperor grew older the responsibilities that he had to deal with rapidly developed the strength and decision of his character, and by the time that he was eighteen he was able to rule by himself. The invaluable services of Bahrám Khán could not atone for the intolerable presumption that he displayed, and Akbar was deeply offended by his acts of gross heartlessness. With wise tact and delicate gracefulness Akbar sent him a message telling him that thus far he had been occupied in education, but that it was now his intention to govern his people according to his own judgment. He advised his well-wisher to give up worldly affairs and spend the rest of his days in prayer at Mecca. Bahrám started on his pilgrimage, but on the way abandoned his peaceful intentions and raised a rebellion against Akbar. He was unsuccessful, and he besought the emperor to forgive him, and Akbar restored him to his former honours. After a time he once more started for Mecca, but was murdered in Guzárát.

It has been said that the Moghal empire at its commencement was weaker than those that preceded it. Akbar had smaller armies than earlier conquerors, and their discipline was exceedingly lax. His generals on gaining victories acted not as if they were officers but rather as independent chiefs. Akbar had a way of his own in dealing with them, and he generally managed to obtain their submission without punishment or reproofs, but by the soft answer that turneth away wrath. His whole policy was at first incomprehensible, both to Muhammadans and Hindus; and though when necessary he could deal a prompt and crushing blow upon open rebellion, he preferred to gain his ends by conciliation rather than by brute force. His marriage with a Rájput princess pointed out the object which he had in view. The dream of his life was to fuse into one nation the Hindus and Muhammadans of India. The subversion of Hindu chiefs was followed almost invariably by their enrolment as nobles of his court, and this generally had the effect of bringing about their co-operation with his policy. By these means, in a few rapid campaigns, he extended his dominions to Málwa, and the frontiers of Khándesh and the Deccan. But the obstinate defence of the Hindu stronghold of

Chittur in 1567 by the Rájput clans, rendered a different treatment inevitable. Desperate at the loss of their leader the Rájputs slew their women and children, and burnt them with his body; and on the storming of the fortress they one and all perished, rejecting all offers of quarter.

Rájputána brought into submission the emperor marched upon Áhmadábád; Mozáffar Sháh made his allegiance and was enrolled as a noble of the empire. In quelling some resistance to the imperial armies in Guzárát, Rájput chiefs fought side by side in the fray with Akbar's Muhammadan commanders. Returning to the Panjáb the emperor had scarcely reached Ágra when he heard that Guzárát had risen against him. The rainy season which generally puts a stop to all military operations in India had set in, but he made a rapid march, doing the last 450 miles in nine days. With reckless courage he led his troops in person against the insurgent forces, and Guzárát was again in his hands. A few years later Mozáffar Sháh the ex-king of Guzárát rebelled, but after some protracted operations the imperial general completely defeated him and his ally the chief of Junagahr, in 1584. Mozáffar Sháh lived for a few years in exile and perished by his own hand.

About this period the attention of Akbar was drawn to the political state of the Deccan by refugees from the state of Áhmadnagar. By this time not only were the Deccan monarchies in a chronic state of warfare with each other, but the very foundations of their existence were rotting away under the influence of internal dissensions. Áhmadnagar in particular was well-nigh rent asunder by the contests of two parties, one headed by a Hindu, the other by Abyssinian nobles who were related to the wives of the Nizam Sháhi kings. Refugees of the Hindu faction were

FOUNDATION OF THE MOGHAL EMPIRE.

the first to call upon Akbar to move on their behalf; and some of them lived long enough to rue the day that they had adopted that course. The state of the Deccan was in every way favourable to a general who might wish to bring it under his power. The Portuguese had thrown away an unrivalled opportunity of founding an empire, but Akbar had widely different views as to the expediency of extending his dominions. In 1590 he sent ambassadors to each of the Deccan kings with demands that they should acknowledge his supremacy. His arms were for the time being occupied in other places among which was Kábul. It is noteworthy that no Hindu of any caste then objected to cross the Indus and serve in the Áfghán mountains, although in after years sepoys of the British army pretended that they had lost caste by proceeding beyond Átak. Akbar's empire was steadily increasing. In 1590 his general captured Junagahr, and the rest of Káthiáwár submitted. In Sind the Árghun dynasty had been succeeded by one of Persian extraction. There was, as a matter of course, a series of dissensions in the family; but the harbouring of malcontents gave to the officers of Akbar a pretext for interference which may or may not have been in truth a necessity. Sind was attacked both from the sea and from the Panjáb. Its prince was, in 1592, induced to submit, and he was thereupon enrolled amongst the imperial nobility. In the same year Burhán Nizám Sháh of Áhmadnagar made a furious attack upon Chául, but the results were disastrous to himself. His commander Farhád Khán was made prisoner, 75 pieces of cannon taken, and a loss of 12,000 men is acknowledged by the Muhammadan historian.

Akbar had now, in 1593, ruled for thirty-seven years. His empire included Kábul, Kándahár and the whole of Hindustún with Sind and Guzárát. On the East of India, Oudh, Bengal and Orissa owned his sway. The Rájputs too, though under their own chiefs, were mostly connected with the empire by marriage, and were thoroughly loyal to it. But the ambition of Akbar was deeply mortified at the return of his envoys from the Deccan with the news that each of the kings evaded or refused his demands; and he ordered an army southwards to enforce his authority. The army marched through Málwa and Khándesh, the ruler of which state placed his submission in the hands of the general and joined him with 6,000 horse. At Galna additional forces from Guzárát, under Akbar's son Murád, the viceroy of that province, formed a junction with the main body, and the united armies marched upon Áhmadnagar.

To women is assigned but a scanty rôle in the drama of Indian history, but every now and then one has stood forth to show what splendid deeds her sex is capable of. Such a one was Chánd Bibi of Áhmadnagar, who now opposed the imperial forces. This celebrated lady, who is still the heroine of Deccan story and Deccan song, was the daughter of Hussein Nizám Sháh of Áhmadnagar. She had been given in marriage with the long disputed fort of Sholápur as her dower to Ali Ádil Sháh of Bijápur, in 1564, in order to cement the alliance of those two states which was formed to crush the Hindu kingdom of Bijanagar. Her husband died in 1579, and Chánd Bibi was left as regent on behalf of her little son Ibráhim Ádil Sháh. In a time of incessant turmoil she ruled wisely and well, though she was more than once deprived of power by rival factions in the state. In 1584 she returned to Áhmadnagar and took up her abode there. This noble queen succeeded in uniting together the discordant factions that raged in the Nizám Sháhi capital;

and inspired by her enthusiastic courage they offered a bold front to the enemies of Akbar. Chánd Bibi was the life and soul of the defence. With the valour of Joan of Arc she put on armour, and sword in hand led the defenders against the foe. Again and again the Moghals were beaten back with immense loss, and the vast ditch of the fort was filled with dead (1595). The crisis was passed and the state for a time saved. Allies came up from Bijápur and Golkonda, and prince Murád was compelled to withdraw his troops and to be contented with the cession of Barár. For a short period indeed it seemed that the rival Deccan States were to form a confederacy which would drive the Moghals from Western India for good and all. On the excuse that prince Murád had annexed other districts besides Barár the confederate troops of the three states marched to expel the invaders from the province. It was, in fact, a national contest for supremacy between two Muhammadan races. The battle was fought at Supa on the Godáwari. After horrible slaughter on both sides the Moghals were left in possession of the field, but they found themselves too weak to follow up their advantage. Murád proceeded to subdue Gáwilgahr and other forts in Barár, but he died in 1599, having made little permanent impression on the troops of the Deccan kings. A few more united efforts against the Moghals might have changed the history of the Deccan. But party spirit was stronger than patriotism. With nothing short of insanity the late confederates recommenced their favourite pastime of cutting one another's throats, while the enemy collected his forces for a final spring upon his victim. The Muhammadan kingdoms were doomed, and when the Moghals were driven from all but a comparatively small portion of the Deccan it was not by them but by the Maráthas.

Dissatisfied with the progress that had been made Akbar himself took the field, and Áhmadnagar was a second time besieged. The queen defended the fort with her former bravery, but treachery was at work and her ungrateful troops put her to death. The besiegers pressed the siege with greater vigour than ever. Their mines were sprung and the breaches stormed and scant mercy was shown to the garrison. Having taken the fortress the emperor consolidated under one government Áhmadnagar, Barár, and Khándesh. His favourite son Daniel was made viceroy and wedded to the daughter of the king of Bijápur. Akbar was not happy in his sons. Murád was dead, Daniel died soon after his marriage from excessive drinking; and now his eldest son Silim who was also a drunkard raised a rebellion against him in the North of India. To quell this Akbar had to leave the Deccan without absolutely extinguishing the vitality of the Áhmadnagar State. The fort was held by the imperial troops, but an Abyssinian noble named Málik Ambar, one of those who little better than savages in their own country developed in the Deccan into soldiers and statesmen, established the capital of the Nizám Sháhi kingdom at Daolatábád, of which city he had been governor. Ostensibly in the name of the young king but practically on his own behalf he formed a bulwark against the Moghal invaders almost till his death in 1626. This great man not only defended the frontier and even for a time recovered the fortress of Áhmadnagar, but he found means to reduce the finances of the kingdom to a complete and admirable system. The assessment of the land revenue was made fixed instead of fluctuating. At first it was made payable in kind, but latterly commuted to a money payment, and the amount of assessment was moderate. He abolished revenue farming, and appointed Brahmans who were rapidly increasing in importance to collect the revenue under Muhammadan supervision. Altogether the districts under his rule became thriving and populous. The Golkonda State had suffered less from war and schism than its two rivals in the Deccan. In 1589 the king moved its capital to a healthier site, and built the city which is now called Hydarábád, but which he named Bhágnagar. Many noble buildings still survive to attest the splendour of his reign. But to the South of his kingdom there were still a number of petty Hindu States, and Moslem rule was not firmly established between the Krishna and Cape Comorin.

Hastened by grief at the conduct of his sons Akbar's death took place in 1605 after a reign of 51 years. His possessions in Bombay consisted of Sind, Guzárát including Káthiáwár, Khándesh, Barár, the fort of Áhmadnagar and some neighbouring districts. With the Portuguese his troops had not come into collision. That nation, unlike those that followed it, had refrained from all interference with the new empire, except for a short period, when, in order to obtain possession of Diu, they assisted the king of Guzárát against Humáyun. But before the first century of Portuguese conquest was completed a new power began to despatch ships from Europe to the East. In 1595 two Dutch vessels were sent to the Indian Archipelego; and the naval supremacy of the Portuguese was first disputed and then destroyed by the Dutch and their successors the English. The first defeat of the Portuguese in Indian waters by an English fleet took place at Surat in 1612.

Thus before the English reached India the greatest of the Moghals had passed away. Weaker at the beginning of his reign than former Muhamadan rulers, Akbar had brought his empire to a pitch of greatness that none of his predecessors had attained. No mere ambition for success in battle, no mere lust of empire or plunder actuated him; he had no wish to slay his prisoners of war by the thousand to attest his greatness, it was no pleasure to him to sell their women and children into slavery. Such deeds, on the contrary, were absolutely forbidden. Conquered chiefs had no need to fear death or torture or forcible conversion to Muhammadanism; they had only to submit and they were sure to be exalted to a high position in the imperial nobility. In many cases all their possessions were confirmed to them. Akbar anticipated the edict of Lord William Bentinck that abolished Sati, only permitting it when the widow deliberately chose it herself. He allowed the remarriage of widows, and, what the British Government has not yet dared to do, he forbade the marriage of little children. He abolished the jazia or capitation tax that was levied on all Hindus. They were unmolested in the ordinary practices of their religion; their priests, temples and endowments, were vigilantly protected. Rájput princes were numbered among his courtiers and soldiers; and his great finance minister, Todar Mal, whose revenue settlement of the country has been maintained as a basis upon which the existing system has been built up, was a Hindu. Not only were Hindus allowed the exercise of their own faith but even the administration of their own laws, and they were employed in all branches of the public service except as judges. Akbar drew up a code of laws relating to the army, justice, police, and general state policy, known as the Ayn Akbari. Its ordinances are eminently practical, and in them, from beginning to end, justice is tempered with mercy.

It could not be expected but that Akbar's liberal sentiments and breadth of view should escape opposition from the bigoted and intolerant Moslems, who formed his subjects.

The very fact that he could overcome their opposition and silence the lying charges which said that he persecuted the followers of the prophet makes the picture of his life more wonderful than ever. His perfect tolerance is the more admirable when it is remembered that at the same era the Christian churches of Europe were burning and torturing all whom they deemed to be heretics, and in England and Scotland men and women were being drowned and hanged on ridiculous charges of witchcraft. The fact is that Akbar was in reality not a Muhammadan. There was no God but God, he declared, and Akbar was his caliph; and as all men are liable to err no creed or ritual propounded by man was infallible. Akbar was a theist in whose sight all seekers after God were of equal worth as long as they sought to live righteously and do good to their fellow-men. Whatever may be said on behalf of a somewhat vague belief in a benevolent providence with but few characteristic points to seize the imagination of the multitude, it is quite certain that it is not Muhammadanism. Beautiful as the system may have been, it began with Akbar, and even he can have hardly hoped that it would endure after he had passed away. On his deathbed he repeated the confession of faith and died in the forms of a good Mussalmán. As with his religious convictions so it was with his political reforms. They were his and his only; they belonged to the man and not to the age. It cannot be reiterated too often that there can be nothing permanant in the reforms of a benevolent despot. If it is possible to impart a firm and lasting character to reforms forced upon a people without reference to their will it must be by their belonging to a system and not depending upon the idiosyncracies of a single man. The English love of law and order which embues generation after generation of administrators has given to the inhabitants of India almost all that was given them by Akbar, only very much more has been added. The ranks of the civil service are open to Europeans and Natives alike, if only they can pass the competitive examination in London; and if natives cannot command British brigades they can rise to be judges in the High Courts of Calcutta, Bombay and Madras.

In Akbar's reign beautiful buildings sprang up in the cities of India, and his court was one of the most magnificent in the world. In jewels and decorations, in cloth of gold and velvet, in the equipage of the camp and the trappings of the army, splendour could hardly go further. In ability of character, in breadth of view, in genius and ability Akbar has few rivals in any country, while in the history of India, the great Moghal emperor stands out absolutely unique and unrivalled.

VII.—COMING OF THE ENGLISH.

UPON the death of Akbar, his eldest son, Silim was crowned at Ágra under the title of Jahángir, or conqueror of the world (1605). Gifted with a keen political discernment he was able to carry out some useful reforms, but the mantle of his father did not fall upon his shoulders. He adopted to the letter the orthodox formulas of Islam, and the jazia or poll-tax was replaced upon Hindus. The love of drink ran strong in his family, Akbar alone having withstood the temptation; and the effect of the vice upon Jahángir was to render him a cruel and sullen tyrant. The stern edicts which he issued forbidding the use of wine to others were never binding on himself. He was capable of the most revolting cruelty. His eldest son Khosru rebelled against him in the Panjáb but was taken prisoner; and Jahángir caused 700 of his followers to be impaled in a line from the gate of Láhur. While they were writhing and shrieking in their death-agony he had his son placed on an elephant and carried down the line. Such was the successor of Akbar. The change was indeed startling, and it demonstrates the futility of building up reforms unless the rulers themselves are subject to the reign of law.

Jahángir had reigned three years when there arrived at his splendid court at Ágra the first representative of the future rulers of an empire greater than his own; and Captain Hawkins, the commander of the first English ship that reached India, came from Surat to crave the emperor's permission to establish a factory at that port.

The nation which was to surpass all other European peoples in the contest for supremacy in the East was slow to commence its task. The brilliant success that attended early Portuguese enterprise was not vouchsafed to it. The Portuguese had been lords of the Indian seas for a hundred years, and the Dutch had firmly planted their footing on the rich islands of the Indian Ocean before the first English mariners sailed to the shores of India. A few attempts had latterly been made to reach India or China by the North-west passage. In striving to make his way to India by sailing round Cape Horn Sir Francis Drake's little fleet circumnavigated the world for the first time, but never reached the country to which it had been sent. His expedition however called for remonstrances from Spain against his interference with the fancied rights of its flag. But Queen Elizabeth stoutly declared that the sea like the air was common to all men, and her subjects were free to sail where they pleased. Several expeditions were now sent, but owing to the mismanagement and want of enterprise of their commanders no success was achieved. One captain named Lancaster managed to reach Ceylon, but his vessel was lost and he eventually returned home alone in a French ship. The Dutch were altogether more fortunate, and in 1599 several rich cargoes were brought to Holland. Three years later the various companies which had been engaged in the venture united under a single charter.

A like method was adopted in England. A company was embodied by royal charter in 1600, under the title of "The Governor and Company of the Merchants of London trading to the East Indies"; and a letter was drawn up by the Queen recommending her subjects to the care of all monarchs and peoples whose shores the expedition might visit. Five ships were despatched in 1601 under Lancaster, who was destined never to reach India. But he obtained a valuable cargo at Sumatra, and added to the wealth thus obtained by the capture of a Portuguese ship laden with spices. Queen Elizabeth did not live to see his return, but a second expedition under Admiral Middleton to Sumatra in 1604 was even more successful. The Dutch, however, though they received the new arrivals with friendly greetings, showed unmistakably that they meant to keep the monopoly of the spice traffic to themselves. However, by collecting their cargoes at other islands the English gave no room for interference. The ships returned in 1606 without having as yet visited India proper.

The success of these enterprises led the company to undertake a third venture, and early in 1607 three ships were despatched under David Middleton. The goal aimed at was still the spice islands of the Indian Archipelago, but one of the ships named the "Hector," under Captain Hawkins, parted from her consorts and sailed to Surat. The "Hector" was thus the first English ship to reach India. Hawkins remained at Surat to make arrangements for future commercial operations, but despatched his vessel to Bantam in Sumatra; and the three ships reached England with large profit. Two vessels despatched from England before their return were wrecked; but nothing daunted the company sent another expedition to Bantam which resulted in a profit that surpassed their highest expectations. They considered it advisable to strengthen their positions by obtaining from James I. a new Charter which confirmed their existing privileges. Upon this three ships were despatched under Sir Henry Middleton, one of them the "Trades' Increase" being of 1,000 tons burden, a very different vessel from the slender craft of the earlier attempts. The "Trades' Increase" had an adventurous voyage. She visited Aden and Mocha, and at the latter port was run ashore by an Arab pilot, and her crew and commander imprisoned. By extraordinary good fortune they obtained their release. The "Trades' Increase" was floated, only for the crew to find a considerable Portuguese fleet waiting to oppose them. Force on this occasion was not used; but Middleton let the Portuguese know that their opinion as to their sole right to trade in those waters hardly coincided with his own, and that he meant to trade where he liked. From the Red Sea he made his way to Surat. However at the Guzárát emporium he found the native authorities so impressed with the fear of the Portuguese that for the time being trade was impracticable. He therefore followed the advice given him at Surat and sailed to Gogo, some miles northward on the Káthiáwár coast, where he was less likely to be interfered with.

He took with him Hawkins, the Captain of the "Hector," who had just returned from Ágra with an Armenian wife bestowed upon him by the emperor. Hawkins had a wonderful tale to tell. When he despatched his ship to Bantam he speedily found that he would be unable to establish a factory or create a trade without the emperor's sanction. Taking King James' letter addressed to the Great Moghal he adventured on the long journey to Ágra, travelling hundreds and hundreds of miles where the face of no Englishman had yet been seen. Jahángir received him with every attention and courtesy; he lodged him sumptuously and bestowed on him high marks of favour. The emperor showed himself well disposed to the stranger who sought his aid, and expressed a wish to welcome an ambassador from the Court of London. For the present however the imperial permission to trade was not granted, but Hawkins went away astounded at the magnificence of the court life of Jahángir and the civilized nature of his rule. What stood in the way of more substantial results was the presence at the imperial court of some Portuguese Jesuits, who frustrated his efforts to obtain a firmán; and even contrived to prevent the payment of a handsome salary promised him by the emperor. These narrow-minded priests did not even hesitate to attempt the life of a man who was interfering with the commercial monopoly of their nation. Failing to obtain his object Hawkins, not without considerable difficulty, made the long and hazardous journey back to Surat.

Sir Henry Middleton had been sent to trade by the East India Company. This errand he had no intention of leaving unaccomplished merely because circumstances stood in the way of peaceful commerce by land. He betook himself to the mouth of the Red Sea and there seized vessels laden with Indian produce. He placed their cargoes on board his ships and gave the masters in return the goods that he had brought from England, whether the exchange was to their liking or not. The result was a rich gain to the Company. About this time an English ship sailing up the Eastern coast of India found the Dutch established at several native ports by permission of the king of Golkonda. The English captain managed to plant a small factory at Másulipatam.

From Sir Henry Middleton's voyage the English learnt the lesson that in the face of the superior strength of the Portuguese the only way to establish a trade with India was by force. Accordingly in 1612 a fleet of four ships fully armed made direct for Surat, and were about to open trade, seemingly, by permission of the local authorities. At that moment four Portuguese men-of-war and a convoy of merchant ships entered the harbour. Best, the British Commander, had a fair show of argument on his side; but preferring deeds to words he promptly threw himself upon the Portuguese fleet. The Portuguese were utterly defeated. No argument is so convincing to the Oriental mind as physical force, and the effect of this victory was at once apparent. Jahángir concluded a treaty with the English which gave them permission to trade on payment of customs duties at $3\frac{1}{2}$ per cent., and to establish factories at Surat, Cambay, Gogo and Áhmadábád. An ambassador from the English court was to be permanently resident at the imperial capital. Captain Best received this treaty at Surat in February 1613, and the event must be regarded as a famous one in the annals of the English in the East. They were now firmly established and their desultory proceedings at an end.

Meanwhile Jahángir's affairs in the Deccan were not progressing satisfactorily. His army had been defeated by Málik Ambar, the great Áhmadnagar general and minister, who ruled in the name of a fainéant king. The fort of Áhmadnagar had been recaptured in 1610 and the emperor's troops driven back to Burhánpur the capital of Khándesh. The rebellion of Jahángir's son Prince Khosru enabled Málik Ambar to consolidate his power, and carry out his administrative reforms. He rallied round him the chiefs of many Marátha families which were steadily rising in importance, and conferred upon them high military positions. He was playing with edged tools ; and the Hindu chieftains were not always to use on behalf of their Mussalmán rulers the high powers with which they were entrusted. The emperor sent an additional force from Guzárát to assist Khán Jahán Lodi his viceroy in the Deccan in 1612, but the spirited resistance of Málik Ambar drove the united armies from his frontiers.

Jahángir determined to take the field in person against the rebels ; and in 1616 he appointed his son Prince Kharrám who succeeded him as Sháh Jahán, to be commander-in-chief of the Deccan. But before this there had arrived at Ágra Sir Thomas Roe, the English ambassador from James I. In a long residence at Constantinople Roe had acquired a thorough knowledge of Eastern character and manners; but the pomp of the Turkish court had altogether failed to prepare him for the magnificence that he beheld at Ágra. In accordance with the Oriental custom by which no one comes before a monarch empty handed he came provided with gifts. But he could hardly smother a feeling of humiliation when he placed before the emperor the presents sent from England; for all the jewels of the British crown would not compare with those which adorned the throne and robes of Jahángir. Roe, like Hawkins, was admitted to intimacy by the emperor, and the diaries kept by him during his three years' residence at the Moghal Court give a most interesting and valuable picture of the times. Roe left nothing undone to promote the interests of his country. He induced the emperor to extend the permission to trade to the whole of India, and drew up a series of articles regulating the English traffic, most of which were confirmed by the emperor. He was as bold as he was diplomatic, and he sent to the Portuguese viceroy at Goa a document which considerably enlarged that potentate's views on the subject of freedom of trade. The viceroy was plainly told that any attempt to interfere with the English commerce would inevitably bring forth war, revenge and bloodshed. The English intended nothing but free trade open by the law of nations to all men. It was not the purpose of the English to root out or hinder the trade of the Portuguese; and it was strange that people of that nation should dare to infringe upon the free commerce between others. On these liberal views it must be confessed that the policy of the great company for nearly two centuries forms a startling commentary.

In 1616 Sir Thomas Roe accompanied the Imperial army on its march against the Deccan. The emperor himself went no further than the fort of Mándu in Málwa, but his proximity infused energy into his commanders. An alliance was made with Bijápur, and Málik Ambar was driven out of the city and fort of Áhmadnagar. Akbar's conquests were for the time re-established, but in 1620 Málik Ambar again defeated the imperial forces and carried his movements so far to the North as the fortress of Mándu itself. Amongst the Maráthas conspicuous in Málik Ambar's service was an officer named Sháhji Bhonsle. His family had risen into notice under his father Málloji Bhonsle, who held a command of horse in the Áhmadnagar army. Prince Sháh Jahán was again sent against Málik Ambar, but it required well-nigh the full power of the empire to bring him to submission. This was at last done in a general action to the north of the Áhmadnagar territory, in which Sháhji Bhonsle greatly distinguished himself.

Jahángir died in 1627, a year later than his formidable opponent Málik Ambar. That great man was a foreigner, and as such regarded with jealousy both in Áhmadnagar and Bijápur. Had he been an Indian Muhammadan his administrative talent and military genius might have created an impregnable barrier against the Moghal forces. But alike among Hindus and Muhammadans in India political union has always been shipwrecked by private feuds and party feeling. For Jahángir the last year of his life had been embittered by struggles between his own sons and the son of his beautiful and imperious wife Nur Jahán, by her first husband, whom she desired to be proclaimed heir.

VIII.—RISE OF THE MARÁTHAS.

SHÁH JAHÁN surpassed in magnificence all the former emperors of India. He devoted himself to the pursuit of architecture, and it is to him that is due the erection at Delhi of some of the most beautiful buildings in the world. To Delhi he transferred the seat of Government from Ágra; but it was at the latter place that he built in memory of his wife Mumtáz Mahal, the Táj Mahal, the most noble of Indian buildings, alike in its gracefulness and simplicity. European travellers spoke with marvel of the peacock throne, so called from the outspread tail, whose colours were wrought in diamonds and rubies and the costliest of gems. His dominions stretched from Bengal to Persia; and he ruled them with ability and judgment. Without the absolute tolerance of Akbar he was yet free from the narrow orthodoxy of Jahángir, and the fanaticism of Aurangzib. Sháh Jahán had no liking for Khán Jahán Lodi, the commander-in-chief of his forces in the Deccan. That officer had long been bent on making himself independent. His suspicions being aroused by the emperor's treatment of him he openly took up arms against his new master with the aid of the local Marátha authorities. It had taken immense efforts to partially subdue Áhmadnagar. Bijápur and Golkonda had not yet come under the empire. Rightly estimating the efforts that the union of these powers under Lodi might produce, Sháh Jahán proceeded to the Deccan in person in 1629 and directed the policy of the campaign. A hitherto staunch adherent of Lodi was Sháhji Bhonsle who had succeeded to much of the weight and influence of Málik Ambar. He excelled in the art of knowing when to trim his sails, and deeming that Lodi was no match against the emperor now that he had himself come to the Deccan he betook himself to Sháh Jahán. On making his submission he received a patent of nobility and the confirmation of his estates. Other Marátha chiefs followed his example; and the immediate result was to considerably strengthen the cause of the emperor, and proportionately weaken that of Lodi and those who were disposed to aid him. The rebellion was quelled and Lodi slain, after fighting bravely to the last.

Lodi had ineffectually besought the aid of Bijápur to resist the Moghal encroachments, but the Bijápur king was engrossed in the work of adorning and beautifying his city, and he refused to break through the alliance which had been made in the time of Akbar. That alliance had been ratified during the wars of Málik Ambar; and the Bijápur king had entered into a secret treaty with the emperor, by which in return for his co-operation against Áhmadnagar he was to receive the Konkan territory of that state and the fort of Sholápur. But alarmed at the emperor's occupation of the country after his defeat of Lodi, the Bijápur king entered upon an offensive and defensive alliance with Áhmadnagar against Sháh Jahán, receiving from that state the districts which the emperor had formerly engaged to give him. The alliance achieved nothing. The Bijápur army was at once defeated, and the city besieged by the Moghal forces. The siege was not successful but Áhmadnagar was now made over to the emperor by Fatte Khán, the son of Málik Ambar, who was confirmed as regent of the state. This disgusted Sháhji Bhonsle who joined the Bijápur forces against the emperor. Fatte Khán also changed sides and defended himself at Daolatábád, but before long he had to surrender, and was again received into the Moghal service. The last fainéant king of Áhmadnagar, a mere boy, was sent as a state prisoner to Gwálior, and so in 1633 the Nizám Sháhi kingdom came to an end. But Bijápur was unsubdued, and none of the Deccan was really pacified. The emperor was obliged to return to his capital to see after the affairs of the Panjáb, and in his absence his commanders withdrew to Burhánpur.

Sháhji Bhonsle was not slow to take advantage of this opportunity. He proclaimed another prince as lawful heir to the Nizám Sháhi kingdom; and calling himself his guardian collected troops, garrisoned the forts, and occupied the districts of the late kingdom as far as the sea. This insolence could not be tolerated by Sháh Jahán. In 1635 he returned to the Deccan. The country was mercilessly plundered; and though a second siege of Bijápur failed, the king had to sue for peace. He was granted favourable terms and enrolled as vassal of the empire on payment of about £800,000 a year, and the forfeiture of a considerable portion of his dominions, including Sholápur. Shájí had deserted Lodi for Sháh Jáhan, on thinking that course to be favourable to his interest. He left the emperor's ranks when he thought himself able to hold his own in an independent position. He now determined once more to turn with the tide; his submission was received, and he was re-admitted into the imperial service. The Deccan was now for the time being fairly settled, and Sháh Jahán returned to his capital in 1637 leaving his son Aurangzib as viceroy. But Muhammadan rule in that part of India rested upon very insecure foundations. It was composed of elements which not even common interests and a common religion could succeed in uniting. On the one side was the emperor of Delhi, amongst whose forces contention often ran riot, his own sons striving with one another for the mastery. On the other, until the recent extinction of the Nizám Sháhi kingdom by Sháh Jahán, there were the three Muhammadan States of Áhmadnagar, Bijápur and Golkonda who, it has been seen, only laid aside the pleasing occupation of cutting one another's throats for occasional union against a common foe. Meanwhile each was more and more inclined to pamper the Marátha chieftains and soldiery that were ranged under their banners. The movement was steadily gaining strength which brought Shiwáji the son of Sháhji into prominence as a champion of the Hindu faith and a Hindu empire, which should smite down and drive out of the Deccan its Mussalmán rulers, emperors, and kings alike.

Meanwhile English trade was on the whole progressing favourably though not without some fluctuations; and in 1628 a factory was established at Ármagur a town on the eastern coast of India which is memorable as being the first place fortified by the English in the country. At Surat the Dutch entered upon a severe competition with the London merchants. For a time the English commercial supremacy was eclipsed, but the Company's vigour soon reasserted itself. In 1632 important privileges were obtained from the king of Persia for trading in the Persian Gulf, and two years later under a firmán from Sháh Jahán a factory was opened at Pipli near the mouth of the Hughli in Bengal. Less to the liking of the Company than the rivalry of the Dutch was the competition of a new Company from England. King Charles I. did not approve of many of the original Company's actions. He charged them with violation of their privileges, and through under-payment of their servants with conniving at a large amount of private trade. The Company, he contended, had established no permanent forts, and had done nothing towards extending the greatness and wealth of the empire. The real truth was that the king sorely needed the money which the new Company, under Sir Thomas Corten, was prepared to supply. He signed the new charter in 1634, and before the representatives of the original Company at Surat were informed of the transaction, their rivals were at their doors. The time was indeed an ill-chosen one for weakening the East India Company. The Dutch and Portuguese had just agreed to come to terms and strengthen each other's hands. The Corten Company commenced operations brilliantly but its success did not last long, and their predecessors had undoubtedly the advantage in the struggle. In 1646 Fort St. George was founded at Madras to protect a new factory that had been established on the Eastern coast. In 1650 the English Parliament decided that one Company alone was to carry on the trade; but an actual settlement was postponed by war breaking out with Holland. Three ships were captured by the Dutch in the Persian Gulf and the trade of Surat was seriously checked. On the conclusion of peace in 1654 the rival claims of the English and Dutch companies were submitted to the arbitration of the Swiss Cantons. Decision was given in favour of the English, and they were awarded a sum of £88,000, an amount very much smaller than they had claimed. An intense struggle now continued between the two English companies. Finally, under Cromwell, it was determined that the Company and the "Merchant Adventurers" should form one joint stock company, and the amalgamation seems to have been carried out without difficulty. Surat was made the Presidency of Western India with control over the Persian Gulf; while the authority of Madras extended over Hughli, Patna, Kásimbázár and Bálásur.

The submission of Sháh Bhonsle was followed by an interval of peace in the Indian empire of Sháh Jahán. He was nevertheless engaged in sending expeditions to Kándahár and Balkh, but these left him leisure to improve his revenue system and general administration. His son Aurangzib, who had been employed with the army in Kándahár was appointed viceroy of the Deccan. He made his court at the city which Málik Ambar had built near Daolatábád, and changed its name from Kirki to Aurangábád. Under Aurangzib's viceroyalty Todar Mal's revenue system was to some extent introduced into the Deccan. Sháhji meanwhile was permitted to leave the direct service of the emperor for that of his vassal the king of Bijápur, and his talents and genius found him constant employment. In 1627 there had been born to him at Junnar a son named Shiwáji. He was left at Puna with his mother to be brought up under the guardianship of Dádáji Konedew. Dádáji was one of those Brahmans whom all Maráthas of importance retain in their service as writers and men of business. This man showed great skill in the management of Sháhji's estates near Puna, most of which were in the wild valleys of the Western Gháts. As the boy Shiwáji grew up he made friends with other young Marátha chiefs like himself. Animated with an intense hatred of Muhammadanism he and his friends led wild and lawless lives, and issued on plundering raids on the rich lands below the Gháts. An inspiration seized the young Shiwáji that he might smite the Moslem hip and thigh, and bring back the palmy days when the children of Bhawáni and Indra possessed the land, and had not to bow down beneath a foreign yoke. He scorned to learn to read or write, but he attained high skill in all martial exercises. He was equally proficient in the use of the spear, the sword, and the gun, while like most of his countrymen he excelled in horsemanship. He delighted to listen to tales of Hindu chivalry that were recited to him out of the Rámáyana and Máhábhárat. All the religious ideas of a Hindu were strongly developed in his nature, and he was rigidly strict in all caste ceremonies and observances. His mother was a remarkable woman. ' To her he confided all his aspirations, and she worked up his hopes to the highest pitch by telling him of revelations which she had received from the goddess Bhawáni foreshadowing his future greatness as the upheaver of the Muhammadan creed. By the death of his guardian, Shiwáji became the manager of his father's estates. During his life time Dádáji had urged him to give up his schemes and faithfully serve Bijápur. On his death-bed he exhorted him to achieve independence, and protect Brahmans, kine, and cultivators. These dying words were not only an encouragement to Shiwáji, but they gave a sanction to his designs in the eyes of his followers. From his father's estates he gained the means which enabled him to enter upon the mission of his life, while he was daily acquiring a more and more powerful influence over the wild inhabitants of the mountains. Bold and determined as he was he saw the need of caution and wariness. By his politeness and conciliatory manners he gained the good will of the respectable Maráthas of Puna; but his occasional absence into the Konkan were followed by rumours of robberies and dacoities, and it was whispered that Shahji's son shared the profits.

In his wanderings about the wild highlands where he after-

7

wards established himself he not only grew familiar with the paths and tracks, but made himself thoroughly acquainted with the hill forts. These forts had been easily taken by the Muhammadans, and their value being in consequence much under-estimated they were generally neglected. Shiwáji saw that they could be turned to good account. He managed by some means, the particulars of which are not known, to induce the killidár or governor of Torna, a fort about thirty miles to the West of Puna, to give over the place to him. This was in 1646 when Shiwáji was in his twentieth year. He now sent word to the Bijápur authorities of what he had done. He undertook to pay for the tract which he had taken a higher rent than had been received for it in the ten years that it had belonged to Bijápur. No notice was taken of his request, and he proceeded to strengthen and repair Torna. While busied with this task he discovered in the fort a hoard of gold which he attributed to a miracle worked on his behalf by the goddess Bhawáni. This enabled him to purchase arms and ammunition and to build another fort near Torna which he named Rájgahr or the royal fort. Both of them are situated in what is now the Bhor State or Pant Sachiw's territory. The attention of the Bijapur Government was at last attracted. References were made to Sháhji, who replied that doubtless his son was working for the improvement of the estates which he held under government.

Shiwáji next proceeded to win over to his views the Hindu officer in charge of the fort of Chákan, and by a large bribe he secured the important fort near Puna to which he gave or restored the name of Singahr (Shiwagahr) or the lion's den. For his father's estates he was bound to pay revenues to Bijápur. By various excuses he contrived to keep them in his own hands, and use them for his own purposes. A little later by craft and stratagem he occupied Supa, and got possession of Purandhar, another important fortress near Puna. Hitherto these acquisitions were made without stir or bloodshed. Little heed was given to what was being done on or about Sháhji's estates, while Sháhji himself was serving in the immediate presence of the Bijápur king. And so, without let or hindrance, Shiwáji made for himself a splendid base of operations in the fastnesses of the Western Ghâts. When his progress attracted attention, and concealment was no longer possible, he could spring out from his strongholds with a force as irresistible as it was unexpected.

Cautious as he was not to strike before he was sure of his strength, two years had not passed from his occupation of Torna before he was able to show his hand. He had kindled such faith in his followers that he ventured to attack a large convoy of Government treasure on its way from Kályán to Bijápur, and disperse the escort. He divided the treasure amongst his horsemen and conveyed it with all speed to Rájgahr. Rightly judging that this open defiance could not be disregarded by the Bijápur court, Shiwáji at once proceeded to strengthen the position that he had taken up. Such was his activity that before the news could reach the capital he had made himself master of no less than ten forts on the borders of the Deccan and in the Konkan. Some of these were held directly by the Bijápur Government; others were in the little state of Janjira or the island, so called from its fort in the harbour of Danda Rájápuri. The early kings of Áhmadnagar had established Abyssinians as captains of this part of their territories. The appointment became hereditary, the chief being commonly known as the Sidi, a vulgar corruption of Syad, a term of respect for descendants of the prophet. In the ordinary speech of the Deccan Sidi is an equivalent for African, and is used in a contemptuous sense. The Sidi of Janjira was subsequently appointed to be admiral of the fleet of the Moghal empire.

Shiwáji's action had been bold, but his next exploit was still more daring. He pushed his forces on to Kályán, took the governor prisoner, and obtained the surrender of several forts in its neighbourhood. He at once revived ancient Hindu institutions. Endowments were made to temples and assignments to Brahmans. Two new forts were also commenced for the protection of the frontier against the Sidi, who was by no means an unformidable neighbour. Incensed as the Bijápur Government was at being thus defied by Shiwáji the king could not believe that he was acting independently of his father Sháhji. The latter was therefore seized and imprisoned. Sháhji with perfect truth insisted that he had nothing whatever to do with his son's achievements, and advised the king to reduce him to obedience by force. But enraged at what he considered Sháhji's obstinacy the king placed him in a dungeon in which he was all but walled up; and told him that if he did not shortly procure the submission of his son the few remaining bricks would be closed. Shiwáji, seemingly with the deliberate intention of playing the rival Muhammadan powers one against the other, had refrained from any interference with the emperor's territory or subjects; and he now appealed to Sháh Jahán against his vassal king of Bijápur. With a like notion of making use of this daring young Marátha as a check upon his stiff-necked subject, Sháh Jahán admitted Shiwáji into his service, and obtained the release of his father from the dungeon.

RISE OF THE MARÁTHAS.

Sháhji however was detained at Bijápur for two years. During this period Shiwáji was busied with endless schemes, but committed few aggressions. But no sooner was Sháhji allowed to leave the capital and return to his duty in the southern districts than he took to his old courses. He seized fort after fort, and in 1656 made for himself an impregnable stronghold at Pratápgahr, near the heights of Máhábleshwár.

Aurangzib meanwhile, as viceroy of the Deccan, had been waging war against Golkonda, and after sacking Hydarábád he forced the king to pay a fine of £1,000,000 sterling. The death of Muhammad Ádil Sháh of Bijápur, under whose reign the city was one of the finest and most populous in India, formed sufficient excuse for interference in that quarter. Aurangzib chose to say that the selection of a king lay with the emperor. The young king Ádil Ali Sháh offered to pay a sum equal to that exacted from Golkonda, but Aurangzib determined once for all to annex the kingdom to the imperial dominions. The city was invested in 1567, and its capture was only a question of time, when a message reached Aurangzib of the supposed mortal illness of his father. He hurried off to Delhi to secure his succession to the throne and quash the claims of his three brothers. Shuja and Murád, in whom the family vice of drunkenness ran riot, assumed royal titles. Aurangzib cajoled Murád by promising to help him against their eldest brother Dára, a prince who would have been a worthy successor to Akbar. Their combined armies defeated Dára who was forced to flee. Murád, having been used as a tool, was now put aside, and Shuja's efforts were fruitless. On failing to conciliate the emperor, whose illness was after all not mortal, Aurangzib seized the throne in 1658, and kept his father prisoner within the walls of his palace until his death eight years later. Dára and Murád were killed and Shuja only escaped to perish in Arrakhan. Sháh Jahán left no less than £24,000,000 sterling in the public treasury. He had governed his immense dominions wisely and well. The great Deccan kingdom of Bijápur was bound more closely to the empire during his reign than it ever had been before.

Shiwáji had kept a watchful eye on all the movements of Aurangzib. On the commencement of the prince's operations against Bijápur he entered into correspondence with him. Aurangzib listened to his overtures, and consented to his retaining what he had wrested from Bijápur. He even handed over to Shiwáji the port of Dábul and its dependencies on the Ratnágiri coast which were directly under the government of the emperor. Aurangzib was anxious for an interview with the Marátha chief in order to impress upon him how closely their interests were allied. But Shiwáji had no wish to place himself in an equivocal position, being perfectly well aware that the alliance of their interests would last no longer than might seem good to himself. That limit was soon reached, and while writing conciliatory letters Shiwáji made a raid upon Junnar and carried to Rájgahr revenue collections of the Moghal Government worth £120,000. The principle that money is the sinews of war was a maxim that he invariably recognised. But the army of Aurangzib obtained unexpected success at Bijápur, and Shiwáji thought it better to temporise. He wrote in a humble strain begging for forgiveness for what was past; and when Aurangzib journeyed northwards on the news of his father's illness he offered to protect the imperial dominions during his absence. At the same time he pressed his claims to some hereditary estates in the Moghal districts, and solicited the imperial sanction to the transfer of all the Konkan to himself. Aurangzib had no wish that his troops should risk a collision with Shiwáji during his own absence. He judged it best for the time to comply with his arrogant demands, and even deemed it good policy to encourage the Marátha upstart at the expense of Muhammadan vassals. The result showed how fatal was the mistake of allowing an avowed enemy of Islam to consolidate his power, as a means by which the more effectually to bring Bijápur and Golkonda beneath the Imperial sway.

IX.—EXPANSION OF MARÁTHA POWER.

AURANGZIB was forty years old when he dethroned his father and became emperor under the title of Álamgir, and he was to reign like Akbar for half a century (1658-1707). Both were indefatigable workers, both were prompt in action, and both to a certain extent skilful in dealing with emergencies. But Aurangzib had none of his illustrious ancestor's love of righteousness and breadth of sympathy. A bigoted and intolerant follower of the prophet, he has been described as a Puritan Muhammadan monarch. The toleration of Akbar had ended with his life. But it had left a kind of contemptuous half-belief in the state religion among those who carried out its ceremonies to the letter. A period of immorality and licence had sprung up at the court. The great object of Aurangzib's life was to crush this infidelity and licence, to bring Hindus down to their proper level and to subdue the heretical Muhammadan kingdoms of the Deccan. Aurangzib was a Sunni or orthodox Muhammadan; the Deccan kings supported the Shia heresy which refused to recognise as caliphs the first three followers of the prophet who had assumed that title.

Aurangzib loved to enter into the minutest details of his administration. He was fascinated by the individual features of the work of government. He could not throw his gaze over the vast surface of his empire so as to obtain one comprehensive view of the political horizon. His method of rule in Hindustán is not within our consideration here. But his whole history in the West of India with regard to the Maráthas and the Mussalmán kingdoms of the Deccan cannot but fill us with amazement at the praise that has been bestowed on his ability and administration. Daring as he was his boldness was exceeded by his hypocrisy. To advance his ambitious aims no dissimulation was too low to stoop to. He strove to build up a reputation for wisdom; and his successful usurpation of the throne, his close attention to business, the simplicity of his personal habits amidst a court of unparalleled splendour, and the extent of his scholastic attainments sufficed to obtain it for him. That he lacked the affection which Akbar felt for all his subjects is not wonderful; his failure to see that the strongest foundation which his empire could rest upon would be a fusion of all alike into one nationality makes the wisdom of Akbar stand out in yet more vivid relief. In Bijápur and Golkonda he possessed powerful bulwarks which a wise statesmanship might have incorporated into the empire, and bound to it by as warm ties of devotion and interest as those which hold the modern princes of India in allegiance to Queen Victoria.

In most parts of his dominions he smote with an iron rod those who were not followers of the Prophet. The capitation tax on all infidels was stringently collected, and a mass of clamorous petitioners for exemption from the impost were trampled to death by his elephants. Customs duties for Hindus were twofold what they were for Muhammadans, and Hindus were excluded from all public offices except a few military posts. Far from desiring to be a benefactor of mankind, Aurangzib's wish was to establish his title as a Muhammadan saint. Akbar had allied himself to the Rájputs, and Aurangzib had Rájput blood in his veins. But Aurangzib treated this race as enemies of his faith, and goaded them into a rebellion, which was put down with all the ferocity of Islam. The country was laid waste, the men slain, the women and children made slaves. And yet in spite of this mischievous and intolerant bigotry such was his suspicion of the Muhammadan kings in the Deccan who would not bow their heads to the Moghal yoke that he encouraged the rise of the bitterest foe of his and their mutual faith in order to weaken the powers that he should have cherished as the buttresses of his empire. His eyes were partially opened when the mischief was done. But even then, emergent as the crisis was, such was his suspicion and obstinacy that he would not trust his generals with sufficient forces to quell the Marátha power whose growth his policy had stimulated. And at the end, when he himself came to the Deccan for his final efforts at its subjugation, his armies were hampered by their unheard-of pomp and gorgeous equipment, and his treasury exhausted in fruitless display.

When Aurangzib went off from the Deccan to seize the throne at Delhi, Shiwáji promptly went on with his system of conquest. One of his expeditions met with unexpected failure, and an army that he despatched under his Peshwa or chief officer against the little African State of Janjira was signally defeated by the Sidi's forces. Every exertion was used to repair the disaster; and an event shortly occurred which raised Shiwaji's power to the highest pitch. Attracted to his doings in the Konkan and on the Gháts the Bijápur Government, putting aside for a time its endless internal distractions, became sensible of the necessity of subduing the marauder. A splendid army was despatched against him under Afzul Khán, an officer of high rank, who proudly vaunted that he would soon return to his sovereign with the insignificant rebel in chains.

Shiwáji had no intention of risking a battle in the open field. He took up his position at Pratápgahr, and sent pretended offers of submission to the Bijápur commander. Afzul Khán, notwithstanding his contempt for his enemy, was fully aware of the natural difficulties of the country. Halting at Wai he despatched a trusted Brahman named Pantoji Gopináth to receive Shiwáji's submission. Shiwáji gave the Brahman an honourable reception, but assigned him quarters apart from his suite. Secretly in the night he went to him and represented that all that he had done was on behalf of the Hindu faith. It was Bhawáni herself at whose bidding he was making war against the enemies of their religion, the violaters of their temples and gods. It was his mission to free his countrymen from their yoke and to give protection to kine and Brahmans. It was therefore Pantoji's duty to assist him in the divine work. He seconded these arguments with costly gifts, and the Brahman could not resist the appeal.

In order to accomplish their design the false envoy now sent messages to Afzul Khán that Shiwáji was in fear for his safety at the hands of the Bijápur army, but that the personal assurances of the Khán would induce him to surrender. With blind confidence the vain-glorious general took the bait. He led his army into the mountains and walked into the trap that Shiwáji had prepared for him. Shiwáji made ready for the accomplishment of his purpose as though the deed that he proposed to do was the most sacred act of patriotism. He solemnly performed his religious observances, and laid his head at his mother's feet to receive her special blessing on his righteous deed. Under his turban he placed a steel cap, he put on chain armour beneath his cotton gown, and concealed a crooked dagger in his right sleeve. On the fingers of his left hand he fixed a favourite Maráthi weapon known as a wágnak or tiger's claws. His guest was introduced to him. In the midst of the customary embrace Shiwáji stuck the wágnak into his bowels and followed up the blow with his dagger. It was the work of a moment. Afzul Khán's head was severed from his body, and preconcerted signals were given upon which Shiwáji's troops started up from the dense vegetation in which they had been lying in ambush. They mowed down in hundreds the Bijápur soldiers, who never suspected the presence of an enemy, and who had not time to mount their horses or stand to their arms.

The rout of the Bijápur army and the capture of its valuable camp and siege train greatly raised Shiwáji's fame. His subsequent career was by no means unchequered, but he may be fairly said from this date to have created the Marátha nation. He had dealt a deadly blow at Muhammadan power, Delhi and Bijápur alike, and the year of the victory, 1659, is an important date. Almost exactly a hundred years later the battle of Plassey forms another memorable epoch in Indian history. Plassey established as rulers the merchants who for so long had barely sustained a struggle for existence on the sea-coast; and just a hundred years after that the rule of the Company ended in the thunderstorm of the great mutiny only to spring into new life in the mightier rule of the British Crown.

The Bijápur king now took the field in person against Shiwáji and besieged him at Panálla, a strong fort twelve miles from Kolhápur, which the wily Marátha had secured by corrupting its Bijápur commander. Shiwáji escaped from Panálla, and left the king's army to wear itself out in ineffectual efforts to come up with him, while he occupied himself with plundering and robbing right and left. Early in 1661 he appeared before Rájápur on the Ratnágiri coast, plundered the English factory, and imprisoned for several years some of the merchants on the excuse that they had assisted the Bijápur troops against him. Some of his forts were taken by the Bijápur army, but he built new ones, especially near the sea. Observing too the great advantage that the Sidi of Janjira gained from his ships he proceeded to establish a fleet of his own, while he obtained guns and military stores from the Portuguese on condition of leaving them unmolested. The demand it need hardly be said was frequently renewed.

About this period Shiwáji received a visit from his father Sháhji, who was still in the Bijápur service. Shiwáji treated him with profound respect and high distinction. He sent him back to Bijápur with presents for the king, and by his intervention secured an amnesty from the state. The amnesty lasted till Sháhji's death in 1664, and was then not broken by Shiwáji. It was probably at the suggestion of Sháhji that Shiwáji at this time moved his head-quarters from Rájgahr to an impregnable position at Rairi, nearer the sea, in what is now the Kolába district. He changed its name to Raygahr, or the regal fortress, and erected upon it a complete set of public buildings. Shiwáji now possessed a compact territory with a coast line extending 160 miles from Kályán to Goa, and a breadth of 100 miles. His army was a formidable one of some 50,000 foot and 7,000 horse, and his truce with Bijápur enabled him to use it against the Moghals.

The English all this time were steadily improving their position, and a new charter granted them by Charles II. in addition to extending their trading privileges gave them important political and judicial authority. They were empowered to choose their own governors, and to administer British laws within their settlements. They were allowed to make war with any power not Christian—a proviso honoured in the letter rather than in the spirit—to build fortifications, and to suppress the trade of interlopers or unauthorised persons. This greatly raised the status of the Company's settlement at Surat. But a city that was to become the second city of the British empire when the greatness of Surat was well-nigh forgotten was now to come into the Company's hands. In 1661, by the marriage treaty of Charles II. with Catharine of Braganza, the princess of Portugal, the island of Bombay was ceded to the British Crown. The British engaged in return to defend and protect the subjects of the King of Portugal in those parts from the power and invasion of the States of the United Provinces. An expedition was sent to take possession of the island in 1662 under the Earl of Marlborough. The Earl was instructed to convey the Viceroy of Goa from Lisbon to India, and from him to receive the island in possession. He was also directed " to make the most exact observations he could of all advantages which may be secured to His Majesty or his subjects in those parts where he should go, either by treaties with the several Princes of those countries, or by planting of spices in any places which may be or shall be in the king's possession, and of the means of advancing trade and securing navigation in those parts." But owing to a claim to the islands near Bombay which were not specifically named in the concession negociations ensued. The Earl returned to England for instructions, leaving his troops, 500 in number, under the command of Sir Abraham Shipman, on the pestilential island of Anjidiwa near Goa. Sir Abraham and most of his men perished from the climate. However, in 1664 Mr. Cooke, his Secretary, signed a convention accepting Bombay alone, and the island was taken possession of by the crown. Charles II. protested against the action of the Portuguese, and demanded the islands and £100,000 compensation for the loss suffered by the expedition, but nothing came of the remonstrance. Four years later Bombay was transferred to the Company with all the powers of local government. The Company undertook to pay the crown £10 a year rent for the island, and "all persons born in Bombay were to be accounted natural subjects of England." Excepting its magnificent position, which was however greatly reduced in value by the separation of the neighbouring islands of Colaba (now joined to Bombay), Karanja (now mainland), Salsette and Elephanta from its rule, there was little but a few native fishing villages and some small and crumbling Portuguese forts to be taken over by the English. But the fortifications were enlarged and practically rebuilt; and, while Aurangzib was massacring Rájputs, Shiwáji slaying Muhammadans, and the Portuguese allowing none but Christians to sleep within the walls of Bassein, Chául and Goa, a wise policy of religious toleration, freedom of trade and encouragment of native industry, attracted to Bombay persons of all nations. A cosmopolitan population of Europeans, Pársis, Muhammadans and Hindus of all castes rapidly sprang up; each enjoying their own rites and customs and not interfering with each other. Its beautiful and spacious harbour, defended by the powerful fort built for its protection, soon made Bombay a centre of trade. And in spite of attacks from the Moghal, the Dutch, the Sidi, from Marátha and even from English pirates, and a climate whose virulence rested chiefly on an absolute ignorance of sanitary principles, its prosperity steadily increased,

But for the time Surat was the seat of the English administration, and its wealth formed an attraction to the restless Shiwáji. He had been ravaging the Moghal districts in all directions, plundering the villages and levying contributions from the towns. Once, when camped at Singhar, his fort overlooking Puna, a town at this time rising into importance, he performed an exploit which his countrymen for long after his life-time talked of with delight. With a small band of followers he left his fort and slipped into the town, unobserved by the Moghal garrison. He made his way to the general's house, slew his guard and his son, and before it was possible to interrupt him made his way back to Singahr. The glare of torches on the fort expressed to the Moghals at Puna the bravado and defiance of their enemies. Turning aside for a moment from the Moghals the Marátha ruler early in 1664 assembled an army at Kályán, giving out that he meant to attack the Portuguese and once for all reduce the Sidi. His real design was Surat, upon which he made a rapid march. He plundered it for six days and conveyed his spoil to Raygahr. The plunder was great, but would have been greater had not the English under the Governor, Sir George Oxenden, manfully stood on their defence. Shiwáji had on a previous occasion plundered their factory at Rájápur; but he was so impressed by their resistance at Surat that for the future he sought to conciliate them, and on a subsequent raid upon Surat left their factories unmolested. The emperor, on his part, as a mark of his appreciation of their valour, granted the English a remission of a great part of his custom duties.

Not long after this Shiwáji heard of the death of his father. He now assumed the title of Rája, and struck coins in his own name. Some months were spent in arranging the affairs of his government at Raygahr. But he obtained fresh accessions of power. His fleet seized Moghal vessels bound for Mecca, and the rich pilgrims had to pay costly ransoms for their release. He surprised and plundered Aurangábád and Áhmadnagar, and thoroughly defeated a Bijápur army sent against him in the Konkan. In fact, as the English records of the times state, he seemed to be every where and to be prepared for every emergency. His success during this year was astonishing. He levied exactions from the seaports for thirty miles south of Goa, experiencing scarcely any resistance except at Kárwár, from which he had barely time to exact a contribution (1664).

The emperor had no objection to Shiwáji battering to pieces his Muhammadan vassals. But the attack on his own pilgrim ships roused his indignation. A large army under two of his chief generals, one of whom was a Hindu named Rája Jay Singh, was sent to avenge the outrage upon the faith and the insult to the empire. A Hindu of the Hindus, Shiwáji was a slave to superstition. Warned in a dream by the goddess Bhawáni that he could not prevail against this Hindu prince, he entered into negociations with him. Shiwáji ceded a large number of the forts to the emperor on condition of the rest of his acquisitions being confirmed to him as a jághir or estate dependent on the emperor. He then joined his forces to the imperial army and fought with such valour that he was invited to Aurangzib's court at Delhi. He arrived there with his son Sambháji in March 1666. He looked for a reception in accordance with the ideas that he entertained of his own importance. But he felt himself slighted, if not insulted by the position assigned to him, and even in the emperor's presence he could not suppress his resentment at the indignity. He was thereupon placed under guard, and kept in confinement for some months. He at last contrived to escape, and after extraordinary adventures reached Raygahr towards the close of the year. Shiwáji rapidly repossessed himself of his relinquished forts and of the northern Konkan, and Aurangzib in consequence recalled his Hindu general, Rája Jay Singh. The Rája died on his road to Delhi. From Bijapur and Golkonda Shiwáji obtained tribute on condition that he abstained from enforcing his demands for chauth, or a fourth part of the revenue due to Government. At this stage there was comparative peace and quiet in the Deccan; and Shiwáji applied himself steadily to the regulation of his army and civil government. In each of these branches he showed wonderful skill and ability which reached down to the minutest details. His military discipline was excessively strict, especially in the forts; and his troops were punctually paid. The judicial system was founded on that of the panchayet or village council; but as compared with the revenue department the judicial was of slight importance. But though tranquillity existed in the Deccan Shiwáji would not altogether restrain his hands from war. He made some attempts, which however were not successful, on Goa, and the inpregnable Sidi stronghold at Janjira. The Sidi in his need applied for aid to his new neighbours in Bombay. So little value did the English attach to their island that they actually suggested to the council at Surat the advisability of moving their settlement from Bombay to Janjira. The suggestion was treated with the contempt that it deserved.

From the time of Shiwáji's escape from Delhi, there is no doubt that Aurangzib looked with some misgivings upon the rise of the Maráthas which in his folly he had encouraged. He made several changes among his officers in the Deccan. But he wholly trusted none; for he had reason to believe that not a few of them, including his own son Prince Muázim, were in collusion with Shiwáji. There was in truth cause for anxiety. The period of inactivity was past and Shiwáji increased his marauding expeditions to an unprecedented extent. In 1672 he totally defeated in the open field a new army sent against him by the emperor. The army retreated to Aurangábád, and but little was attempted by the imperial forces for ten years. At the end of that time Aurangzib came to command them in person. Shiwáji meanwhile was still at war with the Portuguese and the Sidi, and frequent engagements took place in Bombay harbour. The English deemed it prudent both to further strengthen their defences and to form a treaty with the Maráthas. They endeavoured to secure indemnification for past losses at Rájápur and Surat, and mutual advantages for the future. But Gerald Aungier, the President, a man of great judgement and firmness, refused to enter into any agreement with Shiwáji or the Sidi which would entangle the infant settlement in their quarrels; and only one not very successful attempt was made to dislodge the Marátha fleet from their position near Khánderi (Kenhery) Island off the mouth of Bombay harbour. The plunder of Hubli in Dhárwár in 1673, in which the English factory suffered greatly at the hands of the Maráthas, increased their desire for a definite treaty. Shiwáji, however, protested that in this case his troops had not molested the English. Bombay was seriously threatened in the same year by a Dutch fleet of twenty-two sail, but President Aungier, with the aid of some French ships, made such a brave defence that the attack was abandoned.

Aungier was one of the great men who have helped to create the fabric of the British Indian Empire. When he had built up the fortifications of Bombay he laid out the town, the first street being occupied by silk weavers from the decaying city of Chául. He quelled a mutiny among English soldiers, and under the impartial British law the first man to suffer death on the island was an Englishman. Seeing the mischief that had resulted to the Portuguese by mixed marriages he sent home for English wives for his English subjects. He secured the lives and property of the Company's servants at Surat when a second attack was made by Shiwáji. Bombay became an asylum for the oppressed of all nations, where all might enjoy the free exercise of their religion. All might dispose of their dead with whatever ceremonies they pleased, and none of any nation were to be compelled to embrace Christianity. He secured for Bombay what was then the separate island of Colaba. When confronted with the difficulty of governing the motley population that sprang up he embraced the system of the panchayet, and upon its basis worked up a system of self government. On his death, the judgement of the Council at Surat was, that "amid a succession of difficulties he preserved the English trade for sixteen years." At this time the Company separated their officers into four grades, the junior of whom were writers whose salary together with board and lodging was £10 per annum after three years' service. They rose to be factors, junior merchants, and senior merchants, designations which continued to the last.

Shiwáji had long struck coins and styled himself Rája, but he now determined on having a magnificent coronation at his capital of Raygahr. On the 6th of June 1674, after many solemn rites, the ceremony took place. He openly declared his independence; and assuming the insignia of royalty established the date as an era of his dynasty. His aged mother lived to see this event. The coronation was witnessed by Mr. Henry Oxenden, who had been sent from Bombay on a mission to Shiwáji for the conclusion of the long-wished for treaty. The treaty was signed, and by it Shiwáji gave permission to trade all over his dominions on an import duty of only 2½ per cent.; coins were to pass reciprocally and wrecks to be restored. Indemnification was promised for the losses at Rájapur, and factories were permitted at several new places. The embassy and the administration of Aungier produced a favourable impression; the immediate successors of that able president, who died in 1676, had neither his talents nor his weight.

Shiwáji continued to hold his power for the remainder of his life. The monotonous record of wars and intrigues between the emperor, Shiwáji, and Bijápur, lasted with little intermission to the end. It is varied by an extraordinary expedition that the ever-restless Marátha chief took to the shores of the Bay of Bengal, in which he took Tanjáwar (Tanjore); and by the temporary desertion of his son Sambháji to the Moghal Sidi. When his fortune was still unclouded Shiwáji was taken ill at Raygahr with a painful swelling of the knee joint. This caused a high fever, and he died on the 5th of April 1680 in his fifty-third year.

If he had not altogether realized the dreams of his mother, or literally fulfilled the bidding of Bhawáni, he had risen from a small landholder to be the monarch of a mighty nation which he himself had called into being. He had taught his followers the method by which they were finally to subdue the Moghals. Whenever fortune might for a time desert them, they were to return to their hills leaving their baffled pursuers in despair of finding them. On a favourable opportunity they would dash down upon the plains with the force of a hurricane. And so, when the hand that framed the plans was dust and ashes, the design could bring about its own accomplishment. Shiwáji was a born ruler of men. All can recognise his wonderful genius and admire his undaunted perseverance. But the world cannot endorse the verdict of his nation, who speak of him as an incarnation of the deity, setting an example of wisdom, fortitude and piety. His ruling passion was a love of money. War to him meant plunder; and on his death at Raygahr he left several millions sterling.

X.—DECLINE OF THE MOGHAL EMPIRE.

SAMBHÁJI succeeded to his father's throne. He possessed to the full Shiwáji's audacity and courage, but lacked his discretion. On his succession to power he roused the indignation of his followers by wholesale executions of those whose personal devotion to himself he doubted. Amongst the number of these was the Peshwa or chief minister. As in all Indian dynasties, the system of Shiwáji's rule was a personal one. During his life he maintained it in its integrity; on his death it melted way. The idea of any constitutional form of government, which should pass down unchanged from one ruler to another, is one that is alien to Indian soil. Shiwáji had attached the utmost importance to giving the army regular pay, and to the maintenance of rigid discipline. Under Sambháji, instead of pay the army appropriated as much plunder as they could lay hands on, and discipline was a thing of the past. Shiwáji had been the mainspring of all Marátha action, and he was feared no less by his countrymen than by his enemies. Nothing was done but by his orders. But now the more or less independent Marátha chiefs were a law unto themselves, and each followed his own devices. Yet it will be seen that what looked like weakness became with this singular people a source of strength. But the diverse nature of the Marátha movements and policy makes it impracticable in a limited space to narrate in detail the history of the period that followed the death of Shiwáji; nor would it be profitable to give a circumstantial account of all the events of the time. The country became more and more unsettled. Bitter quarrels sprang up between rival Hindu families as to hereditary rights. National patriotism frequently proved weaker than self-interest, and there are even instances of one party becoming a Muhammadan in order to promote his interests at the expense of his adversary.

Wars went on with the Maráthas and the Sidi. A severe naval engagement in which the latter was victorious took place in Bombay harbour and the Thána creek. Sambháji vowed vengeance against the English for refusing him aid; and he made war against the Portuguese at Chául and Goa. The Viceroy at Goa was not inclined to remain on the defensive. In 1683 he invaded Sambháji's territory; he carried fire and sword through defenceless villages, equalling the Maráthas in cruelty. Those who were taken prisoners were converted to Christianity. The Deccan was thus in anarchy, and Aurangzib determined on a final effort to reduce to obedience both the wild Maráthas and the Mussalmán kingdoms of Bijápur and Golkonda. The emperor was sixty-three years old when he set out from his northern capital, which he was never to see again. The remaining twenty-seven years of his life were to be spent on the march, or in the camp, in a hopeless struggle to bring the Deccan under his control.

Notwithstanding some strange vicissitudes, the last quarter of a century brought considerable advancement to the English in Western India. However in 1683 an extraordinary event occurred which might have lost Bombay to the hostile powers that surrounded it. The president still had his head-quarters at Surat and a deputy resided at Bombay. On account of a reduction in pay and allowances there was wide-spread discontent amongst the servants of the Company at the latter settlement. While the president, Sir John Child, was at Surat, the deputy governor was seized and imprisoned by Captain Richard Keigwin, the commander of the troops and a member of council. He proclaimed the island the possession of the crown and refused obedience to the authority of the Company. Keigwin ruled Bombay for the crown from December 1683 to November 1684. He proved himself a bold and determined man: he obtained from Sambháji not only the confirmation of the agreement made with his father, but considerable additional privileges. After ruling resolutely and well he surrendered the island to Sir Thomas Grantham on condition of a free pardon. Sir Josiah Child was now the head of the Company in England, and he originated a new line of policy which was carried out by his brother Sir John Child. Of the judiciousness of his first proceedings there can be no doubt whatever. From its defenceless position at Surat the Presidency was removed to Bombay where the factors could show a bold front to any who might molest them. But with little regard to the paucity of the means at their disposal, the Childs determined upon a spirited foreign policy. A powerful expedition was sent from England to Bengal; and when it was heard in Bombay that Hughli had been cannonaded and the Moghal viceroy of Bengal repulsed, Sir John Child threw off the mask. The very existence of the English depended upon the Great Moghal. But nevertheless a fleet of Moghal vessels in Bombay was seized, and the emperor's sacred vessels conveying pilgrims to Mecca captured.

The result soon showed the folly of this suicidal policy. The English were driven out of Bengal. The factory of Surat was seized and the goods found there confiscated. The Sidi of Janjira, at the emperor's bidding, occupied a portion of the island of Bombay to the great annoyance and loss of the garrison. For nearly a year his troops held Mazagon, Siwa (Sion) and Mahim, but they could make no impression upon the fort. The English were convinced of their rashness. The President of Bombay dispatched two envoys to the emperor's camp at Bijápur to sue for peace. Their submission was accepted, but to obtain a fresh firmán they had to pay a sum of £15,000. The emperor also demanded the dismissal of Sir John Child who had created this disturbance, but his death occurred before the arrangements were concluded. The Company had indeed enough to do apart from meddling with war. They had to meet severe competition from ships of foreign nations; and rival English traders, known as interlopers, caused them considerable embarrassment. Not content with underselling the Company in the open market the interlopers laid hold of their officers at Surat and handed them over to the Moghal Governor. A Scotch Company which had been founded by James I. issued licenses for free trade. As a natural consequence English markets were glutted with Indian products. The home merchants clamoured for high import duties. The only way to solve the difficulty was to amalgamate the whole of the British traders to India into the "United East India Company." This was done in 1702, and a fresh charter was granted by Queen Anne. Rivalry had been ruining the Company; union and the introduction of fresh blood renewed its strength and prosperity. The reverses in Bengal were repaired, and in 1670 Calcutta was founded by Job Charnock on the little fishing village of Chutanati. Thus the three Presidency towns of modern India are entirely of European origin. In Bengal, in 1698, an Afghán noble rebelled against the Moghal viceroy. In the disturbances that arose the European settlers were told to protect themselves. This event greatly raised their position, and gave them an unassailable precedent for erecting fortifications whenever they liked. Bombay possessed an impregnable stronghold and an unrivalled position for trade. Its subordinate factories of Surat, Broach, Áhmadábád and Suáli in Guzírát, and Kárwár in Kánará, were all in a flourishing condition.

But to the merchants, into whose hands his empire was eventually to fall, Aurangzib gave but scant heed. It was on the conquest and settlement of the Deccan that his vast energies were concentrated. With the flower of his army, a vast array of men and horses splendidly armed from all the provinces of his dominion, he took up his position at Áhmadnagar in 1683. The luxury and magnificence of his camp were almost inconceivable, and formed a remarkable contrast with his simple personal habits. But while this display was designed to strike awe upon all beholders, its extent hindered the movements of the army; and its expense was an insupportable financial burden. Infatuated with the belief in his divine mission of conversion and conquest the emperor proceeded to excite against himself the most intense hostility of the Hindus. He ordered the collection of the poll-tax on infidels to be as strictly enforced in the Deccan as in the North of his dominions. But his designs were in the first place directed to the subjugation of the Muhammadan states. Against the turbulent Maráthas, for whom even yet he entertained a senseless contempt, he neglected the most ordinary precautions. They took advantage of his immoveability, and by a rapid movement sacked Broach and Burhánpur.

Deferring operations against the Maráthas the emperor moved to Bijápur. In 1686, after a brave defence, the city was forced to capitulate. The king was taken prisoner and shortly afterwards died, probably poisoned by Aurangzib. So ended the brilliant Ádil Sháhi dynasty. Bijápur ceased to be a capital, and its inhabitants soon deserted it. Its lofty walls, domes and minarets might still lead the traveller to believe that he was approaching a flourishing city, but within there was nothing but ruin and desolation. Now, after an interval of two centuries, Bijápur is once more rising; not indeed to its former splendour, but to be the centre of a thriving population as the head-quarters of a British district. Its beautiful buildings are carefully preserved, and some of the most suitable have been converted into courts, offices, and dwelling-houses for British officers. And hard by the mighty dome of Sultan Máhmud is heard the shriek of the iron horse.

Within a year Golkonda too fell before the emperor's army, and the last of the dynasties that had risen on the ruins of the Bahmani kingdom came to an end. But for Aurangzib it was one thing to destroy two kingdoms, another to build up his own power. Rebellions of Hindus and Mussalmáns sprang up in every direction. Had Sambháji but possessed his father's genius he might have swept the Moghal forces off the face of the land. But he was wasting his days in debauchery and the people attributed his condition to witchcraft. In fact, as an organized state, the Marátha power appeared coming to an end, and there was thus far some colour for the contempt which it inspired in the emperor. But the form only was changing, the power was still growing. Their military organization might be gone, but their predatory habits, their pride in the memory of Shiwáji, their belief in the strength of their forts was as strong as ever. Far from depending on the existence of any regular or consolidated system, their strength absolutely increased as the system of Shiwáji crumbled away. Their army as a military unit might no longer exist, but their operations took new shapes no less formidable than the old. It booted little if the hydra was deprived of one head when it had a thousand others; and a guerilla war arose, in which chieftains and adventurers led their warlike followers from every quarter against the host of the Moghals. When the odds were too heavy against them they disappeared into the fastnesses of the mountains. One party beaten off it was succeeded by another. Against these foes the unwieldy army of the emperor was of little avail. In fact he had steadily played into their hands. He had destroyed the local powers that had for generations kept them under control, and his bigotry led him to adopt a course of measures which effectually roused their detestation of his rule. He was increasing in years; and, while he trusted none of his subordinates, he could exercise less and less personal control over his colossal administration. His ministers were negligent and corrupt; intrigue ran riot through every department. A partial success was achieved when in 1689 Sambháji fell into his hands, and was led a prisoner into the imperial camp. Overcome with shame at his condition Sambháji longed for death. He was offered life on the condition of embracing Islam. He scornfully replied that the emperor had better give him his daughter, and then he would become a follower of the Prophet. In his rage and impotency he launched furious invectives upon the founder of the faith. Such an insult to the Muhammadan religion had to be avenged with the utmost severity. By Aurangzib's orders, a red-hot iron was drawn across his eyes, his tongue was cut out, and his head severed from his body. The Maráthas had been much estranged from Sambhájí, but they were filled with fury at this brutal execution of the son of their great leader. Rájárám, the half brother of Sambhájí, was declared regent on behalf of Shiwájí, commonly known as Sáhu, the son of Sambhájí, a boy only six years old. Rájárám was formally seated on the throne, and active preparations were made to man the forts and resist the Moghals. The fleet was not neglected. Its admiral Sidoji Guzar was ably assisted by his second-in-command named Kánhoji Ángria, whose father Tukáji Ángria had early distinguished himself in Shiwaji's navy. The Ángria family subsequently gave immense trouble to the Government of Bombay, by its organised system of piracies.

Rájárám possessed no small share of his father's ability. He carried on with marked success the war against the emperor. He even gathered together for a time a larger number of troops under one flag than the great Shiwájí himself. Aurangzib moved against Sátára which he besieged and took. But the Maráthas went about collecting chauth, and plundering and burning towns and villages that resisted them. No Moghal force could overtake or cut off the lightly equipped Marátha horsemen. The emperor might capture some of their forts, but there was an almost endless number to fall back upon. Nearly every hill top in the land was scarped down and protected with bulwarks. In 1700 Rájárám died, but his death was of no more advantage to the emperor than the capture and execution of Sambhájí. His eldest son Shiwájí was declared Rája under the regency of his mother Tárábai, and the struggle was carrried on as keenly as ever. The national spirit was roused in earnest. Aurangzib had exhausted the revenues of the Deccan; the Maráthas intercepted his caravans of treasure from Hindustán. The Maráthas had sometimes to bow before the storm, but they were never broken; and they resisted his final efforts with constantly renewed vitality. Their numbers multiplied and they extended their operations in all directions, plundering wherever their demands were refused. Khándesh and Guzárát were overrun; and over the whole face of the country were seen slaughtered soldiers, homeless ryots, and burning crops.

The Emperor's strength was broken, and the final acts of the tragedy approaching. His empire was unwieldy and rotten to the core, ready to fall to pieces of its own weakness. The Maráthas gave his army no rest, ever baffling the imperial troops. They cut off their supplies, re-captured the forts, and even worsted them in the open field. At last, in 1707, after a quarter of a century of strife, Aurangzib died at Áhmadnagar, hemmed in within his starving camp while the Maráthas feasted around it.

So ended Aurangzib. There is little interest in the history of his successors to the throne of Bábar. Their roll continued until the last was sent across the sea by the English in 1858. Their story is a record of swift ruin. The Hindu martial races closed in upon the empire. Mussalmán viceroys made themselves independent kings. Devastating hosts swept into India from the North, while the merchants on the coast found themselves, almost without knowing it, rulers of the Moghal and Marátha realms alike.

XI.—RISE OF THE PESHWAS AND THE GREAT MARÁTHA HOUSES.

THE Marátha power had a strange habit of constantly shifting its local position and character. It might centre round Shiwáji, forming for a time a real and compact nationality. It might be disintegrated into thousands of predatory bands, each under its petty chieftain. It might amalgamate these miniature communities into a few powerful and independent states. The power might be exercised by the actual king or by an independent minister in the name of a nominal Rája. But in all its changes it never while it lasted ceased to be formidable. In fact, the versatility of its nature added to the difficulties of its opponents. What had seemed the very mainstay of the power might be destroyed; but another head would spring up elsewhere, and the work be no nearer its end than before. For a time after the death of Aurangzib, the form which the strength assumed was that of two great rival parties.

From the time of Akbar, the death of each emperor had been followed by a desperate struggle for the sovereignty between his sons. Aurangzib had hesitated at no iniquity to seat himself on the throne. During his life time his own sons were incessantly at war with each other. His empire was beginning to fall to pieces, and if one thing more than another was needed to preserve its existence, it was that the government should remain in the hands of one strong man.

RISE OF THE PESHWAS.

Notwithstanding all this, Álamgir left behind him a ridiculous and impossible will, dividing his empire between his three sons. The natural consequences followed. Muázim slew his brothers Ázim and Kambaksh, and at the age of sixty ascended the throne as Bahádur Sháh. When Sambháji, the son of Shiwáji, had been captured by Aurangzib, his little son Shiwáji had been taken with him. The boy was brought up in the imperial court under the name of Sáhu, given him by way of a coarse pun by Aurangzib himself. The English, with the astonishing indifference to native languages which marked their early career, chose to regard this name as a title; and they spoke of each successor to the throne as the Sáhu Rája. Ázim set him free, thinking that some of the Marátha chiefs would take up his cause and their temporary union cease. The notion was judicious, but it was Bahádur Sháh who reaped its fruit. Sáhu vowed allegiance to Delhi, and soon gathered round him a large number of adherents who were discontented with the rule of Tárábai, the widow of Rájárám, on behalf of her son Shiwáji. Sáhu obtained possession of Sátára, and was formally enthroned there in 1708. Tárábai continued a fruitless struggle on behalf of her son, taking Kolhápur and Panálla as her base of operations. But her son Shiwáji, who was an idiot, died in 1712 and she was placed under restraint. The party was subsequently revived by a younger son of Rájárám named Sambháji. In 1729 this Sambháji was finally defeated by Sáhu and resigned his pretentions to the Marátha throne. He was allowed to retain the title of Rája of Kolhápur.

During his contest with Tárábai, Sáhu made an application to Sir Nicholas Waite, the governor of Bombay, for a supply of guns, ammunition, European soldiers and money. But a recollection of the result of Sir John Child's foolish policy fortunately led to the request being refused.

The Moghal viceroy of the Deccan, or such of the Deccan as the Maráthas had left to the empire, was at this time Dáud Khán. Seeing the impossibility of resisting the Marátha demands for chauth he adopted the wise policy of admitting them, but he arranged to collect the dues himself and hand them over to the Maráthas. They on their side refrained from plunder, and remained true to the allegiance promised by Sáhu. Thus for a time there was secured in the Deccan a less intolerable state of things than had of late existed.

Bahádur Sháh died in 1712, and the usual contest at once arose between his sons. Jahándár Sháh seized the throne with the aid of Zulfikar Khán, a general who had greatly distinguished himself in Aurangzib's Deccan wars, and who had held the post of viceroy before Dáud Khán. Jahándár Sháh was a typical Eastern tyrant. He immediately massacred all his near kinsfolk, with the exception of his nephew Farokhsir, who managed to escape. Farokhsir's cause was taken up by Syad Hussein Ali, governor of Bahár, and his brother Syad Abdulla, governor of Allahábád. These two brothers were aided by a famous man, Chin Khilich Khán, who under the name of Nizám-ul-Mulk Asuf Jáh, founded the dynasty of the Nizáms of the Deccan at Hydarábád. Zulfikar Khán and his protégé Jahándár Sháh were slain, and Farokhsir reigned in his uncle's stead. Nizám-ul-Mulk was made viceroy of the Deccan, Dáud Khán being transferred to Guzárát. The Maráthas pretended to consider that the arrangement which they had made with Dáud Khán ceased with his transfer to another province. But his successor managed to keep them under a general control, and prevented any dangerous combination by fanning the flames of the struggle between Sáhu of Sátára and Sambháji of Kolhápur. The two Syad brothers ruled at Delhi in the name of Farokhsir, who was, however, by no means a willing tool in their hands. When one of the brothers, Hussein Ali, was nominated viceroy of the Deccan, the emperor sent a secret message to Dáud Khán to intercept him and kill him. The result was Dáud Khán's own death. Hussein secured the viceroyalty of the Deccan, Nizám-ul-Mulk being sent to Morádábád in the North of India. Hussein Ali considered it advisable to side with Sáhu as being the stronger of the rival claimants for power, and as having consistently shown a disposition of friendship to the Moghals. The Peshwa, or prime minister of Sáhu, was now a Brahman named Báláji Wishwánáth, who had risen from the humble position of a hereditary accountant in a village of the Konkan. By his advice, Sáhu demanded from Hussein Ali a recognition of his claims to all the territory that had belonged to Shiwáji, together with his right to chauth and other charges on the revenue. On his part, Sáhu promised to pay tribute amounting to £100,000 a year, to maintain a body of 15,000 horse for the emperor's service, and 'to clear the country of all depredators. The demands were enormous, but they were admitted by the viceroy who hoped thus to consolidate the power of a ruler who seemed a staunch and strong supporter of the imperial interests. Hussein hardly realised the nature of the power of which Sáhu was the head. By thus consolidating the Marátha power he was pulling down and not building up the edifice of the empire.

The Moghal concessions were brought about at the instance of the Peshwa; and the general energy instilled by the astute and able Brahman into the government of Sáhu placed the Marátha affairs in a more favourable condition than they had lately worn. The struggle between the Sátára and Kolhápur parties, encouraged by the Moghal viceroys, who first favoured one faction and then the other, had increased the usual anarchy of the country to an unendurable extent. Many petty depredators had allied themselves to Sambhájí. Of these the most formidable was Kánhoji Ángria. After succeeding to the command of the Marátha fleet this officer, by a series of daring and extensive piracies, made himself practically master of the coast from Bombay to Sáwantwári, near Goa, in his own and not in the Rája's interests. His head-quarters were at the island fort of Kolábá off the town of Alibág, twenty miles south of Bombay. After an ineffectual expedition against this upstart, in which Ángria imprisoned the Peshwa Bairu Pant, Báláji Wishwánáth had been deputed to deal with him. By shrewd diplomacy, the Brahman raised a quarrel between Ángria and the Sidi; then co-operating with the latter he invaded Ángria's territory and compelled him to submit. It was for his services on this occasion that Báláji was promoted to the office of Peshwa in 1714. But Ángria made common cause with Sambhájí or with Sáhu only so long as it suited his own convenience.

Sáhu was not destitute of ability, and under his authority and the guiding hand of Báláji Peshwa, the Marátha power steadily expanded. The legitimate head of the Maráthas, he always styled himself king of the Hindus. But he invariably acknowledged himself a vassal of Delhi, and the importance of his nation was increased by the consideration shown him by the Moghals. Nor was his influence weakened by the fatuity of the emperor, who plotted with the Maráthas against his own viceroy. But in an age of plots, conspiracies, suspicion, and intrigues overtures came from all who had anything to gain to those who had anything to give. The emperor declined to ratify Hussein Ali's treaty with Sáhu. The viceroy therefore promised still greater concessions to the Marátha king if he would but lend him an army to enforce his demands at Delhi. The opportunity was too good to be lost. The Peshwa himself was placed in command of the Marátha forces. He was instructed by Sáhu to obtain the right of collecting tribute in Guzárát and Málwa besides other important privileges. The combined armies marched to Delhi in the year 1720. A tumult arose in the imperial city and the Maráthas lost no less than 1,500 men. But Hussein Ali gained his object. The emperor was first blinded and then strangled by the Syads, who set up in succession two princes each of whom died of consumption in a few weeks. Their third choice was less unlucky, and Ráoshan Akhtar, a son of Jahándár Sháh, was crowned as Muhammad Sháh and reigned till 1748. One of his first acts was to send back the Maráthas to the Deccan, and with them Sáhu's mother and family who all this time had been retained at Delhi. The Marátha soldiers were well paid for their work, and imperial patents were issued confirming all the agreements between Hussein Ali and Sáhu. The Marátha desultory claims, which had hitherto rested on mere force, were thus legalized as a permanent national institution by the imperial government. The amount of tribute which they were entitled to demand from outlying provinces was never exactly defined. The difficulty was easily smoothed over by the simple expedient of exacting as much as they could.

But though Báláji had no desire for an exact definition of the rights thus conferred, he devised a singularly ingenious and systematic method for the collection and appropriation of the revenues. Its intricacy and elaboration rendered the Brahman accountant ever more and more necessary to the illiterate Marátha chief, and so increased the power of the Peshwas. At the same time, it was so contrived that by the sub-division and partition of revenue in each province, or charge, which of set purpose was made to lap over and include one or more others, each chief had an interest in the increase of the whole as well as that which he himself collected, a portion of which he was entitled to retain for the maintenance of his troops. The system was a bar on the independence of each while it encouraged their common encroachments on the Moghal power. Thus a common interest was created and for some time sustained between the Marátha chiefs; and the increasing subjection of Sáhu to the master mind of Báláji Wishwánáth paved the way for the supremacy of the Peshwas. But with all this, although the Maráthas undoubtedly formed a nation in a way that no other body of people in India, except perhaps the Sikhs, ever did, yet their constitution had in it all along the seeds of ultimate dissolution. Their nationality, in order to continue at all, had to be not only aggressive but predatory. Any notion of settling down to the dull life of ordinary farmers or merchants was foreign to their nature. The object of their existence was organised robbery. It could only be a question of time for resistance to arise to such a system and cast off its intolerable burden.

For the time, however, they had their way. The empire was rotten to the core, and the English at Bombay had not yet the strength to oppose them. The English merchants were at present little concerned with the doings of the rulers of Sátára or Delhi. Bombay harbour continued to be the scene of many a fight between the Sidi of Janjira and the Peshwa of king Sáhu, but the policy of discreet neutrality remained unaltered. Their settlement meanwhile flourished almost beyond their expectation. But though they took care not to interfere with others they could not prevent others from molesting them, and for many years their commerce suffered greatly at the hands of the pirate Kánhoji Ángria. While admiral of the Marátha fleet he had shown himself a daring and adventurous leader. He had not hesitated to turn his arms against his master and put the Peshwa in chains. He was the scourge of the Western Coast. His head-quarters alternated between Kolába and Wijaydrug, or Gheria, an impregnable port on the Ratnágiri coast, that has been called the Gibraltar of the east. The decay of the Portuguese power encouraged this daring pirate, and for many years he proved a thorn in the flesh of the English at Bombay. In 1717 he seized the British ship "Success" and beat off an attack upon Gheria. He held the island of Khánderi off Bombay harbour, and a British fleet that sailed against him had to return unsuccessful. In vain did the British and the Portuguese combine to attack him both at Gheria and Kolába. He managed to contrive an intrigue with a Brahman named Ráma Kumpti, who was employed in duties of a confidential nature by Mr. Charles Boone, the governor of Bombay, and who was in command of some native retainers. In reply to despatches from this governor, entreating him to leave off his habits of piracy, Ángria wrote derisive and sarcastic letters. He pointed out that God gives nothing immediately from himself but takes from one and gives to another. As to his government being founded on violence and piracy, he retorted with undeniable truth that Shiwáji's government had commenced in the self-same way, and that, His Excellency would see, seemed likely to endure. In the war between himself and the English there had been loss on both sides, for victories depend upon the hand of God. The governor had told him that he who follows war will find cause to repent. To this Ángria contented himself with replying that he supposed that His Excellency Charles Boone spoke from experience. Encouraged by his successes, Ángria proceeded to take another richly laden Company's ship; and though in 1718 he seemed inclined to come to terms with the English, in the following year he captured the royal galley "King William." His death in 1731 was welcomed as a relief, but though his sons fought with each other for the pirate kingdom, yet the Ángria family did more mischief to the English than ever; and the cost of the fleet that was built to protect the Company's trade amounted to £50,000 a year.

While the fabric of the empire at Delhi was being shaken by revolts in the Panjáb and Káshmir, Nizám-ul-Mulk was adopting a course of action fraught with yet greater danger for his master. Deeply hurt at receiving from the Syads in return for all his services only the governorship of Málwa, he determined to take for himself what he considered due to him from others. He marched south of the Narbada, seized Burhánpur and Asirgahr, and at Bálápur defeated the imperial army that was sent against him. Hussein Ali now determined to march against Nizám-ul-Mulk in person and to take the emperor with him. But the power of the infamous Syads was at an end. With the aid of a courtier, named Muhammad Amin, the emperor procured the assassination of Hussein. He overcame the opposition of Abdulla, whom he imprisoned, and marched back to Delhi which he entered with splendid rejoicings. Muhammad Amin was made minister but almost immediately died. Nizám-ul-Mulk, whose successful revolt was the primary cause of this happy revolution, was summoned from the Deccan to succeed him. Congratulations came to the emperor from all sides, including Sáhu and the chiefs of the European factories, who sent complimentary addresses.

Nizám-ul-Mulk, in accepting the office of Wazir or minister, had been permitted to retain his viceroyalty of the Deccan. His object in accepting office at Delhi had been to bring about sweeping reforms; but the only changes that the emperor cared for were from one form of vice and sensuality to another. Nizám-ul-Mulk was thoroughly disgusted with the state of things in the capital; and finding that a rival had arisen in Hydar Kuli Khán, the late governor of Guzárát, he obtained permission to return to the Deccan, and together with that viceroyalty he received the governorship of Guzárát. He took charge of both provinces, not without opposition in the latter. Then not choosing to remain out of sight, and still half hoping to receive favour at court, he returned to Delhi. Here he found his position insupportable, and once more returned to the Deccan. This act was considered by the emperor as virtually a declaration of independence, and he ordered the governor of Hydarábád to send him the Nizám's head as that of a rebel. A head was sent, but it was that of the Hydarábád governor; and the Nizám offered his congratulations at the suppression of a rebellion which the emperor had not avowed to be of his own making. Nizám-ul-Mulk took possession of Golkonda and Hydarábád. At this place he took up his residence and founded the practically independent dynasty of the Nizáms of Hydarábád which has lasted until now. But the dominions of this house were to be greatly reduced in extent by the Maráthas and the English. Aurangzib had destroyed two great Muhammadan kingdoms in order to plant his own authority in the Deccan. And now, before twenty years had passed after his death, the power of the empire in the Deccan was extinguished, and an independent Muhammadan ruler held a small and decreasing part of the broad dominions that in that part of India had once been subject to Islam. From time to time, however, Nizám-ul-Mulk sent gifts to the emperor whom it suited him to consider nominally his master.

Nizám-ul-Mulk thought to carry on his former system of securing himself by sowing dissension among the Maráthas, but he found a considerable change in the condition of the Hindu power. Báláji Wishwánáth was dead. In his son Báji Rao, who succeeded him in the office of Peshwa, he found a yet more skilful and formidable opponent. Sáhu had to all intents and purposes delegated his power to his minister, and with the rise of what may be fairly called the Brahman dynasty of the Peshwas there rose to power the great Marátha families of Sindia, Holkar, the Gaikwár of Baroda, and the Rája of Barár.* In the battle of Bálápur an officer named Dámáji Gaikwár, serving among the Marátha allies of Nizám-ul-Mulk, had greatly distinguished himself; and the collection of the chauth in Guzárát was made over to him and his lines as an hereditary right. Such is the origin of the reigning family of Baroda. The name Gaikwár is a common one amongst Maráthas and signifies cow-herd. Holkar was a Marátha Dangar, or shepherd, who showed his gallantry in the command of some bodies of horse. He also received the right to collect chauth, and founded the reigning family of Indore. Sindia, though of old family, rose from a still humbler personal position, having attracted Báji Rao's notice by the way in which he filled the office of slipper-bearer. He received a

---

* I have, in accordance with popular usage, written "*the* Gaikwár." It is incorrect, and should be simply Gaikwár, as Sindia and Holkar. His surname was Gaikwár, and his title Rája of Baroda.

similar distinction, and his family became the powerful rulers of Gwálior. Raghoji Bhonsle, the Rája of Barár, obtained like privileges.

Báji Rao was an abler son of an able father. He was not only a statesman but a soldier, and could himself execute the products of his brain. What Báláji had planted, Báji Rao watered. He developed and extended to an extraordinary degree his father's daring plans. He worked out and elaborated his financial schemes, with especial reference to concentrating upon a common object the predatory hordes of Máhárástra. In fact, the wise precautions of the two Peshwas had strongly united the Maráthas; and their common interest in the collection of the revenues bound them together to an extent unsuspected by Nizám-ul-Mulk. Rapidly grasping this fact he proceeded to turn it to his own advantage. While losing no opportunity of creating dissensions among the Maráthas he took care to preserve his general connection with them. He was ready to secure the integrity of his own kingdom by aiding the Peshwa in pulling down the dominions of their common lord. The Peshwa did not stand in need of much encouragement. He understood the materials that he had to deal with. He saw that it was no time for bringing into better order the possessions that the Maráthas had acquired. He could guide but he could not hold in the masses of wild Marátha horsemen who covered the whole country. He pointed out to Sáhu the imbecility of the Moghal authorities and the degeneracy of the empire. Appealing to the name of Shiwáji, he urged him to spread his power over the imperial domain itself. "If we can strike the withered trunk," he said, "the branches will fall of themselves." Sáhu's enthusiasm was kindled. The Nizám received assurances of the Peshwa's good-will as long as he did not interfere with the Marátha invasion of Hindustán. The work was promptly taken in hand. Holkar plundered and ravaged Bengal and Oudh, and Báji Rao himself took the field and marched against Delhi. Striking terror into the emperor, he extorted from him £130,000 for the expenses of the campaign and also the sovereignty of Málwa. But the Nizám had not been true to his agreement. The emperor seeing that his dominions were seriously menaced by the Maráthas had, by profuse promises, induced the aged viceroy once more to operate on his side. Leaving his son Násir Jang in the Deccan, Nizám-ul-Mulk marched to the aid of his nominal master. But he was out-generalled by the Peshwa, and forced to recognise the cession in perpetuity of all the country between the Narbada and the Chambal. He was compelled to purchase exemption from further action against himself by the payment of half a million sterling (1738).

Nor were the operations of the Maráthas confined to the Moghal empire. An army from Goa had assisted Ángria against the Peshwa, and the Portuguese had to pay the penalty. The Maráthas under Chimnáji, the Peshwa's brother, attacked them in the island of Salsette, or Shásthi, between Bombay and the mainland. In 1737 they captured its chief town Thána, and in 1739 drove them out of the island which they had held for more than two hundred years. In the same year, after a brave defence, the fort of Bassein, the Portuguese capital of the North, capitulated to the Maráthas; the Portuguese losing 800 men in killed and wounded and the besiegers 5,000. The English, under the governorship of Mr. John Horne, professed neutrality. But they sold shot and shell to the Maráthas; and, in spite of the danger to their own settlement that the success of the Maráthas might bring, their sympathies evidently lay with them and not with their European rivals. Salsette was the most important of the islands that the English considered had been promised by the Portuguese crown to England with Bombay in 1661, and they had not ceased to resent the non-fulfilment of the contract. The Bombay citizens however hospitably entertained the unsuccessful garrison of Bassein. Thus ended the power of the only formidable European rival to the English that set foot on the western shores of India. The Portuguese strength was broken. They could no longer hold Chául and the fort that they had built for its protection on the opposite rock of Korlai. They handed them over to the English who passed them on to the Maráthas. The Christian population, for the most part, migrated to Bombay and Goa. But the English were awakened by the events at Salsette and at Bassein, to the strength of the Maráthas, and were fully determined not to come to blows with them. They sent a double embassy in the person of Captain Inchbird to Chimnáji at Bassein, and Captain Gordon to Sáhu at Sátára. The latter found that he should have rather addressed himself to the Peshwa who was the real ruler. Both embassies were favourably received and the right of free trade in the Marátha dominions confirmed.

An event now occurred which laid Delhi in ashes and filled the world with horror, and for a moment kindled a flash of national patriotism in the breasts of Maráthas and Mussalmáns alike. Nádir Sháh, king of Persia, came down through the Áfghán passes and invaded the plains of India, defeating the imperial army beneath the walls of Delhi. But the inhabitants murdered the guards that he had placed in charge of the city. Incensed beyond measure at this act, the Persian king gave the signal for a general massacre. The slain amounted to no less than 30,000. The whole city was plundered, and the royal jewels and the peacock throne, itself worth several million pounds, carried away.

Báji Rao and his army were far from Delhi. Had they been nearer the Persian historians might have had another tale to tell. For the completeness of the catastrophe made them forget their quarrels with the Moghals, and realise that there was but one enemy against whom all the inhabitants of Hindustán and the Deccan alike must unite. But patriotism was a plant that could not reach maturity on Indian soil until it grew up later on in loyalty to the British crown. When Nádir Sháh marched away, the old dissensions were renewed. Increasing demands were made by the Maráthas, and Báji Rao was on the point of leading another expedition to Hindustán when in the year 1740 he died. He had spread the Marátha predatory system from province to province till it included the grearter part of the empire. He had built up to be the most powerful people in India a nation whose existence depended upon the confusion of other states. A century before they had not even been heard of and now their name was a terror as far as Delhi and Orissa, Madras and Trichinopoli. The Marátha nation was a tremendous engine of destruction that in Báji Rao's hands was skilfully directed. The Moghal empire was at their mercy. The Portuguese were humbled. The English and French, as yet unaware of their own strength, only sought to increase their trade and privileges by humble submission and the offers of bribes and presents to the native courts. For a time the artificial divisions of revenue cemented with almost unexpected success the union of the Maráthas. But the system was as likely as not in course of time to create rivalry and hostility. Each officer interpreted the amount of his master's claims according to his own pleasure and enforced them according to the extent of his own ability with little reference to their abstract justice.

The Peshwa was succeeded by his eldest son Báláji Báji Rao, better known by the common Marátha name of Nána Sahib. His second son was Raghonáth Rao, who was afterwards so well known to the English as Raghoba. The new Peshwa not without some difficulty crushed the opposition of Raghoji Bhonsle the head of the Barár family and of some other headstrong Marátha chiefs. He obtained greater concessions than ever from the emperor as to the collection of chauth. He sent plundering expeditions from sea to sea. In one expedition alone no less than two and a half million sterling were extorted from the great banking house of Jagat Shet at Murshidábád, the seat of the Moghal viceroy of Bengal. In 1748 Nizám-ul-Mulk was gathered to his fathers at the wonderful age of 104, a few months after his nominal master Muhammad Sháh. The Nizám left a number of sons and was succeeded by the eldest, Násir Jang, who had rebelled against him but been forgiven. The successor of the emperor was his son Áhmad Sháh, and the dynasty became a mere shadow. The following year saw the death of Sáhu. His indolence had not allowed him to use his natural ability. He had come to rely on the Peshwa in every detail of the administration, and in his last years he was in a state of mental imbecility. He partially recovered before he died, and having no sons he adopted as his heir Ráma, a grandson of Tárábai who was still alive. Rámá or Rám Rája had been born in 1712 after the death of his father Shiwáji, the idiot son of Rájárám, in whose name Tárábai had attempted to govern the Maráthas from Kolhápur. One other important act was done by Sáhu before his death. He gave the Peshwa a deed empowering him to manage the whole government of the Marátha empire on condition of his perpetuating the Rája's name, and keeping up the dignity of the house of Shiwáji through the grandson of Tárábai and his descendants. Kolhápur was to continue a separate state. The Peshwa had power to conclude such arrangements, with the jághirdárs or holders of estates under the Rája as might be advantageous for extending Hindu power. In this way the dominions that Shiwáji had created passed from the hands of his family to the Brahman minister who now became hereditary ruler of the nation. But in deference to popular tradition it was expedient to maintain one of his lineage as a nominal king.

XII.—STRUGGLE BETWEEN THE ENGLISH AND THE FRENCH.

IT was now (1748) close on a century and a half since Hawkins had landed at Surat, and nearly ninety years since the cession of Bombay by the Portuguese. The English had built up a vast trade, but their sole territorial possession was the island of Bombay itself. Far from having any idea of creating an empire and conquering the lands upon which they gazed from their factories, their energies were concentrated on the preservation of peace with the Moghals, Maráthas, and Portuguese. They saw the forces of those nations dashing themselves to pieces against each other, and realised how easily they might be turned against their own island. But on the other side of India the keen eye of Dupleix had grasped the possibility of forming a powerful European empire in India. The method to be employed was that of ostensibly working on behalf of rival native princes. And a greater than Dupleix had arisen in Robert Clive, the young English merchant who exchanged the ledger for the sword, and who, by working out the Frenchman's idea, added a continent to the British empire. The decaying Moghal organisation provided an admirable machinery for the purposes of conquest. The empire was ruled by viceroys who were practically independent princes. It was easy to treat them as vassals of the empire which they were *de jure*, or as sovereign powers which they were *de facto*, whichever might be most convenient. Alliances might again be made with a genuine viceroy or a pretender to the throne, according as one or the other could offer the greater advantages. In fact the ruler, whoever he might be, could be used as an instrument to cloak the real designs of the encroaching foreigner. Besides this, the unwieldy armies of native kings were no match for a few disciplined European troops. But Dupleix saw that there existed in the native soldiery magnificent material out of which a judicious military training might elaborate regiments but little if at all inferior to Europeans themselves. So Dupleix raised the first sepoy regiments, and Clive instantly perceiving their value worked out the system with greater success than its originator. Thus in southern India commenced the struggle which was to be fought for the English or French supremacy. While England and France were at war their representatives in India fought for the quarrels of their nations at home. When peace was concluded they ranged themselves on opposite sides under the banners of native princes.

South and West of the dominions of Nizám-ul-Mulk lay the province of the Carnatic. A succession of intrigues, murders and battles had been taking place for years to decide who was to possess its throne, and the English and French supported rival candidates. Nizám-ul-Mulk and the Peshwa had been actively concerned in the dispute. Marátha hordes, under the redoubtable Raghoji Bhonsle, had over-run the country and placed their own partisan on the throne. Chanda Sáhib, who was supported by the French, was a prisoner for some years at Sátára. But though the Peshwa and the Nizám were concerned in the struggle, and the English in Bombay were closely watching its course, yet the events of the war in the Carnatic occurred almost entirely

THE ENGLISH AND THE FRENCH. 147

beyond the limits of the Bombay Presidency, and it would be foreign to my purpose to describe them in detail. The English and French both achieved, with unexpected facility, successes over native armies. Their fortunes alternated, but the English under Clive attained a great military reputation, especially after the famous siege of Arcot in 1751. Under Dupleix and his successor Bussy, the French acquired in the Northern Sirkárs, on the coast of the Bay of Bengal, a territory whose revenue was £500,000 per annum. Dupleix indeed achieved for a while a greater success than he could ever have ventured to hope for. He had made his protégé Chanda Sáhib Nawáb of the Carnatic. His measures had overcome Násir Jang, the young Nizám of the Deccan, and he placed his own candidate Mozaffar Jang, son of Nizám-ul-Mulk's daughter, on the throne. He himself was made governor of all India south of the Krishna on behalf of the Emperor of Delhi. But in 1754 he was recalled and thrown into the Bastille; a fate reserved for Labourdonnais and Lally, two more of France's greatest sons. Mozaffar Jang meanwhile had been killed in battle and Ghází-ud-din, a son of Nizám-ul-Mulk, poisoned. Another brother, Salúbat Jang, was placed on the throne by aid of the French. The Peshwa too had taken advantage of the rival claims on the viceroyalty of the Deccan to add some large slices of territory to his own dominions. In 1753 an agreement was come to between the French and the English which was slightly favourable to the latter. The possessions of each were equalised, and they agreed to refrain from further interference with native powers. At this juncture, Colonel Clive returned to England on furlough. But he came out in 1755 more anxious than ever to dispute the mastery of the Deccan with M. Bussy; for, as he said, "So long as there was one Frenchman in arms in the Deccan. or in India there would be no peace." He probably fully saw that all India must go to the conqueror. But Clive was first to be employed in Bombay, and then after a brief tenure of the governorship of Fort St. David in the Madras Presidency, he had in 1756 to leave M. Bussy in as strong a position as ever in order to repair a tremendous catastrophe that had occurred in Bengal. But before following the adventurous career of Clive it will be convenient to revert to the doings of the Maráthas.

The original capital of Shiwáji's empire had been Raygahr. Under Sambháji it was, if anywhere, Sangameshwár, on the Gháts to the South of Raygahr. Under Sáhu it had been moved to Sátára, Kolhápur being the rival seat of Marátha power. Upon the death of Sáhu and the formal transfer of power to the Peshwa, the seat of empire was transfered to Puna, which remained the capital of the Maráthas to the last. All the chief officers of the state who had been appointed by the Rája were confirmed in their possessions by the Peshwa. Ránoji Sindia died and his son Jyápa succeeded to his jághir. The two houses of Sindia and Holkar divided between them nearly the whole of Málwa, with a revenue of a million and a half sterling. The Gaikwár of Baroda came next in importance of those chiefs whose possessions formed an integral part of the empire. Áhmadábád whose possession had been disputed between the Maráthas and Moghals was finally taken possession of by the former in 1755. The revenues were to be equally divided between the Peshwa and the Gaikwár. The latter's share included the dues from Broach, the port on the Narbada. But he had to content himself with a moiety of the revenues of Surat for the exclusive possession of which city opposing claimants in vain contended. In fact Guzárát was never completely

settled by the Marāthas, and the strangely irregular
appearance on the local maps of the possessions of the
British and Baroda states at the present day points to the
undecided claims to the ownership of the territory. But a
more powerful man than the Gaikwár was Raghoji Bhonsle
of Barár who carried his arms from one end of India to the
other. He collected tribute from the Carnatic and swept
yearly into Bengal which he looked upon as his own peculiar
property. In 1751 the English had to dig a ditch round
Calcutta to protect themselves against his depredations;
and the Marātha forts at places so distant as Katak and
Sahāranpur attest the power that they attained. To collect
revenue and make war were with the Marāthas synonymous
terms. If a village resisted its officers were tortured till they
came to a settlement, and bankers' bills, payable on any part
of India, given up to the marauders. If a fort was unsuccessful in defying them the garrison was put to death with
savage cruelty.

Bálájí Bájí Rao or Nána Sáhib was, if not less able, at all
events less active in disposition than the preceding Peshwas.
He placed the charge of his military arrangements in the
hands of his brother Raghonáth Rao, and the civil administration devolved upon his cousin Sidáshiwa Chimnáji, the son
of Chimnáji Apa who had defeated the Portuguese.
Through all the years of robbery and plunder the system of
village communities had secured some degree of justice for
the people. But it had been supplemented by little
else. The present Peshwa now aimed at a more regular
system, and set his hand to the task of creating a more
orderly administration.

Under Nána Sahib the Marātha power reached its zenith,
and seemed likely to hold permanently within its grasp the

whole of the Indian Peninsula. In the reign of Muhammad Sháh, the last emperor of Delhi, on whose behalf the most ordinary pretensions of respect could be urged, the invasion of Nádir Sháh had been followed by an inroad of the Áfghán Áhmad Sháh Abdali. The Abdali had been driven back by Prince Áhmad who was now the Emperor Áhmad Sháh. In his reign the Rohillas or descendants of old Áfghán invaders of Bengal rose up in Rohilkand, and the emperor adopted the dangerous course of summoning Sindia and Holkar to his aid. The rebellion was quelled, but the Maráthas who had fought for the emperor plundered his country on their own account. This event was followed by another invasion of the Áfghán Áhmad Abdali, to whom the emperor was forced to cede the Panjáb. To this misfortune civil war was added, and the streets of Delhi were deluged with blood. The Maráthas were again summoned to the imperial city, this time against the emperor. It mattered little to these professional robbers on which side they fought. The emperor was deposed and blinded, and another prince raised to the throne in 1754 under the title of Álamgir II. The emperor was a puppet in the hands of his despotic and violent minister Shaháb-ud-din. Under his régime an attempt was made to free the Panjáb from the troops of Áhmad Abdali. The Áfghán promptly came down from his mountains to avenge the insult. He plundered Delhi and the rich city of Mathra, and mercilessly slaughtered thousands of Hindus who were collected there for a religious festival. But the miserable emperor sought from the Áfghán robbers and murderers a defender against his own over-ruling minister, and in 1757 the Rohilla Najib-ud-Daula was left as commander-in-chief of the imperial army. But not even thus could Álamgir escape the tyranny of his minister. Shaháb-ud-din called on the

Maráthas, and Raghonáth Rao in obedience to the summons led his forces against the emperor. In 1758 he entered Láhur in triumph, and the prophecy of Shiwáji was accomplished which said that the Maráthas should water their horses in the Indus and the Hughli. Raghoba left his new possessions in charge of Sindia and Holkar, and himself returned to Puna. But the next year the Áfghán Abdali advanced to recover the Panjáb, and Sindia and Holkar were unsuccessful in their resistance. Áhmad Abdali might have once more placed Álamgir in power. To prevent this possibility his minister murdered him and set up a prince of his own choosing. The real heir Sháh Álam was a fugitive in Bengal. The empire was to all intents and purposes at an end, and the struggle was now directly between the Maráthas and the Áfgháns. Had the warriors from the Deccan driven out the Abdali forces, the emperor of India would have been Máhádaji Sindia, the famous son of Ránoji and the only surviving brother of Jyápa.

News of Sindia's and Holkar's reverses reached the Peshwa at a time when things at home had been greatly prospering. He had been watching the rival candidates for power in the viceroyalty of the Deccan. He had laid plans for obtaining concession of territory by aiding whichever party might from time to time seem stronger. The result was entirely successful. After a short struggle with Nizám Ali, who had put to death his brother Salábat Jang the nominee of the French and made himself Nizám, the Peshwa obtained possession in perpetuity of the important forts of Áhmadnagar and Asirghar, the entire province of Bijápur, and much of Aurangábád with a revenue of £620,000. The Moghal possessions in the Deccan were thus reduced to small dimensions, and the Peshwa's army was free to march upon the Panjáb.

The flower of the Marátha army was accordingly despatched to Hindustán. It was commanded by Sidáshiwa Rao the Peshwá's brother and Wishwás Rao the Peshwa's eldest son. Marátha armies had hitherto been distinguished for the lightness of their equipment and their extraordinary moveability. But success had induced luxury and magnificence; and the army that marched to Delhi rivalled in the splendour of its tents and the magnificence of its equipment the gorgeous camp of Aurangzib. Nor were the Maráthas without allies in their struggle with the Áfgháns. The cause seemed the national one of all Hindus. Rájputs, Pindháris and irregulars of all descriptions flocked to the Marátha standard. The time had come when Hindu authority should reassert itself over the vast empire in which for so many centuries they had been a conquered people. The remembrance of the exploits of Shiwáji, pride in their recent successes in the Deccan, and the hope of extensive plunder in Hindustán, stimulated the various Hindu tribes to join for the moment in a common cause. Not that the Maráthas had any unselfish aims for the advancement of their countrymen. They carried in their sway destruction and rapine. The freedom that they brought to Hindus was limited to that of opinion and the unfettered enjoyment of their religious ordinances. All alike had to pay tribute to the insatiable Maráthas and bow down beneath their yoke.

The army arrived before Delhi in the hot weather of 1760 and took up its quarters there for the rainy season, plundering everything upon which they could lay their hands. They stripped the hall of audience of its silver ceiling which produced £170,000. After the monsoon Áhmad Abdali advanced towards Delhi. The Maráthas moved out to meet him, and the contending forces entrenched themselves opposite each other at Pánipat, the field of so many battles. For nearly three months the armies lay opposite to each other without a decisive engagement being fought. But provisions became scarce in the Marátha camp, and dissension ran high between their leaders. This style of warfare was totally unsuited to them. In January 1761 they were unable any longer to endure their privations. They begged to be led out against the enemy and the generals at last gave the signal for battle. It was a struggle between religions. The fierce shouts of the Muhammadans' "Allah, Allah," and "Din Din," were met by the Hindu "Har Har Máhádew." The battle was furiously contested, but after varying fortune the Afgháns prevailed and the Maráthas broke and fled. Vast numbers of them were made prisoners. The men were butchered in cold blood the day after the battle, and the women made slaves. The corpse of Wishwás Rao was taken to Áhmad Abdali who said that he would have the body of the king of the unbelievers stuffed and taken back to Kábul. The question of Hindu supremacy over India was decided once for all. Hindustán was freed for a time from the ravages of the insatiable Marátha plunderers; and when ten years later Máhádaji Sindia interfered to place Sháh Álam on the throne, he found that he had only done so to benefit the English merchants of Calcutta. But it is now time to return to events elsewhere, which have been passed over in order to give continuity to the doings of the Maráthas in Northern India.

The Maráthas were a nation of plunderers, reaping where they had not sown, carrying fire and sword, desolation and rapine, wherever they went. But all the worst features of the race were reproduced and intensified in the pirate family of Ángria. This detestable brood had established themselves in well-nigh impregnable positions along the coast at Kándheri, Kolába, Sawarndrug and Gheria. Kánhoji Ángria was dead, but his sons Sambháji, Manáji and Tuláji, although they were in disagreement with one another, carried on their father's profession with equal success. From time to time they endeavoured to further their individual aims by inducing the Portuguese, the Sidi, and the Peshwa to interfere in their quarrels; but they took care to give but little in return for the aid which thy sought. They feared neither God nor man. In the foulest treachery and the most bloodthirsty cruelty their history stands unrivalled. The English had not been altogether successful against Kánhoji. The time had now come to try their hand against his sons.

Mr. Richard Bourchier became president or governor of Bombay in November 1750. He at once strove to secure a more intimate intercourse with the Maráthas, for the purpose both of completing arrangements as to Surat and of suppressing the depredations of the Ángria family, especially Tuláji Ángria at Gheria. No ship was safe from these ubiquitous pirates. Not only did the Ángrias follow the vocation, but the Rája of Kolhápur from his fortress Sindidrug or Málwán and the Sáwants of Wári followed their example. From Málwán the English spoke of the pirates indiscriminately as Málwáns. Their general ignorance of native terms was extraordinary. The case of Sáhu has been noticed. Maráthas were commonly styled Shiwájis and latterly Murattoes. Hindus were known as Gentoos, and Mussalmáns as Moors or Moormen, while Bhonsle was written Bouncello. Several years elapsed after Mr. Bourchier's accession to office before operations were commenced, and it was not till the month of March 1755 that an expedition was despatched. It was commanded by Commodore James of the Company's marine, and was to be supported by the Marátha fleet. The support was of the feeblest; but by his judgement and enterprise, Commodore James succeeded in taking the four distinct forts of Sawarndrug. Upon this several forts in the neighbourhood surrendered to the land forces of the Maráthas. That of Bánkot, known as Fort Victoria, at the mouth of the Sáwitri river, together with five villages was handed over to the English in perpetuity. The expedition had been entirely successful; but the monsoon coming on James had to take shelter in Bombay, and further operations were deferred pending the arrival of additional forces under Admiral Watson and Colonel Clive. In the latter part of the year the reinforcements arrived. The force had been sent from England with the object of entering into alliance with the Maráthas for the expulsion of the French from the dominions of the Nizám and the Nawáb of the Carnatic. But the Bombay Government considered that the truce drawn up with the French at Madras precluded this employment of Clive's forces until the views of the home Government should be known. They therefore took the opportunity of sending an expedition to reduce Tuláji Ángria at Gheria.

Clive and Watson started in February 1756. It was agreed that Gheria was to be handed over to the Maráthas, but the English determined to divide the prize-money amongst themselves. Throughout the expedition there was a want of cordiality between the English and their allies which might have endangered its success. It was enjoined upon Clive in the most emphatic manner by the Council in Bombay, that he was to make no terms with the Ángrias. Tuláji, they wrote, was on a footing with no prince in the known world, but a pirate in whom no confidence could be put, who not only robbed and burnt the ships of all nations but even those of his own countrymen to whom he had given passes. He had caused the Company to keep up a fleet to protect their trade at a cost of more than £40,000 a year, and had destroyed innumerable small vessels besides eleven rich ones, the names of which were given in the instructions. On no account was Tuláji to be handed over to the Maráthas who might let him go at some future time.

The fort was bombarded and taken. A shell bursting in the "Restoration," a British ship which Ángria had seized, set her on fire; and the flames spread to Ángria's own fleet, which was totally destroyed. About £100,000 of prize-money was divided between the victors. But the Maráthas secured Tuláji, and Mr. Bourchier waived his objection to that proceeding on the condition that he should never receive any territory within forty miles of the sea. The Maráthas kept their word, and Tuláji died in captivity at Sholápur. The English wished to keep Gheria instead of Bánkot, but after prolonged negociations a treaty was concluded at Puna in October 1756 by Mr. John Spencer and Mr. Thomas Byfield of the Bombay Council by which Gheria was given up, but additional villages were ceded towards defraying the expense of maintaining Fort Victoria. Certain commercial privileges were granted, and the Dutch were excluded from trade within the Marátha dominions. After the taking of Gheria Admiral Watson sailed to Madras, and Clive reverted for a short time to the subordinate position of governor of Fort St. David.

He was not to be left there long, and it is necessary for a moment to leave Bombay and follow him to the other side of India. Early in 1756 the great Bengal Nawáb Aliwardi Khán, who had steadfastly resisted the Marátha invaders, not always without success, had passed away. He was succeeded by his grandson Suráj-ud-daula. The new Nawáb was a mere boy, but at his early age he was already an eastern despot of the worst type. He was brought up with an extravagant idea of the wealth of the English, and he had for them an unbounded detestation. In the furious heat of June he invaded Calcutta. He overcame the resistance of the few who opposed him; and placed in what is known as the Black Hole of Calcutta a hundred and forty-six English men and women, of whom all but sixteen died in the course of the night. The event was a too ordinary one in Indian history to find mention in the annals of native historians. The English presidency in Bengal was for a time destroyed. But the triumph of Suráj-ud-daula was not to last long. Early in 1757 Clive reached Calcutta, cannonaded the fort, and the English flag was once more flying over Fort William. The Nawáb called on M. Bussy from Madras to help him drive out the English from Bengal. Clive anticipated the consent to this appeal by driving the French out of that province. The English flag was planted at their settlement of Chandanagar, and Clive remarked that his standards must advance yet further. In one short year after the horrors of the Black Hole Clive had with the aid of Mir Jáfar, the commander of the Nawáb's forces, won the battle of Plassey, and expelled the miserable Suráj-ud-daula from his capital of Murshidábád. The tyrant was killed by Miran, the son of Mir Jáfar, and Mir Jáfar himself was placed on the throne. A hundred boats conveyed to Calcutta silver worth £800,000 sterling. The battle of Plassey made the English practically, if not in name, masters of Bengal, Bahár and Orissa. The legal possession was to come, not much later. At the time of the battle of Pánipat Sháh Álam the rightful heir to the throne of Bábar fled to Bengal. He made a hopeless attempt to recover that province for himself, but was defeated by the English. He was allowed to return to Delhi after he had offered them the Diwáni or financial management of Bengal. The arrangement was subsequently accepted by Clive in 1765, the Company pledging itself to pay to the emperor an annual tribute of £300,000. The family of Mir Jáfar continued to hold the title of Nawáb Názim of Bengal till 1883, but the power was soon separated from the title. Nor was the suzerainty of the emperor over the English regarded by them any further than was convenient. Sháh Álam turned to the Maráthas to seat him on his throne, and in 1771 Máhádaji Sindia placed him with great pomp on the seat of his ancestors. But it was one thing for the English to pay tribute to the emperor and another to pay it in his name for the benefit of the Maráthas; and Sindia was bitterly disappointed to find that that was not a condition of the bargain. He had hoped to rule Bengal in the name of the emperor; he had only put a large sum into the hands of the English merchants.

Clive had conquered Bengal and driven the French out of it. But his services to his country were not yet ended. Under his directions Colonel Forde defeated the French in successive actions in Madras and the Northern Sirkárs in 1759, and in the next year Colonel, afterwards Sir Eyre, Coote defeated them at Wándiwás. Before the year was out Pondicheri capitulated and its fortifications were razed to the ground. With supreme indifference to the claims of the Nizám Clive obtained from the puppet emperor Sháh Álam a firmán conferring the Northern Sirkárs to the English. The treatment by the Madras Government of this arrangement will be seen later on. In the same year a Dutch fleet of seven ships appeared in the Hughli and began to seize

English vessels. The English promptly resisted, and the Dutch were signally defeated and all their ships taken. But they had landed 700 Europeans and 800 Malays who made their way to their settlement at Chinsura. Colonel Forde asked for instructions. Clive was playing cards when the letter reached him. He wrote on one of the cards, "Fight them at once, I will send you the order in council to-morrow." Before the order in council reached Forde he had engaged and defeated the enemy; and the Dutch were subsequently only permitted to keep 125 Europeans in Bengal for the protection of their factories.

Clive's work of conquest was done. But the country was full of marauding bands of Maráthas and Áfgháns, and it was beyond the power of the Company to arrange for a satisfactory settlement. Clive therefore proposed to Pitt that the nation should take over the sovereignty of Bengal, Bahár and Orissa. The proposal was rejected, and the decision not altered until, a century later, there arose a terrible crisis which might have wiped out British rule altogether from India. But Clive left the Company a power more solid in its foundations than that of the Moghal empire before its decadence began.

Terrible was the grief in Mahárashtra when the fatal news arrived from Pánipat. The first despatch was written in the figurative style not uncommonly used in India when caution is necessary. "Two pearls," it said, "have been dissolved, 27 gold mohurs lost, and of the silver and copper the amount cannot be added up." From these words the Peshwa learnt the fate of Sidáshiwa Rao his brother, and Wishwás Rao his son, together with that of the officers and army. One of the first of the fugitives who confirmed the news was Báláji Janárdin, nephew of Sidáshiwa Rao, who was afterwards famous as Nána Farnáwis. The Peshwa never recovered the shock. It affected his mind and his constitution rapidly sank. He died at the temple of Párbati, a building which he had erected a short distance from Puna. It commands a beautiful view of the city and surrounding country, and from it the last of the Peshwas was to witness the defeat of his army by a British force. Báláji Rao had done something to improve the condition of his subjects, and Marátha power under him had reached its zenith. But it received a shock at Pánipat which negatived the possibility of Hindu supremacy over India. Still the Maráthas remained for a time the most powerful people in the country.

The empire of Delhi had passed away. All that remained to Sháh Álam were a few small districts in the neighbourhood of his capital. The Panjáb had fallen into the hands of the Afghán Áhmad Abdali. The Rohillas, or descendants of former Afghán settlers in Bengal, were powerful in Rohilkand. Oudh nominally a viceroyalty of the empire was really an independent kingdom, and a close ally of the British. In the name of Mir Jáfar the Company was supreme in Bengal, Bahár and Orissa. The Rájput states had long separated from the emperor, and though the Maráthas had imposed upon them demands for chauth they were irregularly paid. The territories of the Nizám or Subadár of the Deccan were considerably reduced in extent. The French power was broken, that of the Dutch destroyed, and the Portuguese reduced to insignificance. In the short space of time from 1755 to 1761 the English, from merchants who maintained a struggle for existence on the coast, suddenly found their strength recognised, and their alliance courted by powers who had regarded them with contempt. In Bengal they were on the high road to the conquest of

India. But as yet in the West they possessed only the island of Bombay, Fort Victoria with a few villages at Bánkot, and the fort or castle of Surat, of which they obtained independent possession after a desperate struggle in 1759. The Maráthas held the Konkan, the Deccan, and Guzárát, with claims over Káthiáwár, Málwa, Khándesh and Barár, Bijápur and most of Aurangábád, and the old Hindu kingdom of Tanjáwar (Tanjor). Besides this their demands for chauth extended over the greater part of India, and they held the town and fort of Katak in Orissa. But Sindia and Holkar, the Gaikwár and the Rája of Barár were serious rivals to the power of the Peshwa. The most important, however, of the late political changes was the fact that it was to be the English and not the French who were to rule in India.

The directors in England of the East India Company looked with no favour on any territorial acquisition. In 1763 they wrote to their representatives in India a despatch which after enumerating their present possessions went on to say:— "The protection of them is easily within the reach of our power, and they may easily support each other without any country alliance whatever. If we pass these bounds we shall be led on from one acquisition to another till we shall find no security but in the subjection of the whole, which by dividing our force would lose us the whole, and end in our extirpation from Hindustán."

XIII.—FIRST MARÁTHA WAR.

ON the death of Báláji Rao shortly after the shock of the terrible news from Pánipat in 1761 where his eldest son perished, he was succeeded as Peshwa by his second son, Máhdu Rao, a boy seventeen years old. Máhdu Rao was invested with the insignia of office by the descendant of Shiwáji, who was a state prisoner at Sátára. Raghoba, the brother of the late Peshwa, assumed the regency, and created general discontent by his arbitrary and high-handed proceedings. The young Peshwa was a boy of spirit and determination, and he attempted to enforce his claims to a share in the administration. He showed his good sense by selecting as one of his officers Báláji Janárdan Bhanu or Nána Farnáwis, the future great Marátha minister. Raghoba, ambitious and unscrupulous, turned to two powers for assistance in his schemes. The Government of Bombay, under Mr. Crommelin, was in the hands of men with clear heads and stout arms. Their gallantry had lately enabled their ally the Sidi of Janjira to hold out against a combined attack of Maráthas and Portuguese. They hoisted the British flag at Janjira and compelled the Maráthas to respect it. Stimulated by the magnificent success of their countrymen in Bengal, and beginning to feel something of their own strength, they cast longing eyes on the island of Salsette which lay between Bombay and the mainland. The Maráthas had conquered it from the Portuguese and the English thought that

FIRST MARÁTHA WAR. 163

Raghoba might hand it over to them as the price of their aid. Raghoba offered to cede territory of greater value in Guzárát, but that was not what the Company wanted and negociations for the time fell through. With the Nizám his overtures were more successful. The Nizám was a far-seeing politician. The flower of the Marátha army had been destroyed at Pánipat, the nation was being torn asunder by rivals for power at home. There could not be a more favourable opportunity for restoring the Muhammadan power in the Deccan. The Nizám at once sent an army to support Raghoba, and the new allies attacked the forces of his nephew Máhdu Rao. With remarkable patriotism the young Peshwa grasped the fact that dissension between himself and Raghoba meant ruin for both. He gave himself up to his uncle who placed him in confinement, and the Nizám's forces were for the present withdrawn. The Nizám was only awaiting a more suitable occasion, and he thought that he had found one in the renewal of dissension in 1762. He led his army to Puna, and the capital of the Peshwa was plundered and burnt. But the Maráthas, indignant at his presumption, threw aside their mutual differences. Raghoba released his nephew, and the Gaikwár and Holkar brought up their forces. The Nizám's army was driven off from Puna, and it sustained a crushing defeat at Aurangábád in 1763.

While the Maráthas were thus occupied in the Deccan there had arisen a new power in Mysur which threatened to become more formidable in India than that created by Shiwáji. Hydar Naik was a man of the same type as the Marátha chief. He could neither write nor read, but he was gifted with great physical strength and activity, and he possessed a commanding nature. He had been a sepoy in the battalions of the French. He left their service and gathered round him a body of men who pledged themselves to follow him on condition of sharing equally in his plunder. With these retainers he served under the Hindu Rája of Mysur at the siege of Trichinopoli. He was to receive a certain sum of money for each soldier and a gift for each man wounded. He doubled the amount thus due to him by making false muster-rolls and bandaging sound limbs. With Hydar, as with Shiwáji, money was power. The Hindu Rája rapidly became one of the fainéant kings that sat on Indian thrones. As Hydar's power grew he dispensed with his nominal master and assumed the title of king. He was to prove himself one of the most powerful antagonists that crossed swords with the English in India. But his first opponents were the Maráthas. He had gradually encroached on their territories, including the fort of Dhárwár, and they were extremely jealous of his power. In 1765, the young Peshwa led an army against the upstart adventurer and defeated him in a severe campaign. Hydar had to release the Marátha districts that he had occupied and pay for the cost of the war.

There now arose a strangely involved series of alliances and confederacies, the threads of which are inextricably entangled with the histories both of Bombay and Madras. The English, the Maráthas, the Nizám, and Hydar Ali were constantly making engagements with and against each other. Besides these factors in the history of the epoch, there was also the party of Raghoba which was in rivalry with that of the Peshwa. There were further the great houses of the Gaikwár, Sindia, Holkar, and Bhonsle of Barár, who were now practically sovereign princes, and who made war or friendship with one another, or any one else, just as it might suit their convenience. The permanent aim of each was his own supremacy. Common danger might for a time bind some of them together; with the need for union the coalition invariably ended. In name the Marátha states continued to be members of one empire. They all acknowledged the supremacy of the Rája of Sátára, whose chief interest in life was to watch the movements of dancing-girls in his state prison. All too recognised the authority of the Peshwa, the only difficulty being to decide whether the youthful heir to the throne, or his uncle Raghoba, had the higher claim to the authority vested in that office.

To follow out the whole cource of this constantly shifting drama would be tedious and useless. Some of the more important scenes only need be lightly sketched. The emperor had conferred on the Company the Northern Sirkárs as a free gift. They had belonged to the Nizám of the Deccan, and the claims of this potentate Clive treated with contemptuous indifference. The Government of Madras, ever distinguished for weakness and incapacity, adopted a contrary policy. They agreed to pay the Nizám a considerable tribute, and concluded with him an offensive and defensive alliance on account of this territory. The Court of Directors commented upon the feebleness and absurdity of this treaty; but it was too late, and its disastrous consequences had to follow. The Nizám chose to make war upon Hydar Ali. The Madras Government joined in the struggle and, in the words of the Directors, plunged into such a labyrinth of difficulties that extrication from them seemed almost impossible. The campaign opened favourably for the English. Hydar, in anticipation of an alliance between the Maráthas and the Company, offered terms. But the Madras Government made such inflated demands that they were rejected with scorn. The fortunes of war turned in Hydar's favour, and the Nizám who had provoked the war changed sides to the stronger. Hydar again made proposals for peace, pointing out that his overtures had been already once rejected. The Council was irresolute and incapable, and made no definite reply. Hydar marched 130 miles in three days and a half; and, camping beneath the walls of Madras, had the Council at his mercy. In fear and trembling they executed a treaty in April 1769 by which mutual conquests were restored; the English were saddled with the expenses of the whole war, and an offensive and defensive alliance was made with the Mysur chief. So ended the first Mysur war, and the prestige of the English sensibly deteriorated. The best excuse that can be made for the action of the Madras Council was that put forward by themselves, that they made peace because they had no money to make war. No sooner was peace concluded with the English than Hydar turned his arms against the Maráthas. But these he found more formidable antagonists. His army was defeated with terrible slaughter in 1771, and he was pursued to Saringapatam and besieged there. In virtue of his treaty, Hydar called on the English for aid. He offered £100,000 for an English brigade, but his request was unheeded in Madras, and he threatened as an alternative to call in the French. Hydar never forgave what he termed the treacherous and cowardly abandonment of him by the English. The English had undoubtedly broken their word. But the treaty had been forced upon them at the point of the sword, and the disgrace was less in breaking than in making the agreement.

During the Mysur war the Bombay Government had sent an envoy to Puna in the person of Mr. Mostyn in 1768. He was instructed both to ascertain the Peshwa's views and, by encouraging domestic dissensions, to prevent the Maráthas joining Hydar and the Nizám. As to their views, the

Marátha court candidly stated that they meant to be guided by circumstances. But Mostyn's task of fomenting dissensions was a sinecure. Raghonáth Rao again rebelled against his nephew, this time unsuccessfully, and was confined as a prisoner at Puna. Wars, plots, counter-plots, cabals, and intrigues between the Peshwa and the great Marátha houses were the order of the day. But young as he was the Peshwa was able, by strength of mind and ability, to hold his own; and the attack by Hydar created a powerful if evanescent union of the Marátha houses. Neither, however, were dissensions at home nor wars with Hydar sufficient to employ the restless Maráthas. Undiscouraged by the defeat at Pánipat, Máhádaji Sindia, with some help from the house of Holkar, was busy at Delhi propping up on his crumbling throne the miserable successor of Aurangzib, and trying to rule Hindustán in his name.

As a ruler, Máhdu Rao Peshwa is entitled to much praise. He strove for justice and equity, and in a rough age supported the weak against the strong, and put down oppressors with a firm hand. But it cannot be repeated too often that the work of a benevolent despot is useless. Something more is needed for good government than the will of one man, whose good deeds may be swept away by his successor. A system is needed and not a person;. and that system has reached India from without in the shape of British law.

Máhdu Rao died of consumption in November 1772 at the early age of 28. He left no children and his brother Nárayan Rao came to the throne. Raghoba had been released by Máhdu Rao before his death. But he was again made prisoner at the instance of the new Peshwa's ministers Sakhárám Bápu, an old and tried officer, and Nánú Farnáwis who was now rising into fame. The new Peshwa had not long to enjoy his power. In August 1773 a mutiny took place amongst his soldiers, and he was himself put to death by a man whom he had once ordered to be flogged. The credit of causing this murder was generally, though unjustly, given to Raghoba. Raghoba was present when it took place and interfered to prevent it. He had, however, previously given a written order that Náráyan Rao should he "seized" and this had been altered to "killed" (dharáwe to máráwe). There was now no heir to the Peshwaship, and Raghoba assumed the title as the rightful successor to his nephew. But a posthumous son was born to Náráyan Rao in April 1774, and was installed as Peshwa when he was forty days old. Raghoba declined to acknowledge his legitimacy, and two great factions sprang up, that of Raghoba who called himself the Peshwa, and that of Nána Farnáwis and other ministers who represented the cause of the son of Náráyan Rao. While these parties were engaged in watching each others' movements, Hydar Ali plundered the Southern Marátha provinces unchecked. Raghoba sought aid from Sindia and Holkar, and again entered into negociations with the English.

The Government of Bombay were ready enough to negociate. They were bent upon securing Salsette, Karanja, and other islands near Bombay. They were, moreover, fully supported in this attempt to gain thus much extension of territory by the Directors at home. In accordance with the Court's instructions Mr. Mostyn had again been sent on an embassy to Puna, where he arrived shortly before the death of Máhdu Rao Peshwa in November 1771. The deliberate object of this mission was to find means of obtaining possession of the islands, the just importance of which to Bombay was indisputable. Bombay is the finest harbour in India. It was already becoming famous for its dockyard, and it was essential for its protection that the English should be the sole possessors of its shores and islands. Nor were the designs of the Bombay authorities confined to Salsette and its neighbourhood. They had already attained the lion's share of the sovereignty of Surat. Surat was paramount over Broach, and the Nawáb of Broach disputed certain claims which were made on him. In 1771 an expedition was sent to enforce them which was not altogether successful; but further operations were for a time deferred by the arrival of the Nawáb in Bombay. The English insisted upon terms which were by no means to the Nawáb's taste; and though he signed the treaty he returned to Broach only to grossly insult the chief of the English factory. This could not be tolerated. A force was sent, and Broach taken by storm on the 18th November 1772, the very day of Máhdu Rao's death. But the brave and accomplished General David Wedderburn was killed, when directing the attack, by a shell shot from the walls of the city.

Mr. Mostyn's first business at Puna was to negociate an exchange of Broach for Salsette. But nothing definite was decided, and upon Nárayan Rao's murder in August 1773, having reason to believe that Raghoba had fallen in his wars with the Nizám, the English determined to possess themselves by force of the long-coveted islands. But Raghoba was not dead, and his applications for aid were welcomed. After a prolonged negociation the Bombay Council, under the presidency of Mr. Hornby, offered in September 1774 to assist Raghoba with all the troops that they could spare which, including some artillery, amounted to about 2,500 men, on condition that he should advance 15 or 20 lakhs of rupees, £150,000 or £200,000, and cede in perpetuity Salsette and the other islands with Bassein and its dependencies. At this memorable meeting of the Council a doubt arose on an important subject. Hitherto the English settlements in India had been independent of each other. But in 1773 an Act of Parliament placed Bombay and Madras in subordination to Bengal; and the Governor of Bengal became the Governor-General of India. Peace or war could not be made without the concurrence of the Governor-General in council. But no intimation had reached Bombay of the arrival of the officers who had been sent out as the members of council; and it was decided that Bombay might act on its own responsibility. But as before, Raghoba refused to give up Salsette or Bassein. He offered other concessions of very considerable value, and the Council were half disposed to accept them, when they received news which at once made them alter their minds.

The Portuguese government had sent a strong expedition from Europe to recover these very islands together with Bassein on the mainland. Prompt measures were necessary. Would the Marátha officer at the fort of Thána, the chief town in Salsette, consent to be bribed? Mr. Hornby offered one lakh. The officer required more, and the Council saw that nothing remained but to use force. By the middle of December 1774 the Portuguese fleet was anchored off the mouth of the harbour, and in answer to the remonstrances of its commander at the aggressive policy of the English, batteries were opened upon Thána. After one unsuccessful attempt, in which 100 Europeans were killed or wounded, the fort was carried by assault; and, incensed at the loss that they had suffered, the soldiers put the greater part of the garrison to the sword. Among the English losses was Commodore Watson, a gallant and experienced officer. Colonel Keating was sent to take the fort of Warsowa on the north of Salsette; and by New Year's day 1775 the whole of Salsette and Karanja were reduced.

The English were now in a position to make what terms they pleased with Raghoba. He had been negociating with Sindia and Holkar without much success, and he now proceeded to Guzárát to obtain the aid of Gowind Rao Gaikwár, who was at war with his brother Fatte Sing at Baroda. In anticipation of the conclusion of a treaty with him the English despatched a force to Guzárát in February 1775 under Colonel Keating, with instructions to aid the Peshwa, as they called Raghoba, against the ministerial forces. He was in sore need of their help. He had been defeated by the ministerial army and had fled to Kathiáwár, whence he sailed to Surat, where he was joined by the British forces. It is difficult to see what value Governor Hornby and Colonel Keating could now set upon his aid, or how he could expect to fulfil his promises. But a treaty was signed at Surat by which Bassein and the islands were ceded in perpetuity together with Jambosi and Ulpár in Guzárát, the revenue of which with other assignments amounted to over 19 lakhs (£190,000). A junction was effected near Cambay with what remaimed of Raghoba's army, and in accordance with his wish the forces marched northwards towards Áhmadábád. The Bombay Council, however, expressed in the strongest terms their opinion that the destination of the forces should be altered to Puna. Their course was accordingly changed, and after ten days' march in the new direction, on the 13th May 1775, they were suddenly attacked near a village called Aras while marching through a narrow road between two high milk-bush hedges. The attack was resisted with spirit, and the enemy three times driven back with great slaughter. The British troops were fighting with splendid courage when some one blundered; the wrong word of command was given and an unintelligible panic ensued, the officers deserted by their troops dying where they stood. But in spite of this deplorable incident, which Colonel Keating frankly described in his despatch, the enemy, as they themselves admitted, sustained a severe defeat. On the 10th of June another opposing force was beaten off with greater success and compelled to throw its guns into the Narbada, Colonel Keating having grasped the secret of success against Maráthas and commenced the attack. Guzárát was now cleared of the enemy; and an agreement was made which patched up the quarrel between Gowind Gaikwár and his brother Fatte Sing, and united them both to the cause of Raghoba. To the English was granted additional territory with a revenue of 3 lakhs (£30,000). Nor were the operations confined to land. The Marátha navy consisted of six men-of-war mounting from 26 to 46 guns each, and ten smaller armed vessels. This fleet was met at sea by Commodore John Moor in the "Revenge" frigate, and the "Bombay" grab. Moor instantly attacked the Marátha fleet which set sail and made off; but he singled out their largest ship the "Shamsher Jang" or Sword of War, and at last brought him to action. After an engagement of three hours the "Shamsher Jang" blew up.

Thus Raghoba's prospects in a few months rose from the lowest to the highest, while those of the young Peshwa seemed correspondingly gloomy. Great promises were made by Nána Farnáwis to Sindia and Holkar to keep them on his side; while the Nizám took advantage of the civil war to extort a cession of nearly 18 lakhs of annual revenue. But Raghoba was personally unpopular and his alliance with the English regarded with dislike and distrust.

The Bombay Council had held that they were at liberty to act independently of the Governor-General and Council at Calcutta. The Council were of a different opinion.

When they heard of the proceedings undertaken by the English in Bombay they peremptorily required that the forces should be withdrawn to garrison in whatsoever state affairs might be, unless safety was endangered by an instant retreat. "You have imposed on yourselves," they wrote, "the charge of conquering the whole of the Marátha empire for a man who appears incapable of affording any effectual assistance in it." The war was pronounced impolitic, dangerous, unauthorised and unjust. The despatch bore the signature of Warren Hastings. But bitter diversity reigned at the Council board, and at that time the great proconsul was hampered and shackled by his colleagues. His personal views were very different. The war had been undertaken without sufficient definiteness of aim, but he held the capture of Salsette an act of necessity and good policy. But, as he himself says, he was not in a position to dictate, and all he could do was to qualify the order with some provisoes.

The Bombay Government accordingly ordered a cessation of hostilities and Colonel Keating and Raghoba encamped about twenty-five miles east of Surat. But they were bitterly indignant at the way in which they had been over-ruled. They sent a report to the supreme government defending their conduct, recapitulating their reasons, and dwelling on the shame and degradation of not fulfilling their solemn agreements. They also sent Mr. William Taylor, a member of their own Council, to Calcutta to advocate their cause. Mr. Taylor ably carried out his instructions. He had an unusual knowledge of the real character of the Marátha empire. He represented that Parliament in arming the Council at Calcutta with controlling powers had no intention that the subordinate presidencies should be made to appear degraded and contemptible in the eyes of the native government. But in spite of the Governor-General's remonstrances the Council insisted upon exercising with the utmost indiscretion their new authority. If the Bombay authorities had been rash it was not by timidity and caution that Bengal had been won. But the Calcutta Council oscillated between rashness and timidity in their Bombay policy, and threw the affairs of that presidency into confusion. One of the members, Mr. Francis, wrote that territorial acquisition on the West of India was inconsistent with the Company's true interest.

Treating with contempt the spirited representations from Bombay, the Bengal Government sent one of their own officers, Colonel Upton, to make terms with the Marátbas. His mild remonstrances were naturally taken for weakness, and the ministers made preposterous demands. Raghoba's cessions were to be void and Raghoba himself given up. Colonel Upton hereupon considered his task at an end. Advice from Bombay had been rejected with scorn at Calcutta, but suggestions from their own officer were received in a different spirit. In February 1776 the Governor-General and Council determined to support Raghoba's cause with vigour, and sent troops and treasure to Bombay. But before the letter could reach Colonel Upton, he had on the 1st March signed the treaty of Purandhar which confirmed most of the cessions to the English, and allowed Salsette to be retained or exchanged for other districts at the pleasure of the Governor-General and Council. The treaty of Surat however was formally annulled; Raghoba's army was to be disbanded and himself to reside as a pensioner at Kopargaum near Áhmadnagar.

It was impossible that this arrangement could secure peace. The English at Bombay were intensely disgusted. They expressed their scorn that a British envoy should suffer the Marátha ministers to secure a peace, on the principle of

Hydar Ali at Madras, by saying that in case of a renewal of the war they would carry fire and sword through all the Company's possessions. Mr. Hastings, though he disapproved of the treaty, was compelled to ratify it. Raghoba could not understand the nature of the interference from Bengal. He offered greater cessions than before, and wrote an appeal to the Court of Directors at home. The Court was in an unusually aggressive mood. In a despatch which reached Bombay in August 1776 they approved under every circumstance of the treaty of Surat, and recommended that the Bombay Government should retain possession of the districts ceded by it. Colonel Upton was after some time recalled to Bengal. Not at all to the liking of the Marátha ministers Mr. Mostyn returned to Puna, and negociations proceeded.

The negociations were considerably protracted. The kaleidoscopic politics at Puna were constantly changing. A rival to Nána Farnáwis had sprung up in his cousin Morába, and the latter had been joined by the veteran minister, Sakháram Bapu, who was jealous of his young colleague's increasing influence. This party was supported by Holkar, and thus consolidated they deemed it advisable to forward their interests by appealing to Bombay to once more assist Raghoba.

Thus the phase of affairs was greatly changed, and in October 1777 Mr. Hornby, the Governor of Bombay, recorded in an able minute on Marátha affairs that "They were fast verging to a period which must compel the English nation to take some active and decisive part in them or relinquish for ever all hopes of bettering their own situation on the West of India." In truth, as Clive had said after the the capture of Chandarnagar, the English standards could not wait where they were. But an event now occurred which vastly accelerated the inevitable interference.

Undefined as their views might be concerning their own ultimate position in India, the English were quite clear on one point that other European nations should not predominate. The British empire was undergoing a formidable crisis. A miserable war was being waged with the American colonists, who were supported by the French. Without allies, England was shortly to carry on a struggle with France, Spain and Holland; and the British flag was with difficulty to protect the English channel. The course of events was not unforeseen even in India. Fortunately in Warren Hastings India possessed a ruler keen to see and prompt to act. Some months before war was declared between England and France a French adventurer named St. Lubin landed at Chául and proceeded to Puna. He had already imposed on the Government of Madras as a man of quality. He even subsequently deceived the French Government so far as to obtain from them an authority to proceed to India. He at once made offer of an alliance with Nána Farnáwis on the part of France. He offered to bring 2,500 Europeans for the support of the ministry and to raise and discipline 10,000 sepoys. Nána may or may not have been deceived as to the authenticity of his credentials and the genuineness of his pretensions to act for France; but he thought him at all events a useful tool to be employed against the English. He hardly realised the danger to which he rendered himself liable by this choice of instruments.

Hastings recognised the gravity of the situation and determined to strike the first blow. The only difference between the new and old policies was that Raghoba was to be considered Regent on behalf of the young Peshwa. News had arrived of the declaration of war with France, an event that was not likely at such a juncture to occasion regret at Bombay or Calcutta. Hastings resolved to support the

Bombay Government with a large body of troops, and six native regiments with artillery and cavalry marched across India under Colonel Leslie, a feat never before attempted by a British force. At the same time an alliance was made with the great Marátha Raghoji Bhonsle of Barár. The French factories in Bengal were seized, and orders sent to Madras that Pondicheri was to be instantly occupied.

On November 23rd 1778 the British troops at Bombay crossed the harbour to Panwel. They were commanded by Colonel Egerton, a man whose weak health unfitted him for active service, and who was totally unacquainted with Indian warfare. He had on a former occasion been set aside in favour of Colonel Keating; but at this juncture Mr. Hornby most unfortunately thought that it was his due to be given the command. The expedition was accompanied by Mr. Carnac of the Bombay Council, Mr. Mostyn, whose services would have been invaluable, having just died. The expedition was a miserable failure. Colonel Egerton and Mr. Carnac wasted time in petty disagreements; and it was not for a month that the army, about 2,500 strong, reached Khándálla at the top of the Bhor Ghát, a distance from Panwel of some forty miles. Thence the advance was slower. On January 9th 1779 they arrived at Talegaum, sixteen miles from Puna. A force of 50,000 Maráthas disputed their advance, and clouds of horsemen harassed their camp. The hearts of their leaders failed them. The guns were thrown into a tank, the stores burnt, and a retreat commenced. On the 11th, at Wargaum, they were surrounded. On the 12th they were attacked. But the soldiers were more valiant than their commanders. Splendidly led by Captain Hartley, his men— Europeans and sepoys alike—fought with steadiness and enthusiasm. The next day the attack was again withstood,

Captain Hartley showing himself the life and soul of the force. But the army got into confusion with its baggage; many European officers were killed, and a large number of sepoys deserted. Further retreat was deemed impracticable. Raghoba, seeing how things were going, had already given himself up to Sindia, and the English came to terms with that chieftain, who acted as representative of the Maráthas. The army was allowed to depart, but an unconditional surrender was made of all acquisitions obtained since 1773. The Bombay Council ignored this shameful convention. They recorded their sense of its disgraceful nature by dismissing Mr. Carnac, Colonels Egerton and Cockburn; while, for his splendid gallantry, Captain Hartley was promoted to the rank of Lieutenant-Colonel.

The Bombay Government had failed. They had attempted a great task without counting the cost. Their irritation at the authority exercised over them from Calcutta had actuated them with the desire of showing what they could do without the assistance that was coming from Bengal. They had learnt the lesson; and though humbled by their misfortunes, their army defeated, their treasury empty, and their reputation dimmed, they set to work under the firm and able leadership of Governor Hornby to retrieve their fortune. This admirable spirit was met by Warren Hastings with the treatment that it deserved. He deprecated the expression of any want of confidence in the Bombay authorities, and preferred to incite them to fresh exertion for the retrieval of their affairs, and to arm them with means adequate to the end.

The Bengal forces, commanded by Colonel Leslie, had procrastinated. Hastings at once superseded him by a dashing officer, Colonel Goddard; but Leslie died before Goddard could relieve him. Goddard soon showed what stuff he was made of.

He marched from Bandalkand to Surat, 300 miles, in twenty days, an achievement which critics in England spoke of as a frantic military exploit. The Bombay Government expressed their gratitude for his activity by offering him a seat in their Council. Mr. Hastings' instructions to Goddard were that he should negociate a new treaty with the Maráthas on the basis of the treaty of Purandhar, with an additional article excluding the French from the Marátha dominions. Nána Farnáwis dallied with these proposals, and vouchsafed no reply until October 1779. Reports were then current of an alliance between the Nizám, Hydar Ali, and the Maráthas, who were binding each other to simultaneous attacks on the English settlements in Bombay, Madras and Bengal. Then the Marátha minister demanded the relinquishment of Salsette, and the abandonment of Raghoba who had thrown himself on English protection. There was no alternative but to recommence the war, and the campaign opened in Guzárát. At the beginning of 1780 Goddard occupied the Peshwa's districts in that province, and in February of that year he made an alliance with Fatte Sing, the brother and rival of Gowind Gaikwár, and proceeded to take Áhmadábád. The wall was breached; the Bombay grenadiers rushed into the opening; and, in spite of a determined resistance by the garrison, which did not cease till 300 of their number lay dead, they made good their entrance.

Máhádaji Sindia and Holkar now advanced, and well-nigh wore out Goddard's patience, first by empty negociations, and, when these came to nothing, by evading all his attempts to bring on a general action. He suggested to the Governor-General the advisability of detailing a force into Málwa to draw them off in that direction, and so leave his division free to advance into the Konkan. He had already sent Colonel Hartley to deal with the Marāthas who were active on the borders of Salsette, and who constantly annoyed the post newly established by the English at Kálýán under Captain Campbell. The result was most successful. Captain Popham, the officer selected for this employment, crossed the Jumna and carried on a brilliant campaign. In August, with equal daring and skill, he captured the celebrated fortress of Gwálior, hitherto considered to be impregnable, while a series of dashing and for the most part successful engagements took place in the Konkan. An attempt to take the two strong forts of Malangaḥr or Bhau Malan—now known from their fanciful shape as the Cathedral Rocks—by Captain Alington partially succeeded. The lower fort was captured, but the upper, an absolutely perpendicular rock, defied all efforts to take it.

During the monsoon the Bombay Government had time to consider their position. They were in great difficulties for want of funds, for which they had looked to Bengal. But in lieu of funds came despatches informing them that the threatened invasion of Hydar had swept over Madras. The Mysur ruler, encouraged by French promises, and his troops drilled by French officers, was stimulated in his disputes with Madras by the Marāthas at Puna. He was ready to accept their help in his crusade against the European settlers; but he meant when he had disposed of the English to make short work of the Marāthas also. France and England were again at war, and there was every possibility of a naval attack upon Bombay. The Bengal Government could give no further assistance. "We have no resources," says Governor Hornby in his minute of the 1st August, "but such as we may find in our own efforts." Whatever brave men could do they did. They raised ten lakhs of rupees by the sale of copper in their warehouses, they managed to negociate loans, and they anticipated the Maráthas in the collection of their own revenues.

The master mind of Hastings perceived that the new struggle with Mysur presented a more formidable danger than immediately pressed on the English from the Maráthas. His plans regarding the Marátha empire were for the time set aside, when they seemed, but for this interruption, not unlikely to be crowned with success. He set himself to break up the confederacy. He detached the Nizám from it by telling him that the emperor of Delhi had granted to Hydar the territories which the Nizám ruled as the Moghal viceroy of the Deccan. By protracted negociations he contrived to obtain the neutrality of the Bhonsle Rája of Barár. The newer and more formidable danger rendered it necessary to make peace with the Peshwa, but not peace at any price; at all extremities there must be no peace not accompanied with honour. With this object in view the Marátha war was vigorously continued. Towards the end of 1780 Goddard took Bassein, which fortified by the Portuguese possessed unusual strength, while Hartley, after covering the siege by six weeks' incessant fighting, repulsed a bold attack of 20,000 Maráthas and killed their commander. After the siege the British forces united.

The Governor-General was anxious that overtures for peace should come from the Peshwa. He suggested through Mudáji Bhonsle, who had succeeded his father Raghoji as Rája of Barár, and who consented to become a mediator, certain conditions which he would accept if the Peshwa's Government would enter upon an offensive and defensive alliance with the Company against Hydar and the French.

But on the news that came from Madras Mudáji declined to continue his friendly offices except on terms that could not possibly be accepted. The news was most alarming. Sir Hector Munro commanded one force, Colonel Baillie another. Instead of uniting and presenting a formidable front to Hydar, they suffered him to attack them separately. Baillie's army, after a brave defence, was almost totally destroyed, the remnant owing their lives to the intervention of Hydar's French officers. Munro was within hearing of the cannonade. He abandoned his equipage, destroyed his stores, threw his guns into a tank, and fled in confusion to Madras. It was a great triumph for Hydar, who decorated his palace at Saringapatam with pictures of the carnage of one English army and the flight of another. The English empire in the south-east of India was within immediate danger of annihilation. But Hastings was equal to the emergency. He suspended the incapable Governor of Madras, and sent the veteran soldier, Sir Eyre Coote, to take command of the army. He soon gave a different character to the operations.

Goddard now considered that an advanced movement, threatening Puna, would be likely to bring about the Governor-General's object. He overrated his ability to menace in sufficient strength. He occupied the Bhor Ghát, and his troops were encamped at Khándálla where the British had been quartered three years before. He thence sent proposals to the Puna ministers for defence and alliance. But Hydar was at that time triumphant. Nána Farnáwis judged him to be more powerful than the Company, and he plainly hinted that he preferred Hydar's friendship to that of the English. It was useless to attempt a treaty with a man in this frame of mind. But the Maráthas were not content with refusing terms. They put forth all their strength, and sixty thousand troops were in readiness to destroy the British army. It was clear that Goddard's movement had failed. The Bombay Government recognised the fact, and Goddard prepared to obey their earnest request that he would withdraw his troops. On the 15th of April a convoy under Colonel Browne, which had fought its way with extreme bravery from Panwel joined his army, and the united forces withdrew towards that town. The movement was conducted with great skill. The enemy swarmed on every side and gave the English no rest. The whole retreat was in fact one protracted battle. Goddard reached Panwel in eight days. He lost in his retreat 461 in killed and wounded of whom eighteen were European officers. He had extricated himself with credit from the dangerous position in which his rashness had placed him, but the Maráthas considered the operations one of their chief victories. The army after halting at Panwel was quartered at Kályan for the rains.

The tide now altogether turned in Madras. Sir Eyre Coote had obtained a magnificent success over Hydar at Porto Novo on July 1st, and with a loss of only 300 destroyed 10,000 of his men. In September he inflicted another terribly severe defeat upon him at Sholinghar, and the campaign was brought to a successful close. The English being at war with Holland, an attack was made on the Dutch settlement of Negapatam; and the garrison, which numbered upwards of 6,500 men, a force greatly exceeding that of the besiegers, capitulated on November 12th. In Málwa too Captain Popham's successes had been followed up by Colonel Camac; and Sindia, effectually excluded from the Deccan, found himself unable to continue operations. In October he made advances for peace. Hastings secured the neutrality of the Rája of Barár by purchasing his forces, and the Rája again offered his services as a mediator. His offer was accepted and he was despatched by the Governor-General to Sindia's camp. Negociations now opened on a wide basis and Hastings, at the beginning of 1782, deputed Mr. David Anderson, in the capacity of Agent to the Governor-General, to the camp of Máhádají Sindia. On the 17th May a treaty was concluded at Sálbai with the English by Sindia on behalf of the Peshwa, Nána Farnáwis and the whole of the Marátha chiefs. The treaty was ratified by Nána Farnáwis, but not before he heard of Hydar's death in December 1782; nor was it finally exchanged until February 1783. By this treaty the English gave up Bassein and other acquisitions made since the treaty of Purandhar, but they retained Salsette, Elephanta, Karanja, and Hog Islands, with absolute possession of the city of Broach. The English were to cease giving assistance to Raghoba, who was to be allowed 25,000 rupees a month if he would reside with Sindia. Hydar Ali was to be made to surrender his conquests from the English and their allies. No factories of any European nations besides the English were to be allowed in the Marátha dominions, except those of the Portuguese already established. The territory of the Gaikwár family, as well as Guzarát in general, was to remain on the same footing as before the war. The English gave Broach to Sindia in recognition of his generous behaviour to their troops after the convention of Wargaum. Raghoba died shortly after the conclusion of the treaty.

The first Marátha war thus ended. The Bombay Government had undertaken it rashly, against a people who, if but united, could have driven all the English of Bombay with ease into the sea. They had been hampered by ill-advised and inconsistent orders of the Bengal Council; but Mr. Hastings from the first personally held that their determination to obtain Salsette and the other islands was indisputably right, and his views were subsequently shared by his Council and by the Court of Directors at home. They had entered upon the war as allies of Raghoba. His aid was altogether inadequate; his faction steadily lost popularity, and long before the close of the war the English were not allies but principals. Their generals had on one occasion disgraced the English name by a cowardly surrender. The Bombay Council dismissed their unworthy officers and another army was sent into the field. For funds they were to great extent dependent on Bengal. When supplies from that Government ceased, by stupendous efforts they raised them for themselves. For seven years they had carried on the war with indomitable fortitude and perseverance. They had been cheered by brilliant successes; reverses had only excited them to renewed exertions. There was none of the cowardice and incompetence of Madras, none of the incredible meanness which in 1756 led the chiefs of the Bengal factory to sail down the river and leave their colleagues to the terrors of the Black Hole. Mr. Hornby and his Council, in dangers and difficulties, displayed the undaunted courage of Warren Hastings himself. Dangers more formidable than that of the Maráthas had compelled them to bring the war to a close before they had achieved the brilliant termination which they hoped for. But on the eve of an alliance of the Peshwa with Hydar, backed up by French influence, against themselves, they won over their Marátha foes as allies against Mysur, and induced them to exclude the French from all their territories. They obtained from the Maráthas in perpetuity the ownership of Salsette and the other islands which they rightly deemed indispensable to Bombay. Salsette was taken under the direct management of the Company. No attempt at double government in the name of any Oriental ruler was made, such as led to confusion and misery in Bengal.

During the war a marked change had been coming over the Marátha empire. The great houses of Sindia, Holkar, the Gaikwár, and Bhonsle of Barár were rapidly growing into independent states, little if at all less powerful than the Peshwa himself. Thus, instead of a single empire, the English had to do with a more or less lax confederacy, each of whose members was actuated by his own personal interests rather than by any spirit of national patriotism. To these factors in the political combination of Western India were to be added the Nizám and Hydar Ali.

XIV.—THEORY OF THE BALANCE OF POWER.

THE Marátha war had been brought to a premature conclusion on account of pressing danger in another quarter. That danger was by no means at an end. The fact was that British power had so far advanced that it must either perish or be supreme in India. The scenes of the long struggle might shift and change; the combatants might vary; and when one enemy was crushed another appear in the field. But for the English there could be no rest, and the general war in India continued with scarcely a break until their supremacy was established. For the present the struggle lay between the English, the Maráthas, and the Muhammadan kingdom of Mysur. There might be convention and truces, but until one or the other emerged as sole victor from the contest they could be only hollow and temporary. The most urgent danger was from the Sultán of Mysur, under cover of whose influence the French were making a determined effort for the recovery of their former ascendancy. Sir Eyre Coote's campaign in 1781 had been signally successful, and the year 1782 opened with like results. But Coote's shattered health compelled him to return to Bengal, and the war with Hydar continued with brilliant actions, but little permanent advantage to either side. The peace with the Maráthas enabled the English to send reinforcements of both troops and ships from Bombay. The ships were greatly needed, for a powerful French fleet under Admiral Suffrein had come to the aid of Hydar. The fleet was altogether stronger than tha[t] of the English under Admiral Hughes, but in several hard fought actions it could obtain no advantage. Decembe[r] brought the death of Hydar, and his son Tipu succeeded t[o] his power. Tipu might not have his father's ability, but h[e] possessed his insatiable ambition and a yet more implacabl[e] hatred of the English. When Hydar died Tipu was conduc[t]ing some distant operations against a detachment of Bomba[y] troops; and, with a capable commander, the Madras arm[y] might have inflicted a crushing defeat on the Mysur force before Tipu could join them. But nothing was done; an[d] Sir Eyre Coote, who was once more despatched by Hasting[s] died shortly after his arrival, worn out by old age and in[-] firmities. The aspect of affairs was not favourable. Th[e] country was ravaged by continual wars, and desolated b[y] famine and hurricanes. And the news came that Bussy wa[s] returning to India with strong reinforcements from France.

Bussy reached India in April 1783, and assumed comman[d] of the French forces. But the Madras commander, Gener[al] Stuart, succeeded in preventing him from co-operating wit[h] Tipu; and in June Bussy was defeated in a general actio[n] though not without a loss of 920 Europeans to the Britis[h] army. Bussy was strengthened by a large number of marine[s] and sailors from Admiral Suffrein's fleet, and he agai[n] attacked General Stuart's camp at night. But he was beate[n] off with heavy loss, and Bernadotte, the future king o[f] Sweden, who was serving with him as a sergeant, was mad[e] prisoner. Shortly afterwards peace was signed between Franc[e] and England, and Bussy agreed to withdraw the Frenc[h] troops in the Mysur service.

The English were thus left to deal with Tipu alone. Bu[t] the task was no light one. He possessed an army of 100,00[0] men. He first reduced, by a siege that lasted five months, the fort of Bednur on the Mysur table-land, which had been gallantly taken by General Mathews with a detachment from Bombay. The garrison made a splendid defence, but were compelled by want of supplies to capitulate. Tipu engaged to send the survivors to the coast. Instead of this he plunged them into the dungeons of Saringapatam. He next marched against Mangalur, which held out nobly until January 30th 1784, when the defenders, who were reduced to the last extremities by famine, were permitted to march out with all the honours of war. Hastings was intent on a vigorous prosecution of the campaign until he could obtain an honourable peace. Two powerful British armies were advancing, and the brutal cruelties of Tipu to Hindus and his forcible conversion of thousands of them were raising against him bitter enemies in his own dominions. Sindia, on behalf of the Maráthas, engaged to join the English, hoping to make Tipu a Marátha tributary. There was every reason to hope that a continuance of the struggle would soon bring a successful ending to the second Mysur war. But the ever-incapable Council of Madras thought otherwise, and determined to sue for peace. In vain did the Governor-General insist that they should imitate the example of Hydar, who had dictated peace under the walls of Fort St. George. Tipu grossly insulted the English Commissioners, and it is impossible to read without shame and humiliation how they stood before him with their heads uncovered, and the treaty in their hands, for two hours, using every form of flattery and supplication to induce compliance; and how their abject entreaties at length softened the Sultán into assent. By the treaty mutual conquests were restored, and the prisoners made by Tipu given up. These included 130 officers, 900

English soldiers, and 1,600 sepoys. Many, including General Mathews, had been murdered, while all had been subjected to most outrageous treatment. There was no element of finality in the convention of Mangalur, and when five years later Tipu once more determined upon war with the English, the only matter for surprise was that he had chosen to observe the agreement for so long. There was no reference in it to Sindia or the Maráthas, an omission regarded by them as singularly offensive. The Governor-General expressed the strongest disapprobation of this humiliating treaty. But as much of it had already been carried into effect before the arrangement was communicated to him, he did not consider himself justified in annulling it.

In April 1783, shortly after the final exchange of the treaty of Sálbai, an unprovoked attack was made by the Peshwa's fleet on a British vessel, which but for the urgent necessity for peace would have probably caused a renewal of the war. Lieutenant Pruen was in command of the "Ranger," a brig carrying twelve guns, which was bound for Kálikat. He was an officer in the Company's service, and he had on board as passengers General Norman Macleod and other officers of the king's service. There was always more or less jealousy between officers of the two services, and Pruen welcomed the opportunity of showing his passengers how a Company's cruiser could fight. He met the Marátha attack of eleven ships with heroic courage. Their shot swept his decks, and their sailors boarded in hundreds. At last, when all his men were killed or wounded, he asked the king's officers if the crew of the "Ranger" could fight, and then struck his colours in order to save the lives of those who still survived. General Macleod was himself desperately wounded while mingling bravely in the fight. The British Government strongly remonstrated at this violation of the treaty; but upon a restoration of the "Ranger" the Peshwa's apologies were accepted.

The treaty of Sálbai had been negociated by the intervention of Sindia. He conceived an exaggerated idea of the value of his services on this occasion, and his ambition rapidly grew. His interests diverged more and more from those of the Peshwa. He had on a previous occasion taken under his patronage the representative of the house of Bábar, and he again turned his attention towards Delhi. His object was to found a great Marátha State between the Ganges and the Jumna. He engaged the Frenchman De Boigne, one of the ablest military adventurers of the time, to discipline his troops; and in accordance with the existing custom in India, by which the name of authority was so often separated from its substance, he sought to make himself master of Delhi by the ingenious contrivance of obtaining for the Peshwa the title of Wakil-i-Mutluk, or supreme deputy of the empire. The title may have been gratifying to the Marátha national vanity at large; but while it gained for the usurpation of Sindia the nominal authority both of the emperor and the Peshwa, it created no small amount of jealousy at his proceedings on the part of Nána Farnáwis, Holkar and other Marátha chiefs (1784). For himself he secured the appointment of deputy to the Peshwa in Hindustán, the command of the emperor's army, and the management of the provinces of Delhi and Ágra. In spite of his jealousy the Peshwa considered it advisable to send off a small body of his troops to preserve the appearance of union between himself and Sindia. In 1785 a Rohilla chief, Gholám Khadir, rebelled against the emperor with temporary success; he put out Sháh Álam's eyes, and brutally outraged his family. Sindia stepped in, and with great ceremony reseated the blinded emperor on his throne. The imperial dominions in Hindustán now practically belonged to the great Máhádaji Sindia. He was inebriated by his own success. Warren Hastings had sailed to England in February 1785, and in the emperor's name Sindia demanded from his successor, Mr. Macpherson, the chauth of the British provinces of Bengal. But the acting Governor-General insisted upon the absolute and immediate withdrawal of the demand, and Sindia found it wiser to obey. The incident showed the English the danger of Sindia's ambitious policy. Considerable attention was paid to other Marátha chiefs, and it was determined again to send an envoy to the Peshwa's court at Puna. Since the treaty of Sálbai Sindia had chosen to regard himself as the political agent between the English and the Peshwa, and his jealousy was accordingly aroused at this proceeding. But Mr. Malet, the officer selected, was sent to Sindia at Ágra to obtain his consent. A tardy acquiescence was obtained from him to a compromise, which arranged for the despatches of Mr. Malet to his Government being sent through Mr. Anderson, the resident at the Court of Sindia, for the information of the Marátha ruler. But Sindia was too busily occupied in Hindustán to be able to pay much attention to affairs at Puna.

Lord Cornwallis, the permanent successor to Warren Hastings, reached Calcutta in September 1786. He found Sindia all powerful in Hindustán; while in the Deccan, the Maráthas under the Peshwa, the Nizám, and Tipu Sultán of Mysur, were the chief actors in the political crisis that he had to deal with.

The power of Tipu was fast becoming intolerable to the Maráthas and the English alike. His father, Hydar Ali, had not been a strict Mussalmán and had left the Hindus unmolested. But Tipu was an orthodox upholder of the faith, and a master of the methods of fanaticism and persecution. He was busily engaged in forcibly converting Hindus to Muhammadanism; he carried off the people of Kurg (Coorg) into slavery, and established a universal reign of terror. Two thousand Brahmans on the borders of the Marátha territory died by their own hand to preserve the purity of their caste. The Peshwa applied for aid to the English, but the treaty of Mangalur had placed them in a neutral position and he had to be content with the alliance of the Nizám. A campaign was opened in 1786, but little was gained on either side, and peace was concluded a few months after the arrival of Lord Cornwallis.

The new Governor-General was a soldier as well as a statesman. He grasped the political situation, and realised that the English could not long remain a neutral power. But his hands were not altogether free. He was sent out to avoid war and to improve the internal administration of the Company's territories. Mr. Pitt's bill of 1784 had forbidden alliances with native princes. Personally, Lord Cornwallis preferred peace, but with admirable statesmanship he prepared everything for war should war be forced upon him. He had not long to wait. By the treaty of Mangalur the state of Travancore was declared to be under British protection. Tipu demanded the submission of the Rája, and in December 1789 he attacked the forces of that state. Lord Cornwallis saw that the time for action had come. If he observed the directions of Mr. Pitt's bill in the letter he certainly broke through them in the spirit. He might not make alliances, but he made treaties to have effect during the continuance of the war. Before Tipu's invasion was an accomplished fact, he had informed him, through Mr. Holland the Governor of

Madras, that he meant to uphold by force the integrity of Travancore. Holland first proceeded to extort money for himself from the Travancore Rája; and when Tipu's attack was made, he deserted his post and sailed for England. On learning of these events, Nána Farnáwis immediately proposed joint action with the English against Tipu. Terms were drawn up in March 1790, and in July of that year the Nizám joined the coalition.

The war was opened with spirit under General Medows, Commander-in-Chief, and now Governor of Madras. He commenced operations in May, and by September he had captured some forts which were deemed impregnable, and possessed himself of the low country of Mysur. In Malabár, Colonel Hartley of Bombay defeated the Mysur general Hussein Ali; and General Abercrombie reduced Kánnanur and secured the coast territory. The Maráthas had given valuable aid, and they captured from the Mysur forces the strong fort of Dhárwár. But the highlands, in which rested the chief strength of Tipu, were in vain attempted; and, disappointed at the result of the first campaign, Lord Cornwallis determined himself to take command in the second. In January 1791 the Governor-General placed himself at the head of the army. The campaign again opened brilliantly, and Lord Cornwallis defeated Tipu in several engagements. The Nizám's forces joined him, but their aid was of little value. The troops were picturesque in appearance but useless except for plunder. Finally, after a splendid victory at Arikera in April, Lord Cornwallis found his supplies to be so scanty and defective that he was compelled to retreat. He had to destroy his batteries and heavy stores, and was only saved from serious disaster by the speedy arrival of his Marátha allies. He took up his position at Bangalur for the remainder of the year, leaving nothing undone to complete his preparations for the overthrow of Tipu in the next campaign. The subsequent operations were crowned with complete success. After capturing several stupendous mountain fortresses Lord Cornwallis advanced on Saringapatam, and on the 5th of February 1792 proceeded to invest it. A few days later he was joined by the Bombay army under General Abercrombie. Saringapatam was now completely isolated, and Tipu felt an alarm at the might of the British power which he had never before conceived. When Lord Cornwallis destroyed his stores and guns after the battle of Arikera he dreamt of no second supply in reserve ; and when he saw a more powerful armament than ever brought against him he exclaimed that it was not what he saw of the English that he feared but what he did not see. Convinced of the overwhelming might of the forces arrayed against him he saw that his only course was that of complete submission; and the third Mysur war was concluded by a treaty in accordance with which the Sultán ceded half his dominions to the allies, and paid the expenses of the war. The Madras Presidency thus gained a large increase of area, including the district of North Kánara with the port of Kárwár, which was handed over to Bombay in 1861. It was subsequently discovered that the British success was no more anticipated by the Nizám and the Marátha troops than by Tipu; and traitorous correspondence was found which showed that only the undaunted vigour and ability of the Governor-General prevented their taking part with the Mysur king against the English.

This triumphant success immensely raised the prestige of the British arms. There is no doubt that they formed the only serious obstacle in the way of Tipu's ultimate conquest of all India. But the most important result of the war was its effect upon the English policy. The system of complete isolation from the other powers of the Peninsula was for the future out of the question. Self-effacement was impossible. The idea of absolute supremacy was indeed not yet come. People in England looked on Native rulers as holders of ancient monarchies, and failed to realise that the Maráthas, the Nizám, and the Sultán of Mysur, not only owed their sovereignty to usurpation and violence, but were no older in the field than the English themselves and had no better right to their conquests. But facts were stronger than preconceived theories. Isolation was dropped and a new theory of a balance of power came in, by which the British Government should hold the scales between the rival candidates for supremacy. This theory soon proved impracticable, but it was an immense step in advance of what preceded it.

Lord Cornwallis sailed for England in October 1793. His reputation rests less on his military achievements than on his courageous reform in the civil service. He bestowed adequate salaries on the Company's servants and put an end to the system of perquisites; and he insisted upon a tone of honour and rectitude which has been the glory of the service ever since. But in making a permanent settlement of the land tenure of Bengal he made a vast mistake, which led to abuses that have not yet passed away. During his tenure of office a change was introduced into the charter of the East Indian Company. A limited amount of free trade was conceded to outsiders, and missionaries and school-masters allowed admission into the Company's territories.

While these events were occurring at Mysur, further changes were taking place amongst the Marátha leaders. Sindia had not joined the Peshwa in his alliance with the English, but he managed his possessions in Hindustán with singular ability and success. His prosperity was the cause of intense jealousy to his great rival Holkar, who was used by Nána Farnáwis as a check upon Sindia's power. Holkar took into his service the Chevalier Dudrenec, and proceeded to raise a disciplined force on the model of Sindia's. Sindia by no means approved of this. He petitioned for Holkar's recall, and himself proceeded to Puna with the ostensible object of investing the young Peshwa with the insignia of his office which he had obtained from the emperor. His ulterior motive was to increase his influence and popularity with the Maráthas of Máháráshtra, from whom his long absence might have in some degree estranged him. He reached Puna in June 1791 and pitched his camp with magnificent state on the Sangam, or junction of the rivers Muta and Mula. Nána Farnáwis intensely disliked Sindia's proceedings, and dreaded his increasing influence; but the ceremony was carried out with regal splendour. The Peshwa was now a high-spirited youth of seventeen. He was greatly attracted by the frank and soldierly manners of Sindia, and the influence of his stern guardian Nána proportionately waned. Sindia utilised to the utmost the Peshwa's liking for him. He had extended at his own risk the dominion of the Maráthas to Hindustán, and he now put forth a request that he might be reimbursed for the costs which he had been compelled to incur. Nána Farnáwis retorted that he had now held the conquests for some time, that the territories were wealthy, and that he ought now to render an account of his stewardship to his master the Peshwa. While Nána and Sindia were thus intriguing at the Peshwa's court, news reached Puna that Sindia's army in Hindustán had inflicted a crushing defeat on the forces of Holkar. The triumph of Sindia seemed assured, and in the crisis that ensued Nána Farnáwis besought his master to let him retire to Banáras. But Sindia almost immediately died of fever near Puna, and his nephew, Daolat Rao, a boy of fifteen succeeded to his sovereignty.

Máhádaji Sindia was one of the most daring and able men of his age. He was held by a great proportion of the Maráthas in almost as great veneration as Shiwáji himself. He was a consistent opponent of the ascendency of the Brahmans. While striving for his own independence, he aimed at a Marátha confederacy of which he should be the leader. At one time, when defeated by Popham and Camac, his fortunes seemed at a low ebb. But the English, by accepting his mediation at the treaty of Sálbai, recognised his independent position, and from that time he surmounted every difficulty and achieved a task that his enemies might well have held impossible. The progress of the English he viewed with alarm; and he was hostile to the entire demolition of Tipu's power, as he considered it a bulwark against English aggression. But he had in reality by spreading Marátha power over so vast an area considerably sapped its strength; and his system of organising regular infantry and artillery on the European system ultimately led to the ruin of his nation's power. The strength of the Maráthas lay in their irregular cavalry, who could fight or flee as might be most expedient. Infantry and guns might compel them to stand their ground when retreat was more judicious. The Maráthas were a martial rather than a military people. Every member of a peasant's family had carried arms, but of discipline and technical skill they had little. Pitched battles and regular warfare were unsuited to their style of fighting. What gave them their tremendous power was their surprising activity and mobility. These qualities were destroyed by the introduction of a more cumbersome organisation. Their courage was never a very conspicuous quality. There was a change, too, at this time in the reigning house of Baroda. Fatte Sing Gaikwár, the regent, died; and, after some intrigues and disputes his brother, a former rival, Gowind Rao, was accredited by Nána Farnáwis as his successor. Throughout the Mysur war the curse of piracy had clung to the western coast. Raghoji Ángria of Kolába professed submission to the Peshwa, but practised it only so far as suited his convenience. The Sidis of Janjira plundered the ships of all nations with the exception of the English, nor did this exception always hold good. Nána Farnáwis attempted to take advantage of revolutions in this petty state and annex the unconquerable island to the Peshwa's territory. In 1791 an agreement was actually signed by which the heirs relinquished their right in favour of the Peshwa. But the island fort was never reduced. The empire of the Peshwas has perished, but the principality of Janjira has endured. The pirates also of Málwán, Sáwantwári and Kolhápur swarmed along the coast. An armament was made ready against Kolhápur in 1792; but it was not despatched as pardon was asked, an indemnity promised, and a treaty concluded. But little result came of the agreement, and it was not till 1812 that the Bombay Government finally put an end to piracy. The pirate strongholds now contain English life-boats; and the rock of Kándheri, in lieu of a nest of robbers ready to plunder the mariner, now bears a lighthouse to warn him off the reefs and shoals.

After the death of Sindia, Nána Farnáwis managed the affairs of the Marátha States. Daolat Rao Sindia was too young to interfere, and Nána kept the Peshwa in rigid tutelage. His first measures were taken against the Nizám, upon whom the Maráthas considered that they possessed no small claims. Whatever just claims they may have had, the demands urged were preposterous, and the Nizám appealed to Calcutta. Sir John Shore, who was afterwards Lord Teignmouth, had succeeded Lord Cornwallis. But war had again broken out between France and England. Hostilities were again proceeding before Pondicheri, and French influence pervaded many native states. Shore was by no means devoid of courage; but he was not equal to the complications and difficulties of the task before him, and he declined to interfere. A stronger man would have at all events mediated between the contending parties. The Governor-General was fully aware of the dangerous predominance that the defeat of the Nizám would give to the Maráthas. But he held to the policy of non-intervention. The Nizám increased his forces, and with the aid of a French officer named Raymond disciplined twenty-three battalions of infantry and a park of artillery. His efforts were futile. In the battle of Khardla, in March 1795, the troops disciplined by Raymond alone stood their ground; the rest were utterly routed. The Nizám had to surrender frontier districts, including Daolatábád, of the annual revenue of £350,000, and to pay three millions sterling in payment of all the Marátha claims. Nána Farnáwis was now at the height of his ascendency. The young Sindia and Bhonsle of Barár were favourably disposed to him; Tukáji Holkar had grown mentally and physically incompetent to take any part in public affairs. His only anxiety was lest the Peshwa should insist on receiving the authority which was his due. He meant in fact to play the same part with the Peshwa that the early Peshwas had played with the successors of Shiwáji. The fainéant Rája at Sátára might be an instrument that would thwart his plans. He consequently increased the severity of his imprisonment and prohibited his relations from going near him. The family of Raghoba was a greater source of danger, especially his elder son Báji Rao. Báji Rao was a graceful and accomplished youth, and his manners gained him the good-will of all who saw him. The young Peshwa was taken by the attractive disposition and the accomplishments of his cousin. Nána Farnáwis therefore had him immured in a hill fort. He treated the Peshwa with extraordinary harshness and severity, but his policy defeated its own object. Rendered desperate by this tyranny, Máhdu Rao Peshwa was overwhelmed with grief and despair. He sank into a fixed melancholy, and in October 1795, in the 22nd year of his age, he threw himself from a terrace in his palace and in a few days expired, living long enough to express a wish that Báji Rao should suceeed him. This catastrophe brought an end to Nána's successful career, and during the remainder of his life misfortunes crowded upon him with but few alternations of prosperity.

Nána had no intention of allowing Báji Rao to succeed. He held that the widow of the late Peshwa should adopt a son, and that son should be Chimnáji Apa, the younger brother of Báji Rao, who would be a more pliant tool in his hands. The extraordinary series of plots, counterplots, assassinations, and massacres which ensued, clearly went to show that the power of the Maráthas was drawing to a close. Báji Rao appealed to Sindia to aid him in securing the throne. Dreading Sindia's power Nána reversed his policy. With the help of Parashrám Bhau, the commander-in-chief, he determined to forestall Sindia, and himself promote the cause of Báji Rao. An objection was now raised by Sindia's minister, and Nána reverted to his original scheme. But growing suspicious he remained aloof; and then, making a fresh departure, he endeavoured to regain his power by setting up the fainéant Rája of Sátára. Meanwhile, Parasbrám Bhau took Chimnáji Apa to Puna where he was invested as Peshwa in May 1796, Parashrám Bhau being at the head of the Government. This was sufficient to attract Nána's sympathies to the cause of Báji Rao. He contrived to enlist Sindia on his side and gained over Raghoji Bhonsle, the son of Mudáji, Rájá of Barár, and he made a treaty with the Nizám at Máhár, by which he cancelled the balance of arrears due to the Maráthas by the Nizám. He also obtained the recognition of the English to the claims of Báji Rao. The adoption of Chimnáji Apa was declared illegal and was therefore revoked; and Báji Rao was proclaimed Peshwa in December 1796.

Beneath his engaging manners Báji Rao concealed the ferocity of the tiger. He bore no love to Nána Farnáwis, and anxious to rid himself of his control he plotted against him with Sindia. In December 1797 he placed him in close confinement in Sindia's fort of Áhmadnagar. Báji Rao had but freed himself from one thraldom to find himself subject to another. Daolat Rao Sindia inherited his father's ambition and love of power. His interference in the state affairs of Puna became more arbitrary than that of Nána himself had been. Tukáji Holkar had died. He left two legitimate sons, one of whom was an idiot. Sindia put the idiot on the throne and murdered the other, and the house of Holkar became for the time subservient to him. But Tukáji left two illegitimate sons, Yeshwant Rao and Wituji; the former of these proved a formidable antagonist, not only to Sindia but to the British power itself, Amongst Sindia's acts of interference the grossest was his capture of the fort of Kolába, the imprisonment of Mánáji Ángria, and the enstalment on his throne of Bábu Rao Ángria, a connection of Sindia's own house. His headstrong and turbulent followers kept Puna in a perpetual state of uproar and confusion. He married in March 1793 the daughter of Shirji Rao Ghatge, one of his officers. The expenses of the marriage were enormous; and he pressed Báji Rao for a reimbursement of the costs which he had incurred in his efforts to place him on the throne. Báji Rao could not raise the amount himself, but he replied that if Sindia would make Ghatge his diwán or minister he might levy his demands upon the rich inhabitants of Puna. The offer was accepted, and in Ghatge there was let loose upon the people of Puna a monster of cruelty whose name is remembered to this day with loathing and execration. His first victims were the former partisans of Nána Farnáwis. He next went to the merchants and bankers, and other rich inhabitants of the city, and by unspeakable tortures, which in many cases ended in death, compelled them to give up their wealth. Báji Rao, whose true character was understood by the British resident, was the real cause of these brutalities; but the popular rage was directed against Sindia, and Báji Rao took advantage of it to plot his assassination. He worked out his plan with his half-brother Amrat Rao, whom he had made his minister in succession to Nána; but at the last moment his courage failed him, and Sindia escaped death by flight.

The plot upon this became more and more involved, and it is almost impossible to follow it out through its intricate twistings and turnings. The whole Deccan became a scene of intolerable disorder. The rupture between Sindia and the

Peshwa widened, and then was healed and opened again. Sindia released Nána Farnúwis and Báji Rao took him back as his minister. The Rájas of Sátára and Kolhápur were incited to aid the rival and ever-shifting parties; fire and sword desolated the country. Each faction sought the aid alternately of the English, Tipu, and the Nizám. The resident at Puna, Colonel Palmer, declined intervention, but endeavoured to mediate, and his advice was not without some effect.

XV.—SECOND MARÁTHA WAR.

WHILE things in the Deccan were going from bad to worse, a new Governor-General arrived in India. Lord Mornington reached Calcutta in May 1798. He came out full of Lord Cornwallis' theory of the balance of power. His first efforts were directed to the renewal of the alliance with the Nizám and the Peshwa against Tipu, and to the driving of the French out of India. With the Nizám the English concluded a most favourable treaty, by promising to mediate on his behalf with the Maráthas. Nizám Ali consented to dismiss his French troops, and to receive in their stead six battalions of English sepoys and a force of artillery, for which he agreed to pay annually twenty-four lakhs of rupees. A similar treaty was offered to but declined by the Maráthas, the Peshwa alleging that previous treaties were sufficient. He however volunteered to assist in the inevitable war with Tipu. But the usual stream of intrigue was in full force. The Peshwa was in his heart of hearts much more inclined to side with Tipu, and he prepared a scheme with Sindia by which the latter should attack the Nizám. Lord Mornington had full information of what was going on and took measures accordingly.

Affairs with Tipu were fast coming to a crisis. His previous lessons had taught him nothing, and he was still bent on driving the English out of India. England and France were as usual at war, and the French were busily engaged in directing the armies and training the troops of Indian princes. Tipu had sent envoys to the Mauritius to bring about an offensive and defensive alliance with France against the English; Napoleon Buonaparte had landed in Egypt with the deliberate intention of invading India. It was generally believed that a French fleet was in the Red Sea on its way to Bombay. It was no time for dilly-dallying. Lord Mornington demanded from Tipu, by Colonel Doveton, a full explanation. Tipu sought time in vain for negociations, and begged immediate aid from the French; and he wrote to Zemán Sháh, the Afghán prince who had crossed the Indus and reached Láhur, to join him in a war of extermination against the infidels. In vain did Lord Mornington assure him that the French fleet had been destroyed in the bay of Aboukir by Admiral Nelson; Tipu was inflexible, and the fourth Mysur war began.

A magnificently equipped army advanced against Mysur in February 1799, under the command of General Harris. Tipu was astonished at the mighty forces arrayed against him. He remembered his former fear of these people who brought their operations to a conclusion by means which he could not see. His generalship deserted him. His army was defeated; the English crossed the Káwari by an unknown ford, and invested him in Saringapatam. On the third day he sued for peace, but the English terms were enormous; and with the brief reply that it was better to die a soldier than to live a puppet king, he prepared to fight to the death. The siege recommenced. On May 2nd the breach was practicable; and on the next day the fort was stormed by troops taken from the three Presidencies in the face of a terrible resistance. It was not easy to restrain the English troops from indiscriminate vengeance, for Tipu had a way of murdering his prisoners, and twelve had been slaughtered the night before. Tipu died a soldier's death, and his body was found beneath a gateway. Crashing peals of thunder mingled with the roar of the English guns that were fired in salute over his grave.

The Governor-General expressed to Mr. Jonathan Duncan, the Governor of Bombay, his appreciation of the merits of Generals Stuart and Hartley and other Bombay officers. He wrote that the distinguished part which the Presidency of Bombay had borne during the late crisis in the labours and honours of the common cause, had repeatedly claimed his warm approbation, and would ever be remembered by him with gratitude and respect. "In your liberal and voluntary contribution," his letter proceeded, "towards the exigencies of your native country and towards the defence of the Presidency under whose government you reside, in the alacrity with which you have given your personal services for the military protection of Bombay, I have contemplated with pleasure the same character of public spirit, resolution and activity which has marked the splendid successes of the army of Bombay from the commencement to the close of the late glorious campaign."

The home Government had fully approved of the policy of Lord Mornington. The title of Marquis of Wellesley was conferred on him, and General Harris was raised to the peerage. The family of Tipu was pensioned. So much of his dominions as had formed the ancient Hindu kingdom of Mysur was ruled by the English in the name of the real Rájá of the country, a boy five years of age, whose descendant now holds his dominions. The rest was divided between the English and the Nizám, the Nizám's portion reverting shortly to the English on condition of their strengthening their contingent at Hydarábád and protecting him from all oppression. The Peshwa and Sindia were astounded at the magnitude of the English success. The former anticipated a share of the partitioned kingdom, and made excuses for the inactivity of his troops in support of the English. The Governor-General was prepared to gratify the Peshwa's wishes; but, as he would not abate his claims on the Nizám, and only proposed to accept his share as a discharge of his claims for chauth on Mysur, Lord Wellesley brought the matter to a simple ending by the annulment of all the Peshwa's claims.

The Marquis of Wellesley's career in India, short as it had been, was already long enough to convince him of the hopelessness of the theory of balance of power. Things had come to such a pass that the permanent existence of the English in India depended upon their absolute supremacy. Lord Wellesley henceforward steadily acted on the assumption that in return for British protection each state must surrender its independence. All these incessant and intolerable wars were to be brought to a close; no state was to make wars or alliances, nor employ Europeans, not English, in their service without the consent of the paramount power. For the French intrigues were still rampant and French military adventurers abounded. Lord Wellesley's singularly clear military insight led him rather to over-estimate than under-value danger from this source, for his own splendid achievements led him to see what determined perseverance could effect. He may have also unduly dreaded the power of the Áfghán Zamán Khán, who had prayed him for help to drive Sindia out of Hindustán. To counteract the schemes of Napoleon Buonaparte and of the Áfghán prince there must be a united India, and where was the possibility of such a union apart from the absolute predominance of British rule? The Governor-General's plan then was that each of the larger states should maintain a force commanded by British officers, and cede in full sovereignty an assignment of territory for its maintenance. The Nizám had accepted the position. The Peshwa and Sindia had yet to be convinced of its necessity.

Both these potentates steadily behaved in a manner that hastened the day when their backs should bow beneath the British yoke. In March 1800 Nána Farnáwis died. "With him," wrote Colonel Palmer the British resident, "has departed all the wisdom and moderation of the Marátha government." He had been a great statesman, and shown himself a worthy and honourable foe of the British Government. He watched with a keen and jealous eye the progress of their arms, and had consistently opposed the admission of a body of English troops. For twenty-five years he had conducted with ability the internal affairs of the Peshwa's empire. But the last portion of his life was embittered by the intrigues which hurled him from power; and, though he died in harness, his reputation was sullied and his influence dimmed. Weakened as his power was, its loss soon made itself felt. Disorder was supreme in the Deccan. Ghatge was pursuing his brutal cruelties wherever it pleased him; the Rája of Kolhápur was at war with the Peshwa, while a military adventurer of the time named Dhondia Wág, who had passed from Tipu's service to that of Kolhápur, was now plundering on his own account.

Dhondia Wág's proceedings passed the bounds of all endurance. The Peshwa was too much occupied with Sindia to be able to check him. A British force was therefore sent after him—with scant recognition of the Peshwa's independent sovereignty—under Major-General Arthur Wellesley, brother of the Governor-General, who had already foreshadowed the reputation that he was to gain at Waterloo as a Colonel in the last Mysur war. He pursued Dhondia Wág for four months; and at last, in September 1800, brought him to an action in which he was cut down in a charge of the 19th Dragoons.

Since Nána's death Sindia exercised complete control over the Peshwa, and Báji Rao watched with secret joy the rise of a rival in Hindustán whose progress would inevitably summon his oppressor away from Puna. This was Yeshwant Rao Holkar, the half-brother of the idiot whom Sindia had placed on the throne of Tukáji, and of the other brother whom he had murdered. Yeshwant Rao betook himself to the jungles, and rapidly gathered around him a horde of such as delighted in war, and scorned to work when it was possible to plunder. He soon had an army of 20,000 men, and he was joined by the Chevalier Dudrenec and his battalion. It was not long before he directed his energies against the dominions of Sindia, and Sindia was compelled to leave Puna for the defence of his own districts. An obstinate war ensued, and numerous bloody battles were fought with varying success. At last, in October 1802, fortune favoured Holkar, who attacked Sindia's possessions in Khándesh, and extended his operations almost to Puna; and he gave out that as head of the house of Holkar he meant to protect the Peshwa from the usurpation of Daolat Rao Sindia.

Báji Rao had been delighted at getting rid of Sindia. But when left to himself he showed that other occupations were more to his taste than so serious a business as the administration and consolidation of his empire. He preferred to pass his time in destroying and robbing all such families as he believed to have been at any time opposed to his interests. Among his victims was Wituji, brother of Yeshwant Rao, who had been taken prisoner during the war. Wituji was brought before the Peshwa and tied to the foot of an elephant, and Báji Rao looked on gleefully as the animal dragged off its shrieking victim to a lingering death in the public streets. He was therefore hardly prepared to welcome Yeshwant Rao when he appeared before his capital. In his consternation he besought the aid of the British Government; but the only terms on which they would give it were those prescribed in the case of the Nizám, and these he refused to accept. It only remained to fight; and when the united forces of the Peshwa and Sindia marched out for battle on October 25th, Báji Rao felt that he might yet be saved. The combat was terrific. Holkar himself headed charge after charge; the impetuosity of his attacks at length broke through Sindia's disciplined battalions, and the rest of the army fled. The spoil was immense, the victor obtaining the whole of the guns and stores of the defeated army. Báji Rao fled to the fort of Singahr; and in his despair sent a letter to Colonel Close, the new resident at Puna, professing his willingness to conclude a treaty with the English for the maintenance of six battalions of sepoys. He then went to Máhár, near the old English settlement of Dasgaum, and applied to the Presidency of Bombay for ships to take him and his followers to that Island. Mr. Jonathan Duncan, who was Governor from 1795 to 1811, possessed a clear and acute intellect. He had been a civilian in Bengal; and had, as Commissioner of Banáras, done valuable service in checking the prevailing social crime of infanticide of female children. As Governor of Bombay he continued this useful work in Kachh, Guzárát, Málwa and Rájputána; and though the cruel rite was by no means stamped out, the thin edge of the wedge was introduced by which it has since been eradicated, and many children were preserved by Governor Duncan's efforts. He saw the importance of this crisis. Báji Rao went to Rewadanda, a modern village on the site of Chául, and thence sailing to Bombay was received by Mr. Duncan on December 6th. After a few days' stay he proceeded to Bassein, where he was followed by Colonel Close, and by December 31st 1801 the treaty of Bassein was completed. Lord Wellesley considered that the state of things afforded a most favourable opportunity for the complete establishment of the interests of the British power in the Marátha empire. The Peshwa was no longer in a position to discuss the terms which the English offered him. Like the Nizám he professed his readiness to cede territory for the maintenance of a force of 6,000 regular infantry, together with proportionate artillery, to be stationed in his dominions. He was to allow no Europeans, not English, within his territories, and to have no intercourse with native states without the consent of the Governor-General. His claims on the Nizám and on the Gaikwár were to be settled by the British Government, and with regard to the latter he recognised the convention lately drawn up between the British and Ánand Rao Gaikwár. The increasing disorder throughout Guzárát had compelled the interference of the Governor of Bombay. In 1799 the Nawáb of Surat died. The English had long held the castle; but the revenues and possession of the city had been for many years shared between the Nawáb, the Maráthas, including the Gaikwár and the Peshwa, and the English. Commissioned by the Governor-General, Mr. Duncan proceeded to Surat, assumed sole charge of the city, and pensioned the Nawáb's brother who was the heir to the Nawábship. Gowind Rao Gaikwár assented to this arrangement, merely provising that the Peshwa's consent was necessary. This was now obtained. But meanwhile

Gowind Rao died, and the English supported his eldest son, Ánand Rao, against various claimants to the throne who took the field in support of their claims. Considerable force had to be exercised to reduce the insurgent forces. The Arab mercenaries, who had for some time ruled at Baroda, made extravagant demands for arrears of pay and seized the person of Ánand Rao. A European regiment was sent from Bombay to Baroda. The town was invested by Colonel Woodington, and taken after a ten days' siege. The finances of the Baroda Government were in hopeless confusion, and the whole province was in a state of anarchy. The result was inevitable. The Bombay Government took the matter in hand. Five battalions were subsidised; and, like his master the Peshwa, Ánand Rao Gaikwár became a vassal of the British Government, and his dominions were speedily brought into order. This arrangement was ratified by Báji Rao in the treaty of Bassein. In short, he yielded up his authority and his suzerainty over the great Marátha houses in order to be secured in the semblance of his ancient dignity. The cup was a bitter one. In his humiliation he had to drain it; should fortune change, he meant to cast it from him.

Sindia was deeply mortified at the execution of the treaty of Bassein. The treaty of Sálbai had been negociated by the late head of his house. Here was a treaty in which his existence had been absolutely ignored, and which was in defiance of the old Marátha policy that come what might they would have no foreign intervention. He was still more incensed when Lord Wellesley proposed to form a similar arrangement with himself, and he perceived that the encroachments of the English threatened the very foundations of Marátha power. Raghoji Bhonsle of Barár was imbued with similar sentiments. Both of them gave evasive replies to the Governor-General's overtures, while they endeavoured to form a wide confederacy against their common foe. If Yeshwant Rao Holkar would join them their way would be clearer. But Yeshwant Rao prepared to watch the course of events, and throw in his lot with the winner. Baji Rao, however, alarmed at the action of the vast machinery which he had put in motion, entered into secret correspondence with Sindia and Barár, encouraging their plans at the very moment when a British force was about to replace him on his throne.

The conspiracy was formidable enough, but its gravity was immensely increased in the Governor-General's view by the presence of French intrigues and French officers. An intense hostility to the designs of France, the danger of which he possibly over-rated, was the keynote of Lord Wellesley's policy. Napoleon had in 1800 landed in Egypt, and there was no reason why the attempt should not be repeated. Lord Wellesley had himself sent an expedition of 7,000 troops from Bombay to Suez under Sir David Baird, who made a memorable march across the desert and descended the Nile to Rosetta. The conclusion of peace with France prevented their meeting the French troops in action, but the fame of the expedition increased the estimate of British power in India. Bombay had been in no little excitement and alarm and, stimulated by the supposed urgency of the danger, the patriotism of the citizens had provided Government with the money needed for its operations. The revenues of the Doáb, or land between the Ganges and the Jumna, were still collected by French officers for the maintenance of the French battalions of Sindia under Perron; and Broach, the port at the mouth of the Narbada, was in Sindia's possession. Lord Wellesley pictured to himself the possibility, if not the likelihood, of a French army landing at Broach, and co-operating with Perron at Ágra to achieve a French conquest of Hindustán.

Lord Wellesley had complete information as to the doings of Sindia and his allies. They would not ratify the treaty of Bassein; so he proceeded to put it in force with a strong hand without reference to their pleasure, and to replace the Peshwa at Puna. The Hydarábád subsidiary force, under Colonel Stevenson, accompanied by 1,500 of the Nizám's regular troops, took up a position on the river Sina that formed the eastern boundary of the Peshwa's dominions. Major-General Arthur Wellesley was detached from the Madras army that was guarding the borders of Mysur. He marched towards Puna with 8,000 infantry and 1,700 cavalry, adding to his strength on the way 10,000 horse contributed by the feudatories of the Southern Marátha Country, to aid in the Peshwa's restoration. The length of his march was nearly six hundred miles, in the worst season of the year, through a country which had been destroyed by Holkar's army. But he travelled with heavy guns an average of thirteen-and-a-half miles a day. Holkar meanwhile, and his son Amrat Rao, whom he chose to proclaim as Peshwa in Báji Rao's absence, had been mercilessly plundering the unfortunate inhabitants of Puna, and the country round was devastated. But neither of them awaited the arrival of the British troops, Holkar retreating to Málwa and his son to Násik. General Wellesley however, hearing that they were likely to burn Puna, made a forced march of sixty miles in thirty-two hours up to the city; but on his arrival on April 20th he found it evacuated. Amrat Rao subsequently joined the British troops.

On May 13th 1803 the Peshwa, escorted by British troops, reached Puna from Bassein, and was placed upon his throne with every ceremony of rejoicing. To mark the happy occasion, a salute of nineteen guns was fired at Bombay and the principal military stations of the Company.

While Holkar was watching the issue of events from a distance, and rejecting overtures from Sindia and the English alike, the attitude of the confederates Sindia and Barár became more and more threatening. The Governor-General called upon Sindia for a definite explanation of his intentions, and at the same time made every preparation for war. He replied that he could not make an explicit declaration until he had met the Rája of Barár; after meeting him he would inform the resident at his court whether it would be peace or war. The reply was sufficiently menacing; but commentary was needless when Sindia's army advanced to the borders of the Nizám's territory and Bhonsle's forces took up a position near his camp. But a further period of grace was accorded the confederates. Colonel Stevenson crossed to the north of the Godáwari and General Wellesley moved to within a few miles from Áhmadnagar. The Governor-General appointed his brother plenipotentiary for all political and military matters in the Deccan; and between General Wellesley and the Marátha chieftains a prolonged series of negociations ensued. They professed friendly intentions which their conduct belied; and in a remarkably able document General Wellesley told them that if they meant anything by their professions of good will they must withdraw their troops within their own borders, upon which he promised in like manner to withdraw the British troops. The only answer to this proposal could be "yes" or "no;" a subterfuge attempting to evade compliance could not but be regarded as a refusal. General Wellesley's reply speaks for itself. "Your Highness," he wrote, "will recollect that the British Government did not threaten to commence hostilities against you; you threatened to commence hostilities against the British Government and its allies; and when called on to explain your intentions, you declared it was doubtful whether there would be peace or war; and in conformity with your threats and declared doubts you assembled a large army in a station contiguous to the Nizám's frontier. On this ground I called upon you to withdraw that army to its usual station if your subsequent pacific declarations were sincere; but instead of complying with this reasonable request you propose that I should withdraw the troops which are intended to protect the territories of our allies against your designs; and that you and the Rája of Barár should be suffered to remain with your troops assembled in readiness to take advantage of their absence. This proposition is unreasonable and inadmissable, and you must stand the consequences of the measures which I find myself compelled to adopt in order to repel your aggression. I offered you peace on terms of equality, and honourable to all parties; you have chosen war and are responsible for the consequences."

The Governor-General was fully prepared for war and he resolved to strike his enemy on every side at once. To General Lake he intrusted the task of occupying Sindia's possessions between the Jumna and the Ganges, and of crushing the battalions disciplined by De Boigne and his successor Perron. Colonel Woodington was sent against Broach and Sindia's forts in the direction of Guzárát; on the other side of India, Colonel Harcourt invaded Katak and the remainder of the Barár Rája's territories, while General Wellesley and Colonel Stevenson had to deal with the main body of Sindia's army in the Deccan. Lord Wellesley had led a splendidly equipped force against Mysur. His present forces were arrayed on a more stupendous scale, and his armies were sent into the field with resources hitherto unknown in Indian warfare. His wise selection of leaders, and his confidence in his agents, roused the enthusiasm of all to the highest pitch. The various British forces amounted to 55,000 men, of whom 8,930 were under the personal command of General Wellesley and 7,920 under Colonel Stevenson. The armies opposed to them were about double their number.

On the 3rd of August the resident withdrew from Sindia's camp, an act equivalent to a declaration of war. Wellesley was encamped at Wálki, eight miles south of Áhmadnagar; and, after a few days' delay caused by heavy rain, he marched against the city of Áhmad on the 8th of that month. He first took the town, which was surrounded by a mud wall and obstinately defended by Sindia's troops. The promptness of this proceeding filled the enemy with consternation. "Who could withstand a people," they said, "who came and looked at the city wall, walked over it, killed the garrison, and returned to breakfast?" On the 10th a battery was opened on the fortress which since the time of Chánd Bibi had the reputation of being almost impregnable. The firing was tremendous, and the commandant desired that it might cease while he treated for terms. He was told that what he chose to say would be heard, but that the firing would only cease when the fort was taken or surrendered. On the 12th it was surrendered. A large tamarind tree is still shown on the glacis under which General Wellesley breakfasted after the fort was given up. The general considered Áhmadnagar, from its strength and position, an excellent base of operations.

Sindia's intention was now to plunder the Nizám's districts towards Hydarábád, but General Wellesley's advance through Aurangábád prevented him from carrying out his plan. Neither Bhonsle nor Sindia were experienced or skilful strategists; and their views as to their operations clashed. The consequence was a series of feeble and inconsistent movements. When Wellesley moved down the Godáwari the Maráthas moved up; and while he was forced to await supplies Stevenson was equally unsuccessful in endeavouring to bring on an action. But on the 21st of September the whole of the Marátha army was encamped near the village of Bokardan; and the two English generals meeting on the same day agreed that they should move separately and attack the enemy on the 24th. On the 23rd Wellesley was about to encamp at the village of Nálni, when he learnt from his spies that the whole of the Marátha army was lying on the Kaitna river, not six miles from where he was. The force with him was only 4,500 men, but it included the 19th light Dragoons and the 74th and 78th Highlanders. This handful of men was opposed to more than ten times their number. But Wellesley knew that there was but one way to meet an Indian foe, and without waiting for Stevenson he instantly attacked the united armies of Sindia and Barár. Had he not done so, he said, he must have been surrounded by the superior cavalry of the enemy, his troops would have been starved, and he would have had nothing left, but to hang himself to his tent-poles. Sindia's cannon and infantry, which Wellesley meant to destroy, were on the Marátha left, near the village of Assaye,* his cavalry on their right, his whole force in the angle between two streams, the Kaitna and its tributary the Jua. The Kaitna was

---

* "This is he that far away,
Against the myriads of Assaye,
Clashed, with a fiery few, and won!"
—*Tennyson's* "*Ode on the death of the Duke of Wellington.*"

between Wellesley and the enemy; the English therefore had to cross that stream and cut their way to Assaye on the Jua. The confined space between the streams would be more suitable to the movements of a small body of troops than the enormous forces of the Marátbas, who were obliged to diminish their front when Wellesley threw his army across the river. As the British lines were forming in their new position a terrific cannonade was opened upon them. The cattle that drew their guns were killed and the guns disabled. To the officer that sent this information Wellesley coolly replied that he must manage to get on without them. The execution in the British ranks was fearful, and the 74th was almost annihilated by the cannonade and a charge of the Marátha horse. For the moment the outlook was gloomy. But Wellesley ordered his cavalry to advance; and with a British cheer the 19th Dragoons, followed closely by the 4th Native cavalry, who proved themselves worthy comrades, dashed at the Marátha horsemen. Cheered by the very wounded of the 74th, they utterly routed the horse and pressed on to the infantry and guns. The British infantry followed them well; the enemy gave way, and were thrust into the Jua at the point of the bayonet. One of the fiercest battles in Indian warfare was won. The result was as decisive as that of Plassey; but the fight was won over an enemy infinitely superior, and the British general lost a third of his forces in killed and wounded. Sindia and Barár fled from the field and left their troops to their fate.

Close to the general in this fight was a young civilian in the Company's service named Mountstuart Elphinstone, who by his coolness in action and thorough knowledge of the native languages attracted Wellesley's notice. He had been assistant to Colonel Close, the resident at Puna; and he was in that city when Wituji Holkar was murdered by Báji Rao, and at Bassein when the treaty was signed with the Peshwa. He subsequently had a most distinguished career, finally becoming Governor of Bombay; and he lived long enough to hear from his nephew Lord Elphinstone in 1858, the result of the Indian mutiny.

As soon as Stevenson joined Wellesley he was despatched in pursuit of the enemy towards the North. He took Burhánpur and reduced Asirgahr without much loss by October 21st, and officers from Hydarábád took charge of the Khándesh districts which thus fell to the disposal of the Company. Meanwhile, Colonel Woodington was equally successful in Guzárát. Broach was stormed and taken before the end of August, and the town and fort of Champaner by the middle of September. General Lake, too, won victory after victory over Sindia's forces in Hindustán under their latest leader Louis Bourquin; Perron having been ousted by intrigues and permitted by the English to retire to Chandarnagar, the French settlement near Calcutta. The fort of Aligahr was taken by extraordinary efforts. Lake defeated the Maráthás under the walls of Delhi and entered in triumph the city of the Great Moghal. Sháh Álam the aged emperor, who for fifteen years had been sightless, received the conqueror in the faded remnants of imperial state, and a second time received the protection of the Company. Lake's work was not yet done. He marched on Ágra and took it on October 18th, and in the most obstinate engagement of the campaign defeated the enemy at Laswári. The victory cost the English army 824 men in killed and wounded; but it overthrew the brigades of Sindia, and the British Government was supreme over Delhi and Ágra, and all Sindia's possessions north of the

Chambal. General Lake became Lord Lake of Delhi and Laswári. The conquest of Katak was effected with equal celerity.

General Wellesley followed up his great victory with spirit and enterprise. Raghoji Bhonsle turned to his own dominions, pursued by the British forces, whose object was to capture the great hill fortresses of Narnálla and Gáwilgahr. Stevenson after his operations in Khándesh rejoined Wellesley in the Deccan; and Sindia now deemed it advisable to sue for a cessation of arms until a permanent arrangement could be entered into. Wellesley granted an armistice until the 22nd of November on condition that Sindia should move considerably to the eastward. To the Rája of Barár no terms were granted. Sindia accepted the truce, but promptly broke its conditions; and the remnant of his forces united with Raghoj Bhonsle. It was necessary at once to crush their resistence, and Wellesley determined to attack them as soon as possible. On the afternoon of November 29th, when at the close of a long march he was halting to pitch his camp, he found himself suddenly opposed by the confederate forces. It was late in the day, but Wellesley declared that there was time enough before night to take the Marátha guns. When night fell thirty-eight of their guns and all their ammunition were in his hands. The defeat of the enemy was complete, and had daylight lasted an hour longer not a man would have escaped. But the English were at one time during the fight in serious danger. "The Native infantry were panic-struck," Wellesley wrote, "and got into confusion when the cannonade commenced. What do you think of nearly three entire battalions who behaved so admirably in the battle of Assaye, being broke and running off when the cannonade commenced at Árgaum, which was not to be compared to that at Assaye? Luckily I happened to be at no great distance from them; and I was able to rally them and re-establish the battle. If I had not been there, I am convinced we should have lost the day. But as it was, so much time elapsed before I could form them again that we had not daylight enough for everything that we should have certainly performed." Elphinstone was again close to Wellesley throughout the fight, and during the subsequent laborious operations by which the stupendous fortress of Gáwilgahr was captured. At this siege Wellesley told him that he had mistaken his profession and ought to have been a soldier. The Maráthas were now thoroughly disheartened and negociations opened in earnest. On December 17th Raghoji Bhonsle Rája of Barár ceded Katak including Bálásur, the whole of Barár lying west of the Warda river, and resigned all claims on the Nizám. Elphinstone, who was only twenty-four, was appointed resident to the Rája, such was the confidence that General Wellesley had in his tact and judgment. Daolat Rao Sindia endeavoured in vain to resist the English demands. On being told that failure to comply with them would be followed by the annexation of all his dominions, he agreed, on December 30th, to accept the terms offered. He relinquished the territory between the Ganges and the Jumna and all but two districts in Rájputána. The forts of Áhmadnagar and Broach with their districts and his possessions on the Godáwari all went; and he resigned all claims on the Moghal emperor, the British Government, the Peshwa, the Nizám, the Gaikwár, or other allies. He agreed to exclude Europeans other than English from his dominions. Major Malcolm, another future Governor of Bombay, was appointed resident. Burhánpur and Asirgahr were restored to Sindia, and he still held a large and compact territory in Central India centring on

Gwálior. In the month of February 1804, by a new article in this treaty, he accepted a defensive alliance.

The first Marátha war had lasted seven years. The whole of the operations in the second were completed in four months and four days. It had been carried on simultaneously in four parts of India, hundreds of miles away from each other with steady and brilliant success. The British Government obtained a vast increase of territory, but chiefly in the North and East of India, a few districts near Surat and Bánkapur in the Southern Marátha Country being ceded to the Peshwa in return for his claims on the new acquisition of Bandalkand. The Nizám gained greatly by this war, the province of Barár being assigned to him as a free gift. But the Peshwa, having failed to furnish the aid which he could have afforded, and having otherwise gained immensely by the campaign, received only the fort and district of Áhmadnagar.

On the 13th of March 1804 Major-General Wellesley made a triumphant entry into Bombay, arriving in the Governor's yacht from Panwel. Mr. Duncan and his Council made splendid preparations to welcome the successful soldier. Bombay had passed through an anxious time. For years past her citizens had been incessantly on the alert for the arrival of a French fleet in their harbour. The period of suspense was at last gone by, and the dream of a French empire in Hindustán was passed and gone. A great storm had wrecked every ship in the harbour and destroyed hundreds of lives; a fire had made havoc of their city; famine had raged in their midst; and in 1802 one of the English sepoys had shot dead the Persian ambassador in their streets. But prosperity was returning to the city and Arthur Wellesley had delivered them from all possibility of danger from without. In reply to the congratulations on his successful campaign, he informed the citizens of Bombay that it was peculiarly gratifying to him to have been instrumental in renewing the benefits of peace to a settlement, from the resources and public spirit of which the departments under his command had derived the most essential aids during the prosecution of the war.

The Duke of Wellington, as he was to be, has left on record some memorable words on the condition of the country. It was a time of misery and oppression, deceit and subterfuge. "From the Peshwa," he wrote, "to the lowest cooly in the bazaar in Puna, there is not a Marátha in whom it is possible to rely that he will perform any engagement upon which he enters unless urged to the performance by his fears." Puna he described as a country which deserved the name of a desert. Famine raged in the Deccan. Habits of industry were out of the question and men had to plunder for subsistence, be destroyed or starve. "There was no law," he said, " no civil government, and no army to keep plunderers in order. No revenue could be collected; no inhabitant could or would remain to cultivate unless protected by an armed force stationed in his village." Báji Rao's government was that of a robber, the Peshwa being callous to everything except money and revenge. In fact, as Sir James Mackintosh, the recorder of Bombay, expressed it, it is difficult to see for what taxes were paid except to bribe the sovereign not to murder or rob the inhabitants. There was no justice save what the system of village communities supplied. The disorder at that time was only an exaggerated phase of its usual and ordinary state. Of Bombay Wellesley wrote, on the other hand, oblivious of some disagreements that he had had with its Government, "This island has now (1804) become the only place of security, in this part of

India, for property and for those who are the subjects of the Peshwa's enmity and vengeance, a circumstance equally honourable to the character of the British nation and advantageous to their interests, and affording the strongest proof of the confidence which the natives repose in the justice and wisdom of our policy and our laws."

In addition to the advantages gained by the war, a further subsidiary treaty of general defensive alliance was concluded at Baroda in April 1805 with Ánand Rao Gaikwár. By various agreements, in 1802 the Guzárát chief had agreed to maintain a contingent of 2,000 men. The force was now raised to 5,000, and districts yielding nearly 12 lakhs of rupees (£120,000) assigned for their support. The districts included Chawrássi, Chikli and Kaira, together with the share of the revenues of Surat which the Gaikwár had received before. Further, no European was to be received into his service, and no act of aggression to be committed against any other power without the sanction of the British Government. Colonel Walker, the resident, directed the affairs of Baroda with singular ability. Thus, at the close of the war, the Bombay Presidency was still very small as compared with Bengal and Madras. The Company's frontier to the east was the fort of Thána on the borders of Salsette, not twenty-five miles from Bombay. In the Konkan they only possessed Fort Victoria at Bánkot, and a few villages for its maintenance which they had held for more than half a century. Above the Ghâts they possessed nothing in what is now Bombay. In Guzárát they had obtained a considerable number of places, but the districts were scattered and far apart. In the South the Company held Kánara with the port of Kárwár, but it formed part of the Madras Presidency.

XVI.—BRITISH SUPREMACY.

WHEN the second Marátha war broke out Holkar had declared his intention of standing aloof from either side. His proceedings afterwards were singularly short-sighted, and foreshowed the insanity which seized him in 1808 and lasted till his death in 1811. Far from taking warning at the crushing defeat inflicted on Sindia, and avoiding a like fate himself, he openly rejoiced at his rival's discomfiture. He determined, as he expressed it, "to fight Lake," and take the place of Sindia in Hindustán. His army was a nucleus for all the disbanded soldiery of the defeated confederates; and they reaped a golden harvest of plunder in Málwa and the Rájput States. Yéshwant Rao had therefore to be put down. General Lake moved into Rájputána and a successful beginning was made before the rainy season. But Colonel Monson, who had gained a great reputation in the previous campaign, wished to effect a junction with Colonel Murray, who was advancing from Guzárát. He proceeded without due caution into Holkar's territory, only to find that Murray was retiring towards Guzárát, and that Holkar was advancing against him in great force. His own supplies were exhausted and could not be replenished. Monson's sole chance of extricating himself from his difficulty was at once to attack the superior forces of the enemy. But he adopted that course which invariably fails, retreat before an Asiatic foe. His retrograde movement stimulated the courage and ardour of Holkar's troops, who attacked him on every side. For three days he retreated in fair order with his baggage and guns, bravely repelling the overwhelming numbers of the enemy. But the rains had set in, and the ground was soft; he was compelled to abandon his baggage, spike his guns, and destroy his ammunition. The wearied troops pursued their retreat, but were allowed no rest by the jubilant enemy; and during their march, on a dark night, they were thrown into hopeless confusion. The retreat became a flight, and the shattered remains of the British force reached Ágra by the end of August.

Lord Wellesley was amazed when he heard of the disaster. As usual in India, the slightest reverse to the British arms raised a host of enemies on every side; and the protected princes began to think that they might yet break the bonds of British supremacy. Yéshwant Rao, who was compared to Shiwáji, marched against Delhi; but his attempt in October to take it and seize the emperor was gallantly resisted by Colonel Ochterlony. Holkar left Delhi and burst into the Doáb harrying and wasting the country. But General Lake was on his track, and his pursuit was as persistent and effective as that of Monson by Holkar had been vindictive. At the battle of Dig, Holkar's forces were routed with a loss of 2,000 men and 87 guns, while the British loss was 643. General Monson, by his splendid bravery in the battle, restored to his name the lustre which his former retreat had sullied. Holkar's troops moved eastward to Farakábád, but Lake overtook them and routed them with a loss of 3,000 of their number. Holkar threw himself into the fort of Dig by December 13th, but Lake took the fort. Holkar himself escaped; and instead of pursuing him, which might have been the wiser course, Lake, in January 1805, laid siege to the strong fort of Bhartpur, whose Rája had signed a treaty that made him a vassal of the British Government, but who had broken through it on the news of Monson's defeat. A large number of Holkar's guns and the remnant of his army were within the fort. Four months were wasted before its huge mud walls, into which the cannon-balls sank harmlessly. In February the Bombay division, under General Jones, joined the Bengal army; and in furious assaults, before and after their arrival, the English lost 3,200 in killed and wounded. The walls were unshaken, but the Marátha troops were incessantly defeated without the fortress. The Rája of Bhartpur realised that he had made a mistake, and seing that their failures were only stimulating the English to fresh exertions he offered terms. He was readmitted into the number of protected princes on payment of £200,000.

Lake moved in pursuit of Holkar, who seemed likely to be joined by Sindia at the urgent entreaties of his brutal father-in-law Ghatge. But Sindia's heart was not in the work; his troops fell back to Ájmir, followed by those of Holkar, over whom Lake was winning victory after victory.

Lord Wellesley would in fact have shortly brought the whole war to a triumphant conclusion. But while his successes had silenced the rising murmurs of the Directors against his forward policy, his first failure was followed by an overwhelming opposition; and in July 1805 the aged Lord Cornwallis arrived at Calcutta with instructions to undo all that the brave and far-seeing Wellesley had done.

The rule of Lord Wellesley was a memorable and glorious one. While India in no sense formed a country or a nation, so neither did the ever-changing states and powers within its borders form nations or powers that could be compared to those of Europe. Some of the reigning Rájput families had in truth ruled for generations prior to the coming of Alexander, three centuries before the Christian era. But such a state of things was entirely exceptional. The empire of Bábar was not yet 300 years old and it had long since crumbled into dust. The viceroys of his empire had formed themselves into independent princes and in their turn were set aside by subjects stronger than themselves. Whatever the origin of European kingdoms, they as a general rule formed societies, in which for a long series of generations the rulers and the people had been one in interest, race, religion, and custom; and to greater or less extent the rulers were the representatives of the people. In India there was nothing of the kind. The existing powers had one and all sprung up since the coming of the English themselves. They were all founded on wrong and robbery, on the simple principle of the spoils to the strongest. Their dominions extended as far as their arms could be carried, their subjects were as many as they could compel by force to obey them. The idea of a government existing for the benefit of its subjects would have been altogether ludicrous. These rulers were ever engaged in war and plunder, and for the very existence of the East India Company it was necessary that this anarchy on its borders should cease. Non-intervention had failed, the balance of power between such seething and shifting forces was absurd and preposterous. Lord Wellesley saw that one course only was possible, and that the English must recognise themselves as the paramount power and with a strong hand put down aggressive warfare and tumult among the rest.

But the Court of Directors at home thought otherwise. They were criminally ignorant of the real condition of India; they shut their eyes to palpable facts. British supremacy was to them a bug-bear. They preferred to remain merchants, dwelling on sufferance on the coasts of the Arabian sea and the Bay of Bengal, to building up a vast empire by expensive military operations. Lord Wellesley's policy was to be reversed; but it was not to be replaced by the balance of power—that humiliation was insufficient—and absolute non-intervention was again to come into force. It is difficult to read of such madness and cowardice without a feeling of shame and indignation. But if the Court of Directors stand condemned at the bar of history, what can be said of Lord Cornwallis, who condescended to do their bidding, who himself as Governor-General had taken command of a magnificent British army and crushed the robber chieftain of Mysur?

Fortunately for India Lord Cornwallis only lived two months, but in that short period he did his best to shatter his reputation as a statesman. He was succeeded by the senior member of Council, Sir George Barlow, who ruled for two years. He had supported Lord Wellesley's policy. He had now no choice except between resigning his office or reversing that policy. He preferred the sweets of office to the interests of the empire, and carried on Lord Cornwallis's retrograde work.

It is not pleasant to linger on the doings of Lord Cornwallis and Sir George Barlow. Sir John Malcolm was instructed to draw up a treaty with Holkar restoring him all his territories except the fort of Tonk Rámpura. But to the upholders of the new regime there was the gall of bitterness in this exception, and Tonk Rámpura was handed over to Holkar too. The alliances with the Rájas of Jaypur and Bundi were dissolved in spite of the earnest remonstrances of Lord Lake, who prophesied the punishment that would fall upon them for their services to the British. Sindia was conciliated by the restoration of Gohad and Gwálior, and all his territory except the Doáb. Delhi was an incumbrance to the British; and Lord Cornwallis proposed to give it up to Sindia and withdraw the emperor to Calcutta. All the sovereign states were to be left to themselves to fight with and plunder each other as they pleased while the English looked on at the imposing spectacle. As Sir George Barlow himself had formerly said, "The national interests of England in India are to rest upon the certain operation of contending and circumscribed interests among the states, whose independence will admit of the individual views of rapine, incroachment, and ambition."

Holkar felt like a prisoner released from his chains. He at once set to work to extort enormous sums from our ally the Rája of Jaypur. In vain could the Rája appeal to Lord Lake. His hands were tied by non-intervention, and in his disgust he resigned his political functions. Lake had promised protection to the Rája of Bundi if he withstood the advance of Holkar. The Rája had resisted him gallantly; but when Holkar ravaged his lands, the fetish of non-intervention prevented the English fulfilling their promise. Lake had to look on with folded hands, and eat his heart with rage and shame. Holkar in fact had a glorious opportunity of indulging the tastes of a wild beast, and he took advantage of it to the utmost. He put his own nephew and brother to death. He cast cannon and greatly increased his army. It was impossible to say to what extent his vagaries might not take him, when his excesses brought on furious madness, and he was placed in restraint until his death in 1811. Tulsi Bai, his mistress, became regent in the name of an adopted child, Malhar Rao Holkar; and bloodshed and anarchy prevailed in the provinces, bribery, intrigue, and murder at the court.

Sir George Barlow had probably some difficulty in digesting the dish that he had prepared. But not even he had drunk to the dregs the Company's policy of self-effacement, and the Directors declared that they would be satisfied with nothing less than the restoration of all territories conquered during the war. This was more than even Barlow could stomach, and he pointed out that such a course would let loose Marátha hordes who would make a desperate struggle to overturn British power in India. The remaining Native chiefs on their part thought it only their due to receive the same liberal treatment granted to Holkar, and the Rája of Barár now generally known as the Rája of Nágpur, from the name of his capital, was bitterly aggrieved that Barlow would not restore him Katak, which the Governor-General deemed essential to the defence of Bengal. One and all, they considered it expedient to open new schemes. At the instigation of the Nizám, the Peshwa, whose very existence depended on the English, plotted with Sindia and Holkar to get rid of their control. Sir George Barlow's eyes were opened to the suicidal nature of his policy, and the new league was promptly suppressed. He did not much longer hold his great office. A horrible mutiny occured at Vellore in Madras, involving the slaughter of the European garrison while they were asleep. Lord William Bentinck, the Governor of Madras — whose injudicious measures had paved the way for it — was recalled, and Sir George Barlow took his place.

XVII.—PINDHÁRI OR THIRD MARÁTHA WAR.

WITH hardly an exception, all Governors-General of India have come out intent upon a peaceful policy. The great majority of them have been compelled to make war. Lord Minto, who arrived in July 1807, was no exception to the rule. He found disorder and anarchy ripe in Bandalkand. Barlow had let things take their course. Lord Minto allowed his common-sense to assert itself; and, declaring that the British Government had no resource but to interfere for the suppression of intestine disorder, sent General Martindell to subdue the fortresses and suppress the banditti. Nor was Bandalkand the only scene of the revival of an intelligent policy. Amir Khán, a Pathán, or Áfghán, and a decendant of the Áfghán soldiers of the empire prior to the Moghals, was a chieftain who had allied himself to Yeshwant Rao Holkar in his marauding expeditions, and now had great influence with Tulsi Bai, the regent for his successor. Besides a large number of his own tribe, he had gathered together a body of irregular horsemen known as Pindháris. The origin of these men is veiled in obscurity; but they were to the Maráthas what the carrion-crow is to the vulture. Their ranks were open to men of any and every caste, and their only bond was that of plunder. They had fought, in large numbers, on the side of the Maráthas at the fatal field of Pánipat. Ranging themselves under the great chiefs, they were known as Sindia and Holkar's Pindháris; and it was often convenient to despatch them on errands of murder and rapine, and then disown responsibility for their actions. The Pindháris were fiends in human shape: Their very name was a terror to the peaceful population. Marching in bands, thirty or forty miles a day, they burnt, plundered, ravished, and slew in every direction. Acting on a regularly-devised plan, their various parties spread over the country, each in its allotted direction, to unite when their work was accomplished and carry home their booty. To extort money, they invented the most awful tortures. The head of their victim was thurst into a bag for feeding horses filled with red-hot ashes, or oil was smeared over his clothes and fire set to them. Sindia and Holkar might be at peace, but these wretches devastated the unhappy country; and Sindia and Amir Khán began to look to them as the basis for building up a new predatory power. The Peshwa's sole idea was to gain all that he could for himself from the combination. In 1809 Amir Khán, having exhausted his preserves nearer home, led his marauding hordes into the territory of the Rája of Barár; and there was no likelihood that his ravages would be limited to that territory. The state of things was intolerable, and Lord Minto put it down. Amir Khán was checked and driven back to Holkar's territory; but Lord Minto's conscience smote him for having disobeyed the non-intervention policy, and in that territory the Pindháris were still allowed to work their will. The Court of Directors, however, with strange inconsistency, censured the Governor-General for leaving his work undone.

He had done something, if not enough. In another case he did nothing. A horrible and desolating war raged between the Rájput kings of Udaipur and Jaypur. The former in his distress applied to the British for aid, using the very argument of Lord Wellesley, that without a paramount power in India there could be no peace, and that no one but the English could act as such a power. But non-intervention stood in the way of granting the prayer, and a great tragedy caused indignation through Western India.

England was still engaged in the long struggle with France. The chimera of a French empire in India was dissolved; but France had occupied Portugal and overrun Holland. So Goa and the other Portuguese settlements in India were garrisoned for the time by British troops, and Lord Minto led a successful expedition against the French in Java, and took possession of the island. The orders of the Court of Directors were that the island should be abandoned in the event of its capture. Lord Minto, with the courage which he frequently but not invariably showed, declined to comply with the request. On his return to India he again found himself compelled to deal with the Pindháris. Emboldened by their success, these loathsome ruffians had spread into British territory plundering unchecked as far as Gáya. Lord Minto, in his bitterness, asked the Court of Directors if he was still to observe neutrality and "refuse to listen to the calls of suffering humanity, and interfere to protect weak native states who call upon us for assistance." Year by year these savages had been increasing in numbers and daring, and spreading desolation over more and more distant countries. The Directors had paid little heed to them, but the invasion of their own provinces opened their eyes to the necessity of at least checking their irruptions. But it was reserved to the Governor-General's successor to stamp them out. Lord Minto left India in 1813, after an efficient administration of the British provinces, and in the belief that there was not a cloud in the sky except the Pindháris.

But Lord Minto was deceived. For there was then rolling up and gathering force a thunderstorm which was shortly to dash down from its pedestal the throne that Shiwáji had founded. Ever since his restoration by their armies, Báji Rao's chief occupation had been to plot against the British. He kept secret agents at the courts of the chiefs who had formed the confederacy against the English; and ascribed his connection with that Government to a deplorable necessity which he trusted would soon come to an end. He had a passion for intrigue and was an adept in the acts of deceit. His engaging manners exercised a persuasive influence over those with whom he had to do, and wormed from them a confidence which he bestowed on none. After dissimulation, his greatest passion was revenge. With short-sighted policy he incited to internecine struggles his feudatory chiefs in the South, who had incurred his dislike or whose loyalty to himself be doubted. He even stirred up the independent Rája of Kolhápur against the vassals of his own empire. The result was an incessant warfare that desolated the whole country. The wild tribe of Bhils had given some trouble in the north of Áhmadnagar. Finding it impossible to reduce them by force, Báji Rao on pretence of a settlement had the whole tribe enticed to an interview at Kopargaum where they were seized and thrown into wells. The Bhils of Khándesh in revenge ravaged the rich plains in the valley of the Tápti. This was only an instance of the treatment constantly extended to the Bhils by the Maráthas. A similar atrocity was perpetrated at Dharamgaum in Khándesh. Hundreds were enticed into a building, of which the doors were closed, and fire set to it and its living contents.

As far as outward appearances went the relations between the British resident and the Peshwa's court were of the most cordial nature. Báji Rao professed warm gratitude to the British Government and friendship to Colonel Close. But he never ceased to engage in plots and conspiracies to free himself from their toils. It is probable that Colonel Close was not thoroughly aware of what was going on. In 1810 he was transferred to the important charge of Hydarábád; and Mountstuart Elphinstone, who had been his assistant in 1802, and had since been on an important mission to Kábul, was after a short interval appointed to succeed him in 1811. With an intimate acquaintance with the native languages, Elphinstone possessed a thorough knowledge of the Marátha character, and he proved himself eminently capable of dealing with the hot-bed of intrigue around him.

One of the first questions that Elphinstone had to settle was the relation of the Peshwa to his feudatory chiefs of the South, whom he was doing his best to rob and ruin. A tolerable settlement was arrived at by the resident's firmness. Some of the chiefs were not unnaturally averse to acknowledging obedience to such a master as Báji Rao; and Elphinstone had to assemble an army at Pandharpur and march to the neighbourhood of the Krishna before they could be brought into any degree of order. The service of their troops as due to the Peshwa was enforced, lands that they had usurped were restored, and they were secured in the enjoyment of their just rights.

In 1812 it was resolved to make a final effort to stamp out once for all the pirates on the Western Coast. The chief offenders were the Rájas of Kolhápur and Sáwantwári. Báji Rao secretly encouraged the Rája of Kolhápur to resist the English demands, and in order to create delay informed the resident that the Rája of Kolhápur was his subject, a statement absolutely untrue. The Rája was compelled to cede the harbour and fort of Málwán on the Ratnagiri coast, and to renounce piracy for good and all, the British Government guaranteeing his possessions. The chief of Sáwantwari by a similar engagement delivered up the fort of Wingurla, and the curse of piracy came to an end. In securing this result admirable work was done by the Indian Navy as also subsequently in the task of rooting out the pirates that infested the Persian Gulf and Red Sea. This navy, which formed the police of the Indian seas, was abolished after the mutiny, when the Imperial Navy undertook the duties which it had performed.

The southern feudatories of the Peshwa had been compelled to bow their necks to his yoke, and Báji Rao, to cease from ruining them; but he had no liking for the troops that they were bound to provide for him. He applied to the English Government to be allowed to raise a brigade of infantry to be disciplined by English officers and regularly paid like sepoys in the British service. The proposition was readily accepted, and Captain Ford who had commanded Colonel Close's escort, was selected as commandant. The force was cantoned four miles to the north-west of Puna. One brigade of British troops was stationed close to the city, while the rest of the subsidiary force was at Sirur, half way between Puna and Áhmadnagar. Báji Rao's action in raising this brigade did not appear inconsistent with good faith to the English. But it was designed to aggrandise his position with them, and pave the way for his ambitious schemes. He gained a further occasion for improving his position by the action of Mr. Elphinstone himself, who pressed upon his attention the inadequacy of the force maintained to protect the country from the Pindháris. It happened that about this time a low retainer of Báji Rao by name Trimbakji

Dainglia, who was originally a spy, had gained the confidence of the Peshwa, and secured his favour by pandering to his vices. This man detested the English. He had risen to be chief director of the Peshwa's councils, and was now appointed his minister in his relations with the British Government. Báji Rao trusted this man as he never trusted anyone else; and beneath his influence his designs against the English gained strength and definiteness. Trimbakji, unscrupulous, treacherous, and violent, gained complete mastery over the Peshwa's mind, and secured immunity for whatever villainy he liked to perpetrate. He even killed with his own hand a rich and respectable Brahman banker, but no notice was taken of the action. By the advice of Trimbakji, Báji Rao prepared his way for rebellion against the English by greatly increasing his army, and consolidating his position as head of all the Maráthas. He was at this time possessed of immense wealth. All his revenue was farmed out, and he saved annually 50 lakhs out of a total of 120. With a strange inconsistency he aspired to a character for sanctity, while at the same time he indulged in the grossest debauchery. Like most of his countrymen, he was a slave to superstition, and he scrupulously observed the ordinances of caste and religion. To complaints of his subjects he gave a deaf ear; and if a villager dared to approach his palace he was lucky if he got away with a whole skin. In a nominal court of justice at Puna, cases were decided by the simple method of giving judgement in favour of the suitor who would pay most to the judge.

Báji Rao's object was two-fold, to revive the old Marátha policy which would make himself the lord over Sindia, Holkar, and other chiefs, and to shake off the British yoke. In fact one plan involved the other, for the fulfilment of the first was incompatible with the relationship which existed between himself and the English. Báji Rao was fully bent upon a course which involved his own destruction. He negociated a secret treaty of general confederacy and support with Sindia, Holkar, and Bhonsle of Barár, and actually with the Pindháris. Their plans were not as yet definitely matured, but a crisis was taking place in Bengal towards which all their eyes were strained.

In 1813 Lord Minto had been succeeded by Lord Moira, or, as he may at once be called by his more familiar name, the Marquis of Hastings. Like his predecessor, he came out imbued with the notion of the merits of non-intervention. Like his predecessor, he speedily learnt the folly of the idea; but unlike him he consistently acted upon his opinions. Lord Minto had left him a hard task to accomplish in the mountain-kingdom of Nepál; and for a time the success of the British arms was doubtful. As usual on similar emergencies enemies showed themselves broadcast. Danger threatened from Ranjit Sing and his Sikhs in the Panjáb, from the Maráthas and the Pindháris. But fortune once more smiled on the Company's forces; Nepál was subdued, and the hostile combination sank for a short time into masterly inactivity.

But Lord Hastings realised that the Pindháris at all events must go; and he wrote an earnest despatch to the Court of Directors in September 1815 to impress upon them the absolute necessity for action. There are none so blind as those who refuse to see; and the Directors, while ordering the protection of their own dominions, replied that the Governor-General was not at liberty to engage in operations with the Pindháris either with a view to their utter extirpation or in anticipation of expected danger. So for the moment they were spared, only to await the destruction destined at once for them and the Peshwa who lured them on. The Peshwa, meanwhile, turned his attention to Guzárát. The government of Baroda had practically fallen into the hands of the resident, Colonel Walker. This able officer had done much to settle the affairs both of that province, and of the adjacent peninsula of Káthiáwár, whose Rájput States paid tribute to the Gaikwár. In 1804 an arrangement had been made by which the Gaikwár paid for ten years an annual revenue of five-and-a-half lakhs to the Peshwa for the district of Áhmadábád. The ten years had now expired, and the Peshwa resolved to take the opportunity of extending his influence in Guzárát. He accordingly made considerable claims on the Baroda state, while the Gaikwár on his part raised counter-claims. It was at last determined to send a confidential agent to Puna to negociate the whole matter with the Peshwa. The officer deputed was Gangadhar Shástri, a man of great shrewdness and talent, who in conjunction with Colonel Walker had kept the whole state of Baroda in high order. Though a learned Shástri, he affected English manners—walked fast, talked fast, and mingled colloquial English words freely in his speech. The envoy found the Peshwa in no disposition to arrive at the settlement for which he had pressed. He had not started on his mission with a light heart. He dreaded Trimbakji, and had taken the precaution of obtaining a direct guarantee of safety from the British Government. Realising that he had come on a fool's errand, he determined in June 1815 to return to Baroda, and leave the matter at issue to the arbitration of the British Government.

This was not what the Peshwa wanted, and he induced the envoy to postpone his departure. Báji Rao used his most alluring wiles to bind the Shástri in his own interest and so gain an influence at the Baroda court. He told him that he meant to make him his minister at Puna; and in proof of his sincerity he proposed a marriage between his sister-in-law and the Shástri's son. Preparations were made for the ceremony, when the envoy in sudden dread at losing the favour of his own sovereign broke off the engagement. He gave more deadly cause of offence by refusing to let his wife go near the Peshwa's palace and witness the scenes of debauchery which constantly took place in its precincts. For a time the Peshwa disguised his resentment; and Gangadhar Shástri, not dreaming of danger, accompanied him in blind confidence on a pilgrimage to Pandharpur. On the night of the 14th of July the Peshwa admitted him to unusual intimacy, and parted with him with the heartiest greetings. But the Shástri stepped into the streets only to be hacked to pieces by the agents of Trimbakji Dainglia. Elphinstone was at Ellora. He immediately hurried to Puna; and, on ascertaining the facts, demanded of the Peshwa the prompt apprehension of Trimbakji. "A foreign ambassador," he wrote, "has been murdered in the midst of your Highness' court. A Brahman has been massacred almost in the temple during one of the greatest solemnities of your religion." The public voice of Mahárashtra, shocked at the murder of a Brahman in a place of sanctity, supported the resident in the steps which he took to vindicate the broken guarantee of the British Government.

After a prolonged course of evasion and shuffling, which made it clear that Báji Rao's sympathies lay with Trimbakji, Elphinstone brought matters to a head by saying that if Trimbakji was not given up he would order the subsidiary force to the city, where it would remain till his bidding was accomplished. Trimbakji was at last surrendered at the end of September (1815.) He was confined in the fort of Thána, against the advice of Elphinstone, who recommended that he should be sent to Alláhábád. A year had hardly passed when he contrived to escape, and betook himself to the fastnesses of the mountains (September 1816). The Peshwa did his best by his friendly demeanour to free himself from the suspicion of having aided in his escape; but from this time his plans for a Marátha confederacy against British rule steadily assumed a more definite form. The plot rapidly thickend. There were gatherings of armed men unchecked by the Peshwa's government. Trimbakji was traced from point to point, and Báji Rao openly had an interview with him a few miles from Puna. Remonstrances from the resident were received first with evasions, latterly with impudent denials that troops were assembling, or that the Peshwa had any knowledge of Trimbakji's movements. Elphinstone was told that if he believed in the absurd report of an insurrection he might suppress it himself. In this way the hot weather of 1817 arrived. The Peshwa's object was to gain time while he added to his army, plotted with his confederates, and supplied Trimbakji with money; but he carefully avoided open rupture with the English.

This was not the only portion of Western India where important events were occurring. The state of Kachh was in utter confusion with internal dissensions, and the Rao, or chief, was a confirmed drunkard. Under his rule constant depredations were made by his subjects upon British and protected Gaikwári territory. Remonstrances produced no effect, and force had to be applied. An expedition was accordingly sent in 1816 under Colonel East, and the administration of the state taken in hand by the British Government.

The Peshwa, meanwhile, took no steps to quell the rising which was taking place. Detachments of the subsidiary force under Colonel Lionel Smith, which had been keeping off the Pindháris, were therefore directed against the insurgents. Some Madras troops surprised and killed a party of them, but not before they had seized and murdered Lieutenant Warre of the Madras artillery. The insurgents gained ground in Khándesh, and a fort fell into their hands. It was now palpable that the Peshwa was in the most open way raising levies, repairing his forts, and aiding Trimbakji. Communication with the Governor-General was cut off by a disturbance in Katak, but not before it was known that Lord Hastings insisted on the surrender of Trimbakji. Elphinstone had to act on his own responsibility in the crisis. But he was equal to the emergency. In accordance with his instructions, he insisted on the surrender of Trimbakji, and was not deceived by Báji Rao's warm protestations that he could intend no harm to the British Government to which he owed everything. He distinctly told him that a refusal to give up this cause of all trouble would involve the necessity of immediate hostilities. Twenty-four hours were allowed the Peshwa to decide whether he would accept the terms offered or fight. The conditions were the seizure and surrender of Trimbakji within a month, and the instant delivery of the forts of Singahr, Purandhar, and Raygahr as a pledge of his good faith. On the 7th of May the terms were accepted, and the order for the surrender of the forts placed in the resident's hands. Three days later there arrived instructions from the Governor-General exacting a heavy punishment for the Peshwa's acts of barely disguised warfare. The Peshwa had now to bind himself to hold no communication with any power except the British; he had to admit the guilt of Trimbakji as the murderer of Gangadhar Shástri, the accredited agent of the Gaikwár, residing at Puna under the guarantee of the British Government. All future demands on the Gaikwár were to be relinquished. Instead of furnishing the contingent of 5,000 horse and 3,000 infantry laid down in the treaty of Bassein, he had to cede territory yielding 34 lakhs of revenue. This included Dhárwár and other districts near it that were not clearly defined, the Konkan north of Bombay, and all the Peshwa's revenue in Guzárát, as well as the fort of Áhmadnagar. In the following November, as it was found that the Gaikwár's contingent was inefficient, fresh arrangements were made for a British garrison, territory being assigned for their maintenance.

These were hard and humiliating terms. They reduced Báji Rao's position to so low a degree that he could have continued as the head of his state in name alone. When he learnt them he renewed his preparations for armed resistance, and prepared to leave Puna and join the insurgents. His courage again failed, and he at last sullenly affixed his signature to the treaty. Elphinstone recorded his opinion that if we insisted upon the conditions of this treaty we must be fully prepared for his open hostility should the state of India hereafter favour it; and it is hard to believe that the Marquis of Hastings either expected or wished for any other result. In a despatch of April 12th he had declared his conviction that the Peshwa was engaged in a conspiracy hostile to British honour, and that henceforward our aim must be to strengthen our military position in his territory. He observed:—
"An enforced compliance would be sure to leave a rankling animosity; our foresight must then be directed to the augmentation of the force in the country in our own interests, reform of a part of the establishment, and placing it under a

British officer independent of the Peshwa." The treaty has been condemned as being calculated rather to drive the Peshwa to despair than to assure him a permanent supremacy in his dominions. The fact was that to all intents and purposes he had been at war with the English, and the treaty was such as an unsuccessful combatant might expect. Nor was the question of its observance likely to depend upon its stringency. The Peshwa had shown by a long course of deception, from the date of the treaty of Bassein, that the terms of no convention would be binding on him longer than he could be kept to them by force.

However, the treaty was concluded, and Lord Hastings could turn his attention to the Pindháris, and the Patháns of Amir Khán, who differed from them little but in name. Mr. Canning was now at the head of the Board of Control, and the Governor-General was at last free to act boldly against these incurable savages. He was given authority to repel invasion and chastise the offenders. "We can no longer abstain," added Mr. Canning, "from a vigorous exertion of military power in vindication of the British name, and in defence of subjects who look to us for protection." The Calcutta Council, on their part, resolved that vigorous measures for the suppression of the Pindháris had become an indispensable act of public duty. A defensive alliance was made with Apa Sáheb, who was Regent of Barár, on behalf of Parsáji, who had succeeded Raghoji Bhonsle. It was consequently hoped that the Peshwa and Barár would stand aside; but it was well known that under pretence of suppressing them, Sindia and Holkar were openly countenancing the Pindháris. Military operations, therefore, were taken upon an immense scale, calculated to meet all emergencies. The plan was simple, but vast. The Pindháris were to be completely suppressed by assembling armies round the territories of Holkar and Sindia, and the states of Rajputána, Bhopál, and Bandalkand. Sir Thomas Hislop, Commander-in-Chief of the Madras Army, took command of five divisions prepared in the Deccan; another division was made ready in Guzárát, under General Grant Keir; and the Marquis of Hastings himself took command of four more from Bengal, with two in reserve. Somewhat to the disappointment of Elphinstone, who considered his claims undervalued, Sir John Malcolm was appointed Agent to the Governor-General with the army in the Deccan. The whole British army in the field was not less than 115,000 men, with 300 guns. It was palpable from the magnitude of the forces that Lord Hastings had more in view than the task of eradicating the Pindháris. Nor did he wait until that task was done to deal with those who chose to use them as instruments.

The first to be dealt with was Sindia. Daolat Rao was altogether in the dark as to the immense scale of the British campaign. He was not prepared for operations that caught him as in a net from every side, and when he was requested to issue orders for the free ingress and egress of British troops through his territory he was astounded. He sought to evade compliance, and urged that he had not given up his intention of punishing the Pindháris himself. The contention was treated with contempt. The Governor-General's plans were unfolded to him in detail, and when in open darbár, or council, Captain Close, the British resident, placed in his hands his own intercepted letters to the Nepálese chiefs, proposing a combined attack on the English, he was speechless with confusion. He had little time for consideration. Lord Hastings was rapidly advancing, and in October 1817

Sindia concluded a treaty, which removed the Rájput states from his authority and placed them under British protection, and bound him to maintain a contingent under British officers for the suppression of the Pindháris. As security for the fulfilment of the terms the forts of Hindia and Asirgahr were to be given up. Sindia's forces were closely watched until the end of the contest, and their neutrality assured.

The campaign that had been thus opened against the Pindháris was continued in a similar method. One by one their protectors were humbled to the dust, little being left to be done with the savage Pindháris themselves. The wisdom of the Governor-General's plans in preparing an invincible force and guarding against danger from every quarter was soon manifest. Sindia was accounted for; but the Peshwa, Holkar, and the Rája of Barár were fast hastening to combine.

In the month of July, the Peshwa went on his usual pilgrimage to Pandharpur (page 243). He ostentatiously disbanded a large portion of his cavalry and some infantry; but he advanced his men seven months' pay, and gave them orders to hold themselves in readiness for early recall. From Pandharpur he proceeded to Maholi, near Sátára, and was there met by Sir John Malcolm, who, as Agent to the Governor-General, had visited all the courts of the Deccan, both to consult the residents and to put himself into personal communication with the chiefs. To Sir John Malcolm the Peshwa enlarged on the humiliating conditions of the late treaty. He indignantly denied that he had ever entered into any intrigue against the British Government; and by his cordial professions, and his air of candour and good sense, he completely deceived Sir John Malcolm. That officer returned to Puna convinced that Báji Rao would prove a faithful ally. His forts were restored to him in August and he was encouraged to raise troops. Elphinstone made no secret of his very contrary opinions, but could not oppose this liberal system. But he did not disguise his anxiety at the exposed state of the handful of troops at Puna, after the advance of General Smith's division to the frontier. He therefore requested that the Company's European regiment from Bombay should join the detachment at Puna. The Peshwa did not return to Puna till the end of September. Trimbakji had been succeeded in the post of general adviser and confidant to the Peshwa by a man named Bápu Gokla; and by his counsel Báji Rao determined to enter upon open hostility as soon as his designs were prepared. The recommendation of Sir John Malcolm that he should recruit his army against the Pindháris was an excellent cloak under disguise of which he could increase his forces against the English. Gokla was the leader of all his measures, and he received an advance of nearly a million sterling to complete his warlike preparations.

But the Peshwa's pet schemes were the assassination of the resident and the corruption of his native troops, and even of their European officers. He commissioned a man named Yeshwant Rao Ghorpure, who was intimate with these officers, to carry out this plan. Yeshwant Rao had no objection to receiving an advance of 50,000 rupees. But he kept the money, and warned Elphinstone of what he was likely to expect. Gokla, too, much as he detested the English, disdained to commit so base a crime as that proposed by Báji Rao, that he should entrap the resident to a conference and murder him. But Báji Rao was bitterly hostile to Elphinstone, and he endeavoured to get Trimbakji, with a body of Bhils, to surprise the residency by night and carry out his infamous design. On the 14th of October an interview took place for the last time between the Peshwa and the resident. The Peshwa was still profuse in his professions of loyalty, and repeated his assurances that his troops should be promptly sent against the Pindháris.

On the 19th of October the festival of the Dassara took place. In every Hindu state it is the regular time for the annual muster of troops, being as it is at the close of the rains, and the commencement of the season for military operations. It is also an occasion for military display as the anniversary of the mythical capture of Ceylon by king Ráma. A magnificent gathering of troops was held by the Peshwa, no ceremony that could add to the pageant being omitted. The resident was treated with marked discourtesy, and a large body of cavalry galloped up as if to charge the British troops, but wheeled aside at the very moment when the charge seemed about to be delivered. It was a piece of swagger, which may have been called to mind on both sides, when a few months later one of the three weak battalions then present repulsed the whole Marátha army. It was a time of intense anxiety. The Peshwa's troops were crowding into Puna. General Smith was at a distance, and the European regiment from Bombay could hardly arrive before the 5th of November. Parties of the enemy hustled and crowded on the British troops in their cantonments. The Peshwa knew of the coming reinforcements from Bombay, and deliberated on the advantage of attacking the resident before their arrival. On the night of the 28th his guns were yoked, horses saddled, and infantry under arms. At midnight Elphinstone received the information. Should he not anticipate the attack? But he knew that directly the Peshwa engaged in open hostilities, Sindia and others would at once show their true colours. It was advisable to wait unless compelled to fight. While Elphinstone stood thus deliberating on his terrace the din in the city died away; the Peshwa's attack was postponed. The next day the crowding of the Marátha cavalry upon the English brigade was more offensive than ever. Elphinstone sent a message to the Peshwa, pointing out the intolerable nature of these proceedings, and confined his own men to their quarters to prevent any premature contest. To Gokla the message seemed one of insufferable insolence. He wished to attack the English at once while the European regiment was still at a distance. But the Peshwa hesitated. A night was wasted in consultation; and at four o'clock, on the morning of the 30th, the European regiment under Major Wilson, who was apprised of the crisis, by incredible exertions marched into the cantonment. The English at Puna could once more breathe freely. But the position which they occupied was bad, and on November 1st they moved out to Khirki, a village four miles off. The Maráthas promptly plundered the old cantonment, and commenced their former tactics of pressing upon and hustling the British in their new position. Elphinstone remained for the time at his residency on the Sangam. Meanwhile, General Smith had been informed of the impending struggle. He therefore sent back his light battalion to Sirur, and concentrated his force at Phultamba on the Godáwari. On the 3rd Elphinstone summoned the light battalion to Puna. The Peshwa at last made up his mind to attack. By the morning of the 5th his preparations were made. Even then he once more attempted to negociate. He sent a message to Elphinstone, desiring him to send away the European regiment and reduce his native battalion, as such a large assembly of troops near Puna was offensive to him.

Elphinstone's sole reply was that a removal of troops must commence on the Peshwa's side. Báji Rao therefore warned him of the consequence of his proceedings, and threatened that he himself would leave Puna and never return should the resident continue obstinate. The conversation was prolonged as far as possible by the Marátha messenger. At last he withdrew. The Peshwa's officers left their quarters at the palace and placed themselves at the head of their troops. Báji Rao proceeded to the temple of Párbati, which his ancestor had built, whence he could from a safe distance command a view over the undulating plain of Khirki. Elphinstone and his party left the residency and joined the British forces at Khirki. The Marátha army was between the residency and the camp. He therefore crossed the river Mula by a ford which then existed—the present dam at Puna not having been built—marched up the left bank of the river, and recrossed it at Khirki by a bridge.

It was the afternoon of a sultry Deccan day. The heat was almost stifling. There was not a breath of wind to blow aside the clouds of dust. The Marátha army poured out from Puna in the direction of Khirki through fields where the rich grain stood ready for the harvest. The spectacle was most imposing. The low hills that edged the plateau were covered with infantry. Endless streams of horsemen issued from the city, and covered the whole surface of the plain. The air was filled with the trampling of horses and the rumbling of cannon. The peasants fled from their work in the harvest fields. Their bullocks broke off from their yokes and raced away in terror. The mighty wave of soldiers moved onward in all the pomp of war with apparently irresistible force. But the battle was not to be to the strong. Nothing daunted at this vast host, which out-numbered them almost twelve to one, the English force of 2,800, of whom 800 only were Europeans, was eager for the fray. At the earnest advice of the resident they did not wait to be attacked. Gallantly led by Colonel Burr, they dashed at the advancing enemy. The Maráthas were astounded by this act of daring. Their spirits were already damped by an evil omen, for the staff of their Jári Patka, or national standard, had broken in twain ere they left the city. Gokla did all that a brave soldier could do to encourage his troops, and he led in person a brilliant cavalry charge. But before a company of the European regiment could come near, the heroic Seventh Bombay Native Infantry, under Colonel Burr himself, hurled back the ranks of the horsemen beneath the hill of Ganesh Khind. The battle was won. The Marátha army was utterly disconcerted by the unexpected onslaught of the British forces. The guns were driven off, and the field of battle was cleared. The British loss was trifling, that of the Maráthas 500 men. The British returned after night-fall to their position at Khirki, and the next morning the light battalion and some auxiliary horse joined them from Sirur.

While the battle was being fought the residency, by Báji Rao's orders, was plundered and burnt; of the resident's own apartments and library not one stone was left upon another. The families of sepoys in the English ranks were robbed and mutilated, trees torn up, and graves demolished. Two British officers, brothers, named Vaughan, taken prisoner at Talegaum, were barbarously hanged.

Bitter was the despair of the Peshwa as he witnessed the battle of Khirki from his temple at Párbati, and he poured out terrible upbraidings on those who had urged him to defy the British power. The Marátha empire was at an end. It had been founded by the massacre of Afzul Khán at Pratápgahr; it fell with the attempted massacre of the British resident at Puna.

Elphinstone hardly realised the momentous result of the battle. With the movements of troops during the action he had not interfered. But it was he who had insisted upon the necessity of commencing the battle by attacking the enemy, and by general consent the honour of the day was his. But from his own description of the battle, it would be supposed that it was solely to Colonel Burr, a gallant but still crippled old soldier, who was suffering at the time from an incurable disease, that the victory was due. In moving a vote of thanks to Lord Hastings and the army at the close of the the war, Mr. Canning said that "Mr. Elphinstone—a man distinguished in the literature as well as the politics of the East—exhibited on that trying occasion military courage and skill, which though valuable accessories to diplomatic talents, we are not entitled to require as necessary qualifications for civil employment."

General Smith was now rapidly returning to Puna, and Elphinstone, as he wrote, fully expected that before his arrival the Peshwa would give them another field day. The Peshwa did not afford them that gratification, and on November 13th, three days after General Smith's return, the Peshwa fled to Sátára and his army evacuated Puna. The city was taken possession of, and the pursuit of the Marátha army commenced. Great exertions were made to come up with the Peshwa, but he continued his flight from place to place amongst the mountains of the Western Gháts; and for some months he evaded pursuit. He sent his wife and much of his property to the fort of Raygahr.

Meanwhile, a small force from Bombay under Colonel Prother was employed in reducing the Konkan; and

General Smith, afraid lest the Marátha army, driven by the English in that direction, should cut off Colonel Prother's detachment, sent reinforcements to him from Puna, and directed the 2nd detachment of the 1st regiment to strengthen Colonel Burr at Puna. This order led to the most vivid episode of the campaign. On the last day of the year the battalion marched from Sirur at eight o'clock in the evening It consisted of 500 men, supported by two six-pounders, manned by twenty-four Europeans of the Madras Infantry. There were also 300 of the newly-raised irregular horse, the whole under the command of Captain Francis Staunton. They marched all night, and on the morning of the New Year's Day the detachment reached the village of Korygaum on the river Bhima, and found encamped before it the whole of the Peshwa's army of 25,000 horse and a large number of Arabs under Báji Rao in person. Captain Staunton took up his post in the village and placed his guns where they could do the greatest execution. The Maráthas endeavoured to storm the English position, and they obtained possession of a strong square enclosure commanding the village from which they could not be dislodged. A terrible struggle was then waged. Captain Staunton's men had marched all night. They were cut off from the river; they had neither food nor water. But in vain did the Marathás and the fiercer Árabs hurl themselves time after time upon the devoted band. Every foot of ground was disputed. Hardly any of the European officers were unwounded. The wounded men and officers were in agonies of thirst which could not be relieved. The surviving combatants were fainting and nearly frantic for want of water. Some of the gunners, all of whom fought heroically, proposed to sue for terms. But Captain Staunton pointed out to them the dead body of their officer

Lieutenant Chisholm, who had been shot, and whose head the enemy had then severed from his trunk. "Such was the way," he told them, "in which all would be served who fell dead or alive into the hands of the Marathas." They replied that they would die to a man, and the unequal conflict was continued all that terrible day. Towards sunset their plight seemed well nigh desperate, but their efforts were not slackened. As night fell the attack became less fierce. By nine o'clock the artillery fire ceased, and the village was evacuated by the Peshwa's troops. The men were able at last to alleviate their intense thirst. The next day the Peshwa's troops refused to fight, and gradually withdrew. Captain Staunton had lost 175 men besides a portion of the auxiliary horse. The Maratha loss was between 500 and 600 men. A monument, erected upon the spot, tells the traveller of the fierce fight that was waged where he stands; and Maratha minstrels, be it told to their credit, sing of the glory of the defence.

The Peshwa, as at Khirki, surveyed the battle from a distance. He had brought with him the Raja of Satara, his nominal master. A screen had been erected to ward off the rays of the sun. The Raja begged that it might be taken down, "Otherwise the English would send a cannon-ball through it." Gokla and Trimbakji directed the Maratha attacks, and the Peshwa impatiently asked his commanders, "Where were their boasts of defeating the English if they could not overcome one battalion?"

The Governor-General shortly afterwards conferred on Captain Staunton the important command of Ahmadnagar, and repeated the observation of General Smith, that the action at Korygaum was "One of the most brilliant affairs ever achieved by any army, in which the European and Native soldiers displayed the most noble devotion and most romantic bravery, under the pressure of thirst and hunger almost beyond human endurance." And two years afterwards, in presenting to him a valuable sword voted by the Court of Directors, he said, "In that hour of difficulty and danger, surrounded by implacable enemies, and cut off from all hope of succour, it was your firmness that afforded to your brave companions an opportunity of displaying that devotion and gallantry which terminated in their triumph over the vast forces opposed to them, and not only established for ever their own reputation, but threw a lustre over their own establishment, and added to the glory of the Indian army." In the House of Commons Mr. Canning extolled the glory of the little band which had kept at bay the Peshwa's 25,000 horse and masses of Arab infantry.

The Marquis of Hastings resolved that the Peshwa should be the last of his line. To appoint a successor would be only to revive the old pretensions to Marátha confederation and supremacy, which experience had shown to be incompatible with the very existence of the English as a power in the land. The dynasty was to be done away with, and the dominions annexed to the Company's possessions. But with consummate statesmanship the Governor-General resolved to conciliate the Marátha nation by a graceful concession; and the imprisoned Rája of Sátára, the descendant of Shiwáji, was to be given the nominal sovereignty of the district of Sátára. Mr. Elphinstone was wisely selected to carry out this policy and settle the annexed territory, and two divisions of the Deccan army under Generals Smith and Pritzler were withdrawn from Sir Thomas Hislop's control and placed at his disposal. Captain Grant Duff, the talented historian of the Maráthas, was made resident at Sátárá, which was taken on February 10th, 1818, by General Smith with little difficulty. The British flag was hoisted on the fort; but the day after replaced by the Bhagwa Jenda, or standard of Shiwáji. A manifesto was at the same time published by the Commissioner, setting forth the intentions of the British Government and stating the reasons which had rendered their action inevitable. The document was admirably calculated to promote the end in view. "There was to be no interference," it said, "with religion, gifts of Inám or rent-free land, or allowances from the state, provided that those concerned accepted the sovereignty of the Company." Farming of the revenue was to be abolished, and a moderate assessment collected by British officers. Thus the petty chiefs and landholders were confirmed in their possessions which became an invaluable security for their allegiance to the new régime.

The campaign had, however, yet to be concluded. General Smith continued the pursuit of the Peshwa. General Pritzler attacked and took the hill-forts of Purandhar, Singhar and others south of Puna. General Thomas Munro, from Madras, captured the strong hill-fort of Badámi in the district of Bijápur, and then marched on Sholápur and took that fort after a short siege. In the Konkan, General Prother took fort after fort, including the stronghold of Raygahr the mighty fortress-capital of Shiwáji. After a rapid march, in furious heat, through Indápur and Máhár, he got his guns in position on an almost inaccessible mountain-ridge opposite Raygahr. The bombardment was opened with spirit. The firing was extremely accurate, and nearly every building in the fort was laid in ruins. At last a shell burst over the citadel and set fire to the houses; and the Peshwa's wife induced the Arab commandant to surrender. Fifty thousand pounds sterling was found in the fort. The Peshwa's wife was escorted to Puna and subsequently to Wai. In the Ratnágiri district

Colonel Kennedy, with a detachment fitted out by Sir Evan Nepean, the Governor of Bombay, was occupying the country with equal success. All over the country fortress after fortress fell in a few weeks, most of which, with Shiwáji as a master, would have withstood the whole British army.

General Smith, though unsuccessful in his pursuit of the Peshwa, managed to overtake a large part of his army at Ashta, and with hardly any loss put them to flight. At Ashta, Gokla, whose personal valour was undaunted, fell fighting bravely. He had pledged himself to die sword in hand, and he kept his word. The Maráthas were pursued for miles, and the engagement hastened the termination of the war. On this occasion General Smith, who was himself wounded, captured the Rája of Sátára and his family. They expressed unbounded joy at the rescue from their Brahman masters. They were placed in charge of Mr. Elphinstone, and the Peshwa continued his flight towards Nágpur. At Nágpur, Apa Sahib the regent had made a subsidiary treaty with the English. He promptly proceeded to break it. He murdered the boy on whose behalf he was ruling, plotted with the Peshwa, sent his family and treasure out of the city, and ordered his troops to attack Mr. Jenkins' small detachment of sepoys. Owing to the heroic courage of Captain Fitzgerald, who was in command of some Bengal horse, and the enthusiasm which he instilled into his men, the attack, although made by numbers that appeared overwhelming, was beaten off; and Marátha singers mingle with the fame of Korygaum the magnificent exploit of Sitabaldi. Apa Sáhib disavowed any share in the attack, but refused to disband his troops. Another action was required; his guns were taken, and he surrendered unconditionally. For the murder of his nephew he was sent a prisoner to Alláhábád; but he escaped on the road, and after nine years' misery in the Windhya mountains, found at length a refuge with the Rája of Jodhpur, and was there left undisturbed. An infant grandson of Rághoji was placed on the throne. Mr. Jenkins administered Barár during his minority, and Nágpur ceased to be a cause of trouble.

Holkar, too, had been effectually dealt with. Tulsi Bai, widow of Yeshwant Rao, was conducting the affairs of the State as regent for the young Malhar Rao, her husband's illegitimate son. Her turbulent soldiery were beyond her control. She was not herself anxious to join the Peshwa, and even made secret proposals to the Governor-General to place herself and the young prince under his protection. But events were too strong for her; and before the end of December 1817 she found herself with her army near Mehidpur on the Sipri river. Here she attempted to negociate with Sir John Malcolm and Sir Thomas Hislop, whose united forces lay in her path. Incensed at this, her officers beheaded her and cast her body into the stream. A few days afterwards, on December 21st, the army of Holkar was utterly destroyed, and sixty-three guns captured with all the military stores and camp equipage. But the British loss was 778 in killed and wounded, of whom thirty-eight were European officers. The submission of the young Holkar was tendered on the 6th of January, and the usual subsidiary treaty entered into. Sir John Malcolm remained as Agent to the Governor-General for the Marátha States of Central India.

Their supporters thus humbled to the dust, the Pindháris could offer no formidable resistance to the invincible British arms. They were struck with terror when they found Sindia compelled to abandon them. They could get no help from any of the Maráthas, and they were unable to protect themselves from Lord Hastings' combinations.

They strove desperately to avoid the retribution that was coming upon them, but their enemies enclosed them on every side. It was in vain that they fled to the North, for the Bengal army was ready for them there; they turned to the South only to lose all their baggage and be worsted in continual small encounters. They were completely dispersed, and most of them came to a miserable end in the jungle— the peasantry showing no mercy after the infamous cruelties which they had formerly undergone at their hands. One of their leaders, Chetu, was hunted first through Guzárát and then through Málwa, and at last his body was found near Asirgahr half eaten by a tiger. Another, Wasil Muhammad, betook himself to Sindia, who surrendered him to the English; and, thinking death preferable to captivity, he put an end to his life by poison. Another, named Karim, with leniency altogether undeserved, received an estate in British territory. Amir Khán remained, and as he offered to surrender it was deemed expedient to accept his proposal. Sir David Ochterlony, with no little address and firmness, effected a settlement with his Pathán retainers and obtained their artillery without bloodshed. Pindhári raids were a thing of the past. Those of these banditti who survived, mingled with the population, and many of them became decent and orderly citizens.

There were still a few sieges before the campaign was concluded. Asirgahr was surrendered to Sir John Malcolm in April and garrisoned by British troops. In Tálner, the former Pathán capital of Khándesh, there was a strong force of the Peshwa's Arabs. The commandant surrendered to Sir Thomas Hislop; but when Major Gordon and Captain Macgregor entered the fort they were cut down and killed. The exasperated British troops rushed in; and, of a garrison of 300 men, one only escaped with his life by leaping over the wall. The commandant was hanged—a fate that he richly deserved. At Málegaum in Khándesh, now in the subsequently formed district of Násik, a contrary policy was adopted. The fort was strongly garrisoned by Arabs, who offered to surrender if they were guaranteed arrears of pay and a free passage to Arabia. The offer was accepted, but the generosity was not unnaturally taken for weakness. The Arabs considered that they had achieved a success over British troops, and much harm at Hydarábád and other places resulted from the occurrence.

The war thus came to a triumphant issue. A brief campaign had sufficed to shatter a most formidable confederacy against the British Government. It was owing to the baneful policy of non-intervention that the confederacy had ever been allowed to raise its head. British power was now stronger than ever. There was no longer a question of balance of power. There was to be one supreme authority in India before which all must bow. The Court of Directors denounced the extension of territory, but their words were not followed by action, and they recognised accomplished facts. But even the Directors appreciated the "promptitude and vigour with which Lord Hastings had dispersed the gathering elements of a hostile conspiracy." The verdict of posterity has justified the measures of the statesman, who by a strong hand delivered Central and Western India from the curse of anarchy, which could never cease while rival armies carried fire and sword throughout the land. It is to the Marquis of Hastings that the Bombay Presidency owes almost all its territory.

The pursuit of the Peshwa was carried on with infinite perseverance. Hunted from place to place it was in vain that he applied to his late confederates for succour; and he at last made overtures to Mr. Elphinstone and other officers, but he was told that the only terms that could be accepted were unconditional surrender. He turned his course northwards, intending to cross the Narbada; but the fords and passes were guarded, and he was forced to remain with the 8,000 men who were left to him near Asirgahr in a state of utter despair. Hence he despatched an agent to Sir John Malcolm at Mau. Sir John Malcolm was fully cognizant of Lord Hastings' instructions to Elphinstone—that no conditions were to be made with Báji Rao. His arrest was only a question of time. But Sir John Malcolm, regardless alike of the Governor-General's instructions and the ill-effect which the deputation could not but have on military operations, sent two officers to treat with him. His terms were that Báji Rao should resign his sovereignty and give up Trimbakji and the murderers of the Vaughans. This much being promised, Báji Rao was to separate himself from the remnant of his followers and advance to meet Sir John Malcolm, who undertook to obtain for him from the British Government an ample allowance in any holy city that he might select. Before formally surrendering himself, he had an interview with Sir John Malcolm, and with his usual adroitness and eloquence appealed to him as the last of his three earliest and best friends. Malcolm sank the politician in the man. He remembered the regal splendour in which Báji Rao had lived; and when he saw him now as a hopeless and weary fugitive, he forgot that the Peshwa had rushed upon his fate with his eyes open and that Malcolm himself had been made one of his tools. So when Báji Rao promised to give himself up if he should receive an allowance of £80,000 a year, Sir John Malcolm gave his assent.

The Governor-General was justly indignant at this contempt of orders. But he could not go back from the word of a British officer; and the Peshwa went to reside at Bithur, near Cawnpore, with his stipulated income. The result was disastrous. The largeness of the sum hindered to some extent the liberality that the British Government wished to show in its new territories; and while the agreement obtained favourable terms for many of Baji Rao's people that deserved condign punishment, it also created a spurious and dangerous importance for the dethroned potentate in the eyes of the Maráthas. The full danger of the step was to manifest itself nearly forty years later in the infamous Nana Sáhib of Cawnpore. The surrender of Trimbakji was evaded, but he was finally captured and confined in the fort of Chunar till his death.

In the month of April, Pratáp Sing, the Rája of Sátára—a well-meaning, but weak and vain prince—in his 27th year, was seated on his throne with great pomp by the Commissioner. He issued two proclamations, announcing his connection with the British Government, and putting the entire administration of his kingdom into the hands of Mr. Elphinstone. He dwelt on the injuries that he had received from the Peshwa, and produced an order signed by Báji Rao to put the Rája and his family to death sooner than let them fall into the hands of the English. But circumstances showed that, though the experiment of restoring the Sátára royal family was a wise temporary expedient, it was useless as a permanent measure. The only gratitude shown by the Rája was treachery and plots against the hand that raised him from the dust.

The military operations were no sooner completed than the work of civil administration was taken in hand. Under

Mr. Elphinstone's supervision, Puna was managed by Captain Robertson; Khándesh by Captain Briggs; the central part of the Deccan by Captain Pottinger, and the south by Mr. Chaplain, a Madras civilian. Native officers from the Peshwa's service became their assistants on liberal salaries, and the whole population submitted promptly to the new order of things. So readily did the troops transfer their allegiance to the conquerors, that in many instances soldiers who had been fighting for Báji Rao were within twenty-four hours bearing arms on behalf of the new Government. The first business of the Commissioners was to see that the revenues were duly collected and handed over to the British authorities; to protect and conciliate the people; to show them that no innovation was intended, but that a proper administration of the existing law would be insisted on. It was of the utmost importance to gain the confidence and not to excite the alarm of the natives, and the wise experience of Mr. Elphinstone effectively secured this result. The Maráthas were not disarmed, but armed parties were not allowed to travel without passports; and after the first year this precaution was dropped except in the case of bodies of over twenty-five armed men. Military stations were established at Puna, Sirur, Junnar, Áhmadnagar, Sholápur, Málegaum, Sátára, Karár and Kaladgi. The wild Bhils of Khándesh for a long time could not be reduced to tranquillity, and the steps taken to deal with them will be related further on. One conspiracy only was detected, at Puna, for the murder of all Europeans of that place and of Sátára, and the seizure of the Rája by some Brahmans and men of desperate fortunes. The Brahman ringleaders were blown from guns, an example which had a permanent effect upon that intriguing race. Sir Evan Nepean, the Governor of Bombay, approved of Elphinstone's action; but when he suggested an application for indemnity, Elphinstone replied that if he had done wrong he ought to be punished, if right there was no need of an indemnity.

The Rája of Kolhápur had espoused the British cause, and he was rewarded by the gift of the districts of Chikur and Manáwli, which he had long coveted. Every promise made as to the continuance of pensions, allowances, and free-rent lands was strictly observed. The Pant Sachiw had joined the British cause after the proclamation of Sátára, and he was confirmed in the possession of his territories in the wild mountains above the Bhor Ghát where Shiwáji's power had arisen. Other such chiefs were the Pant Pratinidhi and the Rája of Akalkot near Sholápur. For the decision of civil suits Elphinstone continued the system of panchayats. In the neighbourhood of Sátára criminal cases were settled in the same way; but in most of the new territories individual judges were continued or introduced for this class of work. But Elphinstone knew that the people were not prepared for the elaboration of English law. He gave them its justice without its intricate regulations. By preserving the influence of village officers, he gave the millions under his rule that immense blessing—a simple, cheap, and speedy administration of justice. His plan could be hardly more than a temporary one. The English love of order down to the minutest details could not fail to prevent its being so. But perhaps, with the perfection of the machinery, the element of its adaptability to the conditions of life of a primitive people has to some extent been lost sight of. So liberal was the settlement of the conquered territory that there was little if any saving to the British Government from the Peshwa's revenue; but in a few years, owing to the tranquility and safety of the country, fortunate seasons, and the improvements in agriculture, the revenues largely increased. On the 1st of November 1819 Mr. Elphinstone handed over his commissionership to Mr. Chaplain for the higher sphere of Governor of Bombay. He had endeared himself to the inhabitants of Mahárashtra, who reverence his name to this day. He respected not only the privileges of the people, but even their prejudices, as long as they were not iniquitous or unjust. To Lord Hastings he wrote:—"It is to be remembered that even just government is not a blessing if at variance with the habits and character of the people."

Three years later saw the retirement of Lord Hastings. In spite of his costly wars, his budget had always shown a large surplus. He had followed the footsteps of Lord Cornwallis in purifying the lives and habits of English officers both civil and military. He had devoted himself to the well-being of the natives of India. He set up schools, which were thronged with children, and spared no steps to spread education and knowledge. He allowed the missionaries of Serámpur, near Calcutta, to issue a newspaper, which formed the foundation of the present Native press. Could he have foreseen the existence of newspapers over the length and breadth of the land, steeped in treason and execrating everything that the Government does, he might have hesitated to confer this gift.

The Bombay Presidency had now assumed its present form, with the exception of Sind, Sátára, Ángria's territory of Kolába, and Kánára, which latter belonged to Madras.

XVIII.—MOUNTSTUART ELPHINSTONE.

ALIKE as Commissioner of the Deccan and Governor of Bombay, Mountstuart Elphinstone's whole heart was in the work of restoring order to the new provinces. Tranquillity could not be attained in a day, and there were from time to time disturbances from isolated bands of Pindháris and other marauders. But no native power dared to draw sword against the English. The task that Elphinstone had before him was in truth no light one. He had to spread civilization over a land desolated by anarchy, to afford security to life and property, to usher in a reign of law where law was almost unknown. Sir James Macintosh, who was Recorder or Chief Justice of Bombay from 1804 to 1812, and who made an extended tour in the Deccan, stated it to be his " firm conviction that the first blessing to be wished to the inhabitants of India was that a civilized conqueror might rescue them from their native oppressors, and that they would find better masters in the worst Europeans than in the best of their own countrymen." The Peshwas had done nothing to commemorate their existence. The architecture of the Deccan, that of the fortresses that crowned the heights of Máhárashtra, was of an earlier age. The splendour of Bijápur and the beauties of Áhmadábád raised in the Maráthas no desire to reproduce them. Puna, on the downfall of the Peshwas, did not possess a building worthy of the name. To evade the Pindháris the houses of well-to-do landholders were built so as to resemble on the side from which they were approached the huts of the poorest peasant; and the ryot as he ploughed his field carried his matchlock on his shoulder. Land fetched higher rent in out-of-the-way glens than anywhere near the tracks that were used for roads. As for the common people, Shiwáji contemptuously observed that if they had a dhotar (a waist-cloth) it was all that was needed.

Force might bring peace for the time. Mr. Elphinstone had wider views for the creation of a more far-reaching and lasting reform. He deemed it not impossible to raise the natives by education and public trust to a level with their new rulers. Striving to build up a desire for knowledge, he felt it wisest to begin with the highest classes. To any mingling of religion, even in the slightest degree, with his plans for education, he absolutely and entirely objected. "To introduce Christianity into their schools would be to sound the alarm, and to warn the Brahmans of the approaching danger .... the danger would involve not only failure of our plans of education, but the dissolution of our empire." Missionaries found the lowest castes the best pupils. Elphinstone was careful of offering special encouragement to those castes who were not only the most despised but the least numerous of the divisions of society. To identify education with them would be to make it odious to those who were more fit for it. The soundness of his views are manifested in the result of the labours of missionaries, who are content to take into their fold the lowest of the low in the vain hope that Christianity may spread upwards. Education cannot be expected to flourish without encouragement, and Mr. Elphinstone wished to introduce natives to offices of high rank and trust. But he held at the same time, that very strict supervision was requisite, and that many Europeans were necessary for that purpose. The same spirit of prudence led him to record his emphatic condemnation of the introduction of a free press in a country where freedom has ever been synonymous with license.

The way was thus paved for a system of legislative and judicial reforms. Deprecating a large number of acts, he drew up a code of regulations at once simple and comprehensive, and framed to bring matters to a speedy issue. The language of the court was made the language of the district, the evidence of witnesses taken in their own vernacular. Under the Peshwas there was no prescribed form of trial. A rebel would be executed at once on the ground of notoriety; any Bhil found in a neighbourhood where Bhils had been plundering would be immediately hanged. In doubtful cases, the prisoner was flogged to make him confess. No particular punishment was laid down for particular offences. Where one officer would flog, another would hang, and a third fine. Punishment varied rather with the caste of the prisoner than with the nature of his offence. Mutilation was commonly inflicted. The Hindu law-officer of Áhmadnagar sentenced one man to be thrown from a height upon a spike, and another to be fined a nominal sum for the same offence; because in one case the stolen property had been accidentally recovered, and in the other it had not. The police often shared in the profits of the thieves. Considering this miserable parody of law and justice, and the moral character of the people, whose ranks from the highest to the lowest were pervaded with falsehood, the wonder is not that crime was so great but that it was not infinitely greater.

That European officers should settle every petty dispute and detail of revenue was impracticable. While the status of the village pátil was carefully preserved, equal pains were taken to place on an honourable foundation the position of the Mámlatdár, or subordinate native magistrate and revenue officer, who had charge of a táluka or petty division of a district.

During his tenure of office as Governor of Bombay, Elphinstone twice made a tour through every district in the Presidency. He saw everything for himself, and wrote copious minutes on the condition of each part of the country. These tours were the pleasantest parts of his governorship. He thoroughly enjoyed the bustle and change of camp life. A first-rate horseman, he was an ardent pursuer of the sport of pig-sticking or hog-hunting; and when he was in camp, and heard of any boars being in the neighbourhood, he would proclaim a holiday and devote one or two days to the chase.

Of all the districts in the Presidency, that which most needed regeneration was Khándesh. An extensive plain, watered by the Tápti and surrounded by broad chains of mountains, covered with noxious vegetation, where none but forest tribes can live—Khándesh is rather a province than a district. In area it is to other districts what Yorkshire is to the ordinary counties of England. Its forests are peopled by Bhils, who used to gather together in their inaccessible jungles and burst upon their prey in the plains. Under its Muhammadan rulers the province had been a rich and flourishing garden; under the Maráthas it steadily declined. In 1802 it was ravaged by Holkar's army. A famine followed, and its ruin was completed by the rapacity and misgovernment of the Peshwa's officials. Bhils, Arabs and Pindháris alike robbed and murdered the peaceful inhabitants of the country. On the occupation of the province in 1813, anarchy and oppression had reached a fearful height. Fifty Bhil leaders commanded bands numbering upwards of 5,000 followers, whose subsistence depended upon the fruits of pillage and plunder. The former Native Government had systematically violated its pledges to forest tribes, and they were more than ever suspicious of the foreign conquerors. The Arabs and Pindháris were rapidly suppressed; the Bhils were longer a source of trouble. Many of them were the most uncivilized of all aboriginal tribes. With forms stunted by the deadly climate, they had barely sufficient intellect to comprehend anything beyond the most simple communication. Slaves alike to superstition and drunkenness, they held it degrading to cultivate or labour for wages; no employment was tolerated which interfered with their carrying the long bow and sheaf of arrows. Under the Muhammadans, Bhils had to some extent been employed as village watchmen. That system had been broken up, and no police of any kind existed. In the single táluka of Nandurbár there were, in one month, a hundred cases of murder and robbery.

For several years Colonel Briggs, the political agent, attempted to restore order by a combination of coercive and conciliatory measures. The policy failed; and it was not till banishment, imprisonment, and cognate devices were put aside for ever, and a new system introduced, which gently and kindly persuaded the forest tribes to enter upon a civilized life, that peace was restored to the province. Officers were selected with the title of Bhil Agents, who were to endeavour to inspire these wild men with confidence in the Government, redress all grievances, and in every way ameliorate their condition. Lands were allotted rent-free for those who could be induced to settle on them; and advances of money made for the purchase of seed and cattle, as well as for clothes and food, until they could support themselves. They were still, however, to be restrained—by persuasion if possible; if not, by force—from assembling in masses. The bold idea was conceived of forming these predatory tribes into an irregular corps; and Captain, afterwards Sir James Outram, was the main instrument of carrying out this policy. He delighted the Bhils by joining them fearlessly in the chase in their own wild forests; he entrusted his life to their keeping, and by his hearty sympathy with them, won their confidence first in himself, and then in the Government which he represented. He contrived to raise from their number a body-guard of nine men, and with these marched round the province recruiting more. In a few months he had a corps of sixty men armed with bows and arrows; and subsequently they were all armed and dressed like the Sepoy regiments of the Company. The work progressed beyond expectation. But one of those strange rumours, so common in India, took possession of them. They believed that the Government had formed them into a corps only with the sinister object of linking them in a line, and at one stroke extirpating their race; and their blood was said to be in high demand as medicine in the country of their English conquerors. But time and illimitable patience overcame this and other difficulties; and, though inveterate habits were not changed in a day, by 1826 three hundred ploughs had been established, and the Bhil corps numbered 300 men. A year later it reached twice that number, and a small border disturbance showed that the members of this corps were ready to shed their blood at the bidding of their new masters. In course of time the Bhils were not only able to take the post of village watchmen, but they guarded the Government treasuries and jails; and the regiments of the line were entirely removed from Khándesh. This wise and liberal policy subjected Government to a considerable outlay and some loss by the nonpayment of advances made to Bhils. But very many more repayments have been effected than might have been anticipated, and the same system is still in force. The reformation of this tribe, which no amount of force could subdue, is too inestimable a blessing to be weighed in the scale with pecuniary sacrifice. If British rule had nothing better to show for it than the suppression of the Bhil banditti of Khándesh, and the Ángria pirates of the western coast, it would not have existed in vain.

Lord Hastings was succeeded after a short interregnum by Lord Amherst in August 1823. Though Bombay was in a state of profound peace, the clang of arms soon resounded in other parts of India; and the echoes, rolling to the West, at one time kindled a vein of sympathy that showed a strong hand as well as a just administration to be absolutely indispensable. The catastrophe that had overwhelmed the Pindhári and the Marátha confederacy had taken the light out of the life of thousands and thousands who preferred plunder to industry, and who would have welcomed a return of the anarchy which would follow a reverse to the British arms. Such a reverse they hoped might come from the first Burmese war. The expedition was unpopular with the Sepoys of whom three regiments mutinied; and one, the 47th, was struck off the list of the Company's army. Both to them, and to the natives of India who watched their course, the thought of the power of Burmese magic bore with it a strange terror. The expedition was checked by heavy rains; but the popular belief went abroad that the English were powerless before the Burmese witches, whose incantations prevented them from raising their feet from the ground. A strange crisis of feeling spread over a great portion of India, and it came to a head at Bhartpur. This fortress had been fiercely assailed, but never taken, by the English under General Lake. The ramparts of the Hindu stronghold still rose proudly, and presented an emblem of final victory for the inhabitants of the land. The boy Rája of Bhartpur had been recognised by the British Government; and when a usurper put him aside and seized the throne, Sir David Ochterlony, the resident at Delhi, issued orders for the immediate attack of the fort. Lord Amherst, with a strange infatuity, countermanded the order; and the indignity broke the heart of the gallant soldier, who with a handful of men had defended Delhi against the overwhelming hosts of Holkar after Monson's fatal retreat. As a matter of course, the natives believed that the order resulted from fear. The whole country was in a ferment. Twenty-five thousand men engaged themselves "to fight the Company behind the walls which had defied Lord Lake, the conqueror of Hindustán." There was abundant evidence that Sindia, Holkar, and all the other chiefs were prepared to support the rising if it should meet with any success. Ochterlony was right, and Lord Amherst had been wrong. But he rapidly grasped the emergency of the crisis; and prepared to scatter the delusion which might carry a fire-brand through the peninsula. With stupendous efforts, and a loss of 1,000 men, the fort was taken and its walls razed to the ground.

After the pacification of the Bhils, the only disturbance of any importance which troubled Bombay was an insurrection of the Rámoshis, another aboriginal tribe, in the district of Puna, under Umáji Naik in 1826-27. The Rámoshis were so enterprising and successful that force could not put them down, and the method which had been so successful with the Bhils was applied on a smaller scale to the Puna tribes. An amnesty was granted to all concerned except Umáji, and many were given grants of land and employed as hill-police. Umáji escaped for a time, but was apprehended at Pandharpur and paid the penalty for his crimes.

With two foreign countries the Government of Elphinstone had some dealing. Sind still ranked in that category, and our relations with it were of slender importance. But the frontier was unsettled, and marauders encroached upon British territory. Steps were taken in return to restrain the subjects of the Amirs who ruled in Sind, but for the time the difference was amicably settled. With Persia matters were more serious. The Persian Gulf was infested with pirates, and these had to be put down. A British force, moving inland to capture a pirate stronghold, fell into an ambuscade and was cut to pieces. Another expedition was immediately despatched which avenged the fate of the first and effectually secured its object.

On the 14th of November 1827, Mountstuart Elphinstone sailed from Bombay, after an unbroken service in India of over thirty years. No name is so identified as his with the building up of the Bombay Presidency. Of his Government he was able to write, "It has repelled predatory invasion, restrained intestine disorder, administered equal and impartial justice, and has almost extirpated every branch of exaction and oppression." Writing at Bombay in 1825, Bishop Heber said :—" On this side of India there is really more zeal and liberality displayed in the improvement of the country, the construction of roads and public buildings, the conciliation of the natives and their education than I have seen in Bengal. . . . His policy, so far as India is concerned, appears to me peculiarly wise and liberal; and he is evidently attached to and thinks well of the country and its inhabitants. His public measures, in their general tendency, evince a steady wish to improve their present condition. No Government in India pays so much attention to schools and public institutions for education. In none are the taxes lighter; and in the administration of justice to the natives in their own languages, in the establishment of panchayats, in the degree in which he employs the natives in official situations, and the countenance and familiarity he extends to all the natives of rank who approach him, he seems to have reduced to practice almost all the reforms which had struck me as most required in the system of Government pursued in those provinces of our Eastern empire which I had previously visited." He so distinguished himself in his career that he was twice offered the post of Governor-General; but he felt that his work was done, and that his strength was unequal to the task. Nor could he be prevailed on to accept the peerage which was offered to him. A statue was raised to him in the Town Hall of Bombay, and the Elphinstone College and Elphinstone High School form an eloquent tribute to his name. His views on Indian politics showed a singular foresight. He held that if our Indian empire was to die a violent death, the seeds of its ruin would be found within the native army—a delicate and dangerous machine which a little mismanagement might easily turn against us. "The most desirable death it should die would be," he said, "the improvement of the natives reaching such a pitch as would render it impossible for a foreign nation to retain the government;" but this he acknowledged seemed at an immeasurable distance. He urged always a timely consciousness of danger. And apart from the army, he wrote words of emphatic warning against another danger of yet more tremendous import. "I have left out of the account the danger to which we should be exposed by any attempt to interfere with the religious prejudices of the natives. Our strength consists in the want of energy and the disunion of our enemies. There is but one talisman that, while it animated and united them all, would leave us without a single adherent—this talisman is the name of religion, a power so odious that it is astonishing our enemies have not more frequently and systematically employed it against us." He did not fear any direct attempt of Government to convert the natives; what he dreaded was the suspicion arising from ordinary and indifferent actions that it was disposed to encourage such an object. Prophetic words, that alas! were but too truly realised! The consciousness of danger was ignored, the army by mismanagement turned against us in the name of religion, and well-nigh the whole work of a century of conquest had to be done over again after the tempest of 1857.

Notwithstanding his conviction of the mighty foundations upon which the British empire in India rested, Elphinstone did not regard as an axiom its absolute permanency. In his earlier days he spoke of it as ephemeral, but his opinion considerably altered as he grew older. When he heard of the mutiny of the sepoys ordered to Burma, he wrote—" I used to think our empire made of glass; but when one considers the rough usage it has stood, both in old times and recent, one is apt to think it is made of iron. I believe it is of steel, which cuts everything if you keep its edge even; but it is very apt to snap short if it falls into unskilful hands."

He deprecated entirely all extension of territories beyond India; and from a man who had conducted an embassy to Kábul, and made that country his study, his words are of the utmost weight. As to the native princes of India, " You may leave them to their natural fate. Every Indian Government expires after a short existence. When there are no Europeans at hand, the country passes from the Ghuznevies to the Ghoories, from the Affghans to the Moguls, from the Moguls to the Mahrattas. When there is a stable Government, such as Europeans alone can found, it must necessarily swallow up all the ephemeral governments around it."

His writings, though not brilliant in narrative, give lively and realistic pictures of Indian scenes. Of a Marátha army he writes:—"Camp presents to a European the idea of long lines of white tents in the trimmest order. To a Mahratta it presents an assemblage of every sort of covering, of every shape and colour, spreading for miles in all directions, over hill and dale, mixed up with tents, flags, trees and buildings. In Jones' 'History' march means one or more columns of troops and ordnance moving along roads, perhaps between two hedges; in the Mahratta history, horse, foot, and dragoons inundating the face of the earth for many miles on every side; here and there a few horse with a flag and a drum, mixed with a loose and struggling mass of camels, elephants, bullocks, nautch-girls, fakeers and buffoons; troops and followers, lancemen and matchlock men, banyans and mootasuddies."

Mountstuart Elphinstone lived till 1859, in a pleasant and genial old age, mixing with old friends, and what were scarcely less than friends, his books. He had long since written a history of the Hindu and Muhammadan periods of Indian history. He continued this after his retirement to the period of English rule, but this part of his work was never published.

XIX.—POLICY OF SELF-EFFACEMENT.

IT was a bitter blow to Sir John Malcolm when Elphinstone and not himself was appointed Governor of Bombay in 1819. When Elphinstone retired in 1827, Malcolm, who was then fifty-three years of age, accepted the office in the vain hope that it might serve as a stepping-stone to the Governor-Generalship of India. But he lived to regret that he had undertaken duties which the force of circumstances rendered entirely uncongenial to him.

On July 4th 1827, there arrived at Calcutta, as successor to Lord Amherst, Lord William Bentinck. The eloquent inscription on his statue at Calcutta, by Lord Macaulay, has been read by thousands. "This statue," it runs, "is erected to William Cavendish Bentinck, who, during seven years, ruled India with eminent prudence, integrity and benevolence; who, placed at the head of a great empire, never laid aside the simplicity and moderation of a private citizen; who infused into Oriental despotism the spirit of British freedom; who never forgot that the end of Government is the welfare of the governed; who abolished cruel rites; who effaced humiliating distinctions; who allowed liberty to the expression of public opinion; whose constant study it was to elevate the moral and intellectual character of the Government committed to his charge;—this monument was erected by men who, differing from one another in race, in manners, and in religion, cherish with equal veneration and gratitude the memory of his wise, upright, and paternal administration."

Twenty-one years previously he had been roughly recalled from the Government of Madras. If he was harshly dealt with then, his reputation as Governor-General has been on the other hand altogether over-estimated, and the eloquence of Macaulay is singularly misleading. Of Lord William Bentinck's integrity and benevolence there can be no doubt whatever. Of his prudence there are the gravest doubts, unless it be said that his folly in returning to the policy of non-intervention is removed beyond the regions of all doubt whatsoever. In no land can outward show and the trappings of office be less profitably laid aside than in India; and in scrupulously observing the simplicity of a private citizen he deprived his great office of a dignity which rightly belonged to it. To infuse into Oriental despotism the spirit of British freedom is a task absolutely impossible. Lord William Bentinck did what other Governors-General had done before him, he rooted up the one to make way for the other. Two sentences of the inscription set forth with absolute truth the real glory of his administration. The end of his Government was the welfare of the governed, and he abolished cruel rites. But it cannot be admitted that in the first of these two works his predecessors had not already done much, though it was left to him to do vastly more. In the abolition of cruel rites he stood alone. The effacement of humiliating distinctions refers to his action in the creation of native judges, with primary jurisdiction over civil suits, to whose authority Europeans were subjected. The act excited the most vehement controversy. The fact was that it effaced no humiliating distinction whatever; and its sole effect was gratuitously and needlessly to humiliate Europeans in the eyes of themselves and of natives. It was a small thing that the conquering race, while subject to the same law as their conquered fellow subjects, should have the privilege of being tried by judges of their own race. It was a privilege that not a native in the land would dream of objecting to; his feeling on the subject being limited to surprise that the conqueror should apply to himself the same rigid justice that he enforced upon others. In his efforts to elevate the moral character of the Government—without depreciating what he did—it is due to at least two of his predecessors, Lord Cornwallis and Lord Hastings, to say that they made no feebler efforts in the same direction at a time when their efforts were of immeasurably greater difficulty.

Lord Amherst's wars had been excessively costly, and Lord William Bentinck had to effect retrenchments. Reforms of this nature are never pleasant. But the measures adopted were in the highest degree objectionable both to natives and Europeans. Both were alike dealt with in a spirit of harshness and unreasonableness to produce results utterly inadequate to the discontent that was caused. Europeans cannot be expected to pass their lives in the banishment of India without a remuneration that in some degree makes up for the privations inseparable from the country and its climate. What are luxuries in England are necessities in India; large establishments have to be kept up, constant transfers entail a corresponding expenditure, wives have to be sent home for their health, children for their education. Some Indian officials can save money; many more can, with the exercise of care, live in reasonable comfort on their pay; not a few end their career in the bonds of debt. Very few can be called rich. The expenses of all are heavy. Several times before attempts to cut down their allowances had been met with by action that amounted to mutiny. Knowing all this, in order to save the trivial sum of two lakhs (£20,000) a year for all

India, pay and allowances were cut down in every direction. The measure was met with intense disgust and wide-spread resistance. The retrenchment could not be enforced; and it ended in a miserable compromise, by which stations within 400 miles of Calcutta only suffered while those beyond it were exempted.

While this injudicious course had been adopted with Europeans, natives were incensed by new orders as to rent-free land. The alienations of land under native governments had been large; and on the country coming into English hands a certain amount had been sanctioned hurriedly without due inquiry or the ratification of higher authority. Undoubtedly injustice had thus been done to the state. The fiat now went forth that all such settlements were to be revised, and those persons only would be confirmed in the possession of rent-free lands who could establish their rightful claims. Under Eastern Governments an undoubted title to land is often incapable of documentary or even legal proof. But the order was insisted upon; wide-spread discontent was caused, and some substantial injustice done to save the state £300,000 a year.

The carrying out of these two measures brought vexation to the soul of Sir John Malcolm at Bombay. A man who had all his life been of the most social disposition, who loved gaiety and revelry, found himself in his declining years looked upon as an enemy by every European; and the retrenchments came with an ill grace from an officer who had needlessly laid on the country the burden of paying £80,000 a year to Báji Rao. On other subjects of legal interest he found himself at variance with the judges of the Supreme Court, especially with Sir John Peter Grant, afterwards Lieutenant-Governor of Bengal, who tried to push the power of the

Court so far as to bring the Executive Government into contempt. Malcolm accordingly bitterly condemned himself for having accepted the Bombay Governorship. But though he had no great opportunity of displaying his capacity for Government, and circumstances prevented his being popular, yet in an unpretending way he did much good; and his name in Malcolm Peth, the settlement on the range of Máhábleshwár, must always be remembered with gratitude by Europeans who breathe the pure air of the hills.

In other respects the internal administration of Lord William Bentinck was upright and fearless. The rite of Sati, by which the widows of high-caste Hindus burnt themselves on their husband's funeral pyres, was an abomination to him. In vain did his councillors tell him that to abolish the rite would be dangerous in the extreme. The thing was shameful, and it must go. What previous Governors-General had feared to do was done. Those implicated in Sati were deemed to commit murder; those present were held to abet the act. The law was at once put into force; and all honour is due to the courage of Lord William Bentinck. He did not know that the verse in the "Rig Wed," which the Brahmans used as an authority for the infamous custom, was garbled; and that the real meaning of the text was deliberately misinterpreted by the unscrupulous priesthood to sustain their own importance. But to the Governor-General the genuineness or falsehood of the authority for such an iniquity would have mattered little. The success of this reform enabled the Court of Directors a few years later after his retirement to take a further step which might have offended orthodox Hinduism. Scrupulously avoiding all appearance of religious persecution, the Company had erred in the other extreme; and their troops had been paraded, and offerings made to idols, at great festivals. This bowing down in the house of Rimmon was not only useless but pernicious. It was put an end to once for all in 1840, under the rule of Lord Auckland; but it was Lord William Bentinck's action that paved the way for its abolition.

Sati was done away with in 1829. The following year brought a deliverance from another curse of a very different nature. Over the whole of India there existed a mighty secret society which, like the Pindháris, embraced Hindus and Mussalmans alike. Taking their name from the verb thagna, to cheat, the Thags banded themselves together in the name of the goddess Bhawáni to reduce murder and robbery to a system. Such was their skill that though the association had existed from time immemorial the English had scarcely any knowledge of its existence before the year 1810. But their suspicions were aroused by the disappearance of a large number of Sepoys on furlough. Inquiries were being made in various quarters; and it may have been the consciousness that the English were on his track that induced the leader of one of their bands to give himself up in 1829 to Major Sleeman, the deputy-commissioner of Saugar in the Central Provinces. A strange and terrible tale was unfolded. As the merchant or banker journeyed from one city to another to sell his wares or negociate his bills, or as the soldier proceeded to his native village to enjoy his hardly-earned furlough, they met with other travellers going on similar errands, whose company was gratefully welcomed both for companionship on the journey and for protection on dangerous routes. Charmed with their fascinating manners the travellers journeyed on, delighted with the friends that chance had thrown in their way. But as they sat eating their meal in the shade of the way-side trees by the refreshing stream, the handkerchief of each Thag was round his victim's neck, and in a few short moments their bodies were buried in graves already prepared for them. In the very place where Major Sleeman's tent was pitched, his informant told him that the bodies of many murdered travellers lay concealed. The ghastly tale was only too true. The gang was taken; many more turned informers; and a searching investigation brought to light the immense organisation of the league, and a system of signs and counter-signs used by its members from one end of India to the other. A new department was created for the complete suppression of Thagism, and Major, afterwards Sir William Sleeman, placed at its head. Within six years more than 3,000 Thags were brought to justice, and Thaggi became extinct.

While a great change was introduced into India in 1830 by the navigation of the Ganges by a steamer built at Calcutta, fitted with engines from England, the Court of Directors discouraged steam communication between England and India, which the Governor-General endeavoured to promote. Their nominal objection was the score of expense; but there is no doubt that they strongly disliked a policy which would bring India nearer to England and take its exclusive possession out of their own hands. Their narrow-minded views however could not be sustained; and though regular steamers did not run for some time afterwards, yet when Sir John Malcolm retired from Bombay in 1830 he sailed up the Red Sea in the steamer "Hugh Lindsay," the pioneer of steam navigation in those waters. India was no longer to be a sealed book to all but the servants of the Company. On the renewal of its charter in 1833 it was deprived of the monopoly of its trade to China; and the Court of Directors became an administrative body subject to the Board of Control in England.

In spite of its jealousy of interlopers, the Company was compelled to allow Englishmen generally to reside in India, and hold lands there and develope the resources of the country by their capital and enterprise. Much credit has been given to Lord William Bentinck for sanctioning the admission of natives of all castes, including native Christians whose employment had been expressly prohibited, into the public service. It is difficult to see what change the order effected. To the present day only members of a few higher castes ever fit themselves by education and training for the position of magistrates and other responsible posts, while as messengers and subordinate servants, unless men of inferior caste were chosen, the places could never have been filled. A more salutary measure was that which substituted the vernacular dialects for Persian in the law courts, and encouraged the knowledge of the language and literature of England throughout India. Nor was the spread of English knowledge confined to mere book learning. A medical college was established at Calcutta, and European medical science brought within the reach of the people of India. Hitherto the barber had been the surgeon; and physicians were little but gatherers of simples, while the study of anatomy was unknown.

Much praise, though some blame, is therefore due to Lord William Bentinck for his internal administration. But his policy towards native states was miserably deficient. Each state for good or for evil was left to itself, as though British power were non-existent. In the Nizám's dominions a minister impaired the revenue, and created a horde of usurers and Arab and Pathán free-lances, whose extortions for loans advanced to the minister rendered the life of the people an intolerable burden. Even the Court of Directors remonstrated. "They could not," their despatch ran, "remain indifferent spectators to the disorder and misrule which had so long prevailed in the Nizám's territories." But the Governor-General left the remonstrances to be heeded or not as the minister liked, and the minister treated them with disdain. Anarchy was allowed to grow up and spread in Bhopál. In Sindia's dominions there was a struggle for power between the widow of Daulat Rao and her adopted son Jánkoji, which threatened to disturb the peace of all India. Lord William Bentinck, though he visited Gwálior, declined to interfere. In Jaypur a judicious interference would have checked a commotion which assumed large proportions, and culminated in the murder of Mr. Blake, the assistant resident. Lord William Bentinck may have been actuated by the best intentions. But he desired to make the rulers of native states responsible to their subjects, an idea absolutely unintelligible to the Oriental mind. It is only one instance out of many in which the application of European ideas and systems to India brings out in the strongest relief the impossibility of grafting on the native mind methods for which it is by nature entirely unfitted. India above all places must be dealt with in accordance with facts and not with theories; it is the last country in the world to submit to the experiments of the faddist and the book-worm. The liberty of the press in England degenerates into license in India; a superficial acquaintance with literature is mistaken for knowledge; the clap-trap of professional agitators passes muster for politics. The cause of the "Indian people" is taken up by a band of self-serving graduates who consistently revile the Government to which their class owes its very existence, while contact with the castes whom they designate the people of India means for

19

their self-styled champions contamination. Of all ideas perhaps the most inapplicable was that of the moral responsibility of the ruler to his people, and the hypothesis that a Government existed for the benefit of its subjects. But Lord William Bentinck was convinced of the righteousness of his political creed; and for the sake of his theory anarchy and disorder were suffered to grow up unchecked in one state after another. The British Government had become supreme arbiter in India. Of the duty of that Government to its subjects, the natives states included, there was no doubt whatever; and for his obstinate inaction Lord William Bentinck stands condemned.

XX.—THE AMIRS OF SIND.

WHEN Lord William Bentinck retired to England the north-west frontier of India was a very long way within its present limits. The Panjáb and Sind were as much foreign countries as Kábul. But a glance at the map will show that geographical necessity made it only a question of time for the incorporation of the Panjáb and Sind into the British dominions. And in spite of his non-intervention in the affairs of states that already formed part of the empire, Lord William Bentinck took steps in the case of both the Panjáb and Sind the consequences of which he little anticipated. In 1831 there was seen a magnificent spectacle on the banks of the Satlej when the Governor-General advanced to meet Ranjit Sing, the Lion of the Panjáb. This mighty chieftain had welded into a compact body the loose confederacy of the Sikhs; and the British Government considered him a potentate whose good-will it was advisable to secure. The two rulers parted with mutual expressions of friendship, and Ranjit scrupulously observed the faith which he plighted. In the following year an embassy was sent to Sind under Major Pottinger, who remained as political agent; and a treaty was signed with its rulers the Amirs which precluded the passing of military stores or troops along the line of the Indus by land or water.

In March 1836, Lord Auckland, the new Governor-General, arrived at Calcutta. He had no intention of being bound down by the observance of non-intervention; the errors which led to his calamities were of a very different nature. A year after his arrival a dispute as to the succession of the kingdom of Oudh led to civil war in that state. Lord Auckland promptly revealed his political principles. He took the matter into his own hands, and the crown was placed on the head of Nasir-ud-daula.

In 1839 he was compelled to interfere with a strong hand in the little kingdom of Sátára which Lord Hastings and Mr. Elphinstone had created in 1819. The Rája had for some time reigned quietly and inoffensively. But his weak intellect and extravagant ideas of his own importance were worked upon by the intrigues of Brahmans and the ladies of his court to such an extent that he actually proposed to re-establish the Marátha power, and drive the English out of the country. He was detected on several occasions attempting to corrupt the sepoys of British regiments, and other intrigues were brought home to him. His folly and presumption made warnings useless, and on September 5th 1839 he was finally deposed and sent to reside at Banáras. The state might fairly have been annexed, but a brother of the ex-Rája was invested with his sovereignty on the same conditions as his predecessor. It was owing to the advocacy of Sir James Carnac, Governor of Bombay, that the rebellious prince received such lenient treatment.

But matters of greater import were now being dealt with by Lord Auckland. Sháh Suja the Amir of Kábul had been driven out in 1809, and Dost Muhammad reigned in his stead. The exiled monarch resided under British protection at Ludhiána in the Panjáb. His successor, Dost Muhammad, diligently sought the alliance of the English on condition that they would not attempt to restore Sháh Suja, and would aid him in recovering Peshāwar which had been seized by the troops of Ranjit Sing. But Lord Auckland had no wish to quarrel with the Lion of the Panjáb for the sake of Dost Muhammad, and the dispute between those chieftains continued to smoulder. Meanwhile, Dost Muhammad had received at Kábul, as an envoy from the Governor-General, the accomplished Alexander Burnes. Burnes was empowered only to negociate a commercial treaty; but, judging English by the standard of Oriental diplomacy, Dost Muhammad entertained hopes that trade was merely a screen behind which the politics of the Panjáb and Áfghánistán could be discussed. While he was chafing under the loss of Peshāwar, and vainly seeking the aid of the English to recover it, there arrived at Kábul in 1837 a Russian envoy named Captain Vicovick. Dost Muhammad perceived that the English entertained the gravest anxiety about the Russian advance towards India through Khiva, and he determined to play off one envoy against the other. He hoped that when they saw his alliance sought by a hostile power the importance of his friendship would be magnified in the eyes of the English, and that by dangling with the Russian offers he would stimulate the Governor-General to form the much-desired convention with himself. But Dost Muhammad was playing with dangerous tools. The Russian scare, not without grounds, caused grave uneasiness to Lord Auckland and his Council. Herat was the northern gate of India; and the king of Persia in alliance with Dost Muhammad's brother was laying siege to it with the aid of Russian money and Russian officers. The siege failed owing to the vigour and judgement of Eldred Pottinger, a young artillery officer who happened to be travelling in Central Asia. The result of Dost Muhammad's policy was not what he looked for. Lord Auckland made up his mind to expel the chief who sought his alliance by flaunting the Russian overtures in his face; and, by restoring Sháh Suja to his throne, he hoped to secure a friendly Áfghánistán as a barrier against Russian aggression. At the same time all risk of a struggle between the Áfgháns and Ranjit Sing, which might involve the English, would be done away. In April 1838 Burnes returned to India, and Vicovick remained for the present triumphant.

It was necessary to demonstrate to Persia that no interference at Herat or elsewhere would be tolerated, and Lord Auckland instructed the Bombay Government to send an expedition to Karrak an island in the Persian Gulf. The Persian king understood the warning thus conveyed, and a treaty was signed which guaranteed Herat from any further molestation from that quarter. It was urged upon Lord Auckland and his Council that Russia could only act through Persia, and that Persia being now dealt with nothing further need be done, and Dost Muhammad should be left in peace at Kábul. Subsequent events have shown what Russia can do without aid from Persia; and of the ultimate Muscovite aims upon India there can be no manner of doubt. But that does not justify Lord Auckland for restoring by force an unpopular king whom his subjects had expelled from the throne, and whose repeated attempts to regain it they had invariably resisted. The war was condemned by Lord William Bentinck, the Duke of Wellington, Lord Wellesley, and Mountstuart Elphinstone; but the die was cast, and in November 1838 a magnificent army assembled at Ferozpur on the borders of the Panjáb, and was there inspected by Lord Auckland and Ranjit Sing. Ranjit Sing had a very clear idea of what was likely to be the final extent of the British possessions in India. On seeing a map of India with the

Company's possessions coloured red, he is said to have exclaimed—" Sab lál hojáega!" it will all become red. But he was not going to hasten the inevitable process, and not a British regiment was to march through his territories. Through the Panjáb the line to Kábul would have measured 500 miles, or from Átak on the Indus 300. But the Bengal army assembled at Ferozpur was to march to the south of the Panjáb, down the valley of the Satlej and the Indus to Rori. Thence it was to cross the river, and advance through the furious heat of the Sind desert and the terrific defiles of the Bolán pass round to Kándahár and Ghazni, a route not less than 1,500 miles. Ranjit Sing was strong and his territory had to be respected. The Amirs were supposed to be weak, and the troops were sent through their dominions. The details of the Áfghán campaign are without the limits of Bombay history. But the invasion brought in its train the conquest of the province of Sind.

The course of Bombay history had for many generations separated itself from Sind, a land which historically and geographically belongs to the Panjáb. From the time of its conquest by the Muhammadans it had been ruled by a succession of foreign governments. In the beginning of the 18th century the Kalloras, military fanatics from Persia, obtained the sovereignty and for a time retained hereditary power under the title of Mias. In 1771 the Beluch tribe of Tálpuris settled in the plains of Sind. They obtained the chief offices of the state and became the soldiers of the country. The Kallora prince jealous of their power put the chief of the tribe to death. A terrible series of murders, assassinations and massacres ensued. At length the Tálpuris made themselves rulers of the land, and drove the son of the last Kallora into exile in the Panjáb. The first Tálpuri chief was forced to share his possessions with his brothers. He died in 1800, and his brothers again divided the country, but unequally, and called themselves the Amirs or Lords of Sind. From this division sprang the Kyrpur Amirs of Upper Sind, the Hydarábád Amirs of Lower Sind, and the Mirpur Amirs. By a strange order of succession the Rais Pagri, or Turban, of superior rule passed in each family to the brother and not to the son. The Hydarábád family was to some extent obeyed by the others. The Amirs soon called down more of the hill Beluchis, giving them land on military terms; and with their aid they considerably extended their frontiers. From the Áfgháns they took Shikárpur, and the fortress of Bakar that was built on a rock in the middle of the Indus. In few places has Oriental despotism assumed a more terrible aspect than under these rapacious usurpers. "Give the poor a dhotar, it is enough," Shiwaji had said. "What are the people to us," observed the Amir Nur Muhammad to Lieutenant Eastwick in Sind. The policy of William the Conqueror of England was imitated; and the most thriving villages were depopulated to make Shikárgáhs or hunting-grounds. Slavery existed in the most repulsive form, while the Amirs collected from their subjects the uttermost farthing to pile up their swollen coffers.

In 1775 an English factory was established at Tatta on the delta of the Indus. It was abandoned in 1792 owing to the pressure of the Tálpuris, but in 1799 Lord Wellesley made an effort to restore it. The reigning Tálpuri prince appeared favourable to its maintenance, but the influence of Tipu from Mysur and the jealousy of traders at Hydarábád were too powerful to be resisted, and Mr. Crowe, the superintendent of the factory, was in 1800 peremptorily ordered to quit the country. In 1807 the Amirs were prevailed on to execute a treaty which provided for intercourse with the English by envoys, and for the exclusion of the French. This was renewed in 1820 for the purpose of settling border disputes with Kachh, where it had been necessary to send an army from Bombay in 1816. In 1831 a closer communication was made with Sind at the express wish of Lord Ellenborough, then President of the Board of Control; and, for the ostensible purpose of conveying presents to Ranjit Sing, Alexander Burnes was sent to explore the Indus and ascertain its commercial capabilities. He succeeded with great difficulty, and the advantages of the trade route became known. What was likely to come of this exploration by the English, in the interests of commerce, was speedily realized. "The mischief is done; you have seen our country!" cried a Beluchi soldier, when Burnes entered the river. "Alas! Sind is gone, since the English have seen the river which is the high road to its conquest," was the observation of a wealthy Muhammadan near Tatta. The following year Captain Pottinger was sent to survey the course of the lower Indus, and to negociate the treaty that has been already referred to. He found the lower country governed by the Amirs of Hydarábád, the chief of whom was Ali Murád.* In Kyrpur, the capital of Upper Sind, Mir Rustam was chief, and practically independent, though he faintly acknowledged the superiority of Hydarábád. Identical treaties were formed with Ali Murád and Rustam. Free passages were granted through Sind for travellers and merchants; but no vessel of war was to float on the Indus or military stores to be conveyed by it. A reasonable tariff was to be proclaimed. In 1834, by another commercial treaty, the tariff was fixed, and Colonel Pottinger appointed political agent for Sind.

---

* Not the well-known Ali Murád of Kyrpur.

The tolls taken at the mouth of the Indus were to be shared by the British Government; for did not their own river the Satlej flow to the sea mingled with the waves of the great river of Sind? A year later a steam-boat from Bombay navigated the Indus.

In 1836 Ranjit Sing threatened an invasion of the Amir's territory. Lord Auckland welcomed this opportunity for interference. His whole policy turned on counteracting the increasing influence of Russia in Central Asia. That policy it has been seen, was to be effected by obtaining control over the intervening country of Áfghánistán. The ruler of the Panjáb was too wary to be coerced into furthering this project; Sind was another affair altogether. Lord Auckland pressed the Amirs to receive a British force in their capital to protect them against the Lion of the Panjáb, and Colonel Pottinger went to Hydarábád to negociate the proposition. The peculiar constitution of the Amirs rendered all negociation with them difficult. The chief Amirs of each branch was always willing to consent, but there was invariably a strange difficulty in obtaining the compliance of the inferior nobles, each of whom was independent of the rest. The territories of the three chiefs were mixed and confused in the most bewildering way, and this labyrinthine system they had no wish to disentangle for the benefit of the encroaching foreigner.

Colonel Pottinger reached Hydarábád in September 1836; but, though he reported in December that his negociation was successful, no ratified treaty appears to have been concluded until a year and a half later. It was then made only in consequence of significant hints that Ranjit Sing would, to say the least, not be discouraged from working his pleasure in Sind. The argument did not lose force from the notorious fact that the connection between Ranjit Sing and the Governor-General had been cemented by a personal interview. Thus was obtained the ratified treaty of April 1838, providing for the mediation of the Indian Government and the permanent residence of a British political agent at Hydarábád; and that officer was to be at liberty to move about the country attended by such an escort of troops as his Government should consider suitable. In other words, the county was to be occupied by British troops. Lord Auckland believed, not without grounds, that Russian agents were busily engaged in combining the nations of Central Asia against the British empire in the East. The Persians, he knew, were besieging Herat with their assistance. Whether by appealing to the self-interests of those races—cultivating the good-will of the Áfgháns, Sindis, Turkmáns, Persians—he might have counteracted the Muscovite designs it is impossible to say. Lord Auckland's proceedings, whatever else they did, succeeded in rendering the English name odious to one and all of these peoples.

In June 1838 a tripartite treaty was drawn up between the English, Ranjit Sing, and Sháh Suja, part of which had reference to Sind, whose rulers were not consulted in the matter. The Amirs of Sind were considered to be vassals of the kingdom of Kábul. As *de jure* ruler of Áfghánistán, Sháh Suja had long-standing claims against them to supremacy and tribute. By the treaty he now relinquished these claims, on condition of the payment of a sum of money to be determined by the English. The Sháh, the Amirs were told, would arrive at Shikárpur in November supported by a British army. The money must then be paid, or in lieu of payment the Sháh would take military possession of the town and district of Shikárpur. The amount was left undetermined, but it was significantly observed " the Amirs must be wealthy." The claim was obsolete, and the Ámirs retorted plainly that it was not made by Sháh Suja, but that the demand was entirely that of the English by whom he had been supported for twenty-five years. The Amirs were also told that the article of the former treaty, which forbade the transmision of military stores up the Indus, must be suspended in favour of the English. As regards this particular measure, it is manifest that in drawing up the former treaty an exception was intended in favour of those who had the provision inserted.

Whatever the Amirs might think of the proceedings of the English it must have been clear to them that arguments were useless. Five thousand men were ready to sail from Bombay, and the Bengal army was coming down the Satlej, without the form of asking leave, to occupy their territories. It was chiefly the Amirs of Lower Sind who were pressed for money for the Sháh's army, and for the admission into their country of a subsidiary force, with the certain result of the whole of their dominions being subdued. But it was in Upper Sind that the Bengal army would cross the Indus. In the middle of the river was the rock and fortress of Bakar. Sir Alexander Burnes was ordered to negociate a treaty with the Kyrpur Amirs for the loan of the rock and fortress. It was now said, and undoubtedly not without some reason, that the Sind authorities had violated the commercial treaties. Lord Auckland displayed intense indignation, and at the same time pity, for the distracted government; and declared that 5,000 troops should seize Shikárpur, and such other strategical positions as might be necessary. Those of the Amirs who had shown any unwillingness to aid the invasion of Áfghánistán were to be displaced from power; but they were all assured that the seizure of their territories meant nothing injurious to their interests. Menaces, flattery, promises, and evasions were alike in vain. The Amirs then offered personal violence to Colonel Pottinger, and this failing to intimidate him was followed by abject apologies. The iron screw was indeed being twisted on Hydarábád by Pottinger, and Kyrpur by Burnes. From one demand indeed Pottinger recoiled. How could he demand money from the Amirs, on a claim due to Sháh Suja, when they produced formal discharges of all claims written in Koráns duly signed and attested? His scruples were set at rest by instructions that that part of the transaction would be arranged by another officer. The whole course of the negociations was in fact sickening, and it is needless to follow it through its humiliating details. Both Burnes and Pottinger advised open war in preference to this diplomatic hypocrisy.

In December 1838, Sir John Keane arrived at the mouth of the Indus, and in January 1839 marched up to Hydarábád. Driven to despair, the Kyrpur chief, Rustam, gave up Bakar, or, as he phrased it, "the heart of his country," and admitted Upper Sind to be a British dependency. The Amirs of the lower provinces, exasperated beyond endurance, plundered the stores collected at Hydarábád, chased Lieutenant Eastwick ignominiously from the residency, and put 20,000 Beluchis in motion against the Bombay army. Karáchi was instantly seized by the English and an advance ordered, when the Amirs, quailing at the storm which they had raised, signed a new treaty, and for the indulgence paid £200,000, half of it on the instant. The treaty brought Sind as entirely into the British power as was possible without absolute annexation. Stringent as the document was it did not satisfy Lord Auckland. Without the slightest reference to the Amirs he retained Karáchi, and altered the treaty to that effect.

The treaty had been made in the names of Hydarábád and the Indian Government. But that implied a paramount chief of Sind. A separate treaty was therefore made with each Amir, and they were told that " they must consider Sind to be, as it was in reality, a portion of Hindustán, in which the British were paramount, and entitled to act as they consider best and fittest for the general good of the whole empire."

The only palliation of these negociations is the score of necessity. If the invasion of Áfghánistán was an act of self-preservation the injustice in Sind may be condoned as pardonable, though even then it would have been less ignoble to seize the country without the miserable pretexts that were stooped to. As to the facts about self-preservation, they need not be considered in the history of the Bombay Presidency. But one consideration cannot be too strongly insisted on. Bad as all this was, the transgression was not against a nation: it was against Amirs who had usurped the country within the memory of living men, and who were the most atrocious tyrants that can possibly be imagined. The British camps offered an asylum to thousands; and of the Queen's subjects in India none have gained more from the British Government than the peaceable inhabitants of Sind. The Amirs and the fierce Beluchi warriors, who lived on the spoil of the Sindis, suffered. But even this defence cannot be pleaded on behalf of Lord Auckland, for his treaties left the people in the absolute power of their rulers.

The armies now passed on to Kábul; the subsidiary force entered Sind, and the Amirs passively recognised the treaties. Colonel Pottinger, created a baronet, continued resident in Sind until the beginning of 1840. He was then replaced in the lower country by Major Outram, Mr. Ross

Bell taking charge of the upper country. This officer died in 1841, and Major Outram became agent for the whole of Sind and Beluchistán. But while the Amirs continued apparently submissive they evaded payment of the tribute. Territory is more valuable than tribute, and Lord Auckland in 1841 seized Shikárpur, then the largest city in Sind. Bakar was theirs already; and with these places in the North and Karáchi, the only good port in the South, the English held the Amirs in a grasp of iron.

Nor were the military operations then going on confined to India itself and countries connected with it by land. In 1837 a ship was wrecked at Aden, and the crew plundered by Arab subjects of the Sultán of Laling. The demands of the Indian Government were evaded, and Aden was therefore bombarded and taken. Peace was made in 1843, but Aden was retained and strongly fortified, and it is garrisoned by the Bombay army. It is curious to note that in the time of Lord Wellesley, he and his Council recorded their opinion that the proposed measure (to occupy Aden) was in no respect eligible (1800). The overture of the Sultán of Aden was therefore declined in conciliatory terms. Perim, too, the island at the mouth of the Red Sea was stated not to possess the advantages expected of it, and it was not thought proper that it should be occupied by British forces.

XXI.—CONQUEST OF SIND.

UNTIL the beginning of 1842 Sind reposed in apparent quietude. British stores passed up the river unmolested, for none dared meddle with the irresistible British strength. But the fire of revenge smouldered in the hearts of the humiliated Amirs, and the blast was springing up to fan it into flame. A terrible tragedy had occurred at Kábul. England's generals had blundered—her soldiers had forgotten of what race they sprang. In January 1842, the whole army at Kábul capitulated; and 4,500 soldiers and 12,000 followers marched back towards India. Of these only one, a doctor named Brydon, survived to tell of the awful catastrophe by which every soul but himself perished in the defiles of the Khyber Pass.

Lord Auckland was stricken down in mind and body when he heard the miserable news. But a new and more vigorous man was fortunately on his way; and on the 28th of February his successor, Lord Ellenborough, who had already been President of the Board of Control, arrived at Calcutta. He found the public mind confused with terror at the Kábul vicissitude. Nothing was being done to retrieve the misfortune. The soldiers were depressed in spirit, and smarting under the deprivation of their just allowances. But the sky was not all gloomy. Apart from Sind, and the country beyond the frontier, India was in profound peace. No conquered state lifted its head; no chief attempted to rally round him the thousands of unquiet spirits that ever exist in Oriental states, or drew his sword against the supreme power. Ranjit Sing was dead, but the Sikhs as yet continued his friendship with the English; the Maráthas, under a firm and liberal rule, had turned their swords into ploughshares. So Lord Ellenborough could concentrate his entire energy on remedying the evils that his predecessor's policy had brought upon the empire.

A heavy blow had been struck at British supremacy. It was absolutely necessary to show the Eastern world that a reverse did not mean defeat. The English arms must for the safety of the empire be borne triumphantly through Afghánistán, and the British hold on Sind must be maintained. Lord Ellenborough had not come out to pass judgement on his predecessor's political morality; he had to accept accomplished facts, and to insist upon the observation of existing treaties. It was as much beyond the range of practical politics to retire from Sind because Lord Auckland had seized it under a guise of friendship, with a velvet glove on an iron hand, as to give up Bengal on account of Clive's dealings with Mir Jáfar and Umáchand. He sent a solemn warning to the Amirs. "On the day," he wrote, "on which you shall be faithless to the British Government, sovereignty will have passed from you; your dominion will be given to others." Major Outram at an early period informed Lord Ellenborough that "He had it in his power to expose the hostile intrigues of the Amirs to such an extent as might be deemed sufficient to authorise the dictation of any terms to those chiefs, or any measure necessary to place British power on a secure footing;" and he advised the assumption of the entire districts to render British power invulnerable. Major Outram's deliberately expressed opinions are noteworthy in view of the embittered controversy which subsequently sprang up between himself and Sir Charles Napier, whom he accused of intentionally bringing on an inexcusable war. Outram's proofs of the hostile disposition of the Amirs were ten in number. They were undoubtedly numerous and strong; they showed positive violations of the treaties made with Lord Auckland, and a wide-spread conspiracy to destroy the British troops in Sind. It has been said that some of the papers proving the conspiracy were forgeries. That tolls were being levied and other articles of the treaties broken was beyond dispute. In forwarding his report Outram recommended a new treaty of very stringent terms. Lord Ellenborough accepted the facts, but drew up a milder treaty. He proposed to punish the Amirs for their infidelity by taking from them the districts of Sabzalkot and Bhung Bhara in the north of Sind, and restoring them to the chief of Bahawalpur, from whom they had been wrested thirty years before by Rustam and the other Amirs. The right of cutting fuel for the steamers on the banks of the Indus was insisted upon. Instead of the tribute, Sakar, Rori and Bakar in Upper Sind, and Tatta and Karachi in Lower Sind, were to be ceded in perpetuity. This secured the absolute military command of the Indus and freedom of trade on its course. Arrears of tribute were to be forgiven.

It was hardly to be supposed that the Amirs would yield to these terms without a murmur. The progress of the avenging army through Kábul might cause them to bide their time, but the final desertion of that country in September 1842 appeared to them a proof of weakness. The victorious Áfgháns reminded them that they were feudatories of the Áfghán kingdom, and incited them to act boldly in the common cause; and the Amirs consulted together how they might best act against the English. At this juncture Major Outram was replaced in political charge of Sind by Sir Charles Napier. "I will present your treaty to the Amirs," Sir Charles Napier wrote to the Governor-General; "I will spare no pains to convince them that neither injury nor injustice are meditated, and that by accepting the treaty they will become more rich and more secure of power than they are now. If they refuse to listen to reason, if they persist in sacrificing everything to their avarice and hunting-grounds, they must even have their way, and try the force of arms at their peril, if they are so resolved." Among the many Amirs of the three branches it was unlikely that all would be actuated by patriotism. Rustam of Kyrpur was an old man. His younger brother, Ali Murád, determined to obtain for himself the Kyrpur turban of supremacy; and with this view he threw himself into the arms of the English. Sobdár of Hydarábád adopted a somewhat similar course. Ali Murád induced Rustám to come to him at his strong fort of Diji, and there resign to him the pagri or turban of command, with all the rights and lands attached to it. Sir Charles Napier had meanwhile crossed the Indus with a considerable body of troops in the middle of December, and was proceeding to take possession of Sabzalkot and Bhung Bhara. He was now close to Diji; and, seemingly entertaining some doubt as to the voluntary nature of this cession, he proposed to Rustam to visit him, and offered to restore him to his dignity if he had been coerced. Rustam would have nothing to do with the English leader. He fled into the desert with his treasure, two guns, and several thousand followers. From this flight the Sind war may be said to be dated.

In order to conduct the details of the new treaties, the Governor-General had permitted Sir Charles Napier to name a commissioner. He selected Major Outram, and Lord Ellenborough, in spite of his having no personal predilection for that officer, sanctioned the nomination. Major Outram was accordingly recalled to Sind. He had to deal with the three sovereign families of Kyrpur, Hydarábád, and Mirpur, and the separate members of those families who claimed more or less independent power. The flight of Rustam secured the alliance of Ali Murád; and while it forced the other princes of the Kyrpur family to display their hostility, it effectually prevented their union whether with one another or with the chiefs of Lower Sind. Of their hostility there was no doubt. It might have been unreasonable to expect anything else. Rustam denied his cession of the turban to Ali Murád, but refused to meet Sir Charles Napier. The English general's first step was to disperse the armed bands which had gathered in clouds around Kyrpur. A strong demonstration effected this without the need of striking a blow. But the crisis was only deferred. The whole country was rising, and it was known that the Amirs counted on having 70,000 men and thirty pieces of cannon. The slightest advantage to their cause would bring down in myriads the Áfghans and Beluchis from the mountains. Besides these forces, they counted on the fierce heat of their climate, their arid deserts, and the deadly miasma of the swamps along the Indus as allies whose aid could not fail them. And they had two stupendous fortresses at Hydarábád and Imámgahr.

By the beginning of January 1843 it was evident to the English general that while the Amirs were amusing themselves with protracted negociations they had no intention of signing the treaty. They were with rapidity and energy concentrating their forces to attack him at the close of the cold weather. But while he gave them every opportunity of signing the treaty, he had not the least intention of letting the cold weather pass, and be compelled to carry on a campaign under a sun more formidable than the weapons of the enemy. A son of Rustam, named Muhammad Khan, had thrown himself with 3,000 men and treasure into Imámgahr, which he had stored with grain and gunpowder, and was making the basis of operations for the army of Upper Sind. The fortress was in the heart of the desert. Its exact position was not known, and no European had ever set eyes on it. It was said to be eight long marches distant. In several of the marches there was no water. The Amirs had absolute faith in the desert and believed the fort to be impregnable. Sir Charles Napier's political career in Sind has been bitterly attacked. But on his daring courage and military genius no doubt whatever has been cast. The Amirs had not realised the nature of their opponent. He resolved to capture Imámgahr.

The task was hazardous for his army of 3,000 men. But a native agent brought such a tale of arid sand and dried-up springs that the general accepted the impossibility of moving his whole army through the desert. He selected 250 irregular cavalry, put 350 of the 22nd Queen's Regiment on camels, loaded ten more camels with provisions and eighty with water and plunged into the desert. The march began on the evening of the 5th of January. Ali Murád, as the chief of Kyrpur in alliance with the British, accompanied the force. The night was dark, the sand deep, and the guide missed his way. But before they halted the troops had moved twenty-five miles. The next day's march was shorter; forage failed, water was scanty, and three-fourths of the cavalry was sent back.

Nor was the march unmolested. Rustam and his armed followers were on the flank of the English with seven guns. Major Outram was sent to bring him to reason, while Napier pushed on with his fifty horsemen, two howitzers, and his 350 Irish infantry. The country through which their route lay was a succession of sand-hills, some so steep that the howitzers could only be dragged up by men. The solitude of the waste was unbroken. They were not even sure of the right course; food and water were doled out in scanty portions, but they marched on with unimpaired energy. On the eighth day they reached Imámghar to find that Muhammad Khán, in spite of having a strong fortress, abundant supplies, and a garrison six times as numerous as the little band coming against him, had fled with his treasure. The fortress belonged to Ali Murád the ally of the English. But it might again be seized by a hostile party. The general therefore determined to destroy it utterly, and Ali Murád fired the first gun against its walls. The grain was distributed to the troops, the stores of powder employed to load twenty-four mines for the blowing up of the fortress. This work was carried out by Major Waddington, the chief engineer. The matches were all lighted and the assistant engineer took refuge behind some cover, but he perceived his chief bending over the train of one mine. He eagerly called out to his chief to run as the other mines were about to burst. "That may be," was the reply, "but this mine must burst also." Major Waddington deliberately arranged his match to his satisfaction and walked away, marvellously escaping injury from the huge fragments which the bursting mines hurled around him. Flushed with success, the gallant band marched back to the Indus without the loss of a man; their object was completely attained, the enemy's plan of campaign baffled. In the House of Lords the Duke of Wellington thus described the exploit. "Sir

Charles Napier's march upon Imámghar is one of the most curious military feats which I have ever known to be performed. He moved his troops through the desert against hostile forces; he had his guns transported under circumstances of extreme difficulty, and in a manner the most extraordinary, and he cut off a retreat of the enemy which rendered it impossible for them ever to regain their positions."

On the 23rd of January the general brought his troops to Pir Abu Bakr, in the valley of the Indus. He had already invited the Amirs of Lower and Upper Sind to send envoys to Kyrpur with full powers to sign the treaty. From Upper Sind none came; from Lower Sind the envoys sent by only one of the Amirs had the requisite powers. By the end of January there was no change in the situation. The general knew that the hot season was rapidly approaching and no time was to be lost. While he hoped for peace he had no reason to expect it. The conduct of the Amirs was suspicious. Armed men were gathering from every quarter. It was beyond all manner of doubt that the Amirs of all Sind were making common course. Major Outram held that he could bring the Amirs to submission, and was therefore allowed to proceed to Hydarábád while the general slowly moved his forces in that direction. Everything was done to delay his movements. The Amirs imagined that by continually promising to sign the treaty, and then by delaying on all possible pretexts, they could procrastinate till their fierce sun drove the British troops out of the field to take shelter in cantonments. They protested that if the general advanced southwards they could not restrain their Beluchi warriors, whose very existence they had previously denied. They sent a secretary to Outram to sign a promise to accept the treaty, and at the same time assembled a large army four miles north of Hydarábád. By the 12th of February that army amounted to 60,000 men, but on that day the Amirs signed and sealed the new treaty with great formalities. The result proved that the Amirs were right in one thing. They could not restrain their wild Beluchi warriors. Whether they had any wish to restrain them is another question. Their subsequent behaviour hardly warrants the supposition that they did. But Outram, quite inconsistently with his policy in Lord Auckland's time, would see or hear nothing to their disadvantage, and he besought Sir Charles Napier to leave his army and come alone to Hydarábád and settle the whole matter. The advice was fortunately not accepted. On the 14th of February the Amirs bribed Outram's native secretary into giving them the treaties which they had solemnly signed and sealed; they tore them to pieces and trampled them under foot in the darbár in which they had signed them. But the wild Beluchis were furious at the disgrace which had accrued to their rulers by the signature of the treaty, and were not to be pacified by its destruction. Incensed beyond measure, they attacked the Residency on the 15th; and Outram, a magnificent soldier if a doubtful diplomatist, after making a spirited resistance, took refuge in a steamer which the general had sent in anticipation of danger.

Both sides prepared for battle. The forces of the Amirs took up a splendid position at Miáni, a few miles north of Hydarábád. On the night of the 16th the British army marched to meet them, and at eight o'clock next morning the advanced guard discovered the Amirs' camp. Their front was upon a natural rampart, formed by a sand-bank lining the nullah or dry bed of the river Falaili, a connection of the Indus. Their wings rested on large Shikárgáhs, or wooded hunting-grounds, dense with jungle and trees. The natural strength of the position was increased by skilful military appliances. The enemy numbered thirty-five thousand, the British less than twenty-four hundred, and from this small number a guard had to be taken to protect the followers and baggage. Sir Charles Napier had twelve guns flanked by fifty Madras Sappers and Miners, the 22nd Queen's Regiment of impetuous Irishmen, the 1st Grenadiers and the 22nd and 25th Bombay Infantry, the 9th Bengal Cavalry, and the Sind Horse led by Captain Jacob. A plain, a thousand yards wide, separated the armies, and the Beluchis' cannons were already firing across it. The advance was ordered full against the enemy's front. In the Shikárgáh, on their left, the general detected an opening, which had been prepared to allow the Beluchis to pour out on the flank and rear of the advancing British line. The inspiration of genius seized him. He ordered Captain Tew with eighty men of the 22nd to block up the entrance, and if need be die at his post. He did die at his post; but the opening was defended, and the action of 6,000 men paralysed by that of eighty.

A magnificent spectacle was now seen. Dashing across the plain, swept by the Beluchi cannon and matchlocks, the British troops pressed eagerly on to close with the numberless masses of the enemy. When they were within a hundred yards of the high sloping bank, over which the heads of the Beluchis could be seen, they wheeled into line. The voice of the general, shrill and clear, commanded the charge; with a British shout the guns were brought into position and the infantry rushed up the sloping bank. For a moment they staggered back at what they saw beyond it. Far as the eye could reach thé wild Beluchi warriors covered the ground, brandishing their sharp swords. With wild yells and frantic gestures they dashed with awful ferocity at the devoted band that dared to fling itself against them. But a moment later the Irish, and the Bombay sepoys, with cheer upon cheer, met their charge and sent their foremost masses rolling back in blood. For three hours and a half the furious contest raged. Never more than three yards apart, the adverse ranks were borne this way and that, as Barbarian might and British discipline for a time swayed the scales. The savage Beluchis, with unabated but vain fury, tried to drive back the English troops. They leaped upon the guns and were blown away by twenties at a time; the bayonet and small arms sent the dead in hundreds down the slope—ever more and more came on. The English general seemed everywhere, cheering and rallying his men.

Nearly all the English officers were slain or wounded, and victory had not yet shown itself. Napier saw that in another twenty minutes the battle must be lost or won. He had hitherto kept in reserve his Bengal and Sind horsemen under Colonel Pattle, the 2nd in command. These he ordered to turn the enemy's position on their right. So rough was the ground over which the cavalry had to advance, and so cut up by ditches, that fifty of the Sind troopers were thrown from their horses by the leaps. But rapidly mounting, they crossed the bed of the nullah, gained the open plain beyond, and charged with irresistible fury. At last the Beluchi swordsmen wavered. The 22nd saw their masses shake; they hurled themselves upon them with the shout of victory; the gallant sepoys by their side pushed their opposing forces into the ravine and renewed the fierce struggle. The battle was won. Doggedly and slowly the Beluchis retreated, still glaring with fury as the victors poured in volley upon volley into their ranks till they were weary of slaughter. The carnage on both sides was awful. The enemy lost 6,000 men, or three to each man of the British force. Napier lost 270, including twenty officers of whom four were field-officers.

The next morning at daybreak the general sent to the Amirs to say that he would immediately storm Hydarábád if they did not surrender. Six sovereign princes entered his camp and offered themselves as prisoners, laying their swords at his feet. Out of pity for the fallen their swords were restored to them. On the 19th the army took possession of Hydarábád, the Amirs being left in full enjoyment of their palaces and gardens, while the conquering general contented himself with a small field-tent. His work was by no means over. The chiefs of Kyrpur and Hydarábád were settled with. There remained Sher Muhammad of Mirpur, who was only six miles off from Miáni with 10,000 more men whom he was bringing up to the aid of the other Amirs. Napier intended to suppress opposition from this quarter immediately after the occupation of Hydarábád. But Outram begged leave to negociate with Sher Muhammad, whose temper he understood thoroughly and who, he affirmed, never meant to fight. Napier gave a reluctant consent, and the Amir promptly rallied round him the Beluchis who had escaped from the late battle. He soon had 25,000 men, and prepared to begin the war again. The captive Amirs did their utmost to aid him by plots and intrigues, so the general put them on board his steamer on the river.

Sher Muhammad was anxious to induce the general to follow him into his deserts, and so have the English troops at his mercy. But Napier was prudent as well as dashing. His army was decimated, more troops were on their way to join him, and while awaiting their arrival he formed a strong intrenched camp not far from the field of battle at Miáni. For more than a month he remained inactive, baffling his enemies' plans and filling them with false hopes that inactivity meant weakness. Napier, meanwhile, obtained six months' provisions, and reinforcements of every kind; and by enticing Sher Muhammad close to his position he saved his men from long marches and was able to choose his own field of battle. Sher Muhammad was totally misled. He sent a message to the general that his army must yield or it would be utterly destroyed. By the 23rd of March Napier had 5,000 fighting men and his preparations were complete. "Tell the Amir Sher Muhammad," he said to the envoys who had brought the insolent message, "that if he chooses to surrender himself a prisoner when I march to attack him to-morrow at the head of my army, without any other conditions than that his life shall be safe, I will receive him."

On the morning of battle, when the British troops were drawn up in line, a messenger reached the General with despatches from Lord Ellenborough. All posts had been intercepted for two months. With an eager hand the general broke the seals, and read the heart-stirring words in which the Governor-General expressed his thanks to the army for its past conduct, and the victory at Miáni, and assured them that honour and rewards would wait on that great battle. Instantly the general made known the despatches to his men, and a great shout rose up to heaven of pride and exultation, and of honour for the leader who had not forgotten to name the private as well as the officer to the Government whom they all served. The shout was the cry of victory, and each man's heart was full as he marched to meet the foe.

The army marched ten miles and came upon the enemy at eight o'clock in the morning near the village of Dabba, not far from Miáni; but the action that followed is generally known as the battle of Hydarábád. The attack was instantly commenced by the artillery on the British left; and on the enemy's side there was a rush of men from their left to strengthen their right wing that was thus menaced. Napier's cavalry was on his right, and he suddenly perceived them dashing full speed against the enemy opposite them, whose movement towards the centre they had taken to be a flight. The advance at that moment was in entire disregard of Napier's plan. He gallopped off to stop it; but it was too late to remedy the error, and he resolved to utilise it. After watching the cavalry for a moment careering wildly against the foe, whirling their swords above their heads and pealing their war cries, he turned back to his own left, put himself in the front of his foremost ranks, and in a clear high-pitched voice gave the word to charge. The bank before them was steeper than that of Miáni, but the fiery soldiers were over it in a moment, and with a mighty cheer leaped into the midst of the swordsmen. For three hours the battle raged desperately, but at last the enemy were driven back, their infantry fighting valiantly to the last. Their cavalry were less plucky, and were pursued by the Bengal and Puna horse for several miles into the desert. The number of killed and wounded on either side were much the same as at Miáni.

With Sir Charles Napier, nothing was done while anything remained to be done. The dreadful heat was daily increasing. Sher Muhammad had still a force of four to one, and he had two fortified towns Mirpur and Umarkot on which to fall back. Mirpur was forty miles from the field of battle. The next day the Puna horse were at its gates, which were opened by the Sindis, who welcomed their deliverers from the

Beluchi yoke. Sher Muhammad had fled from Hydarábád to Mirpur. He now fled on to Umarkot. He was not left undisturbed there. Within ten days after the battle, Umarkot was reduced and garrisoned by a British detachment, though one hundred miles distant in the heart of the desert. The exertions required to effect this were indescribable, but Sher Muhammad again anticipated the arrival of the troops and fled into the desert. On the 3rd of April Sir Charles Napier marched back into Hydarábád master of Sind, having in a short campaign fought two such battles as are without parallel in the history of the Bombay Presidency.

Lord Ellenborough annexed Sind, and made Sir Charles Napier Governor, independent of the Presidencies and responsible only to himself. He was instructed to abolish slavery and ameliorate the condition of the people as far as possible. The captive Amirs, eleven in number, were transferred to Bombay. The highest rewards and honours were liberally apportioned by Lord Ellenborough to all who had shared in the arduous campaign. Outram considered the final attack on the Amirs inexcusable and declined to receive his share of prize-money. The Kyrpur family, on account of the loyalty of Ali Murád to the British, were confirmed in possession of a considerable portion of territory as a dependent state. Ali Murád himself, whose conduct has been stigmatised as base and treacherous to his own people in the highest degree, was subsequently convicted of perjury and forgery, and was punished for his offences; but the punishment has been condoned and he still lives in Upper Sind. Sher Muhammad was pursued relentlessly till June, when the remnant of his forces were dispersed by Jacob and his Sind horse, and the Amir fled into Beluchistán with only ten followers. "We have taught the Beluchi," said the general, "that neither his sun, nor his desert, nor his jungles, nor his nullahs can stop us; and he will never face us more."

The policy of Lord Ellenborough and the exploits of Sir Charles Napier were vindicated and accepted by the sovereign and both Houses of Parliament. Whatever be the injustice of Lord Auckland—who coerced the Amirs for the purpose of his Áfghán war and compelled them to sign treaties which destroyed their independence—Lord Ellenborough had no choice when, after acquiescing in the treaties for three years, the Amirs proceeded to violate them and prepared to drive the English troops out of the land. He was compelled for the safety of the empire to punish the transgression of the treaties and impose new conditions. After every kind of evasion, the Amirs signed the new treaty only to tear it in pieces as soon as it was signed, and attack the British troops, not in despair, but in every confidence of destroying them. Sind had to be conquered. The only people who have suffered for it are the Amirs and their Beluchi retainers. The peaceable Sindi population have not lost, but immeasurably gained. Sind did not long continue a separate province. The Bengal sepoys strongly disliked garrisoning the valley of the Indus, and the task was handed over to troops from Bombay, and Sind became part of that Presidency.

But while the Bombay Maráthas had been loyal and quiet during the warfare in Sind and Kábul, the same could not be said for Sindia's state at Gwálior. Jánkoji Rao Sindia had died without a male heir, and the usual course of intrigue and rivalry ensued. The Queen-mother dismissed the regent who had been recognised by the Governor-General. This was an insult to British authority and the resident left the court. The affairs of the state fell into unutterable confusion, and the regent, who was supported by the army, showed a defiant attitude to the British Government. The Sikhs of the Panjáb were plotting with the men of Gwálior; and Lord Ellenborough, after earnest remonstrances, in which he stated that the friendly intercourse which had existed for forty years with the house of Sindia could not be allowed to be interrupted, led an army to Gwálior. The Maráthas attacked the English at Máhárájpur, but were defeated, after a desperate battle, by Sir Hugh Gough; the British loss being nearly 800. On the same day at Panniár, twelve miles off, another Marátha army was defeated by Colonel Grey. The Queen-mother was deprived of her regency. The splendid army, which had been disciplined by De Boigne, was reduced to 9,000 men, and a contingent placed in the charge of British officers, a certain amount of territory being ceded for its maintenance. Lord Ellenborough's prompt action against the rebellious army of Gwálior was the salvation of that State. It prevented a coalition with the Sikhs of the Panjâb, whose enmity towards the English was ceasing to be a matter of doubt (1843).

Besides Sind, Lord Ellenborough's rule brought another small addition to the Bombay Presidency. In December 1838 died Raghoji Ángria, the descendant of the pirate princes of Kolába. The family had learnt nothing since Lord Clive battered down the walls of Gheria, and the cruelty and oppression of Raghoji was such that his people remembered his rule as that of Angárak, or Mars, the planet of evil influence. A posthumous son was born to him, who died in 1840, and the legitimate line of the Ángria family became extinct. The Kolába State was annexed and at first administered as an agency, and afterwards formed into the

Kolába district. In the island of Underi (Henery) there was found a loathsome dungeon in which were confined twenty-four prisoners in the most abject misery. They had been denied water except for drinking. They were loaded with fetters, and covered with filth and disease. They had been imprisoned for from three to twenty years. No term of imprisonment had been fixed, and no one knew what offences had been committed. They were of course set free.

An expedition was also needed against the state of Kolhápur. In 1817 the reigning prince had cordially aided the British Government. His successor Báwa Sáhib was a typical eastern tyrant and more than once the Bombay Government had to interfere with force. This Rája died in 1842 leaving two sons, both children. The misrule became so intolerable that the British authorities assumed the management of the state, and a native minister was appointed under the control of the Political Agent at Belgaum. Many reforms were at once introduced, including the abolition of the hereditary garrisons of the strong forts of the state. These measures were resented, and in 1844 an insurrection took place in which the Sáwantwári people joined. So serious was it that it took a force of 10,000 men under Outram to quell the disturbances above and below the Gháts. The fort of Panálla was bombarded and taken, and part of the fortifications demolished. A separate Political Superintendent was then appointed for Kolhápur.

XXII.—THE LAW OF LAPSE.

IN July 1844 Lord Ellenborough was succeeded by Sir Henry, afterwards Lord Hardinge, who reduced the armies of the Panjáb in the first Sikh war. Indian politics centred without Bombay, and the general development of the Western Presidency continued without any specially noticeable events. There was some trouble in 1845 with the warlike Kolis of the Gháts, and an outlaw named Raghoji Bhángria, of Násik, wandered through the Násik and Áhmadnagar districts robbing and mutilating the moneyed classes. The country was in terror of his name, but the police pursued him with such vigour that he broke up his band and disappeared. He was not himself captured till 1847, when Lieutenant (afterwards General) Gell caught him at Pandharpur. He had been guilty of several murders and he paid the penalty on the gallows.

In March 1848 Lord Hardinge returned to England, and Lord Dalhousie succeeded to his post. The second Sikh war soon took place; the army of the Khálsa invading British territory, the Panjáb was again conquered and this time annexed by the proclamation of March 29th 1849. Another addition was also made to Bombay. At the close of the Marátha war of 1817 Lord Hastings had placed on the throne of Sátára, out of sympathy for native feeling, the powerless descendant of Shiwáji. The Rája thus set up by the English had plotted against those to whom he owed everything and was sent to reside at Banáras. His successor died without issue in April 1848. As he lay on his death-bed he adopted a boy, who though distantly connected with him, had no direct claim to the succession of the state. That the boy by Hindu law could become heir to the Rája's private property and perform the necessary ceremonies for the dead there was no manner of doubt. But the state was of English creation, and it was argued that the Rája had no right to adopt an heir to the throne without the consent of the paramount power. Consent had neither been obtained nor asked, and Lord Dalhousie held that the state in consequence lapsed to the British crown. The theory was no creation of Lord Dalhousie's. Under the Moghal empire, viceroys who had carved out in all else an absolute independence, invariably obtained from the suzerain sanction to adoption and succession. Apart from the abstract question of right to annex the state its expediency was unmistakable. The Rája had created no enthusiasm amongst the people of the Deccan; and they were not likely to trouble themselves any more about a boy adopted from a distant family to keep up an empty name. It was altogether beneficial for the Maráthas of Sátára that they should come under a rule which had done so much for the rest of their countrymen. Two succeeding Governors of Bombay, Lord Falkland and Sir George Clerk, argued that the adoption could only be considered applicable to the personal property; and Mr. (afterwards Sir John) Willoughby, a member of the Bombay Council, reviewed the whole subject in an exhaustive minute. Lord Dalhousie's opinion coincided with that of Bombay. "The Government," he remarked, "on such occasions is bound to act with the purest integrity and the most scrupulous good faith. Whenever a shadow of doubt can be shown the claim should at once be abandoned; but when the right to territory by lapse is clear, the Government is bound to take that which is legally and justly its due, and to extend to that territory the benefit of our sovereignty present and prospective." The question was referred to the Court of Directors. On January 24th 1849, the Court, which was supported by the Board of Control, wrote as follows:—"By the general law and custom of India a dependent principality, like that of Sátára, cannot pass to an adopted heir without the consent of the paramount power. We are under no pledge, direct or constructive, to give such a consent; and the general interests confided to our charge are best consulted by withholding it." In accordance with this opinion Sátára was annexed. While the royal line of Shiwáji thus came to an end that of the Peshwa was soon to follow. Báji Rao had been sent to Bithur, near Cawnpore, on a magnificent pension of £80,000 a year. In 1853 he died childless, having adopted as an heir Dhondu Pant, the infamous Nána Sáhib of the future massacres of English women and children at Cawnpore. Dhondu Pant inherited the personal property of Báji Rao, whose private hoards were acknowledged to be more than a quarter of a million sterling, and were proved to exceed half a million. In addition to this private property, Nána Sáhib received the town and territory of Bithur for his lifetime. But he regarded himself as one of the most injured of mankind, because the Government would not continue to him the absurdly lavish pension which Sir John Malcolm had obtained for Báji Rao. He in vain besieged the Indian Government with his complaints, and when that plan failed he sent an agent to

London to obtain redress for his wrongs. The mission was, of course, futile; but the rejection of his claims led to unexpected consequences.

Such were Lord Dalhousie's actions in affairs that concerned Bombay. In other parts of India he acted with no less decision. The Panjáb had been annexed. A fresh cession of territory in Barár was made by the Nizám—in whose dominions law, justice, and government had degenerated into the merest farce—in payment of accumulated debts to the Government of India on account of the contingent force and to provide for the maintenance of that force in future. In Madras, the Nawáb of the Carnatic dying childless, his family was provided for; but, as at Sátára, the sovereignty, nominal as it long had been, came to an end. The states of Jhánsi and of Nágpur, the seat of the Rája descended from Raghoji Bhonsle, lapsed to the Government for want of heirs; and tired out with the monstrous abuses in the kingdom of Oudh, Lord Dalhousie annexed that country to the British Government. Another Burmese war ended in the dethronement of the king and annexation of a large part of his territory.

On the 6th of March, 1856, Lord Dalhousie sailed from India after recording a celebrated minute as to the events of his term of office. He left India with the full assurance that it was in a state of profound and, as he hoped, lasting tranquillity. He was only forty-four years old, and toil had so told on a frame naturally weak that he lived but four years longer. Throughout his career he had laboured incessantly for the bettering of all classes and all ranks in India. The rule of native princes, if the expression can be legitimately applied to lawlessness and anarchy, was miserably bad. He was determined that the British Government should not continue responsible for the upholding of this misgovernment and tyranny; and therefore naturally concluded that the only way to increase the happiness of oppressed millions was to extend the blessings of British rule. An article in the London *Times* ably summed up what he had done. " He, Lord Dalhousie, could point to railways planned on an enormous scale, and partly constructed; to 4,000 miles of electric telegraph spread over India, at an expense of little over £50 a mile; to 2,000 miles of road bridged and metalled, nearly the whole distance from Calcutta to Peshawár; to the opening of the Ganges Canal, the longest of its kind in the world; to the progress of the Panjáb Canals, and of many other important works of irrigation all over India, as well as to the reorganization of an official department of public works. Keeping equal pace with these public works, he could refer to the postal system which he introduced in imitation of that of Rowland Hill, whereby a letter from Peshawár to Cape Comorin, or from Assam to Kurráchee, is conveyed for three farthings, or one-sixteenth of the old charge; to the improved training for the Civil Service, Covenanted and Uncovenanted; to the improvement of education and prison discipline; to the organization of the Legislative Council, to the reforms which it had decreed—such as permitting Hindoo widows to marry again, and relieving all persons from the risk of forfeiting property by a change of religion. Many more items might be added to the list, were it necessary, to prove the largeness and benevolence of the views of this great statesman; and there is no doubt from his recorded opinions, that the annexation measures so bitterly urged against him, were founded on the conviction that in effecting them he had relieved millions from the irregularities and oppressions of native governments, and secured for them the prospective advantages of protection and peace. No one can record, for few know, of his daily toil, or how, with a delicate frame, he overcame it; toil which overworked and destroyed his physical powers, and in 1860 sent him to his grave. 'I have played my part,' he said sadly, in reply to an address from the people of Calcutta, 'and while I feel that in my case the principal act in the drama of my life is ended, I shall be content if the curtain should now drop on my public career.'"

XXIII.—THE SOWING OF THE WIND.

WHEN Lord Canning succeeded Lord Dalhousie as Governor-General, the British army in India consisted of 45,000 European troops and 235,000 sepoys—that is, a proportion of about one-fifth. And in all the battles which the English had won in India, the proportion of sepoys to white troops had been about the same. The discipline, which proved so irresistible against undisciplined hordes of Asiatics when it was confined to Europeans, was just as efficacious when imparted to native troops. An eminent Professor* has therefore argued that our conquest of India is a misnomer. The theory which attributed our successes to any superiority of race is now repudiated. Nay more, according to the same authority, our English writers in describing the English battles in India seem unable to discern the sepoys. The assertion is astounding. From Macaulay's description of the siege of Arcot to Lord Tennyson's siege of Lucknow; at Assaye, Khirki, Miáni and Hydarábád, historians delight to record the exploits of the sepoys who fought side by side with their European brethren. But the difference of the conquerors and conquered, if there were any conquered, is said to lie more in discipline and military science than in difference of race. The English undoubtedly rule India. But the process by which they attained this

---

* Professor Seeley, " Expansion of England."

proud position was not the conquest of one state by another; it was merely an internal revolution in Indian society, and is to be compared to one of those sudden usurpations, or *coups d'état,* by which a period of disturbance within a community is closed. We may suppose, we are told, that a number of Parsee merchants in Bombay, tired of the anarchy which disturbed their trade, had subscribed together to establish fortresses and raise troops, and then that they had had the good fortune to employ able generals. In that case, it is said, they too might have had their Plassey and their Buxar; they too might have extorted from the great Mogul the dewannee or financial administration of a province, and so laid the foundation of an empire which might in time have extended over all India. Parsees are most loyal and exemplary subjects of the Empress of India, but the idea of their merchants trading in a hostile country with their sword in one hand and ledger in the other, and leading sepoy battalions to victory against overwhelming numbers involves an unique power of imagination. In fine, the natives of India were quite capable of receiving European discipline, and learning to fight with European efficiency. This then was the talisman which the Company possessed, and which enabled it not merely to hold its own among the powers of India, but to surpass them—not some incommunicable physical or moral superiority, as we love to imagine— but a superior discipline and military system, which could be communicated to the natives of India.

The contention is wholly false. England did conquer India, or the various powers that occupied the Indian Peninsula, in a series of operations that lasted a century. She conquered it, not by that which she could impart to another race, but by that which could not be imparted. She conquered India by downright hard fighting against enormous odds. True, the king of England did not declare war upon any Nawáb or Rája in India. But England happened to be represented, not by the king, but by the East India Company, and the Company did declare war against both Nawábs and Rájas, though it was generally spared the necessity by Nawábs and Rájas making war upon its armies. But India was conquered by Indians in English pay, just as though at Waterloo the Duke of Wellington led bands of Frenchmen against Napoleon. Again the view is incorrect. There is no India as there is a France; and when Clive led his Madras sepoys at Plassey and Napier his Maráthas at Miáni, the sepoys were as much foreigners to the enemy as the English themselves. It would be idle to discuss the subject further. The English did conquer India, and not solely or in chief part by a superior military system, but by stout hearts and strong arms, and a refusal to acknowledge that they were ever beaten. The military discpline was an admirable, nay an indispensable means to the end; but the means without the instrument were vain; the letter only, not the spirit, could be imparted to the natives of India. The brain that could create was even more powerful than the brain that could merely receive and imitate; the skill that could repair the machinery more valuable than the mere rule-of-thumb knowledge that could put it in motion or stop it when the works were in perfect order. The race with whom military tactics and formations were only the instrument by which the mind that directed them worked its will, could not but prevail over adversaries who looked on military evolutions as possessing in themselves an inherent and all-sufficing virtue.

Already, in wild Marátha battles, the British troops had fought against soldiers disciplined by the skill and genius of

Frenchmen; in the crowning struggle of all, in which the hundred years' conquest had to be well-nigh all done over again, they were to contend with the sepoy troops whom they had themselves taught, trained, and led to victory; troops who possessed to the full the talisman of discipline and military system by which it is stated the Company surpassed the native powers of India, and which would have been no less efficacious in the hands of Parsees.

The Duke of Wellington was of a very different opinion. "The English soldiers," he wrote, "are the main foundation of British power in Asia. They are a body with habits, manners and qualities peculiar to them in the East Indies. Bravery is the characteristic of the British army in all quarters of the world; but no other quarter has afforded such striking examples of the existence of this quality in the soldiers as the East Indies. Those particularly who have been for some time in the country, cannot be ordered upon any service, however dangerous or arduous, that they will not effect, not only with bravery, but with a degree of skill not often witnessed in persons of their description in other parts of the world. I attribute their qualities, which are peculiar to them in the East Indies, to the distinctness of their class in that country from all others existing in it. They feel that they are a distinct and superior class to the rest of the world which surrounds them; and their actions correspond with their high notions of their own superiority. Add to these qualities that their bodies are inured to climate, hardship and fatigue—by long residence, habit and exercise—to such a degree, that I have seen them for years together in the field without suffering any material sickness; that I have made them march sixty miles in thirty hours, and afterwards engage the enemy; and it will not be surprising that they are respected as they are throughout India. Their weaknesses and their vices, however repugnant to the feelings and prejudices of the natives, are passed over in the contemplation of their excellent qualities as soldiers, of which no nation has hitherto given such extraordinary instances. These qualities are the foundation of the British strength in Asia and of that opinion by which it is generally supposed that the British empire has been gained and upheld. These qualities show in what manner nations consisting of millions are governed by 30,000 strangers."

The great storm that burst over India in 1857 at first confined itself to Bengal; and the awful tragedies, the work of vengeance, and the final victories occurred beyond the limits of Bombay. But the tail of the storm spread to the Western Presidency, and Bombay armies won mighty victories over the insurgents in Central India, and the causes that led up to the mutiny must be told here.

These causes were extremely manifold and complex. It is impossible to this day to mention any one particular event which prepared the conflagration, or the absence of which would have prevented it. That the affair of the greased cartridges caused the mutiny is true in no sense whatever. That it was the spark which kindled the mine that was already laid, and whose explosion was only a question of time, there can be no manner of doubt.

. The Government of India had grown up in the form of three Presidencies, and with this disposition of the civil power, there had arisen the three separate armies of Bengal, Bombay, and Madras. Of the 45,000 European troops in India, some 10,000 were soldiers enlisted by the Company for its local European regiments of Bengal, Bombay, and Madras Fusiliers, who had nothing to do with the Queen's army. The native armies, each under its own commander-in-chief, differed widely in their constitution and discipline. The Bengal army was composed for the most part of Brahmans and other high-caste men, while in the other armies men of lower castes predominated. The sepoys of Bengal generally left their wives in their native villages; while in the remaining armies their families were carried about with them, and formed a very weighty guarantee for their good behaviour. But the high-caste men of Oudh and the North-West who filled the ranks of the Bengal army, ready as they were to face any danger, were above the humble duties of the soldier, while their brother sepoys of Bombay and Madras, for whom they had no little disdain, were altogether more amenable to discipline. In the early days of the sepoy army, natives of good family were chosen as officers and trusted with a large amount of authority which their birth and habits of command enabled them to wield. Their position was honourable, their self-respect assured; native officers and privates alike regarded with a devoted enthusiasm their European officers who led them to a succession of victories and respected their caste and religion. But even from the first, incidents occurred which showed how delicate was the link that bound the sepoy army to its masters. Seven years after Plassey five Bengal battalions were discontented with their share of prize-money. They showed a threatening attitude and received their claims; but they had learnt their strength, and a few months later the oldest regiment broke out into open mutiny. The ringleaders were blown from guns and the battalions taught a severe but salutary lesson; the number of English officers with each regiment was increased, and the real power gradually concentrated in their hands. But for many years the command of a native regiment was a coveted appointment, and picked men were chosen for the posts who could keep their men in hand by fear as well as by love. In 1796 there was a further change in the organization. It was a legitimate source of complaint of the veteran officers of the Company that they were superseded and passed over by younger men from the regiments of the King's as opposed to the Company's army. In order to remove this grievance, one regiment was formed out of each two battalions of sepoys, the number of officers assimilated to that of the king's regiments, and all took rank by the date of their commissions. The system of promotion by merit undoubtedly gives rise to occasional jobbery; but still the best man will, as a rule, come to the front, while in the seniority system he is weighed down by an unbending rule which reduces all to a dead level of equality. Thus the command of regiments often fell into the hands of men unfitted for the task; and the decrease in the number of native officers lowered the position of those who remained. The doors of ambition were closed to the sepoy, be he a rival of Hydar Ali in military genius. And at the present day, it may be said, that while the position of the Hindus is on an infinitely higher level under the English than under Akbar himself, that one prospect of high military command, which he trusted to them, is now absolutely precluded. With the new organization the sepoy found that the pay of a boy ensign, just from England, was higher than that of a subadár who had served the Company faithfully for thirty years. Still they were flushed with victory, and had not at first leisure to brood over their grievances. But in Madras that leisure came with the destruction of Mysur; and while the ties of personal devotion which bound the sepoys to their officers were weakened, the evil star of that overrated statesman Lord William Bentinck, who was then Governor of Fort St. George, prompted him to sanction, if he did not originate, some ridiculous orders which interfered with the sepoys' religious prejudices. They were forbidden to appear on parade with caste-marks or earrings; they were to shave off their cherished beards, regulate the length of their moustaches, and exchange their old turbans for leather cockades, which resembled that object of aversion to Orientals the European hat. The leather, made of skins of hogs or cows, was abominable to them; the likeness of the hats to that of Christians not unnaturally made them believe that the change was a preliminary to forcible conversion. What had been done by Aurangzib, Tipu, and the Portuguese was not impossible from the English. Dispirited by their grievances, they were ready to believe anything against their rulers; they gave a ready ear to the tales of religious fanatics who went about the country and told them of the intolerant fanaticism of their conquerors. In Ceylon, they were told, the general had already marched his whole corps to church parade, and they believed that a like fate would soon be theirs. At Vellore was the residence of the pensioned family of Tipu who, state prisoners as they were, still hoped for their restoration to their father's dynasty. Here were the very means to their hands. It is probable that they excited the sepoys to mutiny; that they encouraged their plans, when once formed, is certain. They ridiculed the European appearance of the sepoys, and assured them they would soon have to receive the baptism. The consequence was a horrible outburst at Vellore, which involved the slaughter of the European garrison when they were asleep; and symptons appeared at other places. The mutiny was promptly suppressed and a terrible vengeance accomplished. Lord William

Bentinck managed to quell the storm that he had raised, and persuade the native soldiery that the Government had no thought of interfering with their religion; and the Directors, after recalling the Governor, placed on record a stringent censure of the new generation of commanding officers who had not, like their predecessors, won the confidence of their men. This part of the lesson was taken to heart, and the advantages of a sepoy's career, under officers who were proud to command him and who treated him with paternal kindness, were sufficient to tempt a steady supply of good men. The sepoy received regular pay, an advantage unknown in native states; he retired on a comfortable pension, where a native ruler would let him die in a ditch. He was still a great man in his own family, and he had, what amongst a litigious people was no small privilege, the right of being heard in our courts before other suitors. And a series of victorious campaigns, in which he fought side by side with his European comrade, identified him in no slight degree with the conquering race. But the successful campaigns brought accession of territory, and able men were needed to manage the new acquisitions. Thus the ablest officers were drafted from the regiments to act as political agents and fill other important and lucrative posts; and again the sepoys were quick to see that the fortune of the officers that left the regiments was envied by those who remained. A growing tendency to reduce everything to rules was also springing up, and the paternal and patriarchal power which a colonel possessed was interfered with by a system which centralised military authority at head-quarters, and frequently reversed the decisions of regimental officers. The sepoy was naturally the very last man to mutiny. He entered the army with no rights of his own; he was ready to reverence his colonel as an absolute ruler. But written law, as opposed to personal rule, was unintelligible to him; and when he heard of the articles of war framed in a way which seemed to expect him to break them, and when he learnt the subordination of his colonel to head-quarters in every petty matter, the spell that bound him was broken. And so when the order came to cross the "Black Water" to Burma it came to hearts that were already hardened. Under any circumstances the order would have been distasteful. To cross the sea was against the rules of the higher castes, and of the powers of Burmese magic they had heard strange stories. An exaggerated account of a reverse to some regiments which had already arrived at Burma was credulously swallowed. Three regiments refused to parade for inspection in marching order before proceeding on the voyage. Sir Edward Paget, the Commander-in-Chief, knew that leniency in mutiny means cruelty; that to spare a few lives is to lose many. The sepoys were forced on to the parade-ground, and told to choose between marching or grounding their arms. They refused to do either. Instantly the artillery opened fire upon them with grape-shot; numbers fell dead, and the rest fled. The 47th Regiment was disbanded, the offence of the other two condoned. The lesson was taken to heart, and for years none dared to mutiny.

Lord William Bentinck had done enough harm at Madras. He was to do more as Governor-General. He bitterly offended and aggrieved officers of all ranks by depriving them of a portion of their allowances. In Lord Clive's time such a step was followed by mutiny. To Lord William Bentinck the officers sent a temperate statement of their grievances, which, except in the case of those near Calcutta, was ignored. The futility of the officers' resistance gave another blow to their weakened authority over their men. Not content with this, Lord William Bentinck abolished corporal punishment in the army in defiance of universal military opinion. The native officers, who had all risen from the ranks, were vehemently against it. Well-behaved men had nothing to fear from flogging, the black sheep, who must exist in every regiment, only suffered the punishment if they deserved it. If flogging was abolished, the native officers said, the army will no longer fear and there will be a mutiny. Orientals are excellent judges of their own character. They have a very wholesome regard for fear, and severity based on justness. Of flabbid humanitarianism they have but one opinion, and that is that it proceeds from weakness.

Then came the Áfghán war and its terrible disaster. Here were the ever-victorious soldiers of their masters forgetting that they were British troops, and a whole army capitulating to barbarians. True, the glorious victories that followed over the Amirs of Sind, the rebellious army of Gwálior, and the Sikhs of the Panjáb might well be regarded as more than sufficient to restore the honour of the British arms to its pristine splendour, but the possibility of a British army bowing down before an Asiatic foe was a matter within their actual experience. More than this, they had never received with good grace the orders that sent them beyond the Indus. For the gloomy defiles and barren mountains of Áfghánistán they felt an invincible repugnance. Their hearts burned with indignation against their masters who had led them to defeat in this unknown land, where the bodies of their kinsmen lay unburnt and unburied, food for vultures and beasts of prey, with none to perform funeral rights for the repose of their souls. When Nott and Pollock led the avenging army against Kábul, several regiments refused point blank to enter the dreaded passage of the Khyber Pass, and it was with the utmost difficulty that the mutiny was quelled. Again, as Sind and the Panjáb were annexed to our dominions, new difficulties cropped up. To the sepoy mind the lands beyond the Indus were a foreign country, to garrison which meant for him banishment to distant and often unhealthy places. In a foreign land he was accustomed to receive extra allowances to encourage him to fight the battles of his Government; the annexed countries were no longer foreign, and the extra allowances ceased. When ordered to take their turn of duty in Sind as an ordinary province of India, the 14th Bengal Native Infantry, the 34th and the 61st, the 7th Cavalry, and some artillery mutinied; and the insubordination gained its object, for Bombay troops were sent to Sind. With Madras troops Sind was no more popular, and under the dread of being sent there and to Kábul regiments at Sikandarábad, Nágpur, and other places were within measurable distance of mutiny. But there was as yet no general conspiracy, and an inconsistent policy of punishment and concession was held sufficient to deal with the matter. Of the frightful seriousness of the evil it cannot be said that the Government was not warned. Sir Charles Napier succeeded Lord Gough as Commander-in-Chief of India, and feeling convinced that the native army was in a state of covert mutiny and treachery, he lost no opportunity of impressing his views upon Lord Dalhousie. Napier had failed in Sind to work in harmony with Outram. He failed equally to do so with Lord Dalhousie. Both he and the Governor-General were men of commanding minds not unapt to resent advice or interference; and his arguments failed to take effect. Napier's service had been with the Bombay army, which had a stricter internal discipline than that of Bengal. In the Sikh wars the Bombay sepoys were taunted by the high-caste Brahmans of the Bengal army with performing ordinary duties which had never been imposed upon them. This did not escape Napier's eye. But it was the difficulty about the pay that for the time was more pressing than that of caste. Four regiments refused to accept the reduced rates, and many soldiers were tried and punished. The 66th Bengal Native Infantry, which partially mutinied, was disbanded, and a Gurkha regiment of Nepál Highlanders raised in its place. Sir Charles Napier, on his own responsibility, raised the pay of the army in the Panjáb; but an acrimonious correspondence ensued between him and Lord Dalhousie, and Napier resigned his appointment determined not to be a passive spectator of the ills that he foretold. His opinion may have been exaggerated when he reported to Lord Dalhousie that twenty-four regiments were only waiting an opportunity to rise, but the disaffection of the Bengal army was a notorious fact. As Napier said, to pamper high-caste is to encourage mutiny, and in Bengal it was encouraged to a dangerous extent. It was not that in the other armies the sepoys were free from caste prejudices, but they were not given into. Even in Bengal the caste was not especially obtruded, except when the spoilt sepoys found it could be used as an instrument by which they could exaggerate their own importance or gain their particular ends. Lord Dalhousie may, indeed, be blamed for not going to the root of the matter. But in his busy reign he had a multitude of weighty tasks to do that engrossed the whole of his time; and, while the very existence of the evil was denied by many whose position entitled their opinion to deference, those who recognised the disease proposed diametrically opposite schemes for effecting its cure.

And while their loyalty was undetermined, the disparity of British troops to their own numbers gave them an overweening idea of their own power. Tipu had said that it was not what he saw of the English that be feared, but what he did not see. That his opinion had been handed down shows that it was by no means an ordinary one. The sepoys, unfortunately, judged England by what they saw, and of her vast resources they had no notion whatever. They believed that the whole population of the British Isles amounted to merely a hundred thousand souls. Their notions were not likely to be dispelled by the action of the Home Government, which withdrew two regiments from India for service in the Crimea; and they listened with absolute credulity to stories of the exhaustion of England in the Russian war, and the disease and death of her soldiers in the trenches at Sebastopol. Nay more, with the endless inconsistency of the Oriental mind, Muhammadan sepoys exulted in the reported annexation of England to Russia, though they believed the war to have been undertaken by the Queen of England as a vassal of the Sultán of Constantinople. Against the denuding India of British troops, when many more were urgently needed to guard the new conquests, Lord Dalhousie strenuously protested. But his recommendations were not adopted; and the sepoys, inflated with the idea of their own power, were developing plans, as yet misty and hazy, of taking the government of the country into their own hands.

But if Lord Dalhousie on sailing from India had no notion of the whirlwind that was gathering, there was little likelihood that Lord Canning should suspect it. He was not a weak man, but he was cold and impassive; and he could not bring himself to pass judgement on any question until he had scrutinised it and reviewed it from every point of view with minute carefulness. He wanted the quick insight of the general, who on the field of battle could instantaneously note and resist each movement of his enemy. But, when he had grasped the position, he was keen in judgment and strong in resolve.

The sum of the sepoys' grievances had not yet come. Originally they had been enlisted for service in India alone. The conquest of Burma, and the difficulties of inducing native soldiers to cross the sea, had led to the raising of six regiments for general service. It happened that soon after Lord Canning's arrival none of these were available to relieve those whose time of duty at Pegu had expired. Lord Canning determined to be master of his own army, and in July 1856 issued an order that in future no recruit should be accepted who would not undertake to march wherever he might be wanted. High-caste men at once began to shrink from entering the service, while old sepoys were full of fearful surmises that the oaths of new recruits might be binding upon themselves. With this new order came another, that sepoys declared unfit for foreign service should no longer, as of yore, be retired on invalid pensions, but should be kept on for cantonment duty; and a privilege, which allowed sepoys to send their letters free, was brought to an end upon the completion of the new postal regulations. Another grievance sprang up from the annexation of Oudh, which was a prolific recuiting-ground of the army. Under Muhammadan rule, every complaint of oppression or injustice to the family or kindred of an Oudh sepoy was forwarded to the British resident at Lucknow and promptly redressed by him. This system conferred a valued prestige upon the sepoy as the great man of his family or village. With the introduction of British rule, and the concomitant theory of equality of persons—so unintelligible to the native of India—the family of the sepoy was referred to the ordinary courts; and the sepoy looked on the abrogation of his privilege as a grave indignity.

The sepoys were thus in a mood to believe any lie; the more incredible it might be, the more eagerly would it be gulped down. They were to be superseded by a Sikh army of 30,000 men. Lord Canning had been specially selected by the Queen to convert them all to Christianity, and the General Service Enlistment Act was the first step in the policy of persecution. Missionaries had been becoming for some time past more and more active, and had a year or so before published a manifesto foretelling that the new railways and steamships were destined to accomplish the spiritual union of England and India under one faith. The Commissioner of Patna reported to Government the dangerous feelings which this had caused in his division; a reassuring proclamation from the Bengal Government appeared only a false statement to hide the suspicions that had been raised. Earnest Christian officers unwittingly hurried on the danger by preaching the gospel to the men under their command. The preposterous notion gained strength by the new law which removed legal obstacles to the marriage of Hindu widows, and dealt a direct blow to the integrity of their religious system. Nor did the sepoys fail to supply a reason for the proceedings which they ascribed to Government. Their masters intended to take away their caste and make them Christians in order that they might eat the strengthening beef and drink the commissariat rum of English troops; that they might then embark in ships and go forth with renewed vigour on the endless task of conquest. And while the whole army was seething with agitation, yet still afraid to strike, the slumbering fires that were to burst forth into conflagration had spread beyond the sepoy ranks.

The English were availing themselves of all the resources which the advance of civilization was placing in their hands. The native of India had served many dynasties; but hitherto they had looked on their masters—whether Moghal, Marátha, or English—as people who had vast armies and could use them as they would. Now they had a new and strange experience. The land itself was being bound down in iron bands, over which the fire-chariot sped along at a speed greater than that of the swiftest Marátha horseman. And the lightning posts and wires, set up along the roads, enabled their rulers to know in some mysterious way what was happening at a distance of hundreds of miles. On their rivers, ships moved against the strongest current without oars or sails. That all these devices were new to their rulers they never dreamt. Their own power of invention had been dead for centuries; and they believed that the English had kept hidden these wonderful resources all these years in order to use them the more effectually when the time had come. A yoke was to be fastened upon the land which would never be shaken off, which would destroy their ancient customs, their caste, and their religion. Everything pointed in the same direction. In the Government schools, while their hereditary faith was not directly assailed, the growing generation was filled with a learning which to their parents was new and dangerous, and at variance with their time-honoured notions. The English were altogether changing, and it was impossible to live under their sway. Hitherto the priestly caste of Brahmans had held the keys of knowledge. But they could no more explain the new contrivances than the most ignorant ryot; their supremacy, as the learned class, was threatened; their implacable jealousy was aroused.

By a strange coincidence, this period of their agitation was close to the end of the hundred years which followed the battle of Plassey. By a people, credulous and superstitious in the highest degree, the astrologers were implicitly believed when they prophesied that the anniversary of Clive's great victory would bring to an end the Ráj or rule of the Company. In the most ordinary affairs of life natives consult the astrologers as to a favourable conjunction of the planets; and when it was told them that the year before the end of the Company's ráj there would be terrible outbursts of cholera and flood, and the cholera and floods came, how could they doubt the speedy downfall of the English?

But even yet the tale of the causes that led up to the great tragedy is incomplete. The palace of the Emperor Bahádur Sháh, at Delhi, was a focus of perpetual intrigue. It was also a strategical position of immense value. Lord Dalhousie determined that its possession was essential to the Indian Government, and he bitterly offended the family of the emperor by arranging that Bahádur Sháh should remove his residence to the Kutab, and give up his palace for British troops. Action was, however, deferred for the lifetime of the aged emperor; but before his death the last vestige of the Moghal empire had ceased to be. Bahádur Sháh was an old man; but in the veins of his queen, Zinat Mahal, flowed the blood of Nádir Sháh, and, inspired by her fiery will, the princes of the house of Bábar planned the revival of the Muhammadan empire. The princes, on apparently innocent pretexts, had been allowed by Government to travel about India; and they journeyed hither and thither securing adherents to the throne of Delhi. It was a repetition, very awfully intensified, of the history of Vellore; an army saturated with treason; a royal family encouraging and utilising the treason to further its own ends. A more powerful monarch joined in the fray. In November 1856, an English army had sailed from Bombay against the king of Persia, who had molested Herat; and Sir James Outram, with the Puna Horse and 3rd Bombay Infantry, brought the war to a rapid and successful termination. But it added another element to the danger in India. The Shah of Persia fomented disaffection in Hindustán; and a proclamation—whether genuine or not—was posted on the walls of Delhi in March 1857, in which he stated that a Persian army was coming to expel the English, and called on all the Muhammadans to put on their armour and join the invaders. The representative of another dynasty, too, was wandering about watching the signs of the times, and seeing how best he could make his profit out of them. This was Dhondu Pant, or Nána Sáhib, the adopted son of Báji Rao, the last of the Peshwas. But he veiled the bitter resentment that he felt at the discontinuance of the enormous pension granted to Báji Rao, and mixed freely in English society. His agent, Ázim Ulla Khán, who had pleaded his cause in London, returned to India after visiting the Crimea, and poured into his master's willing ears exaggerated tales of England's weakness.

Early in the year 1857, many Englishmen were warned by native friends to be on their guard and, if possible, retire from India—at any rate to send away their wives and children. Nothing definite was ever stated, and the advice was always received with scorn. At the latter end of February a remarkable anonymous document was received by Lord Elphinstone, nephew of Mountstuart Elphinstone and Governor of

Bombay, containing a solemn announcement of treason, and enumerating reasons for a general discontent. One of the reasons given was the proceedings of the Commission that was investigating the tenures of Inám or rent-free land, and showing the harshness and cruelty of their measures. It was evidently a well-meant warning.

Another strange incident occurred in the early months of 1857. From village to village were passed along chapáties, or flat cakes of flour. Their origin has never been discovered, nor was the token professedly understood even by the natives; but it may have answered to the sending of the Fiery Cross over the Scottish Highlands, and it was at least a signal that grave troubles were impending. Week by week, as the year wore on, the people of Hindustán were more and more carried away by an excitement that was not far removed from madness. At one and the same time, they were overpowered with fear of the yoke that was being imposed upon them, and exulting with triumph at the success that they expected to win. It has been said that it was the duty of the English to take steps to rid the people of the monstrous falsehoods which they accepted as truths. But, on the other hand, India is never free from some absurd ideas of the kind. In Lord Auckland's time, a rumour spread about Simla that the blood of hillmen was wanted to restore him to health, and all the coolies on the hill ran away. When the census was taken at the beginning of 1881, it was widely believed that all the men were to be put in a row and shot, and the women sent up to Kábul as wives of English soldiers.* One

---

* In 1883, when I was in charge of the police on the Southern Marátha Railway, then being constructed, it was rumoured that the English engineers required persons to be buried alive under the foundation of the Málaprabha bridge, and natives would not go near the river except in bodies and in broad daylight.

rumour there was, however, more dangerous than all the rest, which ought to have been dealt with at once. The cartridges of Enfield rifles, then introduced, were in England greased with beef and pork-fat. The order went forth in India that they were to be greased in like manner there. But the pig is abominated by the Muhammadan, the cow sacred to the Hindu. The order brought defilement to both, and it was proof conclusive to all that the cartridges were the means by which the sepoys were to be made Christians, and the conversion of the people speedily brought about. In deadly fear, the sepoys refused to take the cartridges. Yet such is the wonderful inconsistency of the native mind, that the cartridges were used without hesitation or thought of defilement against the English; conspirators took their seats in the trains and sent their messages by the wires that were to bind down the country in bonds of iron.

XXIV.—THE REAPING OF THE WHIRLWIND.

THE first mutterings of the storm were at Barhampur, near Murshidábád. The 19th Bengal Infantry broke into open mutiny on parade; and, though the sepoys were restrained from violence, they were marched to Barrackpur, near Calcutta, and disbanded. The only effect of this measure was to increase the ferment and hasten the evil day.

To the story of the greased cartridges was now added the more horrifying news that the public wells and the flour and butter sold in the markets, in fact, everything had been defiled by bone-dust and that the salt had been polluted by the blood of swines and cows. Now, to a certain extent, but not sufficiently alarmed, Lord Canning issued order after order to satisfy the sepoys; and on the 10th of May he addressed the people at large warning them against false reports and denying that any attempt was being made to interfere with their caste. It was all useless. The documents were looked on as part of the scheme. The fever was at its height and the disease must run its course. Nothing but a fearful lesson could bring the people to their senses; and yet even in the Bengal Army there were regiments found faithful to their masters in the hour of need and darkness.

On the 10th of May, the very day of Lord Canning's general proclamation, the storm burst in earnest at Mirat. It was subsequently discovered that the sepoys had formed a plot to rise together on the last day of that month, but an accident interfered with their preconcerted plans. On the 9th of May some sepoys had been sentenced to imprisonment for refusing to use the cartridges. On the 10th, which was Sunday, at the time of evening-service, the native troops released the convicted mutineers and other prisoners from the jail, rushed through the station cutting down every European whom they met—man, woman, and child. They set fire to the houses; and, to prove the definite and widespread nature of the plot, hurried off to Delhi. There were European troops at Mirat. The imbecility of their commanders allowed them to do nothing, not even to pursue the flying sepoys. At Delhi there were no European troops; but there were three native regiments, and a magazine with immense stores of powder and ammunition in the charge of Lieutenant Willoughby. The sepoys joined the mutineers, and the whole city was in an uproar. The crowd surged about the magazine, and messengers, in the name of Bahádur Sháh, Emperor of India, demanded its surrender. But Willoughby knew his duty. When he and his few comrades could no longer hold out, he gave the command; the train already prepared for the emergency was fired, and with the contents of the magazine and its heroic defenders, some fifteen hundred rebels were blown into the air.

It was this premature rising at Mirat that was the saving of the English. Instead of a simultaneous throwing down of the gauntlet, which would have produced a crisis well nigh desperate, there came a running fire of mutinies; and the telegraph, which Lord Dalhousie's wisdom had spread over the land, warned every station of what was happening. Thus more or less preparation could be made to ward off the coming blow. But the conflagration spread from place to place, and the same horrid drama was repeated. In station after station, the sepoys mutinied, loosed the prisoners from the jails, plundered the treasury, murdered the Europeans, and made off to Delhi. Treacherous as the sepoys were, their treachery was exceeded by that of the princes. At Jhánsi, the Ráni pledged herself by a solemn oath that she would send in safety to another station fifty-five Europeans who had taken refuge in the fort, but who had no store of food. They were to leave the fort two by two, and each couple on coming out was murdered.

It was soon seen that the rebels had no common aim or object. There was no master-mind to direct their efforts, and their leaders soon began to strive after different goals. Muhammadans wished to restore the glories of the Great Moghal. Hindu sepoys had no intention of transferring to Bahádur Sháh the allegiance that they had withdrawn from the English. And Nána Sáhib, at Bithur, meant to strike a blow for himself and renew the Marátha empire of the Peshwas. Had he succeeded, the old story would have been repeated, and Tántia Topi, the only general that the mutiny produced, would have ruled the Peshwa as Nána Fárnáwis ruled Máhdu Rao Náravan. Until the beginning of June he kept the sepoys at Cawnpore quiet, and was lavish in his professions of friendship to the English. At length, on the 4th of June, the native regiments burst into revolt, and set off on the road to Delhi. This by no means fell in with Nána Sáhib's plans. The sepoys already at Delhi would soon bring about the collapse of British power; he wanted an army with which to seize for himself the throne of which his adoptive father had been unjustly deprived. Promising them abundant plunder from the cantonments of Cawnpore he lured back the regiments that had started for Delhi, and on the 6th of June the siege of the British garrison was begun. For nineteen days the English, under Sir Hugh Wheeler, endured fearful sufferings in a heat that even in profound peace, in spite of every comfort, renders life well-nigh unendurable. The numbers of the small garrison were sadly reduced by the enemy's incessant fire; their barrack, which formed their hospital, was burnt; the women and children were stricken with fever and starving for want of food. Were the men only to be thought of, they might have cut their way through the enemy. But the thought of the suffering women and children induced Sir Hugh Wheeler, almost against his better judgement, to accept Nána Sáhib's offer that he would convey safely to Alláhábád all who should lay down their arms. On the 27th the survivors, numbering in all 450, were marched down to the boats which had been prepared for them. No sooner had they taken their places than a murderous fire was opened upon them from the river banks, and the thatched roofs of the boats set on fire. The greater number were killed or drowned; but 122 were carried back to Nána's house, reserved for a more awful fate. Four only escaped to join Havelock's avenging army.

Nána Sáhib now thought that his success was assured. He proceeded to Bithur, and had himself proclaimed Peshwa with magnificent coronation ceremonies. He then returned to Cawnpore where the Muhammadans were already plotting against him. Here he gratified his appetite for blood by murdering all the men out of a party of fugitives from Fatigahr; and he added the women and children to his prisoners, who now numbered over 200. In the meantime, General Havelock was hastening on with strenuous exertions from Alláhábád, winning victory after victory on the road. On the evening of the 15th of July, when he had bivouacked for the night, he heard that the prisoners at Cawnpore were yet alive. He instantly marched fourteen miles further, and was only eight miles from the city when the newly-crowned Peshwa anticipated his arrival by hacking his victims limb from limb and throwing them dying or dead into a well. After issuing proclamations that the infidels had been overwhelmed and sent to hell, he ordered out his troops to meet General Havelock, and a fierce battle was fought. The terrible charge of the British and their Sikh comrades bore down all before them and the sepoys fled. The next morning the British forces beheld the signs of the fearful tragedy, and no one can say that the vengeance was incomplete. The well of Cawnpore is now enclosed with a rich screen carved in stone; and on it the figure of an angel in the attitude of perfect rest, signifies the joyful hope of resurrection to eternal life.

The main features in the struggle in Bengal were now the rescue of the English garrison besieged in Lucknow, and the siege of Delhi by the English armies. After stupendous efforts, a relieving force under General Havelock and Sir James Outram threw itself into Lucknow on the 25th of September. Outram had been sent to supersede Havelock, but he proved himself worthy of the title bestowed on him by Sir Charles Napier, of the Bayard of India, by waiving his rank and accompanying the force as a volunteer. This relief proved to be little more than a reinforcement of the garrison; but by the middle of November Sir Colin Campbell fought his way to the capital of Oudh and withdrew its gallant defenders. It was not, however, till February 1858 that there was strength enough to once more capture and this time to hold Lucknow, and from it begin the conquest of Oudh, the only country in India in which the population as a whole had risen against us.

But it was at Delhi that the bitterness of the struggle was concentrated, and at Delhi that political interest centred. The eyes of all India were turned on the imperial city, in which 30,000 men, trained and disciplined by England, defied the efforts of the 4,000 British troops that attempted to besiege them from their cantonments on the Ridge which overlooks the town. While Delhi remained in the hands of the rebels, the Princes of India looked on bewildered, and the enemies of England exulted; its capture was of the most vital importance to the re-establishment of the British Government in Hindustan, and to the prestige of the English arms. By July 5th two British Commanders-in-chief had died; a fortnight later a third was compelled by ill-health to resign his position, and the command devolved upon General Wilson of the Bengal Artillery. For a time the English were less besiegers than besieged. Assault after assault was made on their lines, and on June 23rd, the hundredth anniversary of the battle of Plassey, the enemy attacked the British position with exceeding courage and skill. But though they were superior in numbers, though they were perfect in discipline and in the inferior details of their military movements, yet the master mind to which military evolutions are but the means to the end was wanting; their fierce onslaughts were of little avail against the indomitable resolution and unattainable military genius of those that had trained them. They realised that the prophecy which had thrilled their blood was at all events not literally fulfilled. As week followed week, the numbers of the besiegers increased; John Lawrence denuded the Panjáb of British troops to hasten the fall of Delhi, and sent his legions of newly-conquered Sikhs to aid their conquerors in the hour of need. On the 6th of September a siege-train arrived from Firozpur, and before dawn on September 14th the assaulting columns were formed in the trenches. Then began a fierce struggle, which was not ended until six days of hard fighting. But before a single soldier of the many hastening from England had set foot in India the climax of the struggle was past. The power of England was again revealed. The head was cut off the rebellious body; waverers were restrained from outbreaks. There was a large dinner given that week at Government House at Puna. A telegram was put into the hand of the Governor while the guests were seated at table. Rising from his chair, Lord Elphinstone read out to the assembled throng the welcome news that Delhi was at length taken and the rebels fled. A deafening cheer of delight and triumph burst from the Europeans, but the scowling faces of native servants in the very house of the Governor of Bombay showed what might have happened had Delhi not fallen. In January 1858 the sovereign to whom the mutineers had sworn allegiance was brought to trial for waging war against the British Government; and with the banishment of Bahádur Sháh into exile in Burma the curtain fell on the great drama of Moghal sovereignty.

If the English had ever doubted of their ultimate success the time for doubt had passed away, and their absolute and complete reconquest of the country was only a question of time. Nor could the blindest of fanatical rebels venture to hope for the restoration of the empire of Delhi. But no small efforts were still to be made to place once more Dhondu Pant, Nána Sáhib, on the throne of the Peshwas at Poona. The causes that gave birth to the Indian mutiny cannot be omitted in a history of Bombay. But the great events of the struggle in Hindustán can only be sketched in the thinnest possible outline. An exception however must be made in the career of the man who attempted to revive the empire that Shiwáji had created. Havelock had scattered the troops of Nána Sáhib at Cawnpore, but they were by no means destroyed. It was impossible to follow them up while matters of more momentous consequence remained to be handled, and for the present they remained unmolested. Defeated as he was for the time, Nána Sáhib did not yet despair of success, and he had the invaluable aid of the Marátha Brahman Tántia Topi, who had superintended the massacre of Europeans in the boats at Cawnpore. The two great Marátha chiefs, Sindia and Holkar, were faithful to the British Ráj; but they could not control their troops, who were smitten with the prevailing contagion. Sindia's troops mutinied in June and shot several of their officers; but Sindia had managed to keep them in a sort of hostile neutrality till after the fall of Delhi. They could then be held down no longer; and, accepting the offer of Tántia Topi to lead them against the English, they marched to join the rebel forces under Nána Sáhib and his brother Bála Sáhib. The Gwálior contingent was one of the finest bodies of men in India; and Tántia Topi, with 20,000 soldiers now under his command, marched against Cawnpore. He was at no great distance from that city when Sir Colin Campbell arrived from Allahábád on his way to relieve Havelock and Outram at Lucknow. Outram, with characteristic unselfishness, wrote to him from the besieged city begging him to effectually destroy the Gwálior rebels before he advanced to their relief. But Sir Colin Campbell persisted in his original intention; and on the 9th of November marched into Oudh, leaving General Windham with a small force to protect Cawnpore. Before he succeeded in his task and returned to Cawnpore, on the 28th of November, amazing events had taken place.

Tántia Topi had been biding his time; and no sooner had Sir Colin Campbell started for Lucknow, than—leaving a strong detachment at Kálpi—he crossed the Jumna and moved on towards Cawnpore, occupying the most important posts on the line of march. Windham was thus cut off from communication with the country which furnished him with most of his supplies. Windham applied for and received permission to detain reinforcements that were reaching Cawnpore from Bengal. But, though his force was slightly increased, he was in serious danger; and information reached him which led him to believe that Sir Colin's force was surrounded by the enemy. Definite action was necessary, and he determined upon a skilful plan for foiling Tántia by taking the initiative against him. The carrying out of the plan involved disobedience to the instructions which Sir Colin had left. He applied for permission to act according to his judgement; but the permission could not reach him, and he shrank from the responsibility of executing in its entirety the plan which he had conceived. The result was half measures and failure. On the 24th he broke up his camp, and left the entrenchment, covering the town on the West, which he had been specially directed to keep, and marched out six miles. The next day Tántia drew near, and on the 26th Windham defeated him, but fell back on Cawnpore. Tántia fully appreciated the necessity of his withdrawal to defend Cawnpore; and on the 27th Windham found that he had been cleverly outflanked, and was assailed by an artillery stronger than his own. The defence was mismanaged. He withdrew in confusion, and the retreat was well-nigh a panic. The tents, camp equipage, and stores fell into the enemy's hands, and Tántia Topí became master of the city. The entrenchment, on which Sir Colin set so much value, was in the greatest danger of suffering the same fate, but that and the bridge of boats across the river to the Oudh shore were saved. Had the bridge, by which alone Sir Colin's force could gain Cawnpore, been cut off it would have gone hard with Windham's force; but hearing the firing of heavy artillery Sir Colin marched on with the utmost speed, regardless of his wearied troops, and arrived in time to prevent this crowning disaster. The non-combatants and wounded were sent off to Alláhábád, and on the 6th of December was fought the third battle of Cawnpore which for a time checked the activity of the wonderful Brahman general. He was to be dealt with later on by Sir Hugh Rose from Bombay. The victory was a brilliant one. The British loss was small. The enemy was pursued for a great distance; and General Hope Grant overtook them at a ferry, twenty-five miles above Cawnpore, and won another success. In these two victories the Gwálior contingent lost thirty-two guns.

It is now time to return to events that disturbed the peace of the Western Presidency, and then follow up the brilliant campaign of the Bombay army under Sir Hugh Rose (Lord Strathnairn) in Central India, against the rebel forces under the Ráni of Jhánsi and Tántia Topí.

XXV.—THE MUTINIES IN BOMBAY.

SIR JOHN LAWRENCE had, with magnificent unselfishness, subordinated the defence of the Panjáb to the defence of the empire, and denuded his own province of troops to hasten the capture of Delhi. Lord Elphinstone, the Governor of Bombay, adopted the same spirited policy. He was a statesman of real ability and possessed a long experience of Indian affairs. Twenty years before he had been Governor of Madras, and had there perhaps distinguished himself as a leader of society rather than as a ruler. But he had since become a wise and enlightened administrator, and by his singular tact and judicious encouragement of merit he had created among his subordinates an enthusiastic confidence for the head of their government. When the news of the outbreak at Delhi reached him he at once directed his efforts to supplement from a two-fold source the British forces in Northern India. The troops which Outram had led to victory in Persia had not yet returned to Bombay. Instead of ordering their return to his own Presidency, he despatched them rapidly to Calcutta; and, promptly grasping the fearful magnitude of the crisis, he enabled Bartle Frere, his lieutenant in Sind, to reinforce Sir John Lawrence in the Panjáb, and helped Colonel George Lawrence, when mutiny broke out at Nimach and Nassirábád in Rájputána to save that province by the aid of Bombay troops from Disa. But the revolt at Nassirábád showed the danger to which the grand trunk road from Bombay to Ágra, through Gwálior and Central India, was exposed. This communication must at all hazards be secured. Lord Elphinstone's resources were not great, but he equipped a column and despatched it to Mau (Mhow), under General Woodburn, with instructions to place his forces at the disposal of Colonel Durand, the Agent to the Governor-General for Holkar's territories at his capital of Indor.

His arrival was sorely needed. Holkar was loyal, but his troops could not be trusted. Not only at Nassirábád and Nimach had the conflagration broken out, but at Jhánsi and Mehidpur; and communication between Indor and Ágra was cut off by the mutiny of Sindia's contingent at Gwálior. Durand's hopes centred in the prompt arrival of Woodburn's column from Bombay, and the mutinous troops hearing of its approach veiled for a time their disloyalty. But Woodburn was not coming. He had found it almost impracticable to get on to Mau at that season of the year; and, on the summons of the British resident at Hydarábád, he turned aside to suppress a disturbance which had broken out at Aurangábád, and remained there even after he had accomplished his purpose. On the 28th of June Lord Elphinstone was forced to telegraph to Durand that the column could not advance. As is always the case in India, such news spreads with mysterious rapidity; and the sedative influence which an unfounded rumour of the fall of Delhi had exercised on the people of Central India being removed by the knowledge that Delhi was still untaken mutiny broke out at Indor. Durand was compelled to flee. He hastened by forced marches to Asirgarh in order to hurry up Woodburn's column to Mau, for the rescue of Central India from anarchy and the restoration of the line of communication. On his way he heard that the column was at last actually advancing under Brigadier Stuart, who had succeeded Woodburn, and the line of the Narbada was fairly out of danger. On July 22nd, Stuart's column arrived at Asirgarh and was there joined by Durand. The force marched to Mau and arrived there on the 1st of August. Heavy rains detained it there for three months. At last the weary season of inaction passed away, and Durand was able to set out with a little army of 1,400 men, of which a large proportion was cavalry and artillery, on a brilliant and successful campaign in Central India. The first place which he moved against was the fort of Dhár, two days' march from Mau. The defendants offered a vigorous resistance, but there was no disputing the advance of the assailants. The 25th Bombay Native Infantry covered themselves with glory, and the fort was taken and destroyed. In November, the little army was reinforced by a detachment of the Hydarábád contingent; and the combined forces defeated the rebels in successive actions at Mandisur and Guráría. This last victory was decisive. Durand marched back to resume his position at Indor, while Stuart's forces returned to Mau, there to await the arrival of a great captain who was advancing from Bombay with an invincible army to war down the hostile forces that still dared to hold up their heads.

But before despatching Sir Hugh Rose to Central India, in December 1857, Lord Elphinstone had had weighty duties to perform in the territories under his charge.

In the recently-annexed province of Sátára, although there was no popular rising or even agitation, there was yet a party which personally favoured the claims to the throne of the adopted son of the late Rája's brother. A wakil, or agent, named Rango Bápuji, who had travelled to England after the annexation of Sátára to advocate the claims of the Rája's brother, plotted in connection with Nána Sáhib of Cawnpore, to release the prisoners in the Sátára jail, plunder the treasury and attack the cantonment. This plot was discovered by Mr. Rose, the district magistrate, on the 12th of June. He at once sent for European reinforcements. The conspiracy was nipped in the bud; Rango Bápuji disappeared; his followers were dispersed by Lieutenant Kerr with a party of the Southern Marátha horse. Seventeen of the conspirators were tried and executed, while the family of the late Rája, who were implicated in the plots, was deported.

There was more serious danger in the districts south of Sátára and the state of Kolhápur. At Kolhápur, Belgaum, and Dhárwár there were native troops. At Belgaum there were about four hundred European women and children, while the British force was limited to a battery of artillery and some thirty infantry. Considerable disaffection, not altogether without reason, had been caused in the Southern Marátha country by the proceedings of the Inám commission. The lapsing of estates consequent on the absence of male heirs, and the refusal to allow adoption, had created wide-spread jealousy and suspicion. Kolhápur was still smarting from the rebellion of 1844, the costs of which the state was ordered to pay to Government together with interest at 5 per cent. Pending the payment in full, the affairs of the state were under the management of a Political Agent. Repayment of so large a sum seemed hopeless, and native rule never likely to be restored. Mr. Seton-Karr, the magistrate of Belgaum, was aware that in his own district—which then included part of Bijápur, as well as in Kolhápur and Dhárwár—considerable excitement had been created among the people by the news of the triumph of Nána Sáhib at Cawnpore, and that the three regiments at Belgaum, Kolhápur, and Dhárwár were intriguing together. It was afterwards proved conclusively that they had plotted to rise on a fixed date; but the sepoys of the 27th Bombay Native Infantry at Kolhápur, discovering that the native adjutant of the regiment, a Jew, was sending away his family, believed that this was preliminary to betraying them, and they resolved to rise at once.

On the night of July 31st, in the height of the monsoon, the outbreak took place, and the native adjutant had barely time to warn the European ladies to flee for their lives when the sepoys came up and poured volleys into their bungalows. Some of the officers escaped into the country, but were caught and shot, and their bodies thrown into the river. Others took refuge in the Residency, about a mile from camp, but not far from the lines of another military body, the Kolhápur Local Corps, commanded by Captain John Schneider. The sepoys plundered the treasury and the station, and then proceeded to the town where they evidently expected to be let in. But the forethought of Colonel Maughan, the Political Agent, had closed the city gates, and this measure checked any movement in their favour on the part of the townspeople. The majority then returned to their lines, but two hundred of them took up a position in an outwork near the town;

and, after repelling the local corps which Colonel Maughan at once led against them, marched off the next day to join a detachment of their regiment at Ratnágiri. On the way, they unexpectedly met with some European troops, and the bulk of the mutineers betook themselves to the jungles of Sáwantwári. But forty, all natives of Hindustán, returned to Kolhápur, and threw themselves once more into the outwork adjoining the town. Here they were attacked on the 10th of August by Lieutenant Kerr, who had marched in twenty-four hours from Sátára, a distance of more than seventy miles, by volunteers from their own regiment and some of the local corps, all under Major Rolland of the 27th. A desperate conflict ensued, almost the whole number of the mutineers being killed. Lieutenant Kerr received the Victoria Cross for his gallantry on this occasion.

The European population of Bombay was seriously alarmed at the news from Kolhápur. Many residents placed their families for safety on the ships in the harbour, and volunteer horse patrolled the streets at night. The anxiety was not lessened by the fact that Mr. Forjett, the energetic superintendent of police, had discovered some of the sepoys in Bombay to be untrustworthy. But Lord Elphinstone, with admirable unselfishness, would not detain troops for the defence of Bombay when they were more urgently wanted elsewhere. He despatched two detachments of the 2nd Europeans by sea to Ratnágiri, a feat hitherto unattempted in the teeth of the monsoon; and he directed them, after taking what measures might be needed to deal with the detachment at that station, to march up the Gháts to Kolhápur. A further detachment was sent by sea to Goa, and ordered to march thence to

Belgaum. And Colonel George Le Grand Jacob, a soldier-politician of great experience, who had just returned with Outram from Persia, was depatched to Kolhápur to restore order, with full authority to act on his own judgement. Jacob started at once; and, after a journey of extraordinary difficulty, in torrents of rain, through a country which then had no roads, he reached Kolhápur on the 14th of August. Order he found had been restored; but the mutinous regiment was still unpunished. A day or two later the European troops arrived from the coast. They had marched over wild mountains, they had crossed swollen rivers, and plodded through deep mud. Their clothes were worn to rags. Some horse artillery also arrived from Sátára, and Jacob determined on the 17th to disarm the native regiment. He made his arrangements admirably. The mutinous 27th was drawn up on the parade-ground with the Europeans and loyal natives on two sides of them. Jacob then addressed the sepoys, appealing to every motive that could lead them to reproach themselves for their conduct, and assured them that none would be punished but those whose guilt should be proved on a fair trial. Before he had finished speaking he observed tears on the faces of some of the sepoys, who are, as he himself states, but children of a larger growth. The order was then given to pile arms, and after a slight but ominous pause it was obeyed. Court-martials were promptly held. The next day twenty-one prisoners were convicted, of whom eight were blown from guns, eleven shot, and two hanged. It was subsequently discovered that the regiment had been in close correspondence with the Bengal sepoys; and that the Bombay regiment was in deadly fear lest the obnoxious cartridge—that powerful fulcrum used by the movers of the revolt—should be served out to them.

The news of the mutiny at Kolhápur was telegraphed to Belgaum, and so was known to Seton-Karr before it was to the sepoys at that station. There had been greater anticipation of danger at Belgaum than at Kolhápur; but Seton-Karr was well acquainted with the designs of the sepoys, and knowing that a certain man had been selected as leader, he sent him off on special duty to a distant town. The absence of their leader paralysed the sepoys, and no outbreak occurred. The detachment of Europeans, despatched by the careful forethought of Lord Elphinstone by way of Goa, arrived on the 10th of August, like their brethren at Kolhápur, in tatters, shoeless, and nearly kitless. Seton-Karr and General Lester then felt themselves strong enough to arrest the conspirators, of whose guilt they had sufficient evidence to bring them to trial. The chief of these was a munshi, a favourite amongst the officers, whom he instructed in Hindustáni. He was a disciple of the head of the Wáhábi sect in Western India, who lived at Puna. Letters were found, which showed the existence of a wide-spread Muhammadan design for a rising in that part of the country, and communications were intercepted between the 29th Bombay Native Infantry and the 74th Bengal Regiment. The plot was mainly brought to light by the Faujdár, or native head of the Belgaum police, whose services were rewarded by the grant of a village. Jacob, meanwhile, remained at Kolhápur, where there were vague rumours of coming disturbance; and the strange movement of the mutineers on the night of July 31st to the town was yet unaccounted for.

The anxiety in Bombay itself was by no means groundless. With a European force of only 400 Europeans, under Brigadier Shortt, there were three regiments of sepoys. The native troops were implicitly trusted by their officers, and the chief danger apprehended by the Government was from the Muhammadans of the town who numbered no less than 150,000. Besides the troops, there were a number of native and sixty European police, under Mr. Forjett, the superintendent. Forjett was born and bred in India, and could disguise himself as a native and mix with the people without any chance of detection. He was convinced that the townspeople would not stir without the sepoys; but he knew that the sepoys were planning mutiny, and much to the disgust of the Brigadier he made no secret of his views. The Muhammadan festival of the Moharam was approaching, always an occasion of anxiety in Bombay even during times of peace. The plans made by Government to keep order involved the splitting up of the European troops and police into small parties; and Forjett by no means approved of an arrangement by which there would be no Europeans to oppose a mutiny of the sepoys at the place where it was likely to begin. As regards the troops he could do nothing, but he told the Governor that he felt obliged to disobey orders as to the location of the police. "It is a very risky thing," said Lord Elphinstone, "to disobey orders, but I am sure you will do nothing rash." Forjett did disobey orders, whether it was risky or not. Going round the city in disguise every night of the Moharam, whenever he heard any one sympathising with the success of the mutineers in other parts of India, he at once whistled for his men, some of whom were sure to be near. The badmáshes and scoundrels of the town were so alarmed at these mysterious arrests, which seemed to show that the authorities knew everything, that they remained quiet. But close at the end of the Moharam, a drunken Christian drummer belonging to one of the sepoy regiments insulted a religious procession of Hindus, and knocked down a god that they were escorting. He was at once arrested and placed in custody; but the men of his regiment, incensed at the action of the police, whom they detested on account of Forjett's hostility to themselves, hurried to the lock-up, rescued the drummer and took him with two policemen to their lines. A European constable and four natives went at once to demand that their comrades should be released and the drummer given up. They were resisted by force; a struggle ensued, and the police fought their way out, leaving two sepoys for dead. The sepoys were in the utmost fury and excitement, and Forjett was summoned by his police. Forjett was equal to the emergency. He ordered his European police to follow him, and galloped to the scene of the mutiny. He found the sepoys trying to force their way out of the lines, and their officers with drawn swords with difficulty restraining them. On seeing Forjett their fury could hardly be controlled. "For God's sake, Mr. Forjett," cried the officers, "go away!" "If your men are bent on mischief," he replied, "the sooner it is over the better." The sepoys paused while Forjett sat on his horse confronting them. Soon his assistant and fifty-four European constables arrived, and Forjett cried, "Throw open the gates—I am ready for them!" The sepoys were not prepared for this prompt action; and in the face of the Europeans judged discretion to be the better part of valour.

A few days later, Forjett erected a gallows near the police-office, summoned the chief citizens whom he knew to be disaffected, and pointing to the gibbet told them that on the slightest sign that they meditated an outbreak they would promptly be hanged. The hint was taken. But there was still danger from the sepoys. Forjett learnt that a number of them were systematically holding secret meetings at the house of one Ganga Prasád. He immediately had this man arrested, and induced him to confess what he knew. The next evening he went to the house, and through a hole in the wall gathered from the sepoys' conversation that they meant to mutiny during the Hindu festival of the Diwáli in October, pillage the city and then leave the island. His report of this to the officers was received with incredulity; but Forjett persuaded Major Barrow, the commandant of one of the regiments, to go with him to the house, and he was aghast at seeing there his own men whom he trusted. "Mr. Forjett has caught us at last," said Brigadier Shortt when this was told to him. Court-martials were held, the two ringleaders executed, and six accomplices transported for life. The Diwáli passed off quietly; and, by the prescience and persistence of the superintendent of police, Bombay was saved.

But in various parts of the Presidency there was still occasion for anxiety. In September, plots to mutiny at Áhmadábád, and Hydarábád in Sind, were nipped in the bud; and at Karáchi the 21st Bombay Native Infantry and three Oudh recruited regiments showed a mutinous spirit and were disarmed. Apart from those mentioned, the Bombay regiments remained staunch during the crisis; those in their ranks who, having been recruited in Hindustán, might have liked to aid their brethren of Northern India being weighed down by the loyalty of the Maráthas. But at Kolhápur, and throughout the Southern Marátha country, where the Inám commission had caused wide-spread disaffection amongst an armed population, there was formidable danger. At Kolhápur Jacob was on the alert for coming disturbance. The Rája was loyal, but indolent. His younger brother, Chima Sáhib, was a man of energy, with the spirit as well as the blood of Shiwáji in his veins; and emissaries from Nána Sáhib stimulated his thoughts of rebellion. On November 15th the Rája acquainted Jacob with a rumour that there was an intention of attacking the camp, and patrols and pickets were doubled. The European force, too, had by this time been increased. On the night of the 5th of December, Jacob was roused from sleep by the clatter of horses' hoofs. Rushing out he met the Rissáldár, or native officer, in command of the Southern Marátha Horse, who told him that suspicious cries had been heard in the town. Jacob directed the Rissáldár to sweep round the city and if possible secure one of the gates, while he himself galloped into the camp and sounded the alarm. Soon after the troops had assembled, the Rissáldár returned to say that the town was in hostile possession and the gates closed against the English. All the gates had evidently fallen into the enemy's hands without opposition; and Jacob concluded that the younger Rája at least was implicated in the plot, and that the camp would be immediately attacked. He determined to forestall the attempt. Leaving the 27th under surveillance, he moved to the city with all available forces. A storming-party was formed. By dawn of day one of the gates was gallantly blown in, and with slight resistance the place was in Jacob's hands. But in the palace there were hundreds of armed men, including a large number of the hereditary garrison of the Panálla fort. These it was who had taken the town by escalade during the night. They had attempted to seize the treasure-chest kept in the palace buildings; but it was guarded by a party of the local corps, who with commendable loyalty fired at the mutineers and killed their leader. All these men were promptly disarmed; thirty-six were there and then tried by a drum-head court-martial, and on their own confession convicted, condemned, and executed. The rest were reserved for subsequent procedure. Jacob's prompt action, while Chima Sáhib was still hesitating to openly commit himself, prevented the full execution of a plot which would have spread mutiny over the whole of the Southern Marátha Country. The explanation of the occurrence was gradually elicited. Chima Sáhib was acting in deliberate collusion with Nána Sáhib. He had had frequent interviews with the native officers of the 27th, and with a deputation of sixty men from Gwálior, whose ostensible object was to congratulate the Rája on his marriage with the daughter of the Gaikwár. A sword had also been received from Lucknow. Chima Sahib was sent as a state prisoner to Sind, and the Kolhápur fortifications were dismantled. The Rája was cleared of all suspicion and confirmed in his sovereignty; but he did not long survive, and was succeeded by his kinsman Rájúrám, a promising and amiable young man, who subsequently died in Italy on his return from a journey to England.

In the Konkan, the remant of the Sáwantwári insurgents of 1844, who had been for a while confined and subsequently given land by the Goa Government, created some agitation, though they got no recruits in Sáwantwári itself. Under Bába Desai, who had been the prime mover in the former insurrection, they broke into revolt in February 1858, harried the country and levied war in the name of the Peshwa Nána Sáhib. But they were hotly pursued, and their depredations confined to a small tract of country. The police in this, as in other operations throughout the Presidency, gave most valuable and efficient assistance. At an outpost at Talliwára, near the Portuguese frontier, a police sergeant and twelve constables defied successfully an attack by a large body of rebels, who actually seized their families and swore that they would murder them unless the place surrendered. The only reply was that the British Government would avenge their deaths, and the threat was not carried out. In the Southern Marátha States a succession of petty outbreaks occurred in the cold weather of 1857-58, owing to the disarming of the people necessitated by their attitude; and Government deemed it advisable to place under one man the turbulent population of the several districts and states. Jacob was accordingly placed in charge of the whole in May 1858, as Commissioner of the Southern Marátha Country; and Charles Manson, who had been assistant to Seton-Karr, was appointed to act under Jacob. Manson had been connected with the Inám commissions; and so was regarded with suspicion by the native chiefs who were up in arms at the assumed right of our Government to disallow succession by adoption. He was thus identified with the harsher features of the policy of the British Government. The principal states were Sángli, Miraj, Kurandwár and Nargund, the last of which was annexed to Dhárwár at the close of the mutiny. The families of Miraj, Sángli and Kurandwár were Brahmans, and related by marriage with Nána Sáhib. The ablest chief was Bába Sáhib of Nargund, and he considered himself grievously wronged by the Inám commission. Others might bide their time till they could see who was winning; he, more daring, threw himself into the insurrectionary movement when its chances of success were at a minimum. On the 26th of May, a few hours after Manson had left Jacob at Kolhápur on his way to visit the northern states of the country, news of the outbreak of the Nargund chief reached the commissioner. Jacob immediately sent a mounted messenger to Manson with the news. He informed him that he had telegraphed to General Lester to send a force to Nargund; and he recommended Manson to return to Kolhápur and consult with himself before joining the forces, with which his proper position would now be. But Manson was blindly confident in his own influence, and replied that he would hasten to Nargund and nip the revolt in the bud, or at any rate save Bába Sáhib's brother, the chief of Rámdrug, from joining in it. He wrote to Colonel Malcolm, commanding at Kaladgi, requesting aid; but Malcolm had gone off to quell a rising elsewhere, and so Manson reached Rámdrug with only twelve wearied troopers. Here he found that he had arrived too late. The Nargund chief had committed himself past hope of recovery. But he saved the chief of Rámdrug, who showed him his brother's letters urging co-operation. He urged Manson not to go to Nargund, as in that case he could not answer for his life; so, after writing to Jacob to throw a garrison into Miraj, or Sángli, Manson went off to join Malcolm. He started that evening, May 27th, and halted at a village on the way, he and his men alike wearied out with marching. In the night the Nargund chief sallied out with 700 or

800 followers, killed the sentry on guard, and rushing upon Manson—who had time to wound one of his assailants with his revolver—killed him and cut off his head, which they suspended over the gateway at Nargund. Bába Sáhib's triumph was short. Malcolm turned back from the rebels in the south, who were disposed of by a Madras force, and with some artillery and infantry from Dhárwár attacked Nargund on June 1st, defeated Bába Sáhib's force with great slaughter, and carried the town by assault. The next day they seized the citadel, a strong place of resistance, but on forcing the gates it was found deserted. The chief had escaped during the night. His track was followed up with extraordinary energy, perseverance and skill by Mr., now Sir Frank Souter, K.C.S.I., Commissioner of Police in Bombay, and in spite of his various devices for throwing the pursuers off the scent, was discovered the same evening with six of his principal followers, disguised as pilgrims. He was soon afterwards tried, condemned, and executed. On hearing of Manson's death, Jacob threw an English garrison into Sángli; and by a skilful negociation induced Bába Sáhib, chief of Miraj, to give up his munitions of war, which consisted of eleven tons of gunpowder and rockets, with arms and cartridges for many thousand soldiers. Part of his fortifications, too, which were of great strength, were dismantled. Mr. Manson was succeeded in his post by Captain Frederick Schneider. Besides the places already referred to, there was considerable disturbance in the hills of Áhmadnagar and it extended more or less into Násik and Khándesh. A man named Bhágoji Naik, who had been dismissed from the Áhmadnagar police, gathered together a number of Bhils and took up an offensive position in September 1857. In October, his

men killed Lieutenant Henry, the superintendent of police, in an action, and the whole Bhil population was greatly excited. In order to check the growing disorder, Captain Nuttall raised a corps of Kolis, hardy mountaineers and hereditary rivals of the Bhils, with eminent success. But the movement was not entirely suppressed for a considerable time, and as late as October 1859 Bhágoji plundered the village of Korkála, in Áhmadnagar, and carried off property worth Rs. 18,000. He was closely pursued by Captain Nuttall, but by rapid and secret marches he managed at first to baulk his pursuers. At last, on November 11th, Mr. Souter, who had been appointed the police superintendent of Áhmadnagar, came upon him in the Násik district; and, in a hand-to-hand combat, Bhágoji and most of his followers were killed and the rebellion brought to an end.

XXVI.—EXPLOITS OF THE BOMBAY ARMY.

IT is now time to relate the doings of the Bombay army under Sir Hugh Rose, which Lord Elphinstone in spite of the danger in his own Presidency nobly sent off to Central India. The plan for the restoration of order in Central India, approved by Sir Colin Campbell, the Commander-in-Chief, was that a Bombay column should start from Mau and march by way of Jhánsi to Kálpi, while a Madras column starting from Jabalpur should march through Bandalkand to Banda. The two columns were to support each other, and form part of a general combination, and, besides pacifying Central India, draw off the pressure of the Gwálior contingent and other rebel forces from Sir Colin's own army. The Madras column was commanded by General Whitlock.

Sir Hugh Rose was a soldier of thirty-seven years' distinguished service. Nor had his career been solely a military one. Besides fighting at the Alma, at Inkerman, and before Sebastopol, he had proved himself a statesman of keen foresight and ripe judgement at Beyrout and as *chargé d'affaires* at Constantinople. Daring in the field, he was a man of polished manners, foremost alike in society and war. But in India he had not served, and there were some who doubted if he would succeed in the conditions of Indian warfare. By Christmas 1857, he was at Mau, and he resolved to begin his march early in January. His operations had to be conducted in one of the most rugged portions of India. He had to traverse the dense jungles and impenetrable mountains and ravines of the Windhya range, and the fastnesses of Bandalkand, whose hardy populations had for centuries defied the efforts of Muhammadan emperors. Sir Hugh's army was divided into two brigades; the first under Stuart at Mau, the second under Stewart at Sihor. There were altogether two regiments of European Infantry, one of Cavalry, four of Native Infantry and the same number of Cavalry, with Artillery, Sappers and Miners, and a siege-train. His first task was to relieve the garrison of Saugar, which was hard pressed. Sending the first brigade against Chandári in Sindia's dominions, he started for Sihor with Sir Robert Hamilton as political officer. On the 16th of January he marched out of Sihor with the second brigade, and after toiling for a week across rivers, hills and jungle the force arrived at Ráthgahr, a fort in the Saugar district, and at once proceeded to bombard it. On the 28th, while the guns were still thundering at the wall, a large force of rebels was seen approaching, and the army of the Rája of Bánpur marched up to relieve the garrison. Without interrupting the bombardment, Sir Hugh sent a detachment to crush his new opponents. Cavalry and artillery dashed against them, and the Bánpur troops flung down their muskets and fled for their lives. By the evening the breach seemed practicable, but ere the assault could be delivered in the morning the garrison had let themselves down by ropes, and eluded the troops that should have intercepted them. The fort was demolished. While the siege was still going on, Sir Hugh heard that the rebels had rallied at a place called Barodia, some fifteen miles off. A portion of the force was detached against them; and, after a difficult march through a dense forest, they scattered the enemy and returned to Ráthgahr. On the 3rd of February, without meeting any further opposition, he succeeded in relieving Saugar. The district was still, however, threatened by the mutineers, who had taken up their position in an almost impregnable fort at Garakota. But they dared not even here await the English; the fort was taken, but the garrison escaped.

The general's object was to press on with all speed to Jhánsi, where the rebellious Ráni had not yet been interfered with. After some delay, for the collection of supplies and for awaiting news of the Madras column, Sir Hugh resumed his march on the 27th. His route had to lie through one of two passes, Nárat or Madanpur. Believing that he would choose the first, the Rája of Bánpur occupied it with the greater part of his forces, but both passes were strongly defended. Making a feint at Nárat, Sir Hugh made his real attack on Madanpur. At five o'clock on the morning of 4th March he moved against the pass, and after a few miles' march entered a deep wooded glen which lay beneath it. Instantly the roar of artillery was heard from the gorge, and a desperate resistance was made to the Bombay column. So strong was the enemy's position, and so stubbornly did they fight, that it required all the efforts of the British force to dislodge them. But the fury of the attack was more than they could endure, and at last they fled, vigorously pursued by the cavalry. The effect of this action was so considerable that none of the forts, nor the river Betwa that lay between the Bombay column and Jhánsi, were defended. On the 17th of March the column crossed the Betwa. The next day news came that the first brigade, under General Stuart, had captured

Chandári. General Whitlock, too, after some delay, was now advancing with the Madras force.

Early on the morning of the 21st the column arrived at Jhánsi. The walls of the fort were 16 feet thick, and armed with powerful ordnance. On three sides it was protected by the city, which was surrounded by a granite wall 25 feet high. The place was almost impregnable, but the general saw a point on the southern side where it might be possible to breach the fortification. The cavalry of the first brigade arrived the same day; and on the 22nd, in order that the garrison, 12,000 in number, should not, as at Ráthgahr and Garakota, escape his clutches, he invested the city and fort with his cavalry. By the evening of the 22nd, four batteries were thrown up. On the 25th they opened fire; and the remainder of the first brigade arriving on that day, fresh batteries were thrown up on the 26th. A struggle now began which rivalled in its intensity the fierce contest that had been waged beneath the walls of Delhi. The besiegers, having always to be ready for action, never took off their clothes. They were almost stifled by the intolerable heat, and they had to fight with wet towels tied round their heads. But their general shared their hardships, and was ever present to cheer them on, and the thought of the awful massacre of English men and women within the walls was constantly in their minds. The defenders, on their part, knew that they could expect no pardon for their crimes, and that the cause of the rebels in Central India depended upon their efforts; and their guns ceased working only at night.

But on the 31st of March the operations on both sides for a moment flagged, when it became known that Tántia Topi was close at hand to relieve Jhánsi. Sir Hugh had now to confront not only 12,000 desperate rebels in one of the mightiest fortresses in India, led by their Ráni Lakshmi Bai, a woman of unbending will and relentless cruelty, but also an army of 20,000 men led by a commander who had defeated a British general at Cawnpore and taken that city from him. Few things in the annals of the British army are more splendid than Sir Hugh Rose's achievements at this crisis. The bombardment was kept up more vigorously than ever, but all the men that could be spared were collected from the two brigades to attack Tántia on the next day. Tántia had detached a portion of his force to relieve the city on the north; the main body was on the right flank of the British, and between them and the river Betwa. The English general also divided his small forces; and the first brigade marched out after it was dark, and lay down to rest unobserved on the right flank of the enemy. The second brigade remained in camp. The enemy swarmed near the English lines, and took up a threatening position. Their sentries kept telling the British that on the morrow they would all be sent to hell, while the garrison shouted, fired salutes and beat their drums. On the morning of 1st April, while the work of bombardment went on as usual in spite of volley upon volley of musketry from the walls, the battle began. The British infantry were ordered 'to lie down, and the artillery opened fire on the advancing enemy. But the fire was insufficient to check them. Seeing this, Sir Hugh sent his horse artillery and some dragoons against their right flank, and himself led the charge of his remaining cavalry against the left. The flanks gave way before the fierce onslaught; the centre halted in bewilderment; the British infantry leaped to their feet, fired a volley, and put the whole of the first line to flight with the bayonet. A moment later, and the force which Tántia had detached the night before came rushing back, pursued by the first brigade, and the rebel army was in full retreat. Even then Tántia displayed his generalship. He set fire to the jungle to hinder pursuit, and took his troops across the Betwa, covering their retreat by an artillery fire. But the British cavalry and horse artillery dashed through the flames, galloped through the river, and when at sunset they returned from the pursuit they had captured twenty-eight guns. In the day's fighting 1,500 of the enemy perished. The next day the breach in the wall was reported practicable; and on the 3rd, at three o'clock in the morning, the men were in their places for the assault. At length the order to advance was given. But silently as their movements had been executed, the gleams of their weapons in the pale moonlight betrayed them; the garrison was prepared, and fierce showers of shot, bullets, and rockets were poured down upon the assaulting columns. As they drew near to the walls, trees, blocks of wood, stones, and pots full of pitch were hurled down with fearful effect. For a moment the troops wavered, but the stormers again pressed on, climbing the ladders which the sappers planted. Three of the ladders snapped, but the check was only momentary. Lieutenants Dick and Meiklejohn, of the Engineers, sprang on to the walls. Their men followed, and dashed into the rebels; but Dick and Meiklejohn fell dead. While the enemy were vainly endeavouring to repel this attack, another party fought their way in on the left; the two bodies joined on the ramparts, and the mutineers fell back. A terrible struggle then took place for the possession of the town. The infuriated soldiers fought their way through an obstinate resistance to the fort, from which a cannonade was still kept up, and put every man in it to the sword. By next morning 5,000 of the rebels were slain; for, remembering the massacre of the English, the soldiers gave no quarter. But the Ráni escaped on horseback, with a small escort, and joined Tántia Topi at Kálpi.

The rebel army at Kálpi again concentrated, and numbered 20,000 men. They had thrown up strong intrenchments on the road from Jhánsi, at a place called Kunch. Kálpi, therefore, must be taken. But fierce as the rebel resistance had been, the British troops had a deadlier enemy in the tropical sun at the summer solstice; and the hardships of the campaign had filled the hospitals. For nearly three weeks Sir Hugh had to remain at Jhánsi to recruit his men, and collect supplies and ammunition. On the 25th he set out for Kálpi, leaving Jhánsi in charge of some reinforcements that had come from Rájputána. Before daybreak, on the 6th of May, he began his march against the stockade at Kunch. The men were wearied out by want of sleep; and, as the sun rose higher and higher in his fiery chariot, they cried hysterically for water and almost broke down with excitement and nervousness. At length, after marching fourteen miles, they halted two miles off Kunch, and recruited their flagging strength with food and rest. Their strength revived, and in the battle that followed the infantry compelled the enemy to retire; the cavalry and horse artillery shattered their ranks; and the 52nd Bengal Infantry, which had mutinied in September, was almost annihilated. The men had marched and fought for sixteen hours with the thermometer at 115° in the shade. More were stricken down by sunstroke than by the enemy; Sir Hugh Rose having four successive attacks of sunstroke during the day. The infantry were much too exhausted to pursue the rebels, but the cavalry followed them for three miles.

A final advance was now to be made for Kálpi, where a nephew of the Nána, known as Rao Sáhib, and the Nawáb of Bánda had joined the forces of Túntia and the Ráni. Kálpi was a fort on a lofty rock on the southern bank of the Jumna, protected by five strong lines of defence. The rebels also fortified the road by which Sir Hugh was expected to advance. But their calculations were vain. Sir Colin Campbell had detached a force from his army in Hindustán, under Colonel Maxwell, to co-operate with the Bombay column; and Maxwell was now at Goláwli on the Jumna, six miles east of Kálpi. Sir Hugh left the fortifications on one side, and effected a junction with Maxwell, on May 15th; by this movement turning the five lines of defence of Kálpi. The troops were terribly exhausted. For five days after reaching Goláwli the enemy harassed them daily; their leaders having issued a general order that, "as the European infidels either died or had to go into hospital from fighting in the sun, they were never to be attacked before ten o'clock in the day, in order that they might feel its force." Meanwhile, Sir Hugh repulsed the attacks while making his preparations for dealing a crushing blow. But the enemy resolved to anticipate his attack. On the 22nd they hurled themselves against him at Goláwli, after swearing on the sacred waters of the Ganges to destroy his force or die. The result was as decisive as in the previous actions. The British troops, exhausted as they were, had strength left to put the enemy to flight, and their vow on the holy water of the Ganges was broken. Throughout the night Kálpi was shelled by Maxwell's artillery; and when on the morning of the 23rd Sir Hugh's forces entered the city, pigs and dogs were fighting over corpses in the streets, but not a sign of the enemy could be seen. Fifty guns and a large amount of stores and ammunition were found in the rebel arsenal. The enemy were pursued and overtaken by the cavalry; the sepoys cut down by hundreds, and all their remaining guns captured.

Sir Hugh Rose had fulfilled his instructions unaided by the Madras column, which arrived a few days later; and, deeming that his labours were over, he issued a farewell order to his army. "Soldiers," it said, "you have marched more than a thousand miles, and taken more than a hundred guns, you have forced your way through mountain passes and intricate jungles, and over rivers; you have captured the strongest forts and beat the enemy, no matter what the odds, wherever you met him; you have restored extensive districts to the Government, and peace and order now reign where before, for twelve months, were tyranny and rebellion; you have done all this, and you have never had a check. I thank you with all my sincerity for your bravery, your devotion, and your discipline. When you first marched, I told you that you, as British soldiers, had more than enough of courage for the work which was before you, but that courage without discipline was of no avail; and I exhorted you to let discipline be your watchword. You have attended to my orders. In hardships, in temptations, and in dangers you have obeyed your general, and you have never left your ranks. You have fought against the strong, and you have defended the rights of the weak and defenceless, of foes as well as friends.

I have seen you, in the ardour of combat, preserve and place children out of harm's way. This is the discipline of Christian soldiers; and it is this which has brought you triumphant from the shores of Western India to the waters of the Jumna, and established, without doubt, that you will find no place to equal the glory of your arms."

The order was issued on the 1st of June. On the 4th, Sir Hugh was astounded by the news that Tántia Topi had formed a new and unlooked-for combination by which to retrieve his fortune and prolong the struggle. Making for the fortress of Gwálior, with the Rání and Rao Sáhib, he stirred Sindia's men to revolt. Sindia marched out to attack the armies that the three leaders brought into his dominions, but his whole army,* with the exception of his body-guard, went over to the enemy, and he himself fled to Ágra. His city and fortress fell into the hands of the mutineers, who once more proclaimed Nána Sáhib under the title of Peshwa. The act was not only of unexpected daring, but of consummate military skill. Tántia had cut in two the line of communication between Bombay and Ágra, gained immense stores and muniments of war, and raised his prestige to an unprecedented height. Fully recognising the magnitude of the emergency, Sir Hugh made his preparations instantly to resume the campaign. On the 6th of June he left Kálpi, and, making forced marches, arrived in ten days at the Cantonment of Morár, near Gwálior, and on the day of his arrival fought another brilliant engagement which made him master of that place (June 16th).

The next day, June 17th, Sir Hugh Rose learnt that

---

* This was Sindia's own army, distinct from the Gwálior contingent, which had long since revolted.

General Smith's column, which had been holding Jhánsi, was advancing to reinforce him. Smith's advance was stubbornly resisted, and an obstinate engagement was fought at Kota-ki-Serai, south of Gwálior. In the last charge by the 8th Hussars, a trooper cut down a woman dressed in male attire, who was no other than the daring Lakshmi Bai, Ráni of Jhánsi, whom Sir Hugh esteemed as "the best and bravest military leader of the rebels."

On the 18th, Sir Hugh marched to join Smith, who had camped not far from Gwálior, leaving General Robert Napier, now Lord Napier of Magdála, who had succeeded to the command of his 2nd Brigade, to hold the Morár cantonment. Late in the evening the troops halted near Smith's position, after a march of twenty miles, in which in one regiment alone the sun struck down no fewer than eighty. Sir Hugh determined to attack the enemy on the 20th. But early on the 19th he saw them moving out from Gwálior against him, and according to his usual custom he attacked them first. The charge was ordered, and the ever-victorious army hurled the rebels back in confusion on the city and vigorously followed up their success. That very day Gwálior was reconquered, and an order sent to Napier to pursue the fleeing enemy. But the mighty fortress of Gwálior, the Gibraltar of India, that loomed 300 feet above the city, still held out, and its guns re-opened fire. Hearing the fire, Lieutenant Rose of the 28th Bombay Native Infantry and Lieutenant Waller, a brother-officer, determined on a daring deed. Taking a blacksmith and a few sepoys, they crept silently to the first gateway, burst it open and passed five more in the same manner. At last the alarm was given, and a fierce struggle took place. The two officers gathered their men together and made a rush that gave them victory. Rose fell dead; and, for his bravery, Lieutenant Waller gained the Victoria Cross. On that day, Sindia was restored with all ceremony to his palace and capital; but the rebels had plundered his treasury of half a million sterling. Napier, meanwhile, overtook the flying rebels at Jura Alipur, slew nearly 400 of them, and took twenty-five guns. Tántiá Topi and Rao Sáhib fled into Rájputána.

It would be tedious to follow the flight and pursuit of Tántia from place to place. From Rájputána to Barár the pursuit never slackened, and the last efforts of his resistance were seen in his junction with the Moghal prince Feroz; but they were hunted down with unsparing efforts, and at last, in April 1859, Tánti was caught during sleep in a Málwa jungle. His military genius had made him a formidable opponent; personal courage he lacked altogether. He had, however, not feared to superintend the massacre of the English on the river at Cawnpore, and he was at once tried, convicted, and hanged. Nána Sáhib and his brother, Bála Sáhib, had been driven into the Terai jungles, at the foot of Nepál, with the remains of their armies. Bála Sáhib, Azim Ulla, and many of the rebel sepoys perished miserably from the pestilential climate. It is probable that Dhondu Pant, Nána Sáhib, who called himself Peshwa, shared the same fate, but nothing has been known for certain of his end. Thus practically ended the rebellion in which, as Sir Colin Campbell recorded, 150,000 native troops had been subdued. The provocation to the English had been terrible; that the punishment was disproportionate none can say.

Peace was proclaimed by Lord Canning on July 8th, 1859, and the 18th of that month was fixed as a day of general thanksgiving—"A humble offering of gratitude to Almighty God for the many mercies vouchsafed." But long before this, people in England made up their minds that the Government of the Company must cease. The Company had had a unique history, and under it had been built up a vast empire. But the mutiny had shown that the empire was too vast to be ruled by a body of merchants; and on the 1st of November 1858, a proclamation was read in every station in India, in the English and the native languages, that the Company was abolished and India brought under the direct rule of the British Crown. From the steps of the Town Hall in Bombay the proclamation was read out to thousands and thousands, who listened to it with demonstrative enthusiasm. In the Bombay Presidency the spirit of the proclamation was carried out first by Lord Elphinstone and then by Sir George Clerk, who for a second time became Governor. Rebellion was pardoned and despairing chiefs allowed to adopt sons. In this way the prophecy was fulfilled which foretold the extinction of the Company's Ráj. Lord Canning, the Governor-General, became the first Viceroy of India. All existing dignities, rights, usages and treaties were confirmed, and the people were assured that the British Government had neither the right nor the desire to tamper with their religion or caste. With the exception of those who had been implicated in the murders, an amnesty was granted to all mutineers. And since the mutiny, no state within the limits of India has been annexed to the British crown, though occasions, which under the old régime would have been promptly followed by annexation, have not been wanting. The present High Courts at each Presidency were created by the amalgamation of the Company's Courts of Sadar Adálat with the Supreme Courts, whose judges were sent out from England. The wisdom of one step that was taken in connection with the transfer of the Government to the Crown has been keenly debated. The Company possessed a European army of 10,000 seasoned veterans. These men would have gladly re-enlisted in the Queen's army for a small bounty; but they were transferred from one service to the other without any reference to their wishes, as they themselves expressed it, like so many cattle. They evinced serious discontent; and one regiment, the 5th Bengal Fusiliers, broke into open mutiny. Fortunately this disturbance was soothed without a resort to force. But they all demanded their discharge, and were sent home to England with a free passage. There, however, they were mostly absorbed into nine new regiments of royal infantry, three of cavalry, and additions to the engineer and artillery corps.

It has been seen that the origin of the mutiny must be ascribed to a combination of causes and not to any one cause in particular. It cannot even be said how far it originated within the ranks of the army, or how far it was due to political intrigues, which worked on men already disloyal. The inhabitants of India as a general rule, except in Oudh, were neutral. The rebellious princes and chiefs—among whom were the Emperor of Delhi and his family, Nána Sáhib, the Ráni of Jhánsi and the Rája of Bánpur—were altogether in the minority compared with those who remained loyal, including the great Marátha chiefs, Sindia, Holkar, and the Gaikwár. England had passed triumphantly through the fiercest ordeal that her arms had ever met with in the East. The loyal classes, if they wanted any further proofs of the beneficial nature of English rule, had an ample demonstration of what the rule which it supplanted was like, in the insecurity for life and property that at once sprang up wherever her authority for a time ceased to be. The old class of hereditary robbers and marauders helped the propertied classes to realise what they gained from the *Pax Britannica*. Shattered as was the hostile combination by the iron hand of the superior race, signs were not wanting that success would have severed its discordant elements as surely as failure. The Muhammadans longed to restore the magnificence of the empire of Aurangzib, and the standard of Bahádur Sháh was a useful rallying-point for all who wished to shake off a foreign yoke. But Nána Sáhib had his own ends in view, the successful accomplishment of which would have soon brought him into conflict with the representatives of Akbar. Nor with the revival of Shiwáji's empire could the Hindus of Northern India have the slightest sympathy. Their historical associations returned to the old condition of things, before Muhammadans had interfered with the Aryan race in India. The lesser Rájas merely wanted an overthrow of the system which prevented them from indulging their taste for tyranny and plunder. The inhabitants of India are singularly wanting in a historical sense, and they looked for the restoration of an imaginary golden age which, as far as is known to us, was a dismal era of aggression, violence and murder. Not even under the far-reaching tolerance of Akbar was there anything like a national administration; nor did either the rulers or the ruled ever contemplate the existence of a Government for the benefit of the people. Splendid palaces and forts were built, and roads were created for the sake of royal processions; neither roads, bridges, nor harbours were made for the general interest of the people at large. Not even under Akbar could the law hold in check the evil-doer; nowhere was there any real security. On the grinding poverty, which from the very nature of things must always exist in India by the side of great wealth—poverty which we have at all events attempted to ameliorate—they bestowed no care whatever. We hear much nowadays of India for the Indian. Imagine for a moment, under Aurangzib, the cry of India for the Hindu!

XXVII.—INTERNAL ADMINISTRATION.

IN 1830, Sir John Malcolm wrote, "I do hope this steam navigation will be pushed through." But the Bombay Government seemingly did not agree with its chief as to the value of this communication. The promoter was informed that "the Government did not look for similar advantages from his success as the other presidencies." But the opening of steam navigation has made Bombay the principal commercial city in India. In 1838, monthly communication between Bombay and England, by the overland route, was established; but the steamers of the Indian Marine, that carried the mails between Bombay and Suez, were often irregular. This arrangement continued till 1855, when the Peninsular and Oriental Company entered into a fortnightly contract for the service. In 1868 Bombay was made the port of arrival and departure for the English mails for all India; and since the opening of the Suez Canal in 1869, all Government troopships with reliefs from England for India disembark their men at Bombay. In 1865 telegraphic communication was established between England and Karáchi by way of the Persian Gulf, and in 1870 between Bombay and Suez. Important as communication with England was, internal communications were scarcely, if at all, less so. In the Marátha wars the difficulty of marching through the Konkan and up the Gháts into the

Deccan was almost insurmountable. In 1803 General Wellesley made a rough track up the Bhor Ghát to Khándálla, but it was subsequently pulled up by the Peshwa. In 1830, Sir John Malcolm opened an excellent road up the same Ghát, and that and his discovery of Máhábleshwár are the principal achievements of his rule. In 1863 Sir Bartle Frere, Governor of Bombay, at the opening of the Bhor Ghát Railway incline—which for fifteen miles takes the locomotive up nearly 2,000 feet, by a series of viaducts and tunnels, through wild and beautiful scenery—quoted Sir John Malcolm's congratulatory address on the completion of the road, and said:—" When I first saw the Ghát, some years later, we were very proud in Bombay of our mail-cart to Puna; the first, and at that time I believe the only one running in India, but it was some years later before the road was generally used for wheeled carriages. I remember that we met hardly a single cart between Khándálla and Puna; long droves of pack-bullocks had still exclusive possession of the road; and probably more carts now pass up and down the Ghát in a week than were then to be seen on it in a whole year. But the days of mail-cart and bullock-cart, as well as the Brinjári pack-bullocks, are now drawing to a close." Bombay can boast that she took the lead in introducing railways into India. The Great Indian Peninsula Railway was projected in 1844. The first twenty miles to Thána were opened in 1853; and in the mutiny Jacob was able to travel by rail to the foot of the Ghats below Khándálla. Through communication was established with Calcutta in 1870, and with Madras in 1871. By the Bombay, Baroda and Central India Railway there is through communication with Delhi; and from Karáchi, by the Indus Valley State Railway, with the Panjáb; while railway enterprise is busy in the Káthiáwár Peninsula, the Quetta territory, and the Deccan. Excellent ordinary roads cover the country. The sepoys of the Bombay army, unlike that of Bengal, have never been unwilling to cross the sea. They have distinguished themselves in many an expedition abroad, whether in China, at Aden, in Abyssinia, Burma or Egypt; while for its extraordinary promptness in despatching troops from its dockyards, at almost a moment's notice, Bombay has achieved no small reputation.

Bombay itself has grown into a city of which its citizens may well be proud. Its beautiful natural position has been embellished by magnificent public buildings, and substantial private dwelling-houses. The view from Malabar Hill over the waters of Back Bay to the Fort has been compared to Neapolitan landscapes, and Bishop Heber's lines—

"Thy towers, they say, gleam fair, Bombay,
 Across the bright blue sea,"

pay a graceful compliment to the beautiful outlines. The population of Bombay is about 775,000 and is rapidly increasing. It forms a cosmopolitan society of the most striking varieties of race, nationality and religion. Of the total number there are 48,000 Pársis, and 10,000 Europeans; the latter, however, including many who are hardly literally entitled to that designation. The Pársis are an enterprising commercial race. They are sprung from the fire-worshipping Persians, who left their country in the seventh century on its conquest by the Muhammadans. They first took refuge at Ormuz, in the Persian Gulf, and afterwards migrated to the Káthiáwár Peninsula and thence to Guzárát. Settling in the country, they adopted many Hindu customs and learnt the Guzárúti tongue. On the arrival of the English they at once attached themselves to that nation. They rose to great importance in Surat: and, when the Company's Government was moved to Bombay, in that island also. A large share of the trade is in their hands, and they own most of the hotels in Western India.

Since the mutiny, considerable advance has been made in the general administration of the Presidency. The administration is carried on by a Governor and three members of Council, one of whom is the Commander-in-Chief of the Bombay Army. Next in the scale come the four Revenue and Police Commissioners, one for Sind and three for the Presidency proper. The unit for administrative purposes is the district which in many respects corresponds to the English county, but is generally the size of Yorkshire. A group of five or six districts is called a division, and placed under a commissioner, who is a supervising and not an executive officer, and who forms a link between the district officers and Government. The executive head of the district is the Collector and District Magistrate. The designation of Collector has been described as unfortunate, since the distribution of the revenue is a more important part of his duty than its collection. He is practically responsible for everything that goes on in the district, and to the great bulk of the population for all intents and purposes he is the government. The magisterial working of the district is entirely under his charge; the strictly judicial work alone is assigned to the district and sessions judge, an officer who has occasionally two districts to work. "Nothing can pass," it has been said, "in the district of which it is not the duty of the Collector to keep himself informed, and to watch the operation. The vicissitudes of trade, the state of the currency, the administration of civil justice, the progress of public works, must all affect most materially the interests of those classes of whom he is the constituted guardian."

What the district is to the State, the village is to the district; and there is a complete series of links from the village pátil, or headman, to the Collector. A certain number of villages, say 200, constitute a táluka, which is under the charge of a native officer called a Mámlatdár, who has revenue and magisterial powers, and in his smaller sphere possesses in the táluka the position that the Collector holds in the district. A district generally contains nine to twelve tálukas. Three or four tálukas form a sub-division (of the district) and are administered by an assistant or deputy-collector. The various departments are represented in each district by officers, who work under the direction or in co-operation with the collector, but are yet controlled by the heads of their own department. The police are in charge of a District Superintendent, who is responsible to the District Magistrate for the efficiency of his force, and is likewise in more professional matters under the orders of the Inspector-General of Police for the whole Presidency. The forests are in charge of a District Forest Officer, who has similar connections with the Collector and the Conservator of Forests. So with the Public Works Department, there is an Executive Engineer, who is responsible for public buildings, roads and bridges; and sometimes a separate officer for irrigation. The Executive Engineer is controlled in technical matters by the Superintending Engineer, and in general matters by the Collector. The health of the district is looked after by a Civil Surgeon, who is controlled by the Surgeon-General with the Government of Bombay. The Educational Department has a Deputy-Inspector, who works with the Collector, and yet under the Director of Public Instruction; and so with other departments, such as the Salt, Telegraph and Post-office.

The system of land tenure has already been referred to (page 30). It is founded on the existing native system, but brought into a more regular and uniform shape by the Survey Department. The Survey Settlement was begun in 1836, and ten years later the various existing surveys were systematised in a regular and definite form. In 1847 a Joint Survey Report was made by Mr. Goldsmid of the Civil Service, Captain (now Sir George) Wingate, and Captain D. Davidson, and these joint rules, which were extremely concise and simple, remained the authority on the subject till 1865. In that year they were again issued, but with considerable modifications; and under the present Land Revenue Code the system has become more intricate and elaborate. Almost the whole of the Presidency has been measured out by the department into "Survey Numbers," and boundary marks, which are carefully preserved, set up between each individual field, and maps of each village prepared in detail. The land having been measured out, it is classed according to the authorised rules with reference to soil, position and other considerations, and its assessment thereby fixed for a term of thirty years.

The Forest Department is of later origin. The first Conservator of Forests was created in 1847, but no staff was appointed for many years later; and the department practically dates from 1865, when it was handed over from the Military Board to the Revenue Department. With the increase of population and the clearance of land for cultivation, it was found that the wasteful use of wood and the indiscriminate cutting down of trees by the landholders and villagers was denuding the country of forests, and even affecting the climate. Forests are now stringently preserved, and the check on the former lavish waste of wood has created considerable discontent. The principles of the department have been thus laid down by Government:—"The true objects for which the Forest Department is organized and maintained are—

"(1st.) To guard and preserve from wasteful destruction the timber growing on defined tracts of land, which may properly be withdrawn from private occupation; and by good management to ensure the supply from those tracts in time to come of the timber needed to meet the wants of the country.

"(2nd.) To combine with the above the realization, by reasonable means, of such a revenue as the Government is fairly entitled to expect from its possession of such valuable property.

"But in striving to attain these ends, Government are bound to pay due regard to the habits and wants of perhaps the poorest class of the population; and they strongly deprecate vexatious and excessive interference with their daily life, for the purpose of enforcing in petty details the so-called rights of the Forest Department."

The forests now bring in a handsome revenue to Government.

Wherever Englishmen govern they will make roads and bridges, and nowhere was there more needed in this way than in the empire that we won from the Peshwa. Public buildings, roads, bridges, wells, or tanks of Marátha origin were, it may be said, non-existent. Their predecessors, the Muhammadans had, on the other hand, left not a few useful memorials of their rule, but their object was almost entirely the convenience of the rulers. Where the king was likely to travel, there would be roads, wells and rest-houses—elsewhere none. The Nawábs of the Deccan made bridges, roads and wells, and planted avenues near their own country seats. The first efforts of the English in this direction were of imperial rather than local convenience; to ensure military communications and advance similar indispensable objects. But as the process of administration ripened into greater completeness, attention was given to the providing means for internal communication in all rural districts as they came under survey. In 1852 Major Wingate submitted a scheme for the creation of local funds for this purpose, and for village schools, which was finally brought into force in Sind in 1865, and in the rest of the Presidency in 1869. The following are the main provisions of the scheme:—

I. "That there should be local funds for the promotion of education in the rural districts, and for the formation and repairs of local roads.

II. "That this fund should be in part at least provided by a local cess, imposed in addition to the ordinary assessments where no pledge expressed or implied to the contrary has been given, and when such a pledge has been given, deducted if Government permit from the land assessment, or levied by a voluntary rate from the payers of land tax.

III. "That the tax-payers should have an influential voice in the disposal of the funds."

It was arranged that the cess should be in the proportion

of one anna to a rupee of the assessment, and that two-thirds of this should go to roads and one-third to education. Other funds, too, were added, such as the surplus from toll and ferry and cattle-pound funds, and the management of these works handed over to the Local Fund Committee. The system has now developed to large proportions.

While self-governing village communities have existed in India from time immemorial, the unit under native rule never ceased to be the village. But besides the system of Local Fund Committees, the British Government has created Municipalities in all towns above a certain size for the management by the citizens in conjunction with the district authorities of the local affairs of the town, such as roads, education, water-supply, and sanitary arrangements.

In order to ensure the proper working of this elaborate system of administration, the Bombay Government insists on District Officers spending a large part of each year on tour. The Collector is on tour in his district for at least four months annually; but directly the dry weather of each year is thoroughly established at the end of October, each Assistant Collector, Superintendent of Police, Forest and Survey Officer moves into camp, and lives in tents till the following June, when the rains drive him into the station. Pitching his camp in one village after another, talking to the people and listening to their grievances, each District Officer gets a thorough acquaintance with the wants of the country, and the state of feeling of the people. He makes the acquaintance of the influential inhabitants of the country, and the lower and more ignorant classes have easy access for the purpose of making known their complaints. Even when the grievance is an imaginary one and it cannot be remedied, it gives immense gratification to the simple ryot to be able to tell his story to the sahib in his own language, and obtain a patient hearing. Thus English officials go everywhere and see everything; they actually live among the people, and see them in their most attractive guise when carrying on their agricultural operations in their villages, and not by any means only when exercising their inimitable talent for swearing that black is white in our law courts.

How far the British system of Government has really affected the mass of the people and taken a hold upon them, whether they are thriving and happy, or poor and miserable under our rule, is a vast subject, and one that can hardly be answered in a moment. It has been reiterated over and over again of late years, by those who dash through India in a flying cold weather tour, or who seek to gain a notoriety by sensational writing, that the condition of the people is getting worse year by year; that under British rule they will soon be all ruined; that they are at present undergoing miseries which are but premonitory to absolute bankruptcy, and that our system is wholly alien to their wants and requirements. Unfortunately, writers of this class generally prove too much, and the mere continued existence of the Anglo-Indian system in spite of their prophecies is enough to demolish their case. But we who live among the people, and week after week never see the face of a fellow-countryman, may at all events have a claim to be heard as to what we are doing.

To compare the position of the ryots and cultivating classes in general with that of corresponding classes in Europe is necessarily futile. They belong to different worlds. An English labourer is extremely badly off on two shillings a day. But a labourer in India is well off on three or four pence. Food is cheap and plentiful; clothes, beyond a girdle round his loins for the greater part of the year, are superfluous encumbrances. From the physical conditions of the country, the rate of wages has been from the earliest times extremely low and the labour market abundant, while interest and rent were always high. And so, from the first, the wealth of the upper classes was excessive; the poverty of the lowest great. That the cultivator can ever be actually wealthy is impossible. Government cannot alter the natural condition of things. But it nevertheless can do, and has done no little for the ryot. It has given him an absolutely fixed tenure, with freedom over his land, such as exists in no other part of the world; it accepts a moderate rent, which is assessed for thirty years in advance; a rent which in fair seasons leaves an ample profit, and in poor seasons enough to live on. In bad seasons, in order to prevent borrowing at high interest from the money-lender, Government makes loans to the ryots for the purchase of seed and cattle, and for assistance under particular distress; and at any time advances money for the construction of wells and improvement of land. If by death, or otherwise, a survey number ceases to be occupied, there is always considerable competition for its lease; and the rent being fixed and unalterable, the right of occupancy is put up to auction for a lump sum, the land at the assessed rent passing to the highest bidder. Judging them by the physical conditions of the country, and taking into consideration the limited extent of their requirements, and not losing sight of their improvident habits, no one who has lived among and known the peasantry of Western India, seen their houses and their fields and their cattle, can say that they do not look well and comfortably off. Apart from their land assessment, the only tax that they need pay is that on salt. Tobacco is untaxed; on their clothes imported from Manchester there is no duty. There are no signs whatever that the people were ever better off than they are now; that they were worse off when the Pindháris burnt their houses and plundered their hardly-gained earnings, when armies devastated the country, and flocks and herds and crops were seized for the soldiery, there is no doubt whatever. And it must be borne in mind that, thrifty and frugal as he is, the ryot is extremely improvident. If people in England marry without an income their conduct is regarded as well nigh criminal by their friends and relations. In India, on the contrary, the question of future provision for the children whose marriages their parents arrange is one that is never so much as thought of. By their religion marriage is necessary for final salvation; and, with perfect trust in Providence to provide, marriages are recklessly contracted, and enormous debts incurred in ceremonies and fees to priests. And so land, which could support two or three families in comfort, has often to support double that number in comparative discomfort. For such a state of things no Government can be blamed, and no ruler be held responsible for its results. In any other country, such reckless increase of population among a people who detest leaving their native villages would infallibly cause utter ruin in a few generations. The native of India is essentially a borrower. It is nothing more to him to be in the money-lender's hands than to an Englishman to know that his country has a national debt. Indebtedness is looked upon as a matter of course. There is no golden road by which to remedy this disease. Improvement may come in time by the spread of education, but the process is necessarily slow. Thus while the standard of prosperity cannot be very high, yet when food is cheap, clothing hardly needed, houses amply suited to the climate built at slight labour and cost, where improvidence recklessly squanders natural advantages, the population are, considering all things, well to do, and most assuredly do not looked starved or unhappy. The people of the roughest lands in the Deccan contrast favourably in appearance with the peasantry in the rich plains of Bengal under the permanent settlement and zemindári system.

That these people have the slightest ambition for anything beyond having enough to eat and drink and giving their sons and daughters in marriage is a supposition which, if entertained at all, is altogether imaginary. What Shiwáji and the Sind Amirs thought of the common people has been recorded. They have always counted for nothing; the idea of their ever having a voice in the management of the state or even of the affairs of their own district, always excepting their villages, would have seemed ludicrous and absurd. They have for century after century toiled and obeyed, giving allegiance to their rulers whoever they might be, and taking little interest in who they were. Therefore, any comparison of them with the English peasant, who wears boots and clothes, reads the newspapers and records his vote for his county or borough, is utterly impossible and misleading. In real truth, the condition of the ryot has steadily improved and is still improving. Whether he realises that fact is quite another thing. The native of India has little historical

INTERNAL ADMINISTRATION. 405

sense or recollection; and, while he forgets all about the Pindháris, he may talk of the good old times, which exist only in his imagination. There are plenty of designing people who are ready to tell him that never before was he so badly off, and that his misery is entirely due to a foreign Government. Natives of the higher and more educated classes are found who, to secure political advancement, journey to England and prate to audiences, who have no means of verifying their statements, of their being the representatives of 250 million people, and incite pity for the wretched peasant who only earns three pence a day and wears only a cloth round his loins. That on three pence he can support his family, and that more clothing would merely be troublesome, they omit to mention. To raise the burden of caste superstition and priestly tyranny these self-dubbed advocates lift not so much as their little finger; and they could not, without being defiled, touch these people whom they profess to represent.

That shortcomings are necessarily incidental to a foreign rule needs no demonstration. The manners of European officials may not always be in consonance with Hindu tastes, but any wish to offend in such a way is a thing almost entirely unknown. "The British Government," a Muhammadan gentleman writes, "and the Europeans employed in carrying it on are foreigners, between whom and the natives there is no social sympathy and fellow feeling. But is that Government tyrannical, or are its servants tyrants? as some persons assert. This question can only be answered comparatively. A comparison instituted between the British and native rule is very much to the advantage of the former. I know a great deal of the British rule, and also of the administration of some native states. We know what the political, moral, and material condition of India was before the British rule. Does any one pretend to say that there were good laws, that there was protection of person and property, that the poor had any remedy against the great and the rich, that there was liberty of action and opinion, that there was peace, that education was provided for the people?

"The administration of many Native States in India has considerably improved of late. But to whom is this due? Surely to the British Government and their Political Agents. I personally know that in certain states even such improvements as good communications, efficient police, equal justice, removal of oppressive taxes, opening of a few schools, and so on were adopted by the chiefs after years of pressing from the Government and its agents; and at last they were adopted to please the British Government.

"It is true that the masses of people in India, both in British India and in the Native States, are poor, ill-fed and ill-clad. But who can say that this is due to the British rule? Their condition was never better; it was perhaps worse before."

A few points may be noticed which demonstrate the improved condition of the people. Men have perished in masses in India from famine, at the very time when in other parts of the country there was a superabundance of food which could not be brought to them. Now railways pour grain by tons into starving districts, and where famine raged a few years ago there remains no sign of the misery that was undergone. But of a great famine that occurred in Khándesh at the beginning of the century the traces, in deserted villages and overgrown fields, have not yet passed away. The financial statements of the Government of India show that the exports and imports of merchandize and treasure increased, from an annual amount of fourteen millions sterling in the early part of the century, to sixty millions in 1859 and 154 millions in 1884. This enormous increase of trade cannot have taken place without an improvement in the purchasing as well as producing-power of the people. This is shown by the increase of imports of cotton-goods from nineteen to twenty-five millions in five years. One noticeable increase in the standard of comfort is, that in a single year nearly four million umbrellas were imported, and sheet glass is wanted more and more for windows in native dwellings. As by railways the wealth of the country can be distributed, so by irrigation works its productiveness is immensely increased. In short, while optimism may be dangerous, yet the pessimist views of ignorant and designing writers are altogether to be deprecated.

I cannot close this sketch better than by an extract from the writings of Sir Henry Lawrence.

"Though compelled in candour to admit that without sword-government the British in India could not maintain their position, we feel strong in our hearts the conviction that one good magistrate may be better than a regiment; one sound law well administered better than a brigade; that a happy mixture of a just civil administration with the strong hand will retain the country in peace and happiness as long as it is good that we should hold it. It is not by believing either ourselves or our laws all purity or all corruption that we are likely to come to a right understanding of what is best for India, but by a close study of its past history; and then by setting ourselves down, each in his own sphere, and honestly working out the details of a code honestly and ably prepared, not shifting and changing from day to day, but founded on experience and suitable to a rude and simple people who, like all people under the sun, prefer *Justice* to *Law!*"

THE END.

INDEX.

A

	PAGE
Abdulla Syad	130
Abercrombie, General	194
Aboriginal tribes	10
Aden captured	303
Ádil Sháhi dynasty	52
Áfghán war, first	294
Afzul Khán	106
Áhmad Sháh	43
Áhmad Sháh Abdali	150
Áhmad Sháh, Emperor	150
Áhmadábád, 44 ; taken by the Maráthas, 148 ; by the English	179
Áhmadnagar, 52, 54 ; end of the kingdom, 93 ; Wellesley at	216
Akbar	69, 71
Álamgír, Aurangzib	104
Álamgír II.	150
Albuquerque	61
Alexander	26
Alibág	132
Ali Murád of Hydarábád	297
Ali Murád of Kyrpur	307
Alington, Captain	180
Aliwardi Khán	156
Alla-ud-din, conqueror of the Deccan	40
Almeida	62
Amherst, Lord	275
Amir Khán	234, 262
Amirs of Sind	296
Ánand Rao Gaikwár	212, 213, 226
Anderson, Mr., envoy to Sindia.	184

	PAGE
Ángria—Kánhoji, 126, 132, 135 ; Tukáji, 126 ; Tuláji, 154, 155 ; . Raghoji	320
Anjidiwa	59, 110
Apa Sáheb, regent of Barár	247, 260
Aras, battle of	171
Arcot, siege of	147
Árgaum, battle of	222
Arikera, battle of	194
Ashta, battle of	260
Asirgahr	46
Asoka	21, 28
Assaye, battle of	219
Auckland, Lord	291
Aungier, Gerald	115
Aurangábád, 96 ; battle of	163
Aurangzib, Viceroy of the Deccan, 96 ; usurps the throne, 101 ; war in the Deccan	127
Ázim Ulla Khán	346, 387

B.

Bába Desai of Sáwantwári	372
Bábar	47, 67
Bahádur Sháh of Guzárát	65
Bahádur Sháh, Emperor	129
Bahádur Sháh, last Emperor, 345, 353.	
Bahmani, kingdom of the Deccan	42
Bahrám Khán	71
Baillie, Col., his defeat	182
Baird, Sir David	214

	PAGE
Bairu Pant, Peshwa	132
Báji Rao (1)	138
Báji Rao (2), 201; flight to Bombay, 211; treaty of Bassein, 212; battle of Khirki, 253; surrenders to Malcolm, 264; sent to Cawnpore, 265; death	323
Bakar, fort of	296
Báláji Báji Rao, 143, 149; death.	160
Báláji Janárdin (Nána Farnáwis	159
Báláji Wishwánáth	131
Bánkot, or Fort Victoria	155
Balance of power	231
Bápu Gokla	250, 254, 257
Barár, 53, 138; ceded to the Nizam	224
Barlow, Sir George	231
Baroda, 3; taken by English	213
Bassein, 70; taken by the English, 181; treaty of	212
Bassora	36
Báwa Sáhib	321
Bednur	189
Bell, Mr. Ross	303
Bentinck, Lord William, 233; Governor-General, 281, etc.; meeting with Ranjit Sing, 291;	335, 337
Bernadotte	188
Best, Captain	87
Bhágoji Naik	374
Bhagwa Jenda	259
Bhartpur, siege of	229, 276
Bhils, 11, 237; pacification of	273
Bhopál, anarchy at	289
Bhor Ghát	177
Bidar	42, 44, 53
Bijanagar	56
Bijápur, 52, 55; its buildings, 57; taken by Aurangzib	124

	PAGE
Black Hole of Calcutta	157
Blake, Mr., murdered	289
Bolan Pass	295
Bombay, ceded by Portuguese, 110; proposal to remove from to Janjira, 114; becomes Presidency, 121; growth of the city	394
Boone, Governor	132
Bourchier, Governor	154
Bourquin, Louis	221
Briggs, Capt	266, 273
British Supremacy	230
Broach, taken by the English, 169; given to Sindia	184
Browne, Col	183
Brydon, Dr.	304
Buddha	2
Burhánpur	4
Burmese war	27
Burnes, Alexander	293, 297, 30
Burr, Col	25
Bussy	147, 18
Byfield, Mr	15

C

Cabral	5
Calcutta founded	12
Camac, Col	183, 19
Campbell, Capt.	18
Campbell, Sir Colin	35
Canning, Mr.	247, 255, 25
Canning, Lord, 328, 341; becomes first Viceroy	38
Carnac, Mr., 177; dismissed	17
Carnac, Sir James	29
Carnatic	15
Caste	1
Chánd Bibi	7

INDEX. 411

	PAGE
Chanda Sáhib	146
Chandra Gupta	28
Chaplain, Mr.	266
Charnock, Job	122
Chául	51, 64, 141
Chauth	114
Chetu, Pindhári	262
Child, Sir John	121
Child, Sir Josiah	121
Child-marriage, forbidden by Akbar	80
Chima Sáhib of Kolhápur	370
Chimnáji	140
Chimnáji Apa	201
Chin Khilich Khán	130
Chisholm Lieut	257
Clerk, Sir George	323, 388
Clive, 145; at Gheria, 155; at Plassey	157
Close, Capt.	248
Close, Col.	211, 238
Columbus	52
Companies, East India, final union of	122
Confederacy, Marátha	186
Coote, Sir Eyre, 158, 182; at Porto Novo, 183; death	188
Cornwallis, Lord 192, etc.: second term of office	229
Corten's, Sir Thomas, new Company	95
Crowe, Mr.	296

D

Dabba	316
Da Gama	51, 60
Dainglia (see Trimbakji)	
Dalhousie, Lord	322, 326, 340

	PAGE
Dámáji Gaikwár	138
Dára	101
Darius	26
Dassara, festival of	251
Dáud Khán	130
Daulat Khán Lodi	47
Davidson, Capt.	397
De Boigne	191, 217
Deccan	3
De Nueva	59
Deshmukhs	33
Deshpands	33
Dhárwár, ceded	246
Dhondia Wág	209
Dhondu Pant (see Nána Sáhib)	
Diaz	52
Dick, Lieut.	381
Dig, fort of	228
District officers	395, 400
Diu, 65; siege of	66
Dost Muhammad, 292, etc.	
Drake, Sir Francis	84
Dudrenec	197
Duncan, Governor	207, 211, 224
Dupleix	145
Durand, Col.	360
Dutch, the, 79; attack Bombay	115

E

East India Company, 84; abolished	388
Eastwick, Lieut.	296, 301
Education	270
Egerton, Col., 177; dismissed	178
Egypt, Bombay troops in	214
Ellenborough, Lord, 297; Governor-General	304

Elphinstone, Mountstuart, 220, 223; resident at Puna, 238, 252; at battle of Khirki, 253; commissioner of the Deccan, 258; Governor of Bombay, 269; his love of sport, 272; policy and views, 279; retirement 280
Elphinstone, Lord 346, 359, 364
European army of the Company. 389
European officials, their position, 283

F

Falkland, Lord 323
Famines 407
Faroksir............................ 130, 135
Fatte Sing Gaikwár 171, 199
Feroz, Prince 387
Fitzgerald, Capt., at Sitabaldi ... 260
Ford, Capt. 239
Forde, Col., defeats French and Dutch............................ 158, 159
Forest Department 397
Forjett, Mr....................... 364, 367
Francis, Mr., his views on Bombay............................. 174
Free press 268
Free trade............................ 196
Frere, Sir Bartle 359, 393

G

Gaikwár, origin of................. 138
Gama da Vasco 51
Ganga Prasád 369
Gangadhar Shástri 242
Gáwilgahr............... 77, 222, 223
Gell, General 322
Gháts, Western 3

Ghatge, Shirji Rao......203, 209, 229
Ghaznevide dynasty 37
Ghazni 36
Gheria, 135; Clive at 155
Gholám Khadir 191
Goa, 63; garrisoned by British troops 236
Goddard, Col. .... 178, etc.
Gokla (see Bápu)
Goláwli, action at.................. 383
Goldsmid, Mr. 397
Golkonda, 53; taken by Aurangzib 124
Gordon, Capt. 141
Gordon, Major..................... 262
Gowind Rao Gaikwár........171, 199
Grant, Sir John Peter.............. 284
Grant Duff, Capt. 258
Grantham, Sir Thomas 121
Gurária, battle of 361
Gujárát, 3; becomes a Muhammadan kingdom..................... 44
Gujaráti language 7

H

Harcourt, Col. 217
Harding, Lord 322
Harris, General 206
Hartley, Capt. 177, 194, 207
Hastings, Marquis of 241, 268
Hastings, Warren, 173, 176, 179, etc.; retires 192
Havelock, Sir H. 352
Hawkins 83, 85
Heber, Bishop.............. 277, 394
Hemu 72
Henery Island 321
Henry, Lieut. 375
Herat, siege of 293

INDEX. 413

	PAGE
Hijira	35
Hindustan	1
Hindustani Language	8
Hislop, Sir Thomas 248; at Mehidpur	261
Holkar, origin of	138
,, Tukáji	200
,, Yeshwant Rao, 202, 210, 214, 227, 232	
,, Wituji, 202; death	211
,, Amrat Rao	215
,, Malhar Rao	232, 261
,, Tulsi Bai	232, 261
Holland, Governor	193
Hornby, Governor, 169, 175, 178, 180	
Horne, John	140
"Hugh Lindsay," the	287
Hughes, Admiral	188
Humáyun	68, 69
Hussein Ali of Mysur	194
Hussein Ali, Syad,	130
Hydar Ali, 163, 182; death	188
Hydar Kuli Khán	137

I

Imángahr, Napier's march against	309
Inám Commission	362, 372
Inámdárs	31
Inchbird, Capt	141
Indus	3
Infanticide	211
Interlopers	288

J

Jacob, Capt	313
Jacob, Col.	365, 370, 372

	PAGE
Jahándár Sháh	130
Jahángir, 83, etc.; treaty with the English	88
Jagat Shet	143
Jains	22, 29
James, Commodore	154
Jangiz Khán	39
Janjira, 99; attached by Shiwáji, 114; never conquered	199
Jári Patka	254
Jay Singh, General	113
Jaypál, King	37
Jazia	80, 83
Jenkins, Mr.	260, 261
Jhánsi, Rani of, 351, 378, 386; siege of	379

K

Kábul, capitulation at	304
Kachh, 3; expedition against	244
Kaira	226
Kálikat	51
Kallora, in Sind	295
Kánara	3, 195
Kánarese language	8
Kanhoji (see Ángria.)	
Karáchi, taken	301
Karanja, taken	170
Karim, Pindhári	262
Karrak, expedition to	294
Kásim conquers Sind	36
Katak, Marátha fort at	149
Káthiáwár	3
Keane, Sir John	301
Keating, Col.	170, 172, 177
Keigwin's rebellion	121
Kennedy, Col.	260
Kerr, Lieut.	362, 364

	PAGE
Khándálla	177, 182
Khánderi (Kenhery)	115
Khándesh, 4; Mussalmán kingdom of, 46; reclamation by the British	272
Khán Jahán Lodi	88, 91
Khardla, battle of	200
Khirki, battle of	253
Khiljy dynasty	39
Khizr Khán	47
Kolába, 132; annexed	320
Kolhápur, Rája of, 129; a separate state, 144; war with	321
Koli rising	322
Korygaum, battle of	256
Kota-ki-Serai, battle of	386
Krishna	4
Kulbarga	44
Kulkarnis	32
Kutab-ud-din	38
Kutab Sháhi dynasty	53

L

Lake, General, 217; at Laswári, 221; war with Holkar	227, 232
Lancaster, Capt.	84, 85
Land tenure	30, 397
Laswári, battle of	221
Lawrence, Col. George	359
Lawrence, Sir John	355
Lawrence, Sir Henry, his views	407
Leslie, Col.	177
Lester, General	366, 373
Lingayats	22
Local funds	399
Lodi dynasty	47

M

	PAGE
Macgregor, Capt.	262
Mackintosh, Sir James	225, 269
Macleod, General	190
Macpherson, Mr., Governor-General	192
Madanpur, battle of	378
Madras, founded	93
Máhúbhárat	13
Máhábleshwár	4, 285
Máhádaji Sindiá, 151 (see Sindia).	
Máhárájpur, battle of	320
Máháráshtra	7
Máhdu Rao Peshwa	162, 167, 201
Málabár	8
Malcolm, Sir John, 223, 231, 248; at Mehidpur	261
Governor of Bombay	281, 392
Malcolm, Col.	373, 374
Malcolm Peth	283
Malet, Mr.	192
Málegaum, surrender of	268
Málik Áhmad	54
Málik Ambar	78
Mámlatdárs	272, 396
Mandisur, battle of	361
Mándu, fort	90
Mangalur, siege of, 189; Convention of	190
Manson, Mr., 372; murdered	374
Mángs	32
Manu, institutes of	15
Maráthi language	7
Marlborough, Earl of	110
Mathews, General, 189; murdered	190
Maughan, Col.	363
Maxwell, Col.	383
Medicine, college of, at Calcutta	285
Medows, General	194
Megadha	23

INDEX.

	PAGE
Megasthenes	28
Mehidpur, battle of	231
Meiklejohn, Lieut.	381
Mhárs	32
Miáni, battle of	312
Middleton	85
Minto, Lord	234, 236
Mirásdárs	30
Mir Jáfar	157
Mir Rustam of Kyrpur	297
Missionaries	196, 270
Moghals	38
Moira, Lord	241
Monson, Col.	227, 228
Mongols	38
Monsoon	5
Moor, Commodore	172
Morába	175
Morár, battle of	385
Mornington, Lord	205
Mostyn, Mr., at Puna, 166, 168, 175; death	177
Mozaffar Khán of Guzárát	44
Muázim, 115; becomes Emperor	129
Mudáji Bhonsle of Barár	181
Muhammad	35
Muhammad Amin	136
Muhammad Ghori	37
Muhammad of Ghazni	37
Muhammad Khán	309 etc.
Muhammad Sháh, 133; Emperor	150
Muhammad Toghlak	41
Munro, Sir Hector's flight from Hydar Ali	182
Munro, General Thomas	259
Murád	101
Murray, Col.	227
Murshidábád	143

	PAGE
Mysur wars—	
1st	165
2nd	180, 189
3rd	194
4th	203

N

Nádir Sháh at Delhi	141
Najib-ud-daula	150
Nána Sáhib 265, 324, 346, 352,	356, 387
Nána Sáhib Peshwa	143
Nána Farnáwis... 153, 162, 200, etc.; death	209
Napier, Sir Charles, 307, etc.	339
Napier, Sir Robert	386
Napoleon Buonaparte	206
Nárayan Rao Peshwa	167
Narbada	4
Nargund, Bába Sáhib of	373
Narnálla Fort	222
Násir Jang	140, 147
Native States	406
Navy, Indian	239
Negapatam, Dutch driven out of	183
Nelson, Lord	206
Nepál, conquest of	241
Nepean, Sir Evan	260, 266
Nizám Ali	151, 207
Nizáms of Hydarábád	137
Nizám Sháhi dynasty	52
Nizám-ul-Mulk	54
Nizám-ul-Mulk	130, 136
Non-intervention	231
Northern Sirkárs	147
Nott, General	338
Nuttall, Col.	375

O

Ochterlony, Col. 228, 262, 276
Omar 35
Outram, Sir James, 274, 302 ; his war with Kolhápur, 321; in Persia, 346 : at Lucknow 353
Oxenden, Sir George 112
Oxenden, Henry 117

P

Paget, Sir Edward 337
Palmer, Col. 204, 209
Panálla 108
Pánipat, battles of 47, 67, 153
Panjáb 2
Panniár, battle of 320
Panwel, Egerton's advance from, 177 ; Goddard's retreat to 183
Parashrám Bhau 201
Párbati 160
Pariahs 17
Parsáji Bhonsle 247
Parsees 329, 394
Patils 32
Pattle, Capt. 314
Peninsular and Oriental Company 392
Perron 214, 221
Persia, expeditions to, 277, 294, 346
Persian Ambassador killed in Bombay 224
Persian language 8
Peshwa, origin of the dynasty, 138 ; rendition of the Government to 144
Pilgrim ships of Aurangzib seized by Shiwáji, 113 ; by the English 121
Pindháris 234, 241

Pirates, 154; stamped out, 239 :in Persian Gulf, 277 (see Ángria).
Plassey 157
Police, bravery at Talliwára ... 372
Pollock, General 338
Popham, Capt. 180
Porto Novo, battle of 183
Porus 23
Pottinger, Capt., 263, 291, 297, 301, 302
Pottinger, Eldred 293
Pratáp Sing, Rája of Sátára 322, 323
Pritzler, General 258
Prophecy about the mutiny 345
Prother, Col. 255, 259
Pruen, Lt., and the "Ranger" 190
Puná, becomes the capital of the Maráthas, 148 ; burnt by the Nizám, 139; taken by Holkar.. 211
Purandhar, 99; treaty of 174

R

Raghoba, 143, 162; his unpopularity, 172, 174;his surrender 178: death 184
Raghoji Bhángria 322
Raghoji Bhonsle 139, 146, 149 ; his alliance with English 177
Raghonáth Rao 143
Railways 393
Rais Pagri of Sind 296
Rájápur 109
Rájárám, son of Shiwáji 126
Rájárám of Kolhápur 371
Rájgahr 98
Ráma Kumpti 135
Rámoshis, rising 276
Rám Rája 143

INDEX.

"Ranger," action with Marátha fleet ... 190
Ranjit Sing ... 241
  his meeting with Lord William Bentinck, 291, 298; death ... 305
Rango Bápuji ... 362
Rao Sáhib ... 383, 387
Ráoshan Akhtar ... 133
Ráthghar, action at ... 377
Raygahr ... 109, 259
Raymond ... 200
Retrenchment ... 283
"Revenge," the frigate ... 172
Revenue, Marátha system ... 133
Robertson, Capt. ... 266
Roe, Sir Thomas ... 89
Rohillas ... 150, 160
Rose, Sir Hugh ... 358, 376, etc.
Rose, Lieut. ... 386
Rose, Mr. ... 362
Russian aims on India ... 293, 294, 299
Ryots, condition of the ... 401
Ryotwár tenure ... 30

S

Sabuktagin ... 37
Saháranpur, Marátha fort at ... 149
Sáhu (Shiwáji) son of Sambháji ... 126, 129, 143
Sakhárám Bápu ... 167
Salábat Jang ... 147
Sálbai, treaty of ... 184
Salsette, 65; taken by the English, 170; retained ... 184
Sambháji, son of Shiwáji, 113; his desertion to the Sidi, 117; war with Portuguese, 120; killed ... 125
Sambháji, son of Rájárám ... 129

Sangameshwár ... 148
Sánskrit ... 8
Saringapatam, siege of ... 166, 182
Sátára, Rája of 258, 265; exiled 292; annexation of the state ... 323
Sáti ... 80, 285
Sawarndrug, fight at ... 155
Scotch East India Company ... 122
Schneider, Capt. John ... 363, 366
Schneider, Capt. Frederick ... 374
Seleukos ... 28
Sepoy regiments, first raised ... 146
Seton-Karr, Mr ... 363
Shaháb-ud-din ... 150
Sháh Beg Árghun ... 53
Sháh Álam ... 151, 153, 157, 191, 221
Sháh Jahán ... 91
Sháji Bhonsle ... 90, 93
Sháh Suja, 292, etc.; his claims on Sind ... 299
"Shamsher Jang," destruction of the ... 172
Shástri, Gangadhar ... 242
Sher Sháh Sur, or Sher Khán ... 68, 69
Shias ... 104
Shipman, Sir Abraham ... 110
Shiwáji, 94, 96, etc.; coronation, 116; death ... 117
Shiwáji, son of Rájárám ... 126, 129
Sholinghar, battle of ... 183
Shore, Sir John ... 200
Shortt, General ... 367, 369
Shuja ... 101
Sidáshiwa Chimnáji ... 149
Sidi of Janjira ... 100
Sidoji Guzar ... 126
Sikh wars ... 322
Silim (Jahángir) ... 78
Silviera ... 65

Sind 2, 36; the Amirs of 277, 291, etc.; annexed 318
Sind controversy .... 305, etc.
Sindi language 7
Sindia, origin of 138
Sindia—
  Ránoji 148
  Jyápa 148
  Máhádaji 151, 167, 191 ; demands chauth from English, 192; at Puna 197; death and character 198
  Daolat Rao 198, 200, 203, 248
  Jánkoji 289, 319
Singhar 98, 112
Sion 122
Siwa 122
Slave dynasty 38
Sleeman, Sir William 286
Smith, Col. Lionel............245, 260
Soarez............................... 62
Souter, Sir Frank.............. 374, 375
Spencer, Mr. 156
Staunton, Capt. 256
Steam Navigation..... .....287, 297, 392
Stevenson, Col. ....215, etc.
Stewart, General 377
St. Lubin 176
Stuart, General 188, 207
Stuart, General 361, 377, 378
Suffrein, Admiral 187
Sunnis.............................. 104
Supa, battle of 77
Sur dynasty 69
Surat, Hawkins at, 83; plundered by Shiwáji, 112; castle taken by English, 161 ; city taken ... 212
Suráj-ud-daula 157
Survey system 397

Syads, the 130

T

Taimur the Tártár 47
Talegaum, retreat from............ 177
Tálner, siege of 262
Túlpuris in Sind 295
Tamerlane.......................... 47
Tántia Topi... 351, 356, 379, 385, 387
Tápti 4
Tarábai, wife of Rájárám... 126, 129
Tatta, factory at................... 296
Taylor, Mr., sent to Calcutta... 173
Tew, Capt. 313
Thags, repression of 286
Thána, 65 ; taken by Maráthas, 140; by English............... 170
Timoja! of Kánara................. 64
Tipu Sultan 188, 193, 206
Todar Mal 80
Toghlak dynasty 40
Tonk Rámpura, fort of 231
Torna 98
Travancore 193
Trimbakji Dainglia... ...240, 243, 257
Tripartite treaty 299
Tulsi Bai Holkar................... 232
Turban of Sind..................... 296

U

Umáji Naik 276
Underi Island 321
Upton, Col. 174
Upris 30

V

Vaughans, murder of 25
Vedas (see Weds).

INDEX.

	PAGE
Vellore, mutiny of	233, 335
Vicovick at Kábul	293
Village communities	29

W

	PAGE
Waite, Sir Nicholas	129
Wakil-i-Mutluk	191
Walker, Col	226, 242
Waller, Lieut.	386
Wargaum, convention of	177
Warre, Lieut., murdered	245
Warren Hastings	173, 176
Warsowa fort	170
Wasil Muhammad	262
Watson, Admiral, at Gheria	155
Watson, Commodore	170
Wedderburn, David	169
Weds (Vedas)	13
Wellesley, Major-General, 209, 215; his opinions of the Maráthas, 225; of the English soldiers	331
Wellesley, Marquis of	207
Wheeler, Sir Hugh	352
Whitlock, General	376
Wijaydrug	135
Willoughby, Sir John	323
Willoughby, Lieut.	350
Wilson, General	354
Windham, General	357
Wingate, Sir G.	397, 399
Wishwás Rao	152, 159
Woodburn, General	360
Wooddington, Col.	213, 217, 221

X

Xavier	71

Y

Yeshwant Rao Holkar (see Holkar).	
Yeshwant Rao Ghorpure	250
Yusuf Ádil Sháh	55

Z

Záffar Khán, Alla-ud-din Hassan Gangu Bahmani	42
Zámorin of Kálikat	59, 61
Zemán Khán	206, 208
Zemindárs, or landlords	31
Zinat Mahal	345
Zulfikar Khán	130

www.ingramcontent.com/pod-product-compliance
Lightning Source LLC
Chambersburg PA
CBHW020536300426
44111CB00008B/694